Joseph DaBoll-Lavoie

About Island Press

Island Press is the only nonprofit organization in the United States whose principal purpose is the publication of books on environmental issues and natural resource management. We provide solutions-oriented information to professionals, public officials, business and community leaders, and concerned citizens who are shaping responses to environmental problems.

In 2000, Island Press celebrates its sixteenth anniversary as the leading provider of timely and practical books that take a multidisciplinary approach to critical environmental concerns. Our growing list of titles reflects our commitment to bringing the best of an expanding body of literature to the environmental community throughout North America and the world.

Support for Island Press is provided by The Jenifer Altman Foundation, The Bullitt Foundation, The Mary Flagler Cary Charitable Trust, The Nathan Cummings Foundation, The Geraldine R. Dodge Foundation, The Charles Engelhard Foundation, The Ford Foundation, The Vira I. Heinz Endowment, The W. Alton Jones Foundation, The John D. and Catherine T. MacArthur Foundation, The Andrew W. Mellon Foundation, The Charles Stewart Mott Foundation, The Curtis and Edith Munson Foundation, The National Fish and Wildlife Foundation, The National Science Foundation, The New-Land Foundation, The David and Lucile Packard Foundation, The Pew Charitable Trusts, The Surdna Foundation, The Winslow Foundation, and individual donors.

About the Scientific Committee on Problems of the Environment

SCOPE, the Scientific Committee on Problems of the Environment, was established by the International Council of Scientific Unions (ICSU, now the International Council for Science), in 1969 as an international, nongovernmental, nonprofit organization with the mandate to advance knowledge of the influence of humans on their environment, as well as the effects of these environmental changes on people's health and welfare, with particular attention to influences and effects that are global or shared by several nations. It serves as a nongovernmental, interdisciplinary, international council of scientists and as a source of advice for the benefit of governments and intergovernmental and nongovernmental bodies with respect to environmental problems. It comprises 40 national committees; the U.S. National Committee organized the symposium on the commons that is the basis for this volume.

Protecting the Commons

PROTECTING THE COMMONS

A Framework for Resource Management in the Americas

Edited by
Joanna Burger
Elinor Ostrom
Richard B. Norgaard
David Policansky
Bernard D. Goldstein

ISLAND PRESS
Washington • Covelo • London

Library of Congress Cataloging-in-Publication Data
Protecting the commons : a framework for resource management in the Americas / edited by Joanna Burger ... [et al.].
    p.   cm.
  ISBN 1–55963–737–4 (cloth : acid-free paper) — ISBN 1–55963–738–2 (paper : acid-free paper)
    1. Natural resources, Communal—America—Management. I. Burger, Joanna. II. Title.
    HC85 .P76   2001
    333.7'097—dc21   00–010487

British Library Cataloging-in-Publication Data available.

Printed on recycled, acid-free paper

Printed in Canada
10 9 8 7 6 5 4 3 2 1

Contents

Preface

The beginning of the new millennium is a proper time to evaluate how we have managed, conserved, and preserved our natural and cultural resources, and the nature of the problems remaining in the wise use of these resources. As populations continue to grow, to disperse over large areas of land, to concentrate in large cities, and to cluster along coastal regions, the management of natural and cultural resources will become even more difficult. With these changes, there are more users, and more uses, of resources held in common.

While there are many paradigms for thinking about resource use, the "commons" paradigm made popular by Garrett Hardin in his influential article "The Tragedy of the Commons" has proven a useful starting point for interdisciplinary collaborations on resource management. In the thirty years since his article was published, numerous studies have confirmed his dire predictions about overexploitation of resources held in common; however, other studies have shown that cooperation and the creation of institutions have resulted in the wise and sustained use of such resources.

In this volume we examine a variety of common-pool resources, from atmospheric and water resources, to fisheries, forests, and medical care, as they apply to the Western Hemisphere. Our goal is to provide a range of examples: from situations for which we have found successful solutions, to those where we are in the infancy of wise and sustainable management. Some problems are as old as civilization, such as dealing with forest products, fisheries, and local water resources. Others are relatively new, such as consideration of the global atmosphere and medical care as commons issues.

The idea for this volume evolved from discussions of the U.S. National Committee for SCOPE (the Scientific Committee on Problems of the Environment) and led ultimately to a symposium titled "Protecting the

Commons: a Framework for Resource Management in the Americas," which was presented at the Tenth General Assembly of SCOPE in June 1998 at the Environmental and Occupational Health Sciences Institute in Piscataway, New Jersey.

The discussions and interest generated by the symposium encouraged us to create this volume, using the speakers as the core. We have added a number of other authors to round out the Americas perspective. Common-pool resources are an integral part of our everyday lives, making the topic far too large for any one volume. Nonetheless, it is our aim to examine a range of natural and cultural resources that are important now, in the hope that they may serve as examples of sustainable resource use in the future.

Acknowledgments

We thank all the members and staff of the U.S. National Committee for SCOPE for helping in the development of ideas for the Tenth Assembly, for providing insights throughout the development of this volume, and for their support of the U.S. National Committee for SCOPE. In addition to those who contributed directly to this volume, we thank A. Davis, E. Bouwer, H. Dowlatabadi, W. J. Mitsch, R. Virginia, A. G. Power, J. Prince, J. J. Reisa, S. Vann, and T. Williams for help with SCOPE, the conference, and the book. We also thank P. Bourdeau (then president of SCOPE), V. Plocq-Fichelet (executive director of SCOPE), J. M. Mellilo, and W. Clark for helpful comments on the symposium and this volume; C. Botnick, B. Davis, M. Robson, and M. Rosen at the Environmental and Occupational Health Sciences Institute for helping to make the SCOPE meeting so productive, efficient, and enjoyable; C. Dixon and R. Ramos for editorial assistance; and finally we are indebted to C. Botnick for her help as managing editor for the final manuscripts. Nearly all authors provided helpful reviews and comments on other chapters; in addition we thank J. Alcorn, N. Dolsak, M. Greenberg, D. Frankford, B. Friedlander, F. Lehoucq, E. Leventhal, B. Palestis, C. W. Powers, and D. Takahashi Kelso for reviews of some of the chapters.

We thank the U.S. Environmental Protection Agency, the National Science Foundation (SBR-9521918), the U.N. Food and Agriculture Organization (FAO), the Ford Foundation, and the National Aeronautics and Space Administration for support of the U.S. National Committee for SCOPE activities; as well as Bristol Myers Squibb Company, Dow Chemical Company, Johnson and Johnson, Merck and Company, New Jersey Public Service Gas and Electric, Schering Plough Research Institute, and World Information Transfer for support of the Tenth General Assembly. We also thank the following for individual support: the U.S. Department of Energy (AI-DE-FC01-95EW55084 and DE-FG-26-OONT-40938), to the Consortium for Risk Evaluation with Stakeholder Participation (CRESP; Joanna Burger, Bernard D. Goldstein), the National Institute of Environmental Health Sciences (ESO 5022; Joanna Burger, Bernard D. Goldstein), and the MacArthur Foundation (Elinor Ostrom).

JOANNA BURGER
ELINOR OSTROM
RICHARD B. NORGAARD
DAVID POLICANSKY
BERNARD D. GOLDSTEIN

Introduction

Common-Pool Resources and Commons Institutions

An Overview of the Applicability of the Concept and Approach to Current Environmental Problems

JOANNA BURGER, CHRISTOPHER FIELD,
RICHARD B. NORGAARD, ELINOR OSTROM,
AND DAVID POLICANSKY

"When the war came to Monterey and to Cannery Row everybody fought it more or less, in one way or another. . . . The canneries themselves fought the war by getting the limit taken off fish and catching them all."

John Steinbeck (*Sweet Thursday*, 1954)

Pasturelands, woodlands, fisheries, and other resources have long been shared, used in common, by local people. To the extent that these resources were sustained rather than environmentally degraded, it was because their common users agreed on the nature of the problem and established and adhered to responsibilities, rights, and other rules. Through extensive case studies, we now realize how the emergence and maintenance of such local and regional commons institutions depend on the coincidence of particular environmental characteristics, social conditions, and technological factors. These advances in our understanding put us in a better position to facilitate the development of

1

commons institutions in the future. At the same time, new conditions are expanding the spatial and temporal scales over which we need to manage common-pool resources, expanding the need for commons institutions, while seemingly reducing the possibilities that such institutions can emerge. These new conditions include

- more rapid rates of population growth;
- higher and continually increasing rates of consumption;
- ever-greater emphases on individualism, materialism, and economic competition;
- greater differences between individuals, locally and globally, in their access to shared resources;
- greater differences between individuals due to specialization in scientific and experiential knowledge;
- more rapid emergence of new technologies affecting our relations with nature and each other;
- broader impacts of new technologies over space and time;
- apparently greater, but difficult to foresee, specificity of impacts of new technologies on ecosystem functioning; and
- greater cumulative effects of human activity and hence tighter regional and global linkages between ecosystem impacts.

As a consequence of these new conditions, the pressure on both long-standing common-pool resources and newly realized ones is unusually high, while the challenges of establishing appropriate institutions seem to have increased. It is by no means clear that we are devising commons institutions to manage and protect common-pool resources sufficiently rapidly to sustain human well-being over the foreseeable future. The purpose of this book is to review and assess the changing nature of common-pool resources and how well developments in our understanding of common-pool resources and commons institutions are helping us meet the social and environmental challenges we face. This chapter provides an introduction.

A Brief Review of the Commons Concept

An individual using a resource in common with others receives the full benefit of using the resource more intensively while the full costs of the increased use are shared with others. Indeed, in the absence of appropriate institutions, it is in the individual's best interest to take as much as possible as soon as possible, damaging the resource further in his or her greed and haste. The resulting tension between individual gain and the collective good encourages resource degradation, perhaps to destruction. This process, however, can be ameliorated, indeed even reversed such that resource improvement occurs, by commons institutions governing individual behavior. The necessarily shared nature of some resources, the tension between the individual and the community, resource degradation, and the possibility of ameliorating institutions have been recognized by moral philosophers and popular orators since early times. The tension has been a central issue of political economy since at least the time of Adam Smith. Thomas Malthus and others (see, for example, the lectures of W. F. Lloyd [1968], given from 1832–1836) added population growth to the argument. Gordon (1954) and Scott (1955) developed formal models of how resources used in common are exploited. Popular and scientific awareness of the interplay between shared resources, institutions, and population was greatly heightened through Hardin's classic article, "The Tragedy of the Commons" (1968).

Hardin used the example of a herder placing one more animal on grazing lands used by multiple herders. The individual herder gains the entire advantage of that animal's grazing while bearing only a small part of the cost of the depletion of the grazing lands. It is always in the individual herder's interest to add one more animal, but additional animals are not in the interest of herders overall. Thus managing common-pool resources comes down to limiting access (who will be excluded and how) and affecting subtractability (how much the taking by one person will impinge on the taking by another). Managing common-pool resources involves various ways of limiting access (deciding who will be excluded and how) and affecting harvesting efforts (how much one actor can take). Both restricting access and limiting subtraction are difficult to achieve (Berkes et al. 1989). The solution, in Hardin's view, was to impose some form of government or private ownership from the outside. His solution, however, neglected the possibility that the herders themselves could agree on common rules and enforce them collectively. Moreover, Hardin confused common property regimes, where a community of individuals have enforceable ways of limiting access and may also have rules affecting harvesting strategies, with open access. Under open access, no one can be excluded and no limits exist on harvesting strategies. This confusion stimulated a collaborative research effort by social and natural scientists to elaborate the range of environmental circumstances associated with common-pool resources as well as social circumstances affecting the development, maintenance, and performance of common-property institutions (National Research Council 1986; Berkes 1989; Ostrom 1990; Feeny et al. 1990; Burger and Gochfeld 1998; Ostrom et al. 1999).

It is important to distinguish between the characteristics of a resource and the property rights regime governing the use of the resource. Some resources, such as the agricultural potential of land, can be divided up and managed as separate parcels by individual owners. To a large extent, the management of agricultural potential by one owner does not affect the potential of the land owned by others. Of course, the introduction of pesticides and other technologies has changed this relationship, making agricultural land less divisible than historically. Fisheries, on the other hand, are much more difficult if not impossible to divide up between users and require some form of collective management. The resource characteristics of anadromous, coastal, lake, and stream fisheries differ significantly, and these differences affect the appropriateness of different commons institutions. It is also important to recognize an asymmetry in the divisible-therefore-private, indivisible-therefore-common institutional spectrum. While divisible resources such as pastureland and forests can be managed successfully in common, less divisible resources cannot be managed successfully through private ownership.

The prototype commons involves people, or commoners, with common interests in meeting similar basic needs for food and fiber, common abilities to exploit the resource, and common levels of power or access to the shared resource. With people and their situations being relatively similar, it seems logical that common responsibilities, rights, and rules would be relatively easy to determine and agree upon. Of course, such perfect conditions have never existed, yet the prototype still serves as a conceptual anchor to much of our understanding about commons. Other social factors being equal, the farther we move from these idealized conditions, the more difficult it would appear to be to develop commons institutions and avoid environmental degradation. Yet other social factors rarely are equal and case studies of common-pool resources and commons institutions have shown that individuals from quite different circumstances have come together and acted collectively to resolve conflicts between individual incentives and the collective good under different social circumstances (Bromley et al. 1992; Ostrom et al. 1994; Agrawal 2000; Baland and Platteau 1996; McKean 2000). In fact, from a rational-choice theory of collective action, resolving such "social dilemmas" is at the root of nearly all governance (Ostrom 1998). Thus we now recognize that our prototypical commons is an interesting conceptual anchor in part because it rests on very simplified liberal-worldview assumptions about individual interests and behavior. While this worldview is certainly dominant in Western political thought, other framings can be used to refine the dominant view, providing substantially richer understandings.

Four general categories of property rights regimes are now recognized: open access, communal, state, and private (National Research Council 1986; Feeny et al. 1990; Bromley 1989, 1991; Hanna and Monasinghe 1995). These regimes differ by nature of ownership, rights and responsibilities of owners, rules of use, and center of control. Box I-1 provides a summary. It is important to keep in mind that actual property rights regimes blur the distinctions, that these categories simply provide additional conceptual anchors. To make matters more difficult, the fourfold classification of property regimes just begins to identify very broad classes of regimes. There are many variants of rules related to access, harvesting, management, determining exclusion, and

---

Box I-I. Property Rights Regimes, after Feeny et al. (1990) and Others

Open access: Absence of well-defined property rights; resource often unregulated and free to everyone.

Communal property (res communes): Resource held by community of users; user community excludes outsiders; users may self-regulate; appropriate uses may still be defined by larger society or external power.

State property (res publicae): Resource rights held by government; government can regulate access and exploitation; general public may have access as granted by government; government can use force to enforce laws and can even subsidize use by some.

Private property (res privatae): Individual has the right to particularly appropriate uses of the resource as socially defined; individual also has the right to exclude others from these uses, perhaps the right to prevent uses by others that interfere with his/her rights, and the right to sell or rent the property to others.

---

transfer of rights. Furthermore, there are rarely perfect matches between resource characteristics and property regimes. Evidence of open-access failure, common-property failure, government failure, and market failure all exist. No simple broad type of property regime fits all common–pool resources. Even similar resource and technology combinations—such as irrigation systems—require variation in the rules that govern access, harvesting, investment, maintenance, monitoring, and sanctioning. Rules that work well for a flat valley-bottom system serving 100 farmers will not work well for a hilly system serving 15,000 farmers. Effective rules help humans cope with the complex characteristics of the resources themselves.

The enrichments in our understanding of common-pool resources and commons institutions, as well as property rights regimes more broadly, came largely through extensive case studies of common-pool resource management around the world. Much of the research on commons has dealt with local and regional fisheries, forests, irrigation systems, groundwater basins, and rangelands (see Alexander 1982; Berkes 1986, 1989; McCay and Acheson 1987; Benjamin et al. 1994; Blomqvist 1996). The case-study approach has proven very useful in identifying and illuminating the questions of common property and the institutional structures that lead to success or failure in dealing with resources used in common. Further, quantitative analyses of multiple resource systems by Tang (1992), Schlager (1990), Schlager and Ostrom (1992), Lam (1994, 1998), and Lam et al. (1997) are beginning to provide a means of examining alternative hypotheses concerning the factors that are associated with the capacity of local users to self-organize and the success or failure of their efforts.

Our understanding of the commons has also been enriched by other lines of research. Insights on the emergence of cooperation have been gained through repeated Prisoner's Dilemma games, a line of research conducted by both biological and social scientists (Axelrod and Hamilton 1981; Axelrod and Dion 1988). Economists, political scientists, and psychologists have conducted experimental research on the factors affecting an individual's willingness to cooperate (summarized in Ostrom 1998). These lines of research cast serious doubt on the presumption that individuals act only in their narrow, material self-interest. New research on civil society and the interdependencies between nongovernmental and governmental organizations further enhances our understanding (also summarized in Ostrom 1998). The emergence of global civil society and its possible future impacts on resource management are also being explored (Young 1989, 1994; Lipschutz and Mayer 1996). While social scientists have increased our understanding of how commons emerge, biologists have argued that natural variation and the limits of scientific and experiential knowledge make it nearly impossible to agree on whether degradation is actually taking place, and hence nearly impossible to derive commons institutions that ensure sustainability (Ludwig et al. 1993). One objective of this book is to bring the insights of social and natural scientists together.

The Applicability of the Concept of the Commons to New Conditions

Our understanding of the commons concept has increased dramatically over the three decades since Hardin's evocative article of 1968. But to what extent does this increased understanding help us address the issues identified in the opening paragraph? Below we elaborate on a few of them.

Expanding Spatial Scales

Part of the reason the commons thinking of the past needs revisiting is that the scale of commons issues has expanded dramatically. Several of the most important commons problems are now truly global in scale. The scale expansion from local and regional to global involves at least three separate kinds of mechanisms. One is the increase in human population, the driver that was the focus of the early commons work and continues to be important. The second critical mechanism is the development of new technologies that change the impacts of individuals and extend the spatial scale of resource consumption. Over the last several decades, growth in human domination of many global commons has been driven more strongly by increasingly powerful technologies and rising expectations than by expanding human population. The third mechanism involves the emergence of commons issues where physical and biological processes impose effects at large spatial and long temporal scales. The global distribution of greenhouse gases and consequent climate impacts is one example, as are impacts of nutrient runoff on downstream water users in large river basins.

Numerous human activities, from the cutting of firewood in rural areas of Central and South America to the regulation of major water systems in all countries of the Western Hemisphere, have causes and consequences measured at small, medium, and large spatial and temporal scales. Commons issues are complicated by the intrinsic relevance of multiple scales of space and time. The physical and biological mechanisms that distribute resources and the consequences of takings range over diverse scales, as do the social and governmental mechanisms that regulate human actions. Many of the most challenging commons problems involve noncongruence, in time and space, between the consequences of an action for multiple resources and between the region affected by an action and the region subject to common governance (National Research Council 1996a).

A particularly important question is whether there is congruence between the spatial scale of the resource system itself and the spatial scale of the jurisdictions able to take governance and make management decisions related to that resource (National Research Council 1996a). Another is whether the temporal scale used by decision makers is similar to the temporal scale of the dynamics of the resource system (National Research Council 1996b).

Property rights systems, and governance systems more generally, tend to be nested in space ranging from the shared properties of individual families, to the shared resources of communities of families or local governments, to much larger regional and national governmental jurisdictions. Multinational protocols for protecting international and global commons present some of the thorniest problems, for at least three reasons. First, the framework for shared stewardship is rarely in place prior to negotiation. Second, the parties often utilize the commons resources for very different purposes. And third, parties with contrasting levels of economic development have access to dramatically different options for protecting the commons. Since the boundaries of governmental units are usually arbitrarily drawn when viewed from the perspective of most natural resources, very often the spatial boundaries of a particular resource are not congruent with any one particular governance unit. Groundwater basins in southern California and Mexico, for example, may underlie many different cities and counties, and developing new institutions to govern and manage any one groundwater basin may involve substantial efforts to use courts, legislatures, and administrative agencies to help constitute new enterprises for the purpose of controlling a particular commons (Blomquist

1992). The watersheds of major rivers, such as the Amazon or the Columbia River, encompass regions located in more than one county, state, or nation. While international treaties can be used for some regulation of major flows between countries, such treaties are inadequate for dealing with many of the relevant problems of regulating smaller sub-basins that do not conform to any particular existing governmental jurisdiction.

A key question in understanding commons is whether one can generalize from one scale to another. Can experience managing a watershed provide guidelines for managing an entire drainage basin? To what extent can short-term, small-scale experiments provide useful guidance for managing resources at the scale of regional and global commons given that long-term, large-scale ecological experiments are relatively rare? Similar questions arise in addressing the scale of commons governance systems. For example, is the theory of collective action relevant to more than one scale of human organization? Are the variables that explain cooperation in social dilemmas of small groups relevant to the study of larger groups and vice versa? Currently, scholars of international relations apply theories of collective action to national or international efforts to overcome social dilemmas. Can findings from analyses of smaller-sized common-pool resources be used to explain the robustness of smaller-scale institutional arrangements, and can these be applied to institutional arrangements for larger common-pool resources (Ostrom 1990; McGinnis and Ostrom 1996; Young 1994)?

Expanding Temporal Scales

When a resource system generates flows of resources in a relatively short time, the time frame of decision makers and of the resource system may be relatively congruent. Thus, households making investment decisions with respect to what crops to plant among those that will mature within a one-year period are likely to make good decisions. They may not, on the other hand, make similarly good decisions with respect to maintaining the soils producing the crop, especially if they share responsibility with many others for soil conditions. It is more difficult to ensure that governance regimes have a sufficiently long time horizon to match resource renewal rates of slow-growing trees, fish, or other wildlife, let alone soil formation. Thus, safeguarding future generations' access to old-growth forests, tropical dry forests, or many species of slow-growing animals is a more challenging task of institutional design.

The problem of temporal congruence is even more difficult for establishing governance of commons resources, especially biological resources that are nonrenewable. With the approach of the end of fossil fuel reserves, alternative technologies present hopeful options. But we have no practical options for restoring biological diversity. Today's exploitation of a common-pool resource can reverberate forever.

Even when resources are divisible and can be privately owned, ensuring environmental sustainability to protect the well-being of future generations cannot be accomplished by individuals acting out of self-interest alone. Even if environmental services could be entirely privately owned, we would need intergenerational commons institutions to ensure sustainability. This is because our children share the resources we pass to them with those they marry. And those they marry may be substantially poorer unless their parents also have, for example, conserved the soil and invested wisely in tree planting so that they could pass on their environmental wealth. Such passing of the environmental wealth must be understood and shared as a common responsibility. One's great-great-grandchildren, for example, have seven sets of other great-great-grandparents in approximately one's own generation besides oneself and one's spouse. One never knows, however, who these other fourteen people are likely to be (Norgaard 1995). Furthermore, even if one could enter into an agreement to sustainably manage one's environmental resources with the other great-great-grandparents, there are descendants in between who must carry out the agreement over time. Thus it is very difficult to ensure the well-being of one's descendants, beyond one's own children, unless the entire community throughout time is playing by a set of rules to achieve sustainability (Howarth 1992). Patrilineal, matrilineal, and other rules of inheritance, awarding of dowries, responsibilities to train youth, land-use restrictions, and diverse other practices and obligations can be interpreted as intergenerational commons institutions that have emerged to facilitate the transfer of environmental assets to the next generation at levels that help ensure sustainability. Note that this problem is not simply related to the transfer of environmental resources to future generations. It is also true for the transfer of knowledge, without which environmental resources would have little value.

Expanding Cognizance

Paralleling the expanding spatial and temporal scales of common-pool resources, we are also experiencing expanding cognizance of resources. Our understanding of common-pool resources and their governance usually entails users who physically use the resources. Box I-1, for example, categorizes stewardship of and access to resources in the proximity of the people who use them. Modern communications and greater understanding of ecological connectedness have caused more and more people to both value and express concern for how resources are used at great distances. Recognition of the existence of physically distant resources brings their stewardship to the attention of a much larger community than the people in the immediate vicinity. For example, following the *Exxon Valdez* oil spill in Alaska, people throughout the world expressed concern for the wildlife living there, even though they may never visit the site (Johnson 1994; National Research Council 1992; Burger 1997). Similarly, interest in the sealing practices of the Inuit peaked when increased communication highlighted the treatment of the seals, leading to a globalization of concern.

We express our concern about such entities through assignment of existence rights and values. This has often led to conflicting priorities between the physically proximate, who control access to resources, and the more distant populace. As an extreme example, charismatic macrofauna are often involved when such issues come to a head (Decker and Goff 1987). For example, the Inuit practice of taking seal cubs to sustain the traditional way of life in the Canadian Arctic was brought to a crashing halt by public opinion mobilized against it in the United States. Many people care about the beautiful rocky shorelines of Maine or Peru, the cuddly penguins of Pumto Tumbo in Argentina, or the fuzzy white baby harp seals of the Canadian maritime provinces.

Resource System Linkages and Cascade Effects

Many common-pool resources are linked to larger, complex ecological systems. Because of these linkages, human exploitation of one common-pool resource may produce a cascade effect of unintended consequences for other components of the ecosystem and for society. These consequences may include declining biodiversity, loss of soil fertility, massive fluxes of nutrients to waters, and alteration of the composition of the atmosphere. This cascade of unintended system-level responses as a common-pool resource is exploited and greatly increases the complexity of the problem of crafting social and political institutions to govern and manage these resource systems.

Cascading ecosystem effects can be seen from local to global scales. The global accumulation of trace gases from agricultural intensification is altering the atmospheric commons, with possible effects on climate. Institutional reactions to this challenge will have to operate at scales from the subsistence farm in developing countries to entire regional agricultural production systems in more developed countries. In both cases, water and nutrients must be managed to generate crop production as well as to prevent degradation of water resources, transfer of nutrients to other land areas, and alteration of the global atmosphere. Some of the best examples of cascading effects are seen following forest harvest and overfishing. Deforestation often results in soil erosion, silting, and eutrophication of surface water, which may lead to declines in fish populations. In grazing systems, overuse of grasslands has led to increased rates of wind erosion, with local losses in soil fertility and regional to global consequences for the atmosphere. Similarly, overfishing of one fish stock influences not only the fish community but also other oceanic communities as well as human activities that depend on the fisheries. When one fish stock is depleted, other human endeavors may suffer, such as bait and tackle stores, hotels and restaurants, recreational fisheries, tourism, and, eventually, the entire local economy where fishing is a significant industry.

Increasing Differences among Users

Our understanding of common-pool resources and institutions for their management has been strongly influenced by historical analysis of nearly ideal commons situations where needs, access, consequences, and other phenomena are common to the users. While we now have case studies of commons institutions emerging with considerable heterogeneity, there is still reason to be concerned that the differences among users, especially as the spatial and temporal scales of common-pool resource problems increase, are well beyond that analyzed in historical local case studies. The modern world is characterized by great inequalities between industrialized and nonindustrialized economies and between resource owners and laborers within each. Equally important, people live increasingly specialized lives with little in common between what is known by farmers, physicists, truck drivers, accountants, and hairstylists. Environmental resources are now shared across cultures that have been in conflict for millennia. To refer to these as commons is to suggest that institutions can be designed to ensure sustainability in which all parties come out ahead. This is clearly not the case; if everyone played by the same rules, some would be major winners, others significant losers. On the other hand, it is difficult to devise and enforce separate rules for people in different circumstances. The promise of transfers of income, for example, between winners in the North and people who are hurt by the agreement in the South, may facilitate agreement, but the transfers are likely going to have to be very large, also tailored to particular circumstances, and their continuance guaranteed before global commons institutions can emerge. Such differences have also made it difficult to negotiate global resource management regimes with respect to fisheries and deep-sea minerals. Deriving a workable combination of rules and income transfers is precisely the exercise in which the world's nations are engaged in their effort to develop an accord to ameliorate global climate change.

The uncommon nature of globally shared resources also produces serious difficulties with respect to monitoring and perceiving environmental degradation. Common pastoralists all see the pasture degrading and, over time, are reasonably likely to agree how much is due to bad weather and how much to excessive grazing. Global environmental degradation, such as climate change or the loss of biodiversity, is not seen in "common." Rather, we have had to develop large teams of specialists over the past two decades to even begin to grapple with the framing and details of measurement. And these large teams of specialists have had considerable difficulty communicating the causes and long-term implications of the problem to other scientists, let alone the public, well enough to affect the development of new institutions to prevent climate change or to preserve our common biodiversity.

Our Objective for This Volume

In light of these new global considerations and the need to further examine the definition and breadth of access and property rights for common-pool resources, we felt it imperative to examine commons issues from a Western Hemisphere perspective. While European and Asian countries have undergone a relatively continuous pattern of human development for centuries, the Western Hemisphere has experienced a disconnect or disjunct in its development because of the European invasion of North and South America that occurred in the 1600s and 1700s. Indigenous methods for dealing with commons issues were often destroyed or greatly modified by this invasion. Furthermore, people migrating to the New World from the Old arrived with divergent views: Some wished to maintain the old land tenure and property rights from their homeland, while others wanted to change the view of the commons. We will concentrate especially on commons experiences that, by failing or succeeding, provide us with understandings that will lead toward a sustainable global ecosystem, from both ecological and anthropocentric perspectives. As McCay (1995) has recently noted, the possibility exists that people who use common-pool resources can also take care of them, including restoring them, and that there can be cooperation between groups of people with very different uses of the same resource (Burger and Leonard 2000). This focus leads to searching for solutions to commons issues rather than merely examining the demise of commons resources. It is this focus that we would like to encourage.

Acknowledgments

We thank M. Gochfeld for bringing J. Steinbeck's quote to our attention.

References

Agrawal, A. 2000. "Small Is Beautiful, but Is Larger Better? Forest-Management in the Kumaon Himalaya, India." In *People and Forests: Communities, Institutions, and Governance,* edited by C. Gibson, M. McKean, and E. Ostrom, 57–85. Cambridge, MA: MIT Press.

Alexander, P. 1982. *Sri Lankan Fishermen: Rural Capitalism and Peasant Society.* Canberra: Australian National University.

Axelrod, R., and D. Dion. 1988. "The Further Evolution of Cooperation." *Science* 242:1385–90.

Axelrod, R., and W. D. Hamilton. 1981. "The Evolution of Cooperation." *Science* 211:1390–96.

Baland, J. M., and J. P. Platteau. 1996. *Halting Degradation of Natural Resources. Is There a Role for Rural Communities?* Oxford: Clarendon Press.

Barker, R., E. W. Coward, Jr., G. Levine, and L. E. Small. 1984. *Irrigation Development in Asia: Past Trends and Future Directions.* Ithaca, NY: Cornell University Press.

Benjamin, P., W. F. Lam, E. Ostrom, and G. Shivakott. 1994. *Institutions, Incentives, and Irrigation in Nepal.* Decentralization: Finance & Management Project Report. Burlington, VT: Associates in Rural Development.

Berkes, F. 1986. "Local-Level Management and the Commons Problem: A Comparative Study of Turkish Coastal Fisheries." *Marine Policy* 10:215–29.

———., ed. 1989. *Common Property Resources: Ecology and Community-based Sustainable Development.* London: Belhaven Press.

Berkes, F., D. Feeny, B. J. McCay, and J. M. Acheson. 1989. "The Benefits of the Commons." *Nature* 340:91–93.

Blomquist, W. 1992. *Dividing the Waters: Governing Groundwater in Southern California.* San Francisco: Institute for Contemporary Studies Press.

Blomqvist, A. 1996. *Food and Fashion, Water Management and Collective Action among Irrigation Farmers and Textile Industrialists in South India.* Linköping, Sweden: The Institute of Tema Research, Department of Water and Environmental Studies.

Bromley, D. W. 1989. *Economic Interests and Institutions: The Conceptual Foundations of Public Policy.* Oxford: Basil Blackwell.

———. 1991. *Environment and Economy: Property Rights and Public Policy.* Oxford: Basil Blackwell.

Bromley, D. W., D. Feeny, M. McKean, P. Peters, J. Gilles, R. Oakerson, C. F. Runge, and J. Thomson, eds. 1992. *Making the Commons Work: Theory, Practice, and Policy.* San Francisco: Institute for Contemporary Studies Press.

Burger, J. 1997. *Oil Spills.* New Brunswick, NJ: Rutgers University Press.

Burger, J., and M. Gochfeld. 1998. "The Tragedy of the Commons Thirty Years Later." *Environment* 40:5–13, 26–27.

Burger, J., and J. Leonard. 2000. "Conflict Resolution in Coastal Waters: The Case of Personal Watercraft." *Marine Policy* 24:61–67.

Cernea, M. 1989. "User Groups as Producers in Participatory Afforestation Strategies." World Bank Discussion Papers no. 70. Washington, DC: The World Bank.

Cordell, J., ed. 1989. *A Sea of Small Boats.* Cambridge, MA: Cultural Survival.

Decker, D. J., and G. R. Goff, eds. 1987. *Valuing Wildlife: Economic and Social Perspectives.* Boulder, CO: Westview Press.

Feeny, D., F. Berkes, B. J. McCay, and J. M. Acheson. 1990. "The Tragedy of the Commons: Twenty-Two Years Later." *Human Ecology* 18:1–19.

Gilles, J. L., and K. Jamtgaard. 1981. "Overgrazing in Pastoral Areas: The Commons Reconsidered." *Sociologia Ruralis* 21:129–41.

Gordon, J. S. 1954. "The Economic Theory of a Common-Property Resource: The Fishery." *Journal of Political Economy* 62:124–42.

Hanna, S., and M. Monasinghe, eds. 1995. *Property Rights and the Environment: Social and Ecological Issues. The Beijer Institute of Ecological Economics and the World Bank.* Washington, DC: The World Bank.

Hardin, G. 1968. "The Tragedy of the Commons." *Science* 162:1243–48.

Howarth, R. B. 1992. "Intergenerational Justice and the Chain of Obligation." *Environmental Values* 1:133–40.

Johnson, G. J. 1994. "Legal Considerations." In *Before and after an Oil Spill: The Arthur Kill,* edited by J. Burger, 44–64. New Brunswick, NJ: Rutgers University Press.

Johnson, R. N., and G. D. Libecap. 1982. "Contracting Problems and Regulation: The Case of the Fishery." *American Economic Review* 72 (5):1,005–23.

Lam, W. F. 1994. "Institutions, Engineering Infrastructure, and Performance in the Governance and Management of Irrigation Systems: The Case of Nepal." Ph.D. diss., Indiana University.

———. 1998. *Governing Irrigation Systems in Nepal: Institutions, Infrastructure, and Collective Action.* Oakland, CA: Institute for Contemporary Studies Press.

Lam, W. F., M. Lee, and E. Ostrom. 1997. "Analyzing Policy Reform and Reforming Policy Analysis: An Institutionalist Approach." In *Policy Studies and Developing Nations: An Institutional and Implementation Focus,* edited by D. W. Brinkerhoff, 51–85. Greenwich, CT: JAI Press.

Lipschutz, R. D., with J. Mayer. 1996. *Global Civil Society and Global Environmental Governance: The Politics of Nature from Place to Planet.* Albany, NY: State University of New York.

Lloyd, W. F. 1968. "Lectures on Population, Value, Poor Laws, and Rent. Delivered in the University of Oxford during the Years 1832, 1833, 1834, 1835, and 1836." Reprints of Economic Classics. New York: Kelley.

Ludwig, D., R. Hilborn, and C. Walters. 1993. "Uncertainty, Resource Exploitation, and Conservation: Lessons from History." *Science* 260 (April 2):17, 36.

McCay, B. J. 1995. "The Ocean Commons and Community." *Dalhousie Review* 74:1–29.

McCay, B. J., and J. M. Acheson, eds. 1987. *The Question of the Commons: The Culture and Ecology of Communal Resources.* Tucson: University of Arizona Press.

McEvoy, A. F. 1986. *The Fisherman's Problem: Ecology and Law in the California Fisheries, 1850–1980.* Cambridge, England: Cambridge University Press.

———. 1988. "Toward an Interactive Theory of Nature and Culture: Ecology, Production, and Cognition in the California Fishing Industry." In *The Ends of the Earth: Perspective on Modern Environmental History,* edited by D. Worster. Cambridge, England: Cambridge University Press.

McGinnis, M., and E. Ostrom. 1996. "Design Principles for Local and Global Commons." In *The International Political Economy and International Institutions,* 465–93. Cheltenham, England: Edward Elgar.

McKean, M. A. 2000. "Common Property: What Is It, What Is It Good For, and What Makes It Work?" In *People and Forests: Communities, Institutions, and Governance,* edited by C. Gibson, M. McKean, and E. Ostrom, 27–55. Cambridge, MA: MIT Press.

National Research Council. 1986. *Proceedings of the Conference on Common Property Resource Management.* Washington, DC: National Academy Press.

―――. 1992. *Restoration of Aquatic Ecosystems: Science, Technology, and Public Policy.* Washington, DC: National Academy Press.

―――. 1996a. *Upstream: Salmon and Society in the Pacific Northwest.* Washington, DC: National Academy Press.

―――. 1996b. *The Bering Sea Ecosystem.* Washington, DC: National Academy Press.

Norgaard, R. B. 1995. "Intergenerational Commons, Economism, Globalization, and Unsustainable Development." *Advances in Human Ecology* 4:141–72.

Ostrom, E. 1990. *Governing the Commons: The Evolution of Institutions for Collective Action.* New York: Cambridge University Press.

―――. 1998. "A Behavioral Approach to the Rational-Choice Theory of Collective Action." *American Political Science Review* 92 (1):1–22.

Ostrom, E., J. Burger, C. B. Field, R. B. Norgaard, and D. Policansky. 1999. "Revisiting the Commons: Local Lessons, Global Challenges." *Science* 284:278–82.

Ostrom, E., R. Gardner, and J. M. Walker. 1994. *Rules, Games, and Common-Pool Resources.* Ann Arbor: University of Michigan Press.

Ostrom E., and M. B. Wertime. 2000. "International Forestry Resources and Institutions Research Strategy." In *People and Forests: Communities, Institutions, and Governance,* edited by C. Gibson, M. McKean, and E. Ostrom, 243–68. Cambridge, MA: MIT Press.

Schlager, E. 1990. "Model Specification and Policy Analysis: The Governance of Coastal Fisheries." Ph.D. diss., Indiana University.

Schlager, E., and E. Ostrom. 1992. "Property-Rights Regimes and Natural Resources: A Conceptual Analysis." *Land Economics* 68:249–62.

Scott, A. D. 1955. "The Fishery: The Objectives of Sole Ownership." *Journal of Political Economy* 63:116–24.

―――. 1993. "Obstacles to Fishery Self-Government." *Marine Resource Economics* 8: 187–99.

Tang, S. Y. 1992. *Institutions and Collective Action: Self-Governance in Irrigation.* San Francisco: Institute for Contemporary Studies Press.

Wade, R. 1994. *Village Republics: Economic Conditions for Collective Action in South India.* San Francisco: Institute for Contemporary Studies Press.

World Commission on Environment and Development. 1987. *Our Common Future.* Oxford: Oxford University Press.

Young, O. R. 1989. *International Cooperation Building Regimes for Natural Resources and the Environment.* Ithaca, NY: Cornell University Press.

―――. 1994. *International Governance Protecting the Environment in a Stateless Society.* Ithaca, NY: Cornell University Press.

Chapter 1

Reformulating the Commons

ELINOR OSTROM

The Western Hemisphere is richly endowed with a diversity of natural resource systems that are governed by complex local and national institutional arrangements. Until recently, these arrangements have been poorly understood. In Mexico, for example, nearly 30,000 *ejidos* and *communidades* serving about 3 million households govern 59 percent of the land area of Mexico and two-thirds of the rural production units. Within these institutional structures, "communities apply an incredible range of innovative, sustainable, locally adapted natural resource management systems in a wide variety of ecosystems, ranging from desert to rainforest" (Alcorn and Toledo 1998: 224). While many local communities that possess a high degree of autonomy to govern local resources have been highly successful over long periods of time, others fail to take action to prevent overuse and degradation of forests, inshore fisheries, and other natural resources (see Gibson and Becker 2000).

The conventional theory used to predict and explain how local users will relate to resources they share makes a uniform prediction that users themselves will be unable to reformulate the rules they face and extricate themselves from the tragedy of the commons (Hardin 1968). Using this theoretical view of the world, there is no variance in the performance of self-organized groups. In theory, there are no self-organized groups. Without externally imposed regulations, jointly used natural resource systems will all be grossly mismanaged. Empirical evidence tells us, however, that considerable variance in performance exists and many more local users self-organize and are successful than is consistent with the conventional theory. The beginnings of an alternative theory are presented in this chapter.

Common-Pool Resources[1]

Most natural resource systems used by multiple individuals can be classified as common-pool resources. Common-pool resources generate finite quantities of resource units, and one person's use subtracts from the quantity of resource units available to others (Ostrom et al. 1994). Most common-pool resources are sufficiently large that multiple actors can simultaneously use the resource system, and efforts to exclude potential beneficiaries are costly. Examples of common-pool resources include both natural and human-made systems including groundwater basins, irrigation systems, forests, grazing lands, mainframe computers, government and corporate treasuries, and the Internet. Examples of the resource units derived from common-pool resources include water, timber, fodder, computer-processing units, information bits, and budget allocations (Blomquist and Ostrom 1985).[2]

When the resource units are highly valued and many actors benefit from appropriating (harvesting) them for consumption, exchange, or as a factor in a production process, the appropriations made by one individual are likely to create negative externalities for others. Nonrenewable resources, such as oil, may be withdrawn in an uncoordinated race that reduces the quantity of the resource units that can be withdrawn and greatly increases the cost of appropriation. Renewable resources, such as fisheries, may suffer from congestion within one time period but may also be so overharvested that the stock generating a flow of resource units is destroyed. An unregulated, open-access common-pool resource generating highly valued resource units is likely to be overused and may even be destroyed if overuse destroys the stock or the facility generating the flow of resource units.

The Conventional Theory of Common-Pool Resources

Since the important early studies of open-access fisheries by Gordon (1954) and Scott (1955), most theoretical studies by political economists have analyzed simple common-pool resource systems using relatively similar assumptions (Feeny et al. 1996). In such systems, it is assumed that the resource generates a highly predictable, finite supply of one type of resource unit (one species, for example) in each relevant time period. Appropriators are assumed to be homogeneous in terms of their assets, skills, discount rates, and cultural views. They are also assumed to be short-term, profit-maximizing actors who possess complete information. In this theory, *anyone* can enter the resource and appropriate resource units. Appropriators gain property rights only to what they harvest, which they then sell in an open competitive market. The open-access condition is a given. The appropriators make no effort to change it. Appropriators act independently and do not communicate or coordinate their activities in any way.

In this setting, as the incisive analysis of Gordon and Scott demonstrates, each fisherman will take into account only his own marginal costs and revenues and ignores the fact that increases in his catch affect the returns to fishing effort for other fishermen as well as the health of future fish stocks. . . . [E]conomic rent is dissipated; economic overfishing, which may also lead to ecological overfishing, is the result. (Feeny et al. 1996: 189)

Many textbooks in resource economics and law and economics present this conventional theory of a simple common-pool resource as the only theory needed for understanding common-pool resources more generally (but, for a different approach, see Baland and Platteau 1996). With the growing use of game theory, appropriation from common-pool resources is frequently represented as a one-shot or finitely repeated Prisoner's Dilemma game (Dawes 1973; Dasgupta and Heal 1979). These models formalize the problem differently, but they do not change any of the basic theoretical assumptions about the finite and predictable supply of resource units or complete information, or about the homogeneity of users, their maximization of expected profits, and their lack of interaction with one another or capacity to change their institutions.

A sufficient number of empirical examples have existed wherein the absence of property rights and the independence of actors captures the essence of the problem facing appropriators that the broad empirical applicability of the theory was not challenged until the mid-1980s. The massive deforestation in tropical countries and the collapse of the California sardine fishery and other ocean fisheries confirmed the worst predictions to be derived from this theory for many scholars. Garrett Hardin's (1968) dramatic article in *Science* convinced many noneconomists that this theory captures the essence of the problem facing most common-pool resources in the world. Since appropriators are viewed as being trapped in these dilemmas, repeated recommendations were made that external authorities impose a different set of institutions on such settings. In some, private property is affirmed as the most efficient form of ownership (Demsetz 1967; Posner 1977; Simmons et al. 1996). Other recommendations are for government ownership and control (Ophuls 1973). Implicitly, theorists assume that regulators will act in the public interest and understand how ecological systems work and how to change institutions so as to induce socially optimal behavior (Feeny et al. 1996: 195).

Until recently, the possibility that the appropriators would find ways to organize themselves has not been seriously considered in much of the economics literature. Organizing to create rules that specify rights and duties of participants creates a public good for those involved. Anyone included in the community of users benefits from this public good, whether he or she contributes or not. Thus, getting "out of the trap" is itself a second-level dilemma. Investing in monitoring and sanctioning activities to increase the likelihood that participants will follow the agreements they have made also generates a public good. Thus, these investments represent a third-level dilemma. Since much of the initial problem exists because the individuals are stuck in a setting where they generate negative externalities on one another, it is not consistent with the conventional theory that they solve a second- and third-level dilemma in order to address the first-level dilemma under analysis.

Until the work of the National Academy of Sciences' Panel on Common Property (National Research Council 1986), however, the basic theory discussed above was applied to all common-pool resources regardless of the capacity of appropriators to communicate and coordinate their activities. The growing evidence from many studies of common-pool resources in the field called for a serious rethinking of the theoretical foundations for the analysis of common-pool resources (see Berkes 1986, 1989; Berkes et al. 1989; Bromley et al. 1992; McCay and Acheson 1987). The consequence of these empirical studies is not to challenge the empirical validity of the conventional theory where it is relevant but rather its generalizability.

Self-organized Resource Governance Systems in the Field

Most common-pool resources are more complex than the base theory of homogeneous appropriators taking one type of resource unit from a resource system that generates a predictable flow of units. The rich case-study literature illustrates a wide diversity of settings in which appropriators dependent on common-pool resources have organized themselves to achieve much higher outcomes than is predicted by the conventional theory (Cordell 1989; Wade 1994; Ruddle and Johannes 1985; Sengupta 1991).[3]

Small- to medium-sized irrigation systems come closer than many biological resources to approximating these conditions and are, thus, an appropriate setting in which to examine these patterns of relationships quantitatively. One resource unit—water—is the focus of efforts to organize and coordinate activities. Recent research on small- to medium-sized irrigation systems in Nepal has found a very substantial difference in performance between systems owned and governed by the farmers themselves and those owned and operated (but in some cases, not governed) by a national governmental agency.

While most farmers own land in Nepal, most own very small parcels of less than 1 hectare. They are relatively homogeneous with similar preferences in obtaining water for rice production during the monsoon and winter seasons and various crops during the spring. Farmers in Nepal have long had the authority to create their own water associations, construct and maintain their own systems, and monitor and enforce conformance to their rules (see Benjamin et al. 1994; Lam et al. 1997). The irrigation systems constructed and maintained by farmers tend to rely on low-tech construction techniques including building nonpermanent headworks from mud, trees, and stones. International aid agencies have provided considerable funding to government agencies in an effort to upgrade the engineering standards.

In a detailed analysis of data from 150 farmer-governed and national government irrigation systems in Nepal, W. F. Lam (1998) developed three performance measures: (1) the physical condition of irrigation systems, (2) the quantity of water available to farmers at different seasons of the year, and (3) the agricultural productivity of the systems. Using multiple regression analysis techniques to control for environmental differences among systems, Lam found several variables strongly related to these dependent variables. One is the form of governance of the system. Holding other variables constant, irrigation systems governed by the farmers themselves perform significantly better on all three performance measures. This variable has the largest explanatory power of any variable in Lam's analysis, including the physical size of the system, terrain characteristics, and the number of farmers.

Thus, farmers with long-term ownership claims, who can communicate, develop their own agreements, establish the positions of monitors, and sanction those who do not conform to their own rules, are more likely to grow more rice, distribute water more equitably, and keep their systems in better repair than is done under government operation. While there is variance in the performance of these Nepali systems, and also among the forty-seven farmer-governed systems in the Philippines described by de los Reyes (1980), few perform as poorly as government systems assuming other relevant variables are constant. Since many of the government systems rely on high-tech engineering, the capability of farmers to increase agricultural production within their "primitive systems," while also providing the labor to maintain and operate the systems, is particularly noteworthy.

On the Origin of Self-governed Common-Pool Resources

Evidence from field research thus challenges the generalizability of the conventional theory. While it is generally successful in predicting outcomes in settings where appropriators are alienated from one another or cannot communicate effectively, it does not provide an explanation for settings where appropriators are able to create and sustain agreements to avoid serious problems of overappropriation. Nor does it predict well when government ownership will perform appropriately or how privatization will improve outcomes. A fully articulated, reformulated theory encompassing the conventional theory as a special case does not yet exist. On the other hand, scholars familiar with the results of field research substantially agree on a set of variables that enhance the likelihood of appropriators organizing themselves to avoid the social losses associated with open-access, common-pool resources (McKean 2000; Wade 1994; Schlager 1990; Tang 1992; Ostrom 1990, 1992a, 1992b; Baland and Platteau 1996; Ostrom et al. 1994). Drawing heavily on Ostrom (1992b: 298–99) and Baland and Platteau (1996: 286–89), considerable consensus exists that the following attributes of resources and appropriators increase the likelihood that self-governing associations will form.

Attributes of the Resource

R1. Feasible improvement: Resource conditions are not at a point of deterioration such that it is useless to organize or so underutilized that little advantage results from organizing.

R2. Indicators: Reliable and valid indicators of the condition of the resource system are frequently available at a relatively low cost.

R3. Predictability: The flow of resource units is relatively predictable.

R4. Spatial extent: The resource system is sufficiently small, given the transportation and communication technology in use, that appropriators can develop accurate knowledge of external boundaries and internal microenvironments.

Attributes of the Appropriators

A1. Salience: Appropriators are dependent on the resource system for a major portion of their livelihood or other important activity.

A2. Common understanding: Appropriators have a shared image of how the resource system operates (attributes R1, 2, 3, and 4 above) and how their actions affect each other and the resource system.

A3. Low discount rate: Appropriators use a sufficiently low discount rate in relation to future benefits to be achieved from the resource.

A4. Trust and reciprocity: Appropriators trust one another to keep promises and relate to one another with reciprocity.

A5. Autonomy: Appropriators are able to determine access and harvesting rules without external authorities countermanding them.

A6. Prior organizational experience and local leadership: Appropriators have learned at least minimal skills of organization and leadership through participation in other local associations or learning about ways that neighboring groups have organized.

The Importance of Larger Political Regimes

It is important to stress that many of these variables are strongly affected by the type of larger political regime in which users are embedded. Larger regimes can facilitate local self-organization by providing accurate information about natural resource systems, arenas in which participants can engage in discovery and conflict-resolution processes, and mechanisms to back up local monitoring and sanctioning efforts. Perceived benefits of organizing are greater when users have accurate information about the threats facing a resource. The costs of monitoring and sanctioning those who do not conform to rules devised by users is very high, when the authority to make and enforce these rules is not recognized. Thus, the probability of participants adapting more effective rules in macro regimes that facilitate their efforts over time is higher than in regimes that ignore resource problems entirely or, at the other extreme, presume that all decisions about governance and management need to be made by central authorities. If local authorities are not formally recognized by larger regimes, it is difficult for users to establish an enforceable set of rules. On the other hand, if outsiders impose rules without consulting local participants in their design, local users may engage in a game of "cops and robbers" with outside authorities.

Toward a Theoretical Integration

The key to further theoretical integration is to understand how these attributes interact in complex ways to affect the basic benefit-cost calculations of a set of appropriators (A) using a resource (Ostrom 1990: ch. 6). Each appropriator i ($i \in A$) has to compare the expected net benefits of harvesting, using the old rules (BO), with the benefits he or she expects to achieve using a new set of rules (BN). Each appropriator i must ask whether his or her incentive to change (D_i) is positive or negative.

$$D_i = BN_i - BO_i.$$

If D_i is negative for all appropriators, no one has an incentive to change. If D_i is positive for some appropriators, they then need to estimate three types of costs:

C1 the up-front costs of time and effort spent devising and agreeing on new rules;

C2 the short-term costs of adopting new appropriation strategies; and

C3 the long-term costs of monitoring and maintaining a self-governed system over time.

If the sum of these expected costs for each appropriator exceeds the incentive to change, no appropriator will invest the time and resources needed to create new institutions. Thus, if

$$D_i < (C1_i + C2_i + C3_i)$$

for all ($i \in A$), no change occurs.

In field settings, everyone is not likely to expect the same costs and benefits from a proposed change. Some may perceive positive benefits after all costs have been taken into account, while others perceive net losses. Consequently, the collective-choice rules used to change the day-to-day operational rules related to appropriation affect whether an institutional change favored by some and opposed by others will occur. For any collective-choice rule, such as unanimity, majority, ruling elite, or one-person rule, there is a minimum coalition of appropriators, $K \subset A$, that must agree before the adoption of new rules. If for any individual k, a member of K,

$$D_k \leq (C1_k + C2_k + C3_k),$$

no new rules will be adopted. And if for at least one coalition $K \subset A$, it is such that

$$D_k > (C1_k + C2_k + C3_k),$$

for all members of K, it is feasible for a new set of rules to be adopted. If there are several such coalitions, the question of which coalition will form, and thus which rules will result, is a theoretical issue beyond the scope of this chapter. This analysis is applicable to a situation where a group starts with an open-access set of rules and contemplates adopting its first set of rules limiting access. It is also relevant to the continuing consideration of changing operational rules over time.

The rule used to change institutional arrangements in field settings varies from reliance on the decisions made by one or a few leaders, to a formal reliance on majority or super-majority vote, to reliance on consensus or near unanimity. If there are substantial differences in the perceived benefits and costs of appropriators, it is possible that K appropriators will impose a new set of rules on the A–K other appropriators that strongly favors those in the winning coalition and imposes losses or lower benefits on those in the losing coalition (Thompson et al. 1988). If expected benefits from a change in institutional arrangements are not greater than expected costs for many appropriators, however, the costs of enforcing a change in institutions will be much higher than when most participants expect to benefit from a change in rules over time. Where the enforcement costs are fully borne by the members of K, operational rules that benefit the A–K other appropriators lower the long-term costs of monitoring and sanctioning for a governing coalition. Where external authorities enforce the rules agreed on by K appropriators, the distribution of costs and benefits is more likely to benefit K and may impose costs on the A–K other appropriators (see Walker et al. 2000).

The attributes of a resource (listed above) affect both the benefits and costs of institutional change. If resource units are relatively abundant (R1), there are few reasons for appropriators to invest costly time and effort in organizing. If the resource is already substantially destroyed, the high costs of organizing may not generate substantial benefits. Thus, self-organization is likely to occur only after appropriators observe substantial scarcity. The danger here, however, is that exogenous shocks leading to a change in relative abundance of the resource units occur rapidly and appropriators may not adapt quickly enough to the new circumstances (Libecap and Wiggins 1985).

The presence of frequently available, reliable indicators about the conditions of a resource (R2) affects the capacity of appropriators to adapt relatively soon to changes that could adversely affect their long-term benefit stream (Moxnes 1996). A resource flow that is highly predictable (R3) is much easier to understand and manage than one that is erratic. In the latter case, it is always difficult for appropriators (or, for that matter, for scientists and government officials) to judge whether changes in the resource stock or flow are due to overharvesting or to random exogenous variables (see Feeny et al. 1996 for a discussion of these issues related to the collapse of the California sardine industry). Unpredictability of resource units in microsettings, such as private pastures, may lead appropriators to create a larger common-property unit to increase the predictability of resource availability somewhere in the larger unit (Netting 1972; Wilson and Thompson 1993). The spatial extent of a resource (R4) affects the costs of defining reasonable boundaries and then of monitoring them over time.

The attributes of the appropriators themselves also affect their expected benefits and costs. If appropriators do not obtain a major part of their income from a resource (A1), the high costs of organizing and maintaining a self-governing system may not be worth their effort. If appropriators do not share a common understanding of how complex resource systems operate (A2), they will find it extremely difficult to agree on future joint strategies. As Libecap and Wiggins (1985) argue, asymmetric private information about heterogeneous assets may adversely affect the willingness of participants to agree to a reduction in their use patterns before considerable damage is done to a resource. Given the complexity of many common-pool resources—especially multispecies or multiproduct resources—understanding how these systems work may be counterintuitive even for those who make daily contacts with the resource. In resources that are highly variable (R3), it may be particularly difficult to understand and sort out the outcomes stemming from exogenous factors and those resulting from the actions of appropriators. And as Brander and Taylor (1998) have argued, when the resource base itself grows very slowly, population growth may exceed the carrying capacity before participants have achieved a common understanding of the problem they face. Of course, this is also a problem facing officials as well as appropriators. Appropriators with many other viable and attractive options, who thus discount the importance of future income from a particular resource (A3), may prefer to "mine" one resource without spending resources to regulate it. They simply move on to other resources once this one is destroyed, assuming there will always be other resources available to them.

Appropriators who trust one another (A4) to keep agreements and use reciprocity in their relationships with one another face lower expected costs in monitoring and sanctioning one another over time. Appropriators who lack trust at the beginning of a process of organizing may be able to build this form of social capital (Coleman 1988; Ostrom 1992a) if they initially adopt small changes that most appropriators follow before trying to make major institutional changes. Autonomy (A5) tends to lower the costs of organizing. A group that has little autonomy may find that those who disagree with locally developed rules seek contacts with higher-level officials to undo the efforts of appropriators to achieve regulation. (See Libecap 1995 for a discussion of efforts to use the courts to challenge the validity of de facto governance of inshore fisheries in the United States; see also Alexander 1982.) With the legal autonomy to make their own rules, appropriators face substantially lower costs in defending their own rules against other authorities. Prior experience with other forms of local organization (A6) greatly enhances the repertoire of rules and strategies known by local participants as potentially useful to achieve various forms of regulation. Further, appropriators are more likely to agree on rules whose operation they understand from prior experience than on rules that are introduced by external actors and are new to their experience. Given the complexity of many field settings, appropriators face a difficult task in evaluating how diverse variables affect expected benefits and costs over a long time horizon. In many cases, it is just as difficult, if not more so, for scientists to make a valid and reliable estimate of total benefits and costs and their distribution.

Appropriators in the field rarely face a setting that generates clear-cut benefit-cost ratios and the collective-choice rules in some settings give a small elite substantial power to block suggested changes that may generate overall positive gains but some losses for those in power. Consequently, the growing theoretical consensus does *not* lead to a conclusion that most appropriators using common-pool resources will undertake self-governed regulation. Many settings exist where the theoretical expectation should be the opposite: Appropriators will overuse the resource unless efforts are made to change one or more of the variables affecting perceived costs or benefits. Given the number of variables that affect these costs and benefits, many points of external intervention can enhance or reduce the probability of appropriators' agreeing on and following rules that generate higher social returns. But both social scientists and policymakers have a lot to learn about how these variables operate interactively in field settings and even how to measure them to increase the empirical warrantability of the growing theoretical consensus.

Many aspects of the macroinstitutional structure surrounding a particular setting affect the perceived costs and benefits. Thus, external authorities can do a lot to enhance the likelihood and performance of self-governing institutions. Their actions can seriously impede these developments as well. Further, when the activities of one set of appropriators, A, have "spillover effects" on others beyond A, external authorities can either facilitate processes that allow multiple groups to solve conflicts arising from negative spillovers or take a more active role in governing particular resources themselves.

Researchers and public officials need to recognize the multiple manifestations of these theoretical variables in the field. Appropriators may be highly dependent on a resource (A1), for example, because they are in a remote location and few roads exist to enable them to leave. Alternatively, they may be located in a central location, but other opportunities are not open to them because of lack of training or a discriminatory labor market. Appropriators' discount rates (A3) in relation to a particular resource may be low because they have lived for a long time in a particular location and expect that they and their grandchildren will remain in that location, or because they possess a secure and well-defined bundle of property rights to this resource (see Schlager and Ostrom 1992). Reliable indicators of the condition of a resource (R2) may result from activities of the appropriators themselves, such as regularly shearing the wool from sheep (see Gilles and Jamtgaard 1981) or because of efforts to gather reliable information by appropriators or external authorities (Blomquist 1992). Predictability of resource units (R3) may result from a clear regularity in the natural environment of the resource or because storage has been constructed to even out the flow of resource units over both good and bad years. Appropriators may have autonomy to make their own rules (A5) because a national government is weak and unable to exert authority over resources that it formally owns or because national law formally legitimates self-governance—as is the case with Japanese inshore fisheries.

When the benefits of organizing are commonly understood by participants to be very high, appropriators lacking many of the attributes conducive to the

development of self-governing institutions may be able to overcome their lia-
bilities and still develop effective agreements. The crucial factor is not whether
all attributes are favorable but the relative size of the expected benefits and
costs they generate as perceived by participants. All of these variables affect the
expected benefits and costs of appropriators. It is difficult, however, particularly for outsiders, to estimate their impact on expected benefits and costs given
the difficulty of making precise measures of these variables and weighing them
on a cumulative scale. Further empirical analysis of these theoretical proposi-
tions is dependent on the conduct of careful comparative over-time studies of
a sufficiently large number of field settings using a common set of measurement protocols (see Ostrom 1998).

On the Design Principles of Robust, Self-governed, Common-Pool Resource Institutions

Of course, the performance of self-governed common-pool resource systems
varies across systems and time. Some self-governed common-pool resource
systems have survived and flourished for centuries, while others falter and fail.
As discussed above, some never get organized in the first place. In addition to the
consensus concerning the theoretical variables conducive to self-organization,
considerable agreement exists about the characteristics of self-governing systems sufficiently to survive for very long periods utilizing the same basic rules
for adapting to new situations over time (Shepsle 1989).

The particular rules used in the long-surviving, self-governing systems varied substantially from one another. Consequently, it is not possible to arrive at
empirical generalizations about the types of rules used to define members of
a self-governing community, what rights they have to access a common-pool
resource and appropriate resource units, and what particular obligations they
face. It is possible, however, to derive a series of design principles that characterize the configuration of rules that are used. By design principles, I mean an
"element or condition that helps to account for the success of these institutions in sustaining the [common-pool resources] and gaining the compliance
of generation after generation of appropriators to the rules in use" (Ostrom
1990: 90). Robust, long-term institutions are characterized by most of the
design principles listed in box 1.1. The farmer-owned irrigation systems in
Nepal analyzed by Benjamin et al. (1994) and Lam (1998), for example, are
characterized by most of these design principles. Fragile institutions tend to be
characterized by only some of them, and failed institutions by very few (see,
for example, Schweik et al. 1997; Morrow and Hull 1996; Blomqvist 1996).

These principles work to enhance participants' shared understanding of the

Box 1.1 Design Principles Illustrated by Long-enduring Common-Pool Resource Institutions

1. Clearly Defined Boundaries

   Individuals or households with rights to withdraw resource units from the common-pool resource, and the boundaries of the common-pool resource itself, are clearly defined.

2. Congruence
   A. The distribution of benefits from appropriation rules is roughly proportionate to the costs imposed by provision rules.
   B. Appropriation rules restricting time, place, technology, and quantity of resource units are related to local conditions.

3. Collective-Choice Arrangements
   Most individuals affected by operational rules can participate in modifying operational rules.

4. Monitoring
   Monitors, who actively audit common-pool resource conditions and appropriator behavior, are accountable to the appropriators or are the appropriators themselves.

5. Graduated Sanctions
   Appropriators who violate operational rules are likely to receive graduated sanctions (depending on the seriousness and context of the offense) from other appropriators, from officials accountable to these appropriators, or from both.

6. Conflict-Resolution Mechanisms
   Appropriators and their officials have rapid access to low-cost, local arenas to resolve conflict among appropriators or between appropriators and officials.

7. Minimal Recognition of Rights to Organize

   The rights of appropriators to devise their own institutions are not challenged by external governmental authorities.

For common-pool resources that are parts of larger systems:

8. Nested Enterprises
   Appropriation, provision, monitoring, enforcement, conflict resolution, and governance activities are organized in multiple layers of nested enterprises.

Adapted from E. Ostrom (1990: 90).

structure of the resource and its appropriators and of the benefits and costs involved in following a set of agreed-upon rules. Design Principle 1—having rules that clearly define who has rights to use a resource and the boundaries of that resource—ensures that appropriators can clearly identify individuals who do not have rights and take action against them.

Design Principle 2 involves two requirements: The first is congruence between the rules that assign benefits and the rules that assign costs. The crucial thing here is that these rules be considered fair and legitimate by the participants themselves (see McKean 1992). In many settings, fair rules are those that keep a relatively proportionate relationship between the assignment of benefits and costs. In irrigation systems, for example, rules that allocate water to different farmers according to the amount of land they own, as well as duties for costs of operation and maintenance using the same formula, are usually considered by farmers to be fair (as well as effective from an agricultural perspective). The second requirement of this design principle is that both types of rules be well matched to local conditions such as soils, slope, number of diversions, crops being grown, and so on.

Design Principle 3 is concerned with the collective-choice arrangements used to modify the operational rules of regular operation of the resource. If most appropriators are not involved in modifying these rules over time, information about the benefits and costs as perceived by different participants is not fully taken into account in efforts to adapt to new conditions and information over time. Appropriators who begin to perceive the costs of their system being higher than their benefits, and who are prevented from making serious proposals for change, may simply begin to cheat whenever they have the opportunity. Once cheating on rules becomes more frequent for some appropriators, others will follow suit. In this case, enforcement costs become very high or the system fails.

No matter how high the level of conformance to an initial agreement, there are always conditions that tempt some individuals to cheat (even when they perceive the overall benefits of the system to be higher than the costs). If one person is able to cheat while others conform to the rules, the cheater is usually able to gain substantially to the disadvantage of others. Thus, without monitoring of rule conformance—Design Principle 4—few systems are able to survive very long. The sanctions that are used, however, do not need to be extremely high in the first instance. The key requirements of a sanction for an appropriator who has succumbed to temptation are that the appropriator's action is noticed and a punishment meted out. This tells all appropriators that cheating on rules is noticed and punished without making all rule infractions into major criminal events. If the sanctions are graduated (Design Principle 5), however, an appropriator who breaks rules repeatedly and who is noticed doing so eventually faces a penalty that makes rule breaking an unattractive option. While rules are always assumed to be clear and unambiguous in theoretical work, this is rarely the case in field settings. It is easy to disagree about how to interpret a rule that limits appropriation activities or requires input resources. If such disagreements are not resolved in a low-cost and orderly manner, then appropriators may lose their willingness to conform to rules because of the ways that others interpret them in their own favor (Design Principle 6).

Design Principles 7 and 8 are related to autonomy. When the rights of a group to devise its own institutions are recognized by national, regional, and local governments, the legitimacy of the rules crafted by appropriators will be less frequently challenged in courts and in administrative and legislative settings. Further, in larger resources with many participants, nested enterprises that range in size from small to large enable participants to solve diverse problems involving different scale economies. In base institutions that are quite small, face-to-face communication can be utilized for solving many of the day-to-day problems in smaller groups. By nesting each level of organization in a larger level, externalities from one group to others can be addressed in larger organizational settings that have a legitimate role to play in relationship to the smaller entities.

Theoretical Puzzles

In addition to the consensus concerning the variables most likely to enhance self-organization and the design principles characterizing successful long-term governance arrangements, many unresolved theoretical issues still surround the self-governance of common-pool resources. Two major theoretical questions relate to the effects of size and heterogeneity.

Size

The effect of the number of participants facing problems in creating and sustaining a self-governing enterprise is unclear. Drawing on the early work of Mancur Olson (1965), many theorists argue that size of group is negatively related to solving collective-action problems in general (see also Buchanan and Tullock 1962). Many results from game theoretical analysis of repeated games show that cooperative strategies are more likely to emerge and be sustained in smaller than in larger groups (see synthesis of this literature in Baland and Platteau 1996). Scholars who have studied many self-organized irrigation and forestry institutions in the field have concluded that success will more likely happen in smaller groups (see, for example, Barker et al. 1984; Cernea 1989).

On the other hand, most of the 37 farmer-governed irrigation systems studied by Tang were relatively small, ranging in size from 7 to 300 appropriators. Tang did not find any statistical relationship within that size range between the number of appropriators or the amount of land being irrigated and performance variables (1992: 68). In Lam's multiple regression analysis of the performance of a much larger set of irrigation systems in Nepal ranging in size up to 475 irrigators, however, he did not find any significant relationship between either the number of appropriators or the amount of land included in the service area and any of the three performance variables he studied (1998: 115). Further, in a systematic study of forest institutions, Agrawal (2000) has not found smaller forest user groups able to undertake the level of monitoring needed to protect forest resources as moderately sized groups.

One problem with a focus on group size as a key determining factor is that many other variables change as group size increases (Chamberlin 1974; Hardin 1982). If the costs of providing a public good related to the use of a common-pool resource, say a sanctioning system, remain relatively constant as group size increases, then increasing the number of participants brings additional resources that could be drawn upon to provide the benefit enjoyed by all (see Isaac et al. 1994). Marwell and Oliver (1993: 45) conclude that when a "good has pure jointness of supply, group size has a *positive* effect on the probability that it will be provided." On the other hand, if one is analyzing the conflict levels over a subtractable good and the transaction costs of arriving at acceptable allocation formulas, group size may well exacerbate the problems of self-governing systems. Since there are trade-offs among various impacts of size on other variables, a better working hypothesis is that group size has a curvilinear relationship to performance.

Heterogeneity

Many scholars conclude that only very small groups can organize themselves effectively because they presume that size is related to the homogeneity of a group and that homogeneity is needed to initiate and sustain self-governance. Heterogeneity is also a highly contested variable. For one thing, groups can differ along a diversity of dimensions including their cultural backgrounds, interests, and endowments (see Baland and Platteau 1996). Each may operate differently.

If groups coming from diverse cultural backgrounds share access to a common resource, the key question affecting the likelihood of self-organized solutions is whether the views of the multiple groups concerning the structure of the resource, authority, interpretation of rules, trust, and reciprocity differ or are similar. In other words, do they share a common understanding (A2) of their situation? New settlers to a region may simply learn and accept the rules of the established group, and their cultural differences on other fronts do not affect their participation in governing a resource. On the other hand, new settlers are frequently highly disruptive to the sustenance of a self-governing enterprise when they generate higher levels of conflict over the interpretation and application of rules and increase enforcement costs substantially.

When the interests of appropriators differ, achieving a self-governing solution to common-pool resource problems is particularly challenging. Appropriators who possess more substantial economic and political assets may have interests similar to those of appropriators with fewer assets or they may differ substantially on multiple attributes. When the more powerful have similar interests, they may greatly enhance the probability of successful organization if they invest their resources in organizing a group and devising rules to govern it. Those with substantial economic and political assets are more likely to be members of K and thus have a bigger impact on decisions about institutional changes. Mancur Olson (1965) long ago recognized the possibility of a privileged group whereby some were sufficiently affected to bear a disproportionate share of the costs of organizing to provide public goods (such as the organization of a collectivity). A theoretical paper by Bergstrom et al. (1986) presents a general model of a public-good setting where wealth distributions that give more assets to a positive contributor to a public good induce a higher level of contribution from that individual. This theory was tested in the experimental lab by Chan et al. (1996) and given modest support.

An alternative theory is presented in Dayton-Johnson and Bardhan (1998), where two players are independently deciding on their harvesting strategies from a fishery. They explore the question of how inequality of assets affects the timing (and thus the conservation) of harvesting activities. They find a nonlinear relationship between increasing levels of inequality and sustainability of resources whereby income inequality is conducive to resource sustainability at very high levels of inequality but harmful over a broad range. Molinas (1998) presents data from a study of 104 local peasant communities in a poorer region of Paraguay that provide empirical support for a curvilinear relationship between income inequality and, in this instance, levels of local user participation and effectiveness of local groups. Molinas finds, however, that moderate levels of inequality, not the extremes, are positively related to performance.

If those with more assets also have short time horizons (A3) related to a particular resource and lower salience (A1), they may simply be unwilling to expend inputs or may actually impede organizational efforts that might ultimately curtail their productive activities. This problem characterizes some fisheries where local subsistence fishermen have strong interests in the sustenance of an inshore fishery, while industrial fishing firms have many other options and may be more interested in the profitability of fishing in a particular location than in its sustained yield. The conflict between absentee livestock owners and local pastoralists has also proved difficult to solve in many parts of the world.

Differential endowments of appropriators can be associated with extreme levels of conflict as well as very smooth and low-cost transitions into a sustainable, self-governed system. Johnson and Libecap (1982) reason that the difference in the skills and knowledge of different kinds of fishers frequently prevents them from arriving at agreements about how to allocate quantitative harvesting quotas (see also Scott 1993). In this case, heterogeneity of endowments and of interests coincide. Heterogeneity of wealth or power may or may not be associated with a difference in interests. As discussed above, when those with greater assets share similar interests with those who have fewer assets, groups may be privileged by having the more powerful take on the higher initial costs of organizing while crafting rules that benefit a large proportion of the appropriators. Appropriators may design institutions that cope effectively with heterogeneities. Thus, when they adopt rules that allocate benefits based on the same formulas used to allocate duties and responsibilities (Design Principle 2A), appropriators who differ significantly in terms of assets will tend to agree to and follow such rules.

Even in a group that differs on many variables, if at least a minimally winning subset of K appropriators harvesting an endangered but valuable resource are dependent on it (A1), share a common understanding of their situations (A2), have a low discount rate (A3), trust one another (A4), and have autonomy to make their own rules (A5), it is more likely that they will estimate the expected benefits of governing their resource to be greater than the expected costs. Whether the rules agreed on distribute benefits and costs fairly depends both on the collective-choice rule used and the type of heterogeneity existing in the community. Neither size nor heterogeneity is a variable with a uniform effect on the likelihood of organizing and sustaining self-governing enterprises. The debate about their effects is focusing on the wrong variables. Instead of focusing on size or the various kinds of heterogeneity by themselves, it is important to ask how these variables affect other variables as they influence the benefit-cost calculus of those involved in negotiating and sustaining agreements. Their impact on costs of producing and distributing information (Scott 1993) is particularly important.

Conclusion

The conventional theory of common-pool resources, which presumed that external authorities were needed to impose new rules on appropriators trapped into producing excessive externalities on themselves and others, has now been shown to be a special theory of a more general theoretical structure. For appropriators to reformulate the institutions they face, they have to conclude that the expected benefits from an institutional change will exceed the immediate and long-term expected costs. When appropriators cannot communicate and have no way of gaining trust through their own efforts or with the help of the macroinstitutional system within which they are embedded, the prediction of the earlier theory is likely to be empirically supported. Ocean fisheries, the stratosphere, and other global commons come closest to the appropriate empirical referents. If appropriators can engage in face-to-face bargaining and have autonomy to change their rules, they may well attempt to organize themselves. Whether they organize depends on attributes of the resource system and of the appropriators themselves that affect the benefits to be achieved and the costs of achieving them. Whether the appropriators' self-governed enterprise succeeds over the long term depends on whether the institutions they design are consistent with design principles underlying robust, long-living, self-governed systems. The theory of common-pool resources has progressed substantially during the past half century. There are, however, many challenging puzzles to be solved.

Researchers interested in these questions need to continue undertaking case studies that enable us to understand the complex interactions that occur within a particular setting. Case studies that follow developments over a long period of time and those that study failed efforts to change are particularly important. More experimental research also allows us to examine the impact of one variable while controlling other variables in a simple setting. In addition, we need many more large N studies to test the relative importance of different variables. Getting a better empirical foundation for which variables consistently are associated with a higher level of success is important for theory development and policy analysis. Most important are over-time studies that enable us to understand the dynamics of these systems.

Further, serious theoretical work is needed to assess how much of the evolving theory of collective action related to small and regional common-pool resources scales up to apply to global commons (see Young 1995; Gibson et al. 2000). Many of the attributes of resources and appropriators that are conducive to self-organization at a local level are frequently *not* present in relationship to global commons (Keohane and Ostrom 1995). These attributes have to be created rather than simply relying on their presence in "natural settings." Achieving trust in the reliability of others to conform to a set of rules once they are devised, when no central authority exists to monitor and sanction nonconformance, appears to be a crucial problem to be overcome. No one wants to be a "sucker" by adopting costly remedial strategies only to find out that others are not following suit. The design principles for robust institutions able to increase the likelihood of sustainable resources do appear to be as relevant to global commons as they are to local or regional commons (see McGinnis and Ostrom 1996). Institutions that are designed in a manner congruent with these principles speak directly to the need to craft arrangements that are perceived by users to be fair and effective. The core problem is finding ways of organizing new institutions at a supranational level that are consistent with the design principles and that complement essential national, regional, and local institutions instead of trying to replace them.

Policymakers can already take some of the important finds and use them immediately. A consistent finding is that having a supportive legal structure at the macro level authorizes users to take responsibility for self-organizing and crafting at least some of their own rules. Constructing more conducive legal structures is justified on the basis of current evidence. In addition to the local units that users may self-organize, it is important for policymakers to create large-scale agencies that monitor performance of both natural resource systems and those who are using them and to compile accurate information that is available to users. Further, low-cost courts and other conflict-resolution mechanisms allow debilitating conflicts to get resolved sooner. Finally, developing programs whereby users gain more benefits from local resources changes the benefit-cost calculus and increases the likelihood of self-organization.

Resource users also face a challenge. They need to be creating associations where they can share with one another information about their own successes and failures. They need to search for ways of increasing the benefit flow from sustainable use of local resources. It is also important to find ways to decrease monitoring and sanctioning costs by involving users in the choice of regulations so that these are perceived to be legitimate. And to do both of these, it is essential to draw on cultural endowments and users' knowledge of local resources to find innovative institutions that fit local conditions.

Thus, there is a lot for all of us to do.

Notes

1. Segments of this chapter draw extensively on a paper titled "Self-Governance of Common-Pool Resources," in *The New Palgrave Dictionary of Economics and the Law*, vol. 3, edited by Peter Newman, 424–33 (London: Macmillan Press, 1998).
2. While all common-pool resources share the attributes of difficulty of exclusion and subtractability, they vary substantially in regard to size, predictability of flow, whether there is storage, and many other attributes (see Schlager et al. 1994).
3. There is also a very rich experimental literature demonstrating that when subjects face analytical problems with the mathematical structure of the conventional theory but are able to communicate, they are able to reach and maintain agree-

ments that come much closer to the optimal use of the resource. Experimental conditions can create predictable variance in the level of efficiency achieved (see Ostrom et al. 1994 for an overview of this literature).

References

Agrawal, A. 2000. "Small Is Beautiful, but Is Larger Better? Forest Management Institutions in the Kumaon Himalaya, India." In *People and Forests: Communities, Institutions, and Governance,* edited by C. Gibson, M. McKean, and E. Ostrom, 57–85. Cambridge, MA: MIT Press.

Alcorn, J., and V. Toledo. 1998. "Resilient Resource Management in Mexico's Forest Ecosystems: The Contribution of Property Rights." In *Linking Social and Ecological Systems, Management Practices and Social Mechanisms for Building Resilience,* edited by F. Berkes and C. Folke, 216–49. New York: Cambridge University Press.

Alexander, P. 1982. *Sri Lankan Fishermen: Rural Capitalism and Peasant Society.* Canberra: Australian National University.

Baland, J. M., and J. P. Platteau. 1996. *Halting Degradation of Natural Resources. Is There a Role for Rural Communities?* Oxford: Clarendon Press.

Barker, R., E. W. Coward, Jr., G. Levine, and L. E. Small. 1984. *Irrigation Development in Asia: Past Trends and Future Directions.* Ithaca, NY: Cornell University Press.

Benjamin, P., W. F. Lam, E. Ostrom, and G. Shivakoti. 1994. *Institutions, Incentives, and Irrigation in Nepal.* Decentralization: Finance & Management Project Report. Burlington, VT: Associates in Rural Development.

Bergstrom, T., L. Blume, and H. Varian. 1986. "On the Private Provision of Public Goods." *Journal of Public Economics* 29:25–49.

Berkes, F. 1986. "Local-Level Management and the Commons Problem: A Comparative Study of Turkish Coastal Fisheries." *Marine Policy* 10:215–29.

———, ed. 1989. *Common Property Resources: Ecology and Community-based Sustainable Development.* London: Belhaven Press.

Berkes, F., D. Feeny, B. J. McCay, and J. M. Acheson. 1989. "The Benefits of the Commons." *Nature* 340:91–93.

Blomquist, W. 1992. *Dividing the Waters: Governing Groundwater in Southern California.* San Francisco: Institute for Contemporary Studies Press.

Blomquist, W., and E. Ostrom. 1985. "Institutional Capacity and the Resolution of a Commons Dilemma." *Policy Studies Review* 5 (2):383–93.

Blomqvist, A. 1996. *Food and Fashion, Water Management and Collective Action among Irrigation Farmers and Textile Industrialists in South India.* Linköping, Sweden: The Institute of Tema Research, Department of Water and Environmental Studies.

Brander, J. A., and M. S. Taylor. 1998. "The Simple Economics of Easter Island: A Ricardo-Malthus Model of Renewable Resource Use." *American Economic Review* 88 (1) (March): 119–38.

Bromley, D. W., D. Feeny, M. McKean, P. Peters, J. Gilles, R. Oakerson, C. F. Runge, and J. Thomson, eds. 1992. *Making the Commons Work: Theory, Practice, and Policy.* San Francisco: Institute for Contemporary Studies Press.

Buchanan, J. M., and G. Tullock. 1962. *The Calculus of Consent.* Ann Arbor: University of Michigan Press.

Cernea, M. 1989. "User Groups as Producers in Participatory Afforestation Strategies." World Bank Discussion Papers no. 70. Washington, DC: The World Bank.

Chamberlin, J. 1974. "Provision of Collective Goods as a Function of Group Size." *American Political Science Review* 68 (2):707–16.

Chan, K., S. Mestleman, R. Moir, and A. Muller. 1996. "The Voluntary Provision of Public Goods under Varying Endowments." *Canadian Journal of Economics* 29 (1):54–69.

Coleman, J. 1988. "Social Capital in the Creation of Human Capital." *American Journal of Sociology* 91 (1):309–35.

Cordell, J., ed. 1989. *A Sea of Small Boats.* Cambridge, MA: Cultural Survival.

Dasgupta, P. S. 1982. *The Control of Resources.* Cambridge, MA: Harvard University Press.

Dasgupta, P. S., and G. M. Heal. 1979. *Economic Theory and Exhaustible Resources.* Cambridge, England: Cambridge University Press.

Dawes, R. M. 1973. "The Commons Dilemma Game: An N-Person Mixed-Motive Game with a Dominating Strategy for Defection." *Oregon Research Institute Research Bulletin* 13:1–12.

Dayton-Johnson, J., and P. Bardhan. 1998. "Inequality and Conservation on the Local Commons: A Theoretical Exercise." Working paper, University of California, Department of Economics, Berkeley.

de los Reyes, R. P. 1980. *47 Communal Gravity Systems: Organization Profiles.* Quezon City, Philippines: Ateneo de Manila University, Institute of Philippine Culture.

Demsetz, H. 1967. "Toward a Theory of Property Rights." *American Economic Review* 57:347–59.

Feeny, D., S. Hanna, and A. F. McEvoy. 1996. "Questioning the Assumptions of the 'Tragedy of the Commons' Model of Fisheries." *Land Economics* 72 (2):187–205.

Gibson, C., and C. D. Becker. 2000. "A Lack of Institutional Demand: Why a Strong Local Community in Western Ecuador Fails to Protect Its Forest." In *People and Forests: Communities, Institutions, and Governance,* edited by C. Gibson, M. McKean, and E. Ostrom, 135–61. Cambridge, MA: MIT Press.

Gibson, C., E. Ostrom, and T. K. Ahn. 2000. "The Concept of Scale and the Human Dimensions of Global Change: A Survey." *Ecological Economics* 32 (2):217–39.

Gilles, J. L., and K. Jamtgaard. 1981. "Overgrazing in Pastoral Areas: The Commons Reconsidered." *Sociologia Ruralis* 21:129–41.

Gordon, H. S. 1954. "The Economic Theory of a Common Property Resource: The Fishery." *Journal of Political Economy* 62:124–42.

Hardin, G. 1968. "The Tragedy of the Commons." *Science* 162:1,243–48.

Hardin, R. 1982. *Collective Action.* Baltimore: Johns Hopkins University Press.

Isaac, R. M., J. Walker, and A. Williams. 1994. "Group Size and the Voluntary Provision of Public Goods: Experimental Evidence Utilizing Large Groups." *Journal of Public Economics* 54 (1):1–36.

Johnson, R. N., and G. D. Libecap. 1982. "Contracting Problems and Regulation: The Case of the Fishery." *American Economic Review* 72 (5):1,005–23.

Keohane, R. O., and E. Ostrom, eds. 1995. *Local Commons and Global Interdependence: Heterogeneity and Cooperation in Two Domains.* London: Sage.

Lam, W.F. 1998. *Governing Irrigation Systems in Nepal: Institutions, Infrastructure, and Collective Action.* Oakland, CA: Institute for Contemporary Studies Press.

Lam, W. F., M. Lee, and E. Ostrom. 1997. "The Institutional Analysis and Development Framework: Application to Irrigation Policy in Nepal." In *Policy Studies and Developing Nations: An Institutional and Implementation Focus,* edited by D. W. Brinkerhoff, 53–85. Greenwich, CT: JAI Press.

Libecap, G. 1995. "The Conditions for Successful Collective Action." In *Local Commons and Global Interdependence: Heterogeneity and Cooperation in Two Domains,* edited by R. Keohane and E. Ostrom, 161–90. London: Sage.

Libecap, G., and S. N. Wiggins. 1985. "The Influence of Private Contractual Failure on Regulation: The Case of Oil Field Unitization." *Journal of Political Economy* 93:690–714.

Marwell, G., and P. Oliver. 1993. *The Critical Mass in Collective Action: A Micro-Social Theory.* New York: Cambridge University Press.

McCay, B. J., and J. M. Acheson. 1987. *The Question of the Commons: The Culture and Ecology of Communal Resources.* Tucson: University of Arizona Press.

McGinnis, M., and E. Ostrom. 1996. "Design Principles for Local and Global Commons." In *The International Political Economy and International Institutions, Volume II,* edited by O. R. Young, 465–93. Cheltenham, England: Edward Elgar.

McKean, M. A. 1992. "Management of Traditional Common Lands (*Iriaichi*) in Japan." In *Making the Commons Work: Theory, Practice, and Policy,* edited by D. W. Bromley et al., 63–98. San Francisco: Institute for Contemporary Studies Press.

———. 2000. "Common Property: What Is It, What Is It Good For, and What Makes It Work?" In *People and Forests: Communities, Institutions, and Governance,* edited by C. Gibson, M. McKean, and E. Ostrom, 27–55. Cambridge, MA: MIT Press.

Molinas, J. R. 1998. "The Impact of Inequality, Gender, External Assistance and Social Capital on Local-Level Collective Action." *World Development* 26 (3):413–31.

Morrow, C. E., and R. W. Hull. 1996. "Donor-initiated Common Pool Resource Institutions: The Case of the Yanesha Forestry Cooperative." *World Development* 24 (10):1,641–57.

Moxnes, E. 1996. "Not Only the Tragedy of the Commons: Misperceptions of Bioeconomics." Working paper, Foundation for Research in Economics and Business Administration, SNF, Bergen, Norway.

National Research Council. 1986. *Proceedings of the Conference on Common Property Resource Management.* Washington, DC: National Academy Press.

Netting, R. M. 1972. "Of Men and Meadows: Strategies of Alpine Land Use." *Anthropological Quarterly* 45:132–44.

Olson, M. 1965. *The Logic of Collective Action: Public Goods and the Theory of Groups.* Cambridge, MA: Harvard University Press.

Ophuls, W. 1973. "Leviathan or Oblivion." In *Toward a Steady State Economy,* edited by H. E. Daly, 215–30. San Francisco: Freeman.

Ostrom, E. 1990. *Governing the Commons: The Evolution of Institutions for Collective Action.* New York: Cambridge University Press.

————. 1992a. *Crafting Institutions for Self-governing Irrigation Systems.* San Francisco: Institute for Contemporary Studies Press.

————. 1992b. "The Rudiments of a Theory of the Origins, Survival, and Performance of Common-property Institutions." In *Making the Commons Work: Theory, Practice, and Policy,* edited by D. W. Bromley et al., 293–318. San Francisco: Institute for Contemporary Studies Press.

————. 1998. "The International Forestry Resources and Institutions Research Program: A Methodology for Relating Human Incentives and Actions on Forest Cover and Biodiversity." In *Forest Biodiversity in North, Central and South America, and the Caribbean: Research and Monitoring.* Man and the Biosphere Series, vol. 21, edited by F. Dallmeier and J. A. Comiskey, 1–28. Paris: UNESCO.

Ostrom, E., R. Gardner, and J. M. Walker. 1994. *Rules, Games, and Common-Pool Resources.* Ann Arbor: University of Michigan Press.

Posner, R. 1977. *Economic Analysis of Law.* Boston: Little, Brown & Co.

Ruddle, K., and R. E. Johannes, eds. 1985. *The Traditional Knowledge and Management of Coastal Systems in Asia and the Pacific.* Jakarta: UNESCO.

Schlager, E. 1990. "Model Specification and Policy Analysis: The Governance of Coastal Fisheries." Ph.D. diss., Indiana University.

Schlager, E., W. Blomquist, and S. Y. Tang. 1994. "Mobile Flows, Storage, and Self-organized Institutions for Governing Common-Pool Resources." *Land Economics* 70 (3) (August): 294–317.

Schlager, E., and E. Ostrom. 1992. "Property-Rights Regimes and Natural Resources: A Conceptual Analysis. *Land Economics* 68 (3):249–62.

Schweik, C. M., K. Adhikari, and K. N. Pandit. 1997. "Land-Cover Change and Forest Institutions: A Comparison of Two Sub-basins in the Southern Siwalik Hills of Nepal." *Mountain Research and Development* 17 (2):99–116.

Scott, A. D. 1955. "The Fishery: The Objectives of Sole Ownership." *Journal of Political Economy* 63:116–24.

————. 1993. "Obstacles to Fishery Self-Government." *Marine Resource Economics* 8:187–99.

Sengupta, N. 1991. *Managing Common Property: Irrigation in India and the Philippines.* New Delhi: Sage.

Shepsle, K. A. 1989. "Studying Institutions: Some Lessons from the Rational Choice Approach." *Journal of Theoretical Politics* 1:131–49.

Simmons, R. T., F. L. Smith, Jr., and P. Georgia. 1996. *The Tragedy of the Commons Revisited: Politics versus Private Property.* Washington, DC: The Center for Private Conservation.

Tang, S. Y. 1992. *Institutions and Collective Action: Self-Governance in Irrigation.* San Francisco: Institute for Contemporary Studies Press.

Thompson, L. L., E. A. Mannix, and M. H. Bazerman. 1988. "Negotiation in Small Groups: Effects of Decision Rule, Agendas and Aspirations." *Journal of Personality and Social Psychology* 54:86–95.

Wade, R. 1994. *Village Republics: Economic Conditions for Collective Action in South India.* San Francisco: Institute for Contemporary Studies Press.

Walker, J. M., R. Gardner, A. Herr, and E. Ostrom. 2000. "Collective Choice in the Commons: Experimental Results on Proposed Allocation Rules and Votes." *The Economic Journal* 110(460):212–34.

Wilson, P. N., and G. D. Thompson. 1993. "Common Property and Uncertainty: Compensating Coalitions by Mexico's Pastoral *Ejidatarios.*" *Economic Development and Cultural Change* 41 (2):299–318.

Young, O. R. 1995. "The Problem of Scale in Human/Environment Relationships." In *Local Commons and Global Interdependence: Heterogeneity and Cooperation in Two Domains,* edited by R. Keohane and E. Ostrom, 27–45. London: Sage.

Part One

LOCAL COMMONS

Chapter 2

When the Commons Become Less Tragic: Land Tenure, Social Organization, and Fair Trade in Mexico

JOSÉ SARUKHÁN AND JORGE LARSON

Common Property versus Communal Appropriation

Widespread and uncritical use of the metaphor of the tragedy of the commons has provoked a confusion that tends to equate *communal* with *common,* although the terms are clearly not synonymous.

Communal land tenure is a form of property rights, while the tragic exploitation of the commons is a problem of poorly defined property rights. The latter is a process of natural resource use that is related primarily with nonsessile wild populations such as fisheries and game. The former is related to a patrimonial view of natural resources, linked to peasant communities with hereditary transmission of property rights over the land. In many peasant and indigenous communities, like those of Mexico, land tenure and the resources the land contains have clearly defined property rights, though it is not an individual who owns them but the community or the *ejido* as a whole. In contrast to open-access resources, in the Mexican communal land property systems, an agreement usually exists about who can use or appropriate the resources.

The issue we address in this chapter is whether the "tragedy of the commons" *sensu stricto* (Hardin 1968) is a fundamental issue to be resolved with respect to the conservation and use of natural resources in Mexico. We present a historical overview of the utilization of natural resources, land tenure, and communities in rural Mexico. We begin by briefly exploring the deep pre-Hispanic roots of our modern rural society. The time span involved and the issues reviewed force us to move from one scale to another and to rely on varied sources. The different sections include information on the pre-Hispanic use of natural resources and social organization related to land tenure and an update on current rural population size and its distribution, land tenure systems, and social organization. We end with a selection of study cases of resource use taken from various regions of Mexico and analyzed from different approaches.

Our point of view stresses that a patrimonial perspective of all land, coupled with a strong social organization, conforms to many of the elements of the design principles for stable and sustainable utilization of communal resources proposed by Ostrom (1990) and discussed in chapter 1 of this book. Assessing the problems and opportunities of the commons at different scales also allows the inclusion of distant beneficiaries. The distant beneficiaries are not only consumers subsidized by natural capital, but they are also coresponsible stakeholders in the stewardship of local, regional, and global commons.

Natural Resources and Land Tenure Systems in Pre-Hispanic Mesoamerica

The brief historical overview of this section has two objectives. First, we explore the importance that *eminent domain*[1] played in the management of natural resources in pre-Hispanic times and its resonance with modern trade privileges. Second, we set a background argument about the role of a culture of rural resistance in ecological and social sustainability.

For the flourishing urban centers of Mesoamerica, an agricultural surplus was a necessity. Among the frequently identified attributes of this cultural region we find cacao, chía, chinampas, coa sticks, corn, and periodic market systems (Porter 1972). A list of goods offered as tributes reveals that besides corn, chía, beans, and squash obtained from agricultural activities, there was also a constant input of products such as honey, firewood, and construction materials; feathers; and chairs made of tule (a reed from freshwater wetlands). These products were derived from extractive activities in wildlands. Thus, the forests (tropical, temperate, or semiarid) were also under human pressure and some kind of management probably existed over these ecosystems.

Although present-day landholding systems in Mexico have undergone recent, profound modifications with potential social, economic, and conservation consequences, they still reflect attributes of the land tenure organization that existed in precolonial times. It cannot be assumed, however, that a direct and univocal connection exists between the two. Historical studies have shown significant differences and discontinuities between essential elements of the indigenous precolonial and colonial rural communities and the peasant communities of today (García-Martínez 1992). The main difference is that in pre-Hispanic times, social linkages and political entities were based to a great extent on the principle of personal association (e.g., trade or government) rather than on territorial association (Hoekstra 1990). Following this line of argument, García-Martínez (1992) concludes that the delimitation of a social or political space was determined by the presence or absence of individuals or groups, which participated in the association linkage, and not by the territorial delimitation of an area. Territorial association was predominantly a result of the colonial period, but the strong association among people remained, derived from common political and cultural links among them.

The historical literature contains little information on how different pre-colonial peoples in Mexico organized their land tenure systems and particularly their modes of utilization of natural resources. The sociological, political, and economic aspects of such groups as the Nahuatl have been studied, but such studies do not cover the forms of appropriation of the natural resources.

In pre-Hispanic Mexico, for each fundamental institution or social rank there were different land tenure systems. In *tlatocamilli* land, the peasants had the obligation to produce goods for the kings, or *tlatoani*. The lords, or *teuctli*, had enough productive land to support their activities and those of their dependents. The next social rank was the *pipiltin*, or nobles, whose land was assigned to them by the *teuctli* to which they belonged. The surplus produced on these lands allowed them to perform their obligations as military personnel, ambassadors, or tribute collectors (Carrasco 1979). As far as we know land tenure was neither communal nor private, but the assignment of land was in a sense a salary for work in public affairs in the three higher social ranks. This means that political and administrative decisions (i.e., personal associations) defined land tenure systems. Although these rights were inherited, to exercise them it was necessary to have approval by a higher authority and to fulfill the obligations related to the possession of land.

Finally, the peasants of the Nahua world were organized around a system of ethnic states called *altepetl*. Lockhart (1992) and García-Martínez (1969, 1992), among others, describe the *altepetl* as a unit which, having a territorial basis, was not restricted to it, but was also built on a personal, social, or political relation. More than a system defined on the basis of strict land-property, the *altepetl* was a unit of jurisdictional rights or eminent domain, which could go beyond the geographic boundaries of a group of land holdings. Trade of specific products was one of the privileges an *altepetl* could exert as part of its eminent domain. This concept is clearly related to jurisdiction, which is fundamental to any politically organized collectivity, and implies the reach of the recognized and legitimate linkages of any human association, especially in the accepted realm of the authority that emanates from such association. The exercise of an eminent domain is a manifestation of a jurisdictional right, as is the application of administrative and justice functions. This eminent domain implied the capacity to rule over the allotment of land to landless people; to regulate uses of the land, water, and other resources for the best interests of the community; and also to exert administrative and legal powers over the members of the *altepetl*.

The *altepetl* in its simplest manifestation—most *altepetl* were much more complex—required minimally a territory, a set of constituent parts named *calpolli,* usually in a given number often associated with astronomical, cosmological, or mythological elements. *Calpolli* were constituted by wards of between 20 and 100 households, the leader of the ward being responsible for land allocation and tax collection among other things. Each *calpolli* was intimately linked to the *altepetl* by a canonical rotation, in a fixed sequence, of duties such as draft labor or delivery of agricultural and forest products throughout the year (see fig. 2.1). The *altepetl* had a dynastic ruler called *tlatoani.* An established *altepetl* would usually possess a main temple as a symbol of its sovereignty and a specific area for the marketing of products (Lockhart 1992). Territory was not restricted to land tenure but included the capacity to govern and manage a cohesive culture and strong social institutions (Alcorn 1994).

Although little is known of the jurisdictional bases on which the indigenous authorities decided the distribution of land, water, and resources, a few examples speak of the way in which indigenous communities regarded natural resources. Gibson (1964) refers to examples of water rights leasing as a means of revenue for a given community. Even more interesting, communities

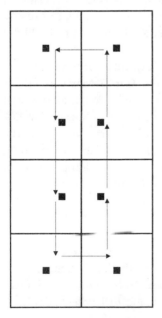

Figure 2.1. An idealized *altepetl* with eight symmetrical *calpolli.* Redrawn from Lockhart (1992). Black squares are the urban centers of each *calpolli* and arrows indicate rotation. In Nahuatl culture, mentions of urban settlements always refer to the *altepetl* as a whole, including its rural areas and component *calpolli.* Moreover, within the *altepetl* the exercise of power was rotated continuously among *calpolli.* When this organizational scheme is visualized in real nonsymmetrical *calpolli* within a complex geography it is clear that natural resource management and trade had strong influences on *altepetl* organization.

under the *altepetl* system considered the land, which was not used for agriculture, part of their communities' patrimony. During the early colonial period, they considered the incursions of Spaniards to poach for lumber and fuelwood illegal and damaging to such patrimony. While the Spanish regarded forested areas as idle lands or wastelands, the indigenous communities valued them as natural resources in reserve, a heritage for the future to be carefully managed, from which they derived a great diversity of needed goods. Clearly, the cultural perception of a natural resource made all the difference in the way conquerors and conquered related to it. In this case, the views of the conquered who survived rested on a culture of a longlasting rural resistance. In contrast, the centralized urban power was dependent on considerable natural capital inputs: tributes, taxes, low prices for nonprocessed goods, and cost-free environmental services.

The jurisdictional and eminent domain characteristics of the *altepetl* had no effect on the Spanish, even when they were living in indigenous territories. They enjoyed, therefore, a status of extraterritoriality (García-Martínez 1992), which allowed them to dispose of new (mostly forested) lands and the resources they contained in the way they deemed most appropriate.

With the conquest began a process of accelerated change in the *altepetl* system. In its attempts to gain full control of the land, the Spanish Crown confiscated the rights of eminent domain of the *altepetl* and the Indian pueblos. Indigenous people were then restricted to the geographical extensions of their land. They lost the capacity to collect taxes, demand religious duties, and administer justice. With the loss of around 75 percent of their population to smallpox, indigenous groups also lost hereditary rights to their former landholdings, and their traditions of jurisdictional domain totally eroded (García-Martínez 1992). It is important to recognize that erosion of the eminent domain occurred through retaining trade privileges for the Spaniards. As early as 1600, the Zoque Indians of Chiapas were constrained to the production of *grana* (a dye obtained from a Coccinnidae that grows on a cactus). The Spaniards allowed them to keep property rights over their *nopaleras* (cactus groves with different degrees of management); in exchange for respecting the land that was already theirs, they agreed not to participate in the commercialization of the dye (García de León 1985). This is a concrete example of the way Spaniards confiscated the eminent domain rights of indigenous peoples.

It is also important to note that development of colonial phenomena such as social stratification and the resulting exploitation of the peasant population, ethnic discrimination, conquest, and tribute were not entirely new to indigenous groups. In fact, according to several historians (e.g., Broda 1979), the peasant egalitarian community results from colonial policies and is not a continuity from pre-Hispanic tradition. In other words, the pre-Hispanic populations that had been socially stratified became obligatorily peasant and "indigenous." Therefore resistance became a *modus vivendi* for almost everyone, regardless of his or her original social status before the conquest. Later recovery of their populations, especially toward the end of the nineteenth century, forced indigenous peoples to obtain land to feed increasing populations. The hacienda system provided many indigenous populations with work as laborers. In many cases the haciendas became important and relatively efficient centers of agricultural production. They also operated as "agricultural experimental field stations" where new and adapted production techniques were tried and their results shared with neighboring production units.

After almost three centuries of colonial rule and nearly one more under independent Mexico, only 1 percent of the agricultural land was in the hands of indigenous communities at the beginning of the twentieth century. However, indigenous people had been the majority of the population throughout these eras (Otero 1989).

Rural Mexico in the Twentieth Century

The process of land recovery for the peasants had extremely high social and human costs in an agrarian revolution that sacrificed at least 1 million lives. The community land tenure structure and many aspects of the traditional political organization of the precolonial indigenous groups were lost in the first revolution of the twentieth century. However, cultural diversity, particularly the part of the culture that defined the relations of societies to nature, remained fairly unaltered in many of the indigenous communities. This was possible largely because the myriad small indigenous groups were shut off from the mainstream of development of the urban centers in a highly centralized country. They depended completely on the wise utilization of their natural resources for subsistence. The basic patterns of population growth, rural/urban coefficients, and the biological and social considerations that show the importance of conservation outside reserves have already been presented in Sarukhán et al. (1996). Characteristics such as spatial extent of the resource, population size, distribution, dependence on a natural system and its resources, shared image of the operation of the resource, and capacity and leadership to organize in a participative form conform to the attributes of resources and appropriators that Ostrom (1992 and in chapter 1 of this book) and Baland and Platteau (1996) recognize as conducive to an increased likelihood that self-governing societies will form. We add to these factors the fact that a *rural resistance culture* has played a historical role in the preservation of the self-governing systems of many rural and indigenous communities.

In our view, success in specific natural resource appropriation scenarios should be measured in three different conceptual frameworks. First, practices should be nondestructive of the resource base; there should be a positive or equal balance between biomass productivity and extraction, with resources remaining biologically diverse. Second, the group should have sociocultural identity. Cultural and political mechanisms for peaceful conflict resolution should remain or be reconstructed. Cultural traits (such as group work, labor division, and collective innovation) related to production processes are vital for continuous adaptation. Language is evidently a fundamental characteristic of culture. However, in rural Mexico some indigenous people retain language without other essential components of communal organization, and some rural communities have lost language identity but are still living under strong communal organization schemes. Third, economic success is very important. Cash crops are essential to all production units because they provide a link with the formal economy that allows resistance and self-sufficiency to become sustainable. A balance must be developed between cash crops and production for self-consumption in order to obtain positive measures of economic success.

Rural Resistance

Rural Mexico is a mosaic of different land tenure systems and strategies for using natural resources that are closely related to local cultural traits and the ecological properties of the land. The Spaniards conquered the Aztecs, who constituted a powerful state that dominated many of the peasant populations and their cultures through warfare and tribute (taxes). The Aztecs had extended their influence to regions as far away as present-day northwestern Costa Rica. Such domination implied diverse impacts on natural resources. Thus the resistance of rural populations to centralized power did not arise for the first time as a result of the conquest. It had existed at the core of the survival strategies of indigenous peoples since ancient times. For example, the Chinantecos, an indigenous Mexican group inhabiting northern Oaxaca and adjoining western Veracruz, are forest people who have resisted the assails of Aztecs and Spaniards and of independent, revolutionary, and modern Mexico. The final result of this resistance is the conservation of most of their forests and the retention of their cultural traits and autonomy. This is not to say that the Chinantecos have done well in every sense. In fact, they remain economically and socially marginalized. However, the natural and human assets they possess are superior to those of other indigenous groups in Mexico that have undergone profound territorial, environmental, and cultural transformations.

The survival of Mayan culture without a centralized Mayan power is another example of the relationship between rural resistance and self-sufficiency. All of the living indigenous and peasant groups of Mayan origin belong to a common cultural matrix, with profound time roots, that has seen the rise and fall of many city-states, both local and foreign. Valuable knowledge and experience of the Maya peoples in the sustainable use of natural resources are only marginally found in archaeological registers. Rather, the Mayan culture has been constantly recreated and kept alive by rural communities and transmitted continuously from generation to generation. A splendid example of this traditional and living culture is the *tzeltal* ethnobotany documented by Berlin et al. (1974).

Rural resistance is organized around self-sufficiency, a concept that clearly resonates with sustainability in productive, social, and ecological systems (García et al. 1991). A culture of resistance, linked to a patrimonial view of the land, is probably one of the most important similarities among precolonial, colonial, and modern rural communities in Mexico. The peculiarities and organization of these communities are the results of social changes that have modified their original historic forms but still allow us to recognize the many strong influences of the past. The most striking characteristic of contemporary Mexico is a large and pluricultural indigenous population that constitutes an enormously important element of Mexican culture and that is, in turn, closely linked to biodiversity. Indigenous communities dominate much of rural landscape in Mexico and help shape the ownership mosaic.

Population Size and Distribution and Their Relation to the Spatial Extent of Resources

The following statistics for Mexico are of high significance in influencing modes of sustainable resource utilization. There are at present around 5.6 million people (of five years of age and over) whose first language is not Spanish. This figure increased between 1930 and 1995 from 2.3 to 5.6 million persons, although the percentage of the total population they represent decreased for the same period from 16 percent to 6 percent (Fernández 1998). They represent at least fifty-four different ethnic groups, which speak more than 240 languages. The rural population in Mexico in 1995 constituted 26.5 percent of the total, down from 71.3 percent at the beginning of the century (Núñez 1998). The greatest relative reduction of rural population took place in the 1950s.

About 90 percent of the 198,430 human settlements in Mexico have 1,000 or fewer inhabitants (INEGI 1995). This figure is similar to or even higher than that of India, where 73 percent of the 557,000 villages have fewer than 1,000 inhabitants (Agarwal and Narain 1989). Figure 2.2 is a map showing localities that have fewer than 100 inhabitants. Including settlements of between 100 and 1,000 persons produces an indiscernible blotch in most of the territory, at the scale permitted by this book. The picture is clear: The rural population of Mexico is atomized, broadly dispersed, and organized in small villages with different levels of community organization and cultural identity. The smallest communities are often isolated from most social services and tend

Figure 2.2. Rural localities in Mexico with populations of a hundred individuals or fewer (INEGI 1995). This figure expresses clearly that the rural population of Mexico is highly dispersed and there are few places with no human settlements. The figure showing localities with populations of 1,000 or fewer was completely saturated with dots.

to maintain their cultural and social organization traits. Many may maintain these traits, despite the efforts of an external higher-level authority to exert influence on the organization schemes or modes of production of these communities.

Types of Land Ownership

There are two types of fundamentally communal ownership: (1) the *ejido* (some 30,000 of them) and (2) communal lands. The latter usually derive from rights recognized by the Spanish Crown to original settlers, and their extent and legal status are highly diverse. Fragmentation of the territory of indigenous peoples is one of the outcomes of a complex historical process of land rights given, taken, and violated many times. *Ejidos,* on the other hand, are clearly a result of the 1910 revolution and its agrarian reform that extended for nearly four decades. They tend to be land assignments to peasants with no specific identity as communities, cultures, or indigenous peoples, who are typically *mestizos.* However, *ejidos* are also managed collectively. More than 90 percent of the indigenous population lives in forested areas, both tropical and temperate, and the rest live in arid and semiarid regions (Toledo 1998). According to Toledo, a little more than two-thirds of all rural production units of the country are owned by indigenous groups; these units represent about 50 percent of the Mexican territory, 70 percent of all forested areas, and 80 percent of land devoted to agriculture. Most of the latter is rain-dependent agriculture. Between 70 percent and 80 percent of Mexico's forest is under the management of some 7,000 to 8,000 *ejidos* and indigenous communities.

Figure 2.3 is a schematic representation of the spatial relationship between the population speaking the indigenous language and conserved vegetation. Although not all indigenous people live in areas classified as conserved, 22 percent of them are immersed in this type of vegetation. For the sake of clarity, we eliminated localities with 75 percent or more indigenous-language speakers who were not within conserved vegetation perimeters, although they could be very close. Consequently, this 22 percent is an underestimation of the extent of spatial correlation between conserved vegetation and indigenous populations. The map shows that many areas of Mexico that still have forests also have many local communities. Arid regions were eliminated from the map because cartographic information is less reliable in these areas regarding the differentiation between conserved and disturbed vegetation.

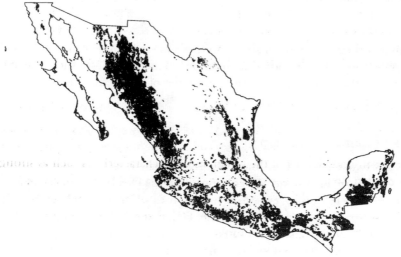

Figure 2.3. Conserved vegetation and localities with high indigenous populations. Gray areas are conserved tropical and temperate forests. Black dots represent localities immersed in conserved vegetation where people speaking the indigenous language represent 75 percent or more of the local population. There are 10,365 localities where 75 percent or more of the population speaks the indigenous language. Twenty-two percent are within vegetation areas classified as conserved.

The *ejido* was defined on the basis of the 1917 constitution, arguably the most sweeping agrarian reform of its time in the world. The constitution established in its Article 27 a juridical context that not only gave heed to the social aspects but also had an environmentally oriented emphasis. Article 27 declared all the land property of the nation, which had the right to transfer it to individuals or communities. Until recently, *ejido* land was devised and operated under this conception as a hereditary and unalienable communal property. Thus it could not be sold, rented, or fragmented. As Córdova (1984) suggests, the 1917 constitution represented a truly progressive position not only from the point of view of social advances, but also in reference to its ecological perspectives (Toledo 1996).

It is interesting to note that almost half of the total number of *ejidos* are located in the biologically richest areas of Mexico. Consequently, either *ejidos* or indigenous communities occupy more than three-fourths of the surface of the Natural Protected Areas of Mexico. Toledo (1998) notes that two-thirds of the territory of the state of Oaxaca, biologically the richest in Mexico, is owned by some 1,400 *ejidos* and indigenous communities. Although Oaxaca has very few protected areas in its tropical or temperate forested areas, it still has much of the remaining tropical rain forest in Mexico.

We have selected some case studies that show where communal properties can be managed effectively, with a social organization that promotes individual participation, based on a common knowledge of the ecological principles that underlie the natural systems on which those societies rely heavily for their subsistence. We also discuss the factors that determine why these systems can break down and cease being self-governing, sustainable models of production.

Selected Examples of Natural Resource Management in Mexico

Specific cases from different parts of Mexico and different perspectives illustrate the complexity of the issues but also illustrate positive experiences. It is important to note that all of these regions share characteristics such as strong social organization (whether strictly indigenous or not), social forms of land tenure, diversified production, and a delicate balance between self-sufficiency and production of cash crops. All of them are also under constant pressure to transform cultural and production traits.

Totonacs in Veracruz: A Diversified Agro-Silvicultural Communal System

One such example has been studied in detail by Toledo et al. (1994) in a region comprising the central part of the state of Veracruz and the northern part of the state of Puebla, bordering close to the northern limit of Neotropical evergreen or semi-evergreen forests in North America. The region, known as

Totonacapan, is inhabited by nearly 200,000 Totonac Indians, descendants of the constructors of the world-famous sites of El Tajín and Río Bobos. They have inhabited this region for at least 700 years and brought to cultivation a worldwide important plant species: vanilla. The region was for a long time the principal production area of this plant.

Until 1940, the area had a relatively large extension of well-preserved tropical semi-evergreen forest and produced maize and beans mostly for self-subsistence purposes, besides the traditional vanilla pods, tobacco, and native rubber (*Castilla elastica*), the latter locally industrialized (Ortiz 1993). Land-use patterns changed significantly in the three following decades with the introduction of citrus, coffee, and banana plantations, as well as an incipient introduction of cattle ranching. The latter has been responsible for most of the forest destruction process. From the 1940s onward, forests have consistently been transformed into extensive, inefficient pastureland or converted to grain production. It is estimated that some 0.5 million ha of tropical forests in this region were lost to agricultural and grazing lands in this period (Ortiz 1993).

The study by Toledo et al. (1994) was centered in an area managed under the *ejido* system in the town of Plan de Hidalgo, with nearly 900 people of whom 80 percent speak Totonac and 7 percent were strictly monolingual. The land of the *ejido* was divided into an area of 122 lots and a communal land territory of nearly 1,500 ha. Each lot has the traditional dimension of 40 × 40 m, which shows the deep roots of the Nahuatl cultural matrix. What is somewhat surprising is that these roots are found in places far from the *ejido's* central political powers at the time of the conquest. The members of the *ejido* provided Toledo and his colleagues with a fascinating description of the *ejido's* physical and biological environment. It included a taxonomy of more than twelve soil types, a classification of landscape units that recognizes vegetation types, successional stages of vegetation and different uses of the land, and, especially, a detailed classification of the major groups of plants, animals, and fungi. This illustrates the people's profound knowledge of the biological diversity available. Landscape management units are identified mostly in relation to the secondary successional processes and whether the units are structurally forest-like or have been transformed (e.g., into pastures). This approach to landscape utilization shows the importance of viewing ecological processes as resources for traditional management schemes (Alcorn 1989).

Totonacs operate in a double economic system including production of commodities for the market and acquisition of merchandise with their proceeds, and production of goods for self-consumption. Shifting agriculture, then, becomes only one of several modes of production for this group. Totonacs use six main landscape units for production purposes: (1) *milpas,* or mixed-maize cropping; rainfed fields, with a rich accompanying plant diversity that serves as a source of food, medicinal plants, biological control, and so on; (2) agricultural monocultures; (3) cash-crop plantations; (4) livestock production areas; (5) managed and unmanaged forests, where vanilla and fuelwood are the main products; and (6) *solares,* or home gardens, backyard agroforestry systems where more than 100 species of plants are used for medicine, food, fuel, construction, and ornamental purposes, and where an array of domesticated and semiwild animal species are kept as food sources.

Households of the *ejido* use the land production units fairly equitably; nearly three-quarters of all households utilize areas of between 7 and 9 ha, less than 10 percent managing more than 9 ha of land. In addition to the equitable use of land, the system in the *ejido* Plan de Hidalgo shows a small-scale use of resources and a multifaceted strategy of resource appropriation. Toledo and his colleagues analyzed the economic aspects of production in the *ejido* and concluded that "the main strategies adopted by the majority of households are economically profitable" with an economic balance that is "always positive." Their calculations on the economy of the system show that, for a typical family of seven members using 8 ha of land and a total of 400 man/days of work, the system "allows both the food and energetic self-sufficiency plus an economic return of over $8,000 US per year."

This example concentrates on the diversified use of the landscape for ecological sustainability and economic bet-hedging to produce a minimum level of social stability and development. These are important traits within qualitative measures of success. The delicate balance between production for the market and for the community shows that the local commons are managed in a sensible way. External market and government forces can dislodge the local balance easily, however. The local ecology and productive system are vulnerable to ecologically insensitive economic incentives (e.g., the stability of cattle price versus unpredictable markets for nontimber forest products). External consumers may be able to value the local ecology if products from it can be certified as coming from sound ecological production systems and adequate social practices. Soft intellectual property rights, such as trademarks and geographical indications of origin, can also help to bridge the distance between local producers and external consumers who value local commons as part of the global commons.

Chicle: A Biological Resource That Raises New Questions about the Commons, Communities, and Intellectual Property Rights

Chicle (natural chewing gum) was originally obtained as the latex from a tree known commonly as *chicozapote,* or sapodilla in the English-speaking world (*Manilkara zapota*). This species is of Amazonian origin and is distributed in

Mesoamerica in what is known as the Gran Petén, a region that covers the southern part of the Yucatán peninsula (the states of Campeche and Quintana Roo), northern Guatemala and Belize, and some marginal areas in Honduras. It reaches the northernmost distribution of the semi-evergreen tropical forests in Mexico, which corresponds to northern Veracruz and the Huastecas (Heaton 1997). This very ample distribution range, particularly to its northern limits, is very probably due to strong anthropogenic activity related to the many uses of the *chicle* tree, which resulted in protection or propagation of *chicozapote* trees for thousands of years (Sarukhán 1968). *Chicozapote* is used not only for its latex, but also for its valued fruit, which has become increasingly improved and commercialized. Its wood is hard and longlasting because of the presence of triterpenoids that provide resistance to insects and rotting (Hart et al. 1973 in Heaton 1997). In fact, many of the support structures of ancient Mayan ruins still standing today belong to this species.

The ecological importance of the *chicle* tree is fundamental to the conservation of the Mayan tropical rain forests. It is an important species in terms of arboreal density and forest structure. Its fruits are an important food source for many species of wild birds and mammals. Consequently, protection of *Manilkara zapota* as a source of latex constitutes a means of protecting an important structural component of the forest. In addition, this form of resource extraction does not involve substitution of homogeneous cultivars for the germplasm diversity of natural stands of forest. In fact, *chicozapote* germplasm has been distributed widely in Asia. India has three times more area producing sapodilla fruit than does Mexico. These Asian regions have much higher yields of the fruit than any other region within the natural distribution area of *chicozapote*. This raises the issue of germplasm diversity as a global common. If we value the genetic pools of marginal crops as global commons, then the local dimension of *chicozapote* conservation also needs to involve distant stakeholders such as consumers in developed countries who value natural products, or the developing nations that benefit from the germplasm pool.

The natural distribution of *chicle* in the Petén area crosses three international borders. The forms of land tenure, social organization, and management schemes differ from country to country. In Mexico the *chicle* tree is distributed within protected areas (e.g., the Calakmul Biosphere Reserve) and in *ejidos* that are owned by local communities, belonging either to the Mayan matrix or to more distant regions such as Veracruz. In fact, many settlers come from the Totonacapan area described in the previous example. In Guatemala, the forest occurs in communal lands and in a very large nationally protected area called the Mayan Biosphere Reserve. In Belize, it is present in nature reserves and private properties. Such a diverse array of social and political situations multiplies the number of stakeholders involved.

However, all of them confront the same challenge: to conserve biological diversity through the sustainable use of forests. Experience has shown that the geology and soils of the greater Petén pose clear limits to agriculture and cattle ranching. This is one reason why *chicle* extraction is now at the heart of the sustainable development efforts in the three countries. In Mexico a *Plan Piloto Chiclero* reorganized latex-tapping activities and established fixed minimum prices and social benefits for resource users. This process derived from the organizational experience of the *Plan Piloto Forestal* of Quintana Roo, where the positive experience of sustainable tropical forest management by rural communities has been well documented (Kiernan and Freese 1997). In Guatemala, the *chicleros* obtain extraction quotas allocated by the government. In Belize, private holders either hire labor or rent the land for *chicle* extraction (Aldrete and Eccardi 1993). A nature reserve in Belize regards *chicle* extraction as a means of obtaining income for the support of its conservation activities (Evans and Hornbostel 1997).

Chicle clearly constitutes a common resource. A walk along any stretch of the Mayan tropical forest shows that most trees have been tapped in the last three or four decades. Besides the problems of quota allocations at a local scale, which are solved differently in each situation, the problem faced by all the stakeholders is that the market is controlled by a few buyers who have the capacity to exert strong control on the price of *chicle*. The potential for organization that the producers have is limited within each country and constrained by national frontiers. This condition allows intermediaries to lower prices and buy from whichever individual, organization, or community is willing to sell. The importance of social organization to the financial viability of sustainable resource use is obvious in the case of *chicle*.

The price of the raw material is only one of the key issues. A high price with no social organization would lead to the typical situation that creates the tragedy of the commons. A high price with social organization can lead to the conservation of the forest and the development of sustainable forestry practices. Low prices, which the intermediaries and buyers seek to increase their private profits, tend to weaken social organization and may lead to a perverse market incentive to transform the forest into uses such as transient agriculture and cattle ranching.

Chicle presents an interesting set of issues. At a very local scale, strong social organization can help solve the problem of excluding potential beneficiaries by incorporating them into communal interests and organization. In fact, many *chicleros* live in communities but have no specific land assignments, because they are either newcomers (*avecindados*) or young members of the community who received very small allotments of land. Thus, communal approaches to natural resource appropriation are a way of diminishing the tragedy of the commons, where once again, the market value of the resource plays a key role in the sustainability of that resource and its conservation.

However, communal organization is not enough for success in production and trade. Technical expertise for transformation from latex to chewing gum is nonexistent locally, chicleros are selling a raw product without much added value, and they are not yet marketing a finished product directly to consumers. This process of vertical integration by chicleros has technical complexities and opportunities on its own, and they will probably need to develop complex alliances with researchers, intermediaries, and industry. In the end, they will also need to communicate with their potential consumers.

It is not easy to lay bridges between distant potential beneficiaries and the owners of local commons. How does an urban consumer of *chicle* in Tokyo, Rome, or Mexico City recognize the link between chewing natural gum and conserving the Mayan forest that houses the largest jaguar and harpy eagle populations north of Panama? How can this fact affect his choice of products as a consumer when he lives in a region that produces the overwhelming majority of synthetic chewing gum sold in the world? Obviously education and public awareness play a fundamental long-term role, but to make a difference within this generation we need to go into product marketing and protecting the trade rights of peasant communities. In this specific case, rights and obligations deriving from the commercial use of the name *Chicle* and its biological content are an appealing alternative. Here again, as in the case of the vanilla or coffee of the Totonacs, soft intellectual property rights may play an important role. Collective trademarks identifying *chicle* with the Mayan forest may help add value and retain it in local communities if the owners of the resource are also the owners of the trademark and the right to license the use of the name *Chicle*. To develop the recognition for a geographical indication of origin, in the meaning given by European countries to Appellations D'Origin Controlles, there will have to be a full transformation of the latex into natural chewing gum or other finished products within the region without foreign materials such as chemicals or synthetic flavors or colors. For the time being such collective trademarks should be used in products containing natural *chicle* in convergence with trademarks belonging to those transforming the raw material and marketing natural gum. This would represent, in a sense, a modern recognition of the eminent domain that the local communities of the greater Petén should have over *chicle*.

Community-based Forest Management Systems

It is important to understand that *ejidos* and communities (UNOFOC 1997) own 80 percent of the remaining temperate and humid tropical forests of Mexico. Within this context, the importance of communal approaches to sustainability in Mexico's rural landscapes is evident, particularly in forests and diverse agroecosystems.

In a comparison of nine communities that manage their forests for timber production, Merino and collaborators (Cabarle et al. 1997) have studied elements of the natural systems as well as those pertaining to the communities. Such elements influence the success with which different groups manage their forest resources sustainably and with a satisfactory economic margin. Communities vary in regard to ethnic origin, population size, economic structure, social organization, the type and extension of their forests, and the different schemes of timber extraction they utilize.

Very often, a major obstacle for the management and conservation of productive forest systems by rural communities is that forests have already been "skimmed" of their best timber, have low levels of economic value, and have deteriorated ecologically. Frequently this problem results in a lowered valuation of the forest resource by the members of the community and in little incentive to invest in and learn adequate forestry management practices.

A clear definition of territorial extension and property was found to be a fundamental condition for achieving stability of forest utilization and to compete successfully with alternative uses of the land, such as agriculture and low-productivity cattle ranching. Some of the factors that help explain why some communities conserve the use of the land under forestry systems and others cede to the temptation to change the forest for other uses are (a) the degree to which forest utilization is a viable economic option, (b) how much control the communities themselves exert over their natural resources, and (c) how convinced the communities are that the forest is a renewable resource that is worth the effort to appropriately manage and preserve (Merino 1997).

The authors found that the majority of the communities they studied derive substantial economic benefit from the forest products extracted when the communities have carried out forest management plans. The forests render to their owners a number of important and appreciated ecological services, such as natural springs, firewood, construction materials, and edible and medicinal products. These services are not in themselves the reason why communities manage and maintain the forests. The economic income produced by the forest products is the main driver for conservation and wise management of the forest systems. Therefore, isolation of the areas does not guarantee forest conservation if it means that the forest products do not have an adequate or economically viable market.

Forest management plans are an important element defining adequate utilization of the forest. At times, these plans are devised solely to comply with bureaucratic requirements. To achieve a well-devised plan requires acquisition by community members of technical capacities for forest management, availability of external advisors on forest management techniques, and resources of sufficient quantity and quality to justify the level of investment necessary for forest management (Merino 1997).

The high levels of biological diversity present in the majority of sites studied by Merino and her group offer little direct social or economic benefit to the owners of the land. As Merino (1997) points out, it is very difficult to generate demand for forest products beyond those very few which already have an established market, such as pine wood, red cedar, and mahogany. In addition, the so-called ecological dumping in the international markets (i.e., the offering of products by companies or communities that do not internalize the ecological costs of timber extraction) poses severe limitations to research and investment in the utilization of many more components of the forest's biological diversity.

An additional obstacle faced by communities that try to manage their forests to achieve an attractive and stable income source is the generalized lack of incentives from the government toward good forest management. For the time being, no more than 10 percent of all forests in Mexico could be certified in the international markets as having sustainably managed forest products (estimation of Castaños [1992], cited by Merino 1997). Governments should stimulate practices that will enable more forests, foresters, and forest product consumers to move in this direction.

Nonwood forest products are different from timber in the ways in which their environmental or social values can be capitalized or protected by soft intellectual property rights. Biological resources such as the honey of melipona stingless bees, understory-grown vanilla, or baskets from vines are candidates to a stronger protection than organic or sustainability certification. Some of them should be identified by collective trademarks, and many comply with the requisites of strict geographical indications.

We could provide additional well-documented examples of the influence of culture and social organization on ecological sustainability (see Oldfield and Alcorn 1991; Reichhardt et al. 1994 for many examples). However, we feel that the cases described have set the stage for the conclusion to this chapter.

Conclusion

We concentrate our final discussion on two different issues that are nonetheless closely related with respect to the commons in modern rural Mexico. The first issue centers on the pervasive political aspects of specific solutions that Mexico must face to achieve a sustainable rural landscape from a socioeconomic and ecological perspective. We then discuss the need for trade policies to address issues surrounding the use of local products processed for national or global markets. Sustainable extraction of these products and their processing depends largely on the access of local people to a fair share of the products' market value.

In Mexico, as in many other countries with widely distributed rural populations that own and depend on the resources of natural ecosystems for their subsistence, the nonconsumptive approach to biodiversity conservation, such as exhibited in isolated and totally protected nature reserves, is fundamental but clearly limited (Sarukhán et al. 1996). Sustainable and diversified processes of extraction and production are necessary conservation alternatives (see Freese 1997 for a critical discussion of the "use it or lose it" debate).

However, based on the cases presented, we cannot claim that land tenure systems such as *ejidos* or communal lands constitute by themselves models of the rational and ecologically sound use of natural resources. In fact, there are many contrary examples in Mexico, where social land tenure regimes remain, but the basic traditional cultural traits have disappeared or been seriously eroded. This alienation comes from internal and external political, social, and economic forces that destroy the inherent social organization of communities and have tended to provoke dependency on an agrarian political and economical bureaucracy, largely ignorant of the ecologically and socially sound use of common resources.

This is painfully and frequently seen in governmental schemes in Mexico and elsewhere. During the last four decades, the resettlement of landless people from the northern and central semiarid regions to the tropical forest areas has resulted in wholesale deforestation, serious forest fragmentation, and establishment of extensive, unproductive cattle ranching. Many socially owned lands failed to be ecologically sound productive units because of erroneous agrarian policies. The private banking system, which never considered *ejidos* as subjects for loans, exacerbated the problem. Recent modifications of land tenure regimes in Mexico will allow *ejidos* and communities to use their land as a guarantee for loans, thus "resolving" one of the problems they have faced, because it may help them capitalize sustainable production projects. The social and economic conditions in which these modifications have taken place, however, do not lead to an optimistic view of future possibilities.

The 1992 changes in the constitution regarding agrarian issues altered the regime of social land tenure. They constitute one of the most serious potential threats to a rural social organization system that has proven in many cases to be successful in providing economic support to its members, with a reduced impact on or even enhancement of natural resources. In the opinion of Alcorn and Toledo (1997), "these recent changes have the potential to undermine the community-based sector and expand the individual property rights to mine resources in ecologically fragile areas, instead of seeking ways to support ecologically sustainable agricultural systems." The new law potentially allows the return of large landholdings or *latifundios,* which were characteristic of the pre-revolutionary period of Mexico.

The new changes to the constitution do not address some of the crucial problems associated with ecosystem deterioration; land erosion; pollution; damage to rivers, lakes, and wetlands; and the loss of biodiversity. In fact, Mexico has laws on forestry, hunting, fishing, wildlife, ecological equilibrium, and environmental protection, but the agricultural sector lacks any such regulations. The agrarian law that existed before the recent amendments focused on models of social organization and land tenure, which we have shown to be key elements for the conservation of natural resources. Their modification leaves rural Mexico lacking any legal or formal sectorial policy in agriculture that may help reduce the effect of the reform. Neither biological conservation nor sustainability issues were considered during the reform. Between 1997 and 1999 there have been discussions and initiatives to regulate access to genetic resources and benefit sharing, biosafety, and rural development. All these initiatives fail to consider a fundamental issue: the conservation and sustainable use of genetic resources. Constitutional reform was inspired by the hypothetical assumption that "efficiency" and "productivity" would result from more "corporate" models of tenure and management. Those who promoted the reform reasoned as if Mexico's landscapes were similar to the homogeneity of the Corn Belt in the United States of America. The threats to the very rich biodiversity of communal lands, mostly those in forested areas and agrosilvicultural systems, are quite obvious.

Abundant literature engages the theoretical debate about the advantages and disadvantages of communal versus private or corporate systems of land ownership (e.g., Pimentel and Pimentel 1979; Netting 1993; Toledo et al. 1985; Toledo 1994; Wilken 1987). From the perspective of sustainability, it is quite clear that communal and small property systems of production using moderate or low external agricultural inputs (e.g., fertilizers, pesticides, improved seeds, machinery, irrigation) are more efficient than large holdings relying on subsidies and high-energy inputs. These examples of efficiency and ecological rationality do not tend to produce changes in policy and regulations because as modes of production they are marginal to financial considerations and politically opposed to centralized powers.

The decisions that eventually define which production systems are promoted by countries immersed in globalization processes should depend on the conception that the rural and urban components of a society have about the type of development they want for their country. At the core of the decision, one needs to ask who is going to pay for the external costs involved in the modes of production favored in that country.

A central issue in evaluating the ecological efficiency of communal property systems as units of production that lead to a more sustainable use of biological resources is whether the considerable human resources and social value of the rural population are brought into the mainstream of development of a country. Substantial human capital is represented by the indigenous and rural communities, which have their own forms of social, political, and productive organization. This human capital has been largely ignored or considered an intractable burden for the modern development of a country. Recent social unrest in rural Mexico is a direct and relevant example of this situation. At the end of the day, this is a decision that must involve not only the idea of sustainable productivity, but also the sustainability of rural societies. Social considerations are at least as important as economic and ecological ones.

We also note that by incorporating indigenous peoples and peasants organized in *ejidos,* we do not disregard other social groups. Rather we need to add their social and biological wealth to enrich the general trends of development of the country. The modern forestry and agricultural sector is part of the mosaic of the rural landscape. This sector is a major stakeholder in economic development as it produces and exports much of the food and raw materials that a predominantly urban Mexico will demand in this new century. However, incorporating the social sector of rural Mexico into the development project must be a priority if we are to deal effectively with ancestral and unsolved social problems and to open more opportunities for biological conservation in our megadiverse country.

Where social organization is active and keeps traditions alive, the exclusion of potential beneficiaries is not a fundamental problem at a local scale. Everyone in the community is expected to benefit from the commons. The problem we should be aware of is the capability of the community for keeping those benefits at a stable and predictable level. This is related to the issues of temporal and spatial scales.

The tragedy of the commons at a local scale is not a fundamental issue in Mexico because social structures still exist that diminish its effects. The issue of scale is crucial because of the need to involve consumers in Mexico and abroad who value the conservation of a lifestyle that results in the conservation of biological diversity at the local scale. The physical distance between the local and external stakeholders is such that direct interaction among them is virtually impossible. If we recognize a common value, then socially and environmentally sensible trade policies need to offer a practical means by which consumers can identify in the global marketplace the products that indigenous peoples and peasants are deriving from socially and ecologically sustainable systems, recognizing those people's rights to a fair share of the economic value of their resources. In Alcorn's (1991) words, "Future humans will nurture these [conservation] systems if they have a moral commitment to both biodiversity and their fellow human beings."

If the biosphere is a global common, then globalized institutions such as the Convention on Biological Diversity, the World Trade Organization, and the World Intellectual Property Organization must recognize that a healthy biosphere is built on healthy local environments. National and international organizations must lay bridges between these two dimensions so as to build up sustainability from local to regional, to national, and finally to global scales. It is our view that many socially organized, sustainable uses of resources are being developed at local scales in many parts of the world, but the next step is to consolidate the capacity of such communities to participate in the global market. The decades-old slogan "act locally, think globally" is still valid, but it is necessary for global and national institutions to complement it by acting globally and thinking locally.

Acknowledgments

The authors thank Eduardo Martínez, Norma Moreno, Enrique Muñoz, and Daniel Ocaña for their support in the elaboration of the maps. José Sarukhán was a Tinker Professor at the Center for Latin American Studies and the Center for Conservation Biology, Stanford University, at the time this chapter was written. Jorge Larson received partial support from a John D. and Catherine T. MacArthur Foundation fellowship (1998–2000) for the writing of this chapter.

Note

1. The concept of eminent domain used in this text is broader than that commonly used in English-speaking North America. The latter refers to the capability of government to condemn a property and pay compensation for it.

References

Agarwal, A., and S. Narain. 1989. *Toward Green Villages: A Strategy for Environmentally Sound and Participatory Rural Development*. New Delhi: Centre for Science and Environment.

Alcorn, J. B. 1989. "Process as Resource, the Agricultural Ideology of Bora and Huastec Resource Management and Its Implications for Research." In *Natural Resource Management by Indigenous and Folk Societies in Amazonia*, edited by D. A. Posey and W. Balee. Advances in Economic Botany Series, no. 7: 63–77.

———. 1991. "Epilogue: Ethics, Economies, and Conservation." In *Biodiversity: Culture, Conservation and Ecodevelopment*, edited by M. B. Oldfield and J. B. Alcorn. Boulder, CO. Westview Press.

———. 1994. "Noble Savage or Noble State: Northern Myths and Southern Realities in Biodiversity Conservation." *Etnoecológica* 2 (3):7–19.

Alcorn, J. B., and V. M. Toledo. 1997. "Resilient Resource Management in Mexico's Forest Ecosystems: The Contribution of Property Rights." In *Linking Social and*

Ecological Systems for Resilience and Sustainability, edited by F. Berkes and C. Folke. Stockholm: Beijer International Institute for Ecological Economics.

Aldrete, M., and F. Eccardi. 1993. "Primer encuentro regional de productores de chicle Guatemala-Belice-México." Manuscript Chetumal, Quintana Roo, México.

Baland, J. M., and J. P. Platteau. 1996. *Halting Degradation of Natural Resources. Is There a Role for Rural Communities?* Oxford: Clarendon Press.

Berlin, B., D. Breedlove, and P. H. Raven. 1974. *Principles of Tzeltal Plant Classification.* New York: Academic Press.

Broda, J. 1979. "Las comunidades indígenas y las formas de extracción del excedente: época prehispánica y colonial." In *Ensayos sobre el Desarrollo Económico de México y América Latina (1500–1975),* edited by E. Florescano. Mexico City: Fondo de Cultura Económica.

Cabarle, B., S. Madrid, F. Chapela, and L. Merino. 1997. "La silvicultura comunitaria mexicana frente a los estándares privados internacionales." In *El Manejo Forestal Comunitario en México y sus Perspectivas de Sustentabilidad,* coordinated by L. Merino. Mexico City: CRIM-UNAM, SEMARNAP, and Consejo Mexicano para la Silvicultura Sostenible. Washington, DC: World Resources Institute.

Carrasco, P. 1979. "La economía prehispánica de México." In *Ensayos sobre el Desarrollo Económico de México y América Latina (1500–1975),* edited by E. Florescano. Mexico City: FCE.

Córdova, A. 1984. "Nación y nacionalismo en México." Mexico City: *Nexos* 8.

Evans, A., and V. Hornbostel. "Protected Areas Management and Geographical Information Systems: A Case Study of Chicle Extraction Management in the Rio Bravo Conservation and Management Area." Master's thesis, Yale University, 1997.

Fernández, P. 1998. "Los montos de la población indígena." *Demos* 11:33–34.

Freese, C. H. 1997. "The Use It or Lose It Debate." In *Harvesting Wild Species: Implications for Biodiversity Conservation,* edited by C. H. Freese. Baltimore: John Hopkins University Press.

García Barrios, R., L. García Barrios, and E. Alvarez-Buylla. 1991. *Lagunas: Deterioro ambiental y tecnológico en el campo semiproletarizado.* Mexico City: El Colegio de México.

García de León, A. 1985. *Resistencia y utopía: Memorial de agravios y crónicas de revueltas y profecías acaecidas en la provincia de Chiapas durante los últimos quinientos años de su historia.* Tomo 1. Mexico City: Ediciones Era.

García-Martínez, B. 1969. *El Marquesado del Valle: Tres siglos de régimen señorial en Nueva España, México.* México City: El Colegio de México.

———. 1992. "Una distinción fundamental en la historia de los pueblos de indios del México colonial." *European Review of Latin American and Caribbean Studies* 53:47–60.

Gibson, C. 1964. *The Aztecs under Spanish Rule: A History of the Indians of the Valley of Mexico, 1519–1810.* Stanford, CA: Stanford University Press.

Hardin, G. 1968. "The Tragedy of the Commons." *Science* 162:243–48.

Heaton, H. J. "A Study of Variation in Chicozapote (*Manilkara zapota*)." Master's thesis, University of California at Riverside, 1997.

Hoekstra, R. 1990. "A Differential Way of Thinking: Contrasting Spanish and Indian Social and Economic Views in Central Mexico (1550–1600)." In *The Indian Community of Colonial Mexico: Fifteen Essays on Land Tenure, Corporate Organizations,*

Ideology and Village Politics, edited by A. Ouwenee and S. Miller. Amsterdam: CEDLA.

INEGI, 1995. *Resultados definitivos del conteo de población y vivienda 1995 de los Estados Unidos Mexicanos.* CD-ROM. Mexico City: INEGI.

Kiernan, M. J., and C. H. Freese. 1997. "Mexico's Plan Piloto Forestal: The Search for Balance between Socioeconomic and Ecological Sustainability." In *Harvesting Wild Species: Implications for Biodiversity Conservation,* edited by C. H. Freese. Baltimore: John Hopkins University Press.

Lockhart, J. 1992. *The Nahuas After the Conquest.* Standford, CA: Stanford University Press.

Merino, L. 1997. *El manejo forestal comunitario de México y sus perspectivas de sustentabilidad,* coordinated by L. Merino, México: CRIM-UNAM, SEMARNAP, and Consejo Mexicano para la Silvicultura Sostenible. Washington, DC: World Resources Institute.

Netting, R. M. 1993. *Smallholders, Householders.* Standford, CA: Stanford University Press.

Núñez, L. 1998. "Los determinantes demográficos del crecimiento de la población rural y urbana." *Demos* 11:6–7.

Oldfield, M. L., and J. B. Alcorn. 1991. *Biodiversity: Culture, Conservation and Ecodevelopment.* Boulder, CO: Westview Press.

Ortiz, B. "La cultura asediada: Espacio e historia en el trópico veracruzano. El caso del Totonacapan." Master's thesis, CIESAS del Golfo, Xalapa, Veracruz, Mexico, 1993.

Ostrom, E. 1990. *Governing the Commons: The Evolution of Institutions for Collective Action.* New York: Cambridge University Press.

———. 1992. "The Rudiments of a Theory of the Origins, Survival, and Performance of Common-Property Institutions." In *Making the Commons Work: Theory, Practice and Policy,* edited by D. W. Bromley et al. San Francisco: ICS Press.

———. 2000. "Reformulating the Commons." In *Protecting the Commons: A Framework for Resource Management in the Americas,* edited by J. R. Burger, R. Norgaard, E. Ostrom, D. Policansky, and B. Goldstein. Washington, DC: Island Press.

Ostrom, E., R. Gardner, and J. M. Walker. 1994. *Rules, Games, and Common-Pool Resources.* Ann Arbor: University of Michigan Press.

Otero, G. 1989. "Agrarian Reform in Mexico: Capitalism and the State." In *Searching for Agrarian Reform in Latin America,* edited by W. C. Thiesenhusen. Boston: U. Hyman.

Pimentel, D., and M. Pimentel. 1979. *Food, Energy and Society.* New York: Wiley Sanderson.

Porter, W. M. 1972. *The Aztecs, Maya, and Their Predecessors: Archaeology of Mesoamerica.* New York: Seminar Press.

Reichhardt, K. L., E. Melink, G. P. Nabhan, and A. Rea. 1994. "Habitat Heterogeneity and Biodiversity Associated with Indigenous Agriculture in the Sonoran Desert." *Etnoecológica* 2 (3):21–34,

Sarukhán, J. "Análisis sinecológico de las Selvas de Terminalia amazonia en la planicie costera del Golfo de México." Master's thesis, Colegio de Postgraduados, Chapingo, México, 1968.

Sarukhán, J., J. Soberón, and J. Larson. 1996. "Biological Conservation in a High Beta-Diversity Country." In *Biodiversity, Science and Development: Towards a New Partnership,* edited by F. di Castri and T. Younés. Wallingford, England: CAB International and IUBS.

Toledo, V. M. 1994. *La ecología, Chiapas y el Artículo 27: Hacia una modernización rural alternativa.* Mexico City: Ediciones Quinto Sol.

———. 1996. "The Ecological Consequences of the Agrarian Law of 1992." In *Reforming Mexico's Agrarian Reform,* edited by L. Randall. Armonk, NY: M. E. Sharpe.

———. 1998. "Biocultural Diversity and Local Power in Mexico: Challenging Globalization." In *Endangered Culture, Endangered Species,* edited by L. Maffi. Oxford University Press.

Toledo, V. M., J. Carabias, C. Mapes, and C. Toledo. 1985. *Ecología y autosuficiencia alimentaria.* Mexico City: Siglo XXI.

Toledo, V. M., B. Ortiz, and S. Medellín-Morales. 1994. "Biodiversity Islands in a Sea of Pasturelands: Indigenous Resource Management in the Humid Tropics of Mexico." *Etnoecológica* 2 (3):37–49.

UNOFOC. 1997. *Forestería comunal.* Special publication of the Unión Nacional de Organizaciones de Forestería Comunal. México City: UNOFOC.

Wilken, G. C. 1987. *Good Farmers: Traditional Agricultural Resource Management in Mexico and Central America.* Berkeley: University of California Press.

Chapter 3

Forest Resources: Institutions for Local Governance in Guatemala

CLARK C. GIBSON

Forests are complex sets of resources. They can generate multiple products, both consumptive and nonconsumptive, that mature at different times. Some may be common-pool resources, while others are private goods, and still others are public goods providing ecosystem services for regions, countries, and continents. Forests may also be valuable for their absence—the land they cover may be worth more to individuals than their trees.

Given the many and possibly overlapping biological and economic characteristics of forests, their effective governance is not a straightforward issue. While in many countries of the Americas ownership by centralized governments has been the norm for at least the last fifty years, few national governments can afford the extensive level of monitoring required by the number and size of their legal forest holdings. Most national governments have discharged their forest duties by selling concessions to logging companies, ignoring many of their other gazetted management duties. The result has been unimpressive forest management and increasing global concern over the fate of forests (Arnold 1998).

The challenges confronting those interested in the governance of forest resources at the local level are also daunting. Individuals living near or in forests face the same large and complex set of forest characteristics as do governments. These individuals must also contend with the varied preferences of others if they seek to manage a community forest. Even if locals develop internal institutional solutions, they may be challenged by various types of outsiders—ranging from predatory governments to other resource-hungry communities living nearby in an ever-changing economic and political arena. The obstacles to constructing effective institutions to manage forest resources at the community level are substantial.

71

Nevertheless, individuals at the local level have successfully constructed institutions in some locations. When will this happen? When will this fail? Ostrom (chapter 1, this volume) provides a general theory of institutional creation for managing common-pool resources. She argues that individuals will create and sustain rules about forests only when they see greater benefits than costs in doing so. Ostrom also provides lists of attributes regarding resources and users that affect the cost-benefit analyses of individuals. Ideally, these attributes can be systematically tested to explore the compelling issues and theories regarding the governance of forests. Such cost-benefit analyses are important steps forward in our understanding of how people interact with their forests, how they might construct rules to govern their forest resources, and how such knowledge may be put to use in advising the governments, donors, and nongovernmental organizations that seek alternatives to conventional models of forest management.

In this chapter I contribute to the analysis of forest governance by identifying the necessary conditions for the creation of institutions regarding the management of common-pool resources. I argue that at least two conditions are necessary: dependence and scarcity (Gibson et al. 1998). I examine and illustrate these two conditions with examples of institutional creation in two communities in Guatemala. The data for this chapter were collected using the protocols of the International Forestry Resources and Institutions Research Program, a collaborative network of researchers. The IFRI program seeks to understand the impact of institutions on forests by collecting and analyzing socioeconomic and ecological data from the local level (Ostrom 1998; see also the IFRI Web page at www.indiana.edu/~ifri). Teams of researchers representing multiple disciplines spent around one month at each site conducting interviews and taking biophysical measurements, including a sample of forest plots (the fieldwork for Morán took place in June and July 1996, Las Cebollas in June 1998).

At each site, the communities possess attributes that many observers believe to be crucial for the creation of self-governance, such as prior experience with building institutions and a general lack of external government interference. The individuals in these cases did not, however, automatically create institutions to govern their valuable common forest resources, even though both communities have the skills and experience to do so. Instead, the communities built institutions where they viewed the resources on which they depend to be scarce.

The Necessary Conditions for Institutional Creation

When do members of a community construct institutions to manage their natural resources? This is a central question for those exploring local-level natural resource management. The answer is, of course, far from straightforward. Scholars have presented many sets of conditions and offered hundreds of cases in their efforts to explain the success and failure of collective action regarding natural resources (e.g., Agrawal and Yadama 1997; Bromley 1992; Gibson et al. 2000; McKean 1992; Wade 1994; Libecap 1989; Ostrom 1990; Baland and Platteau 1996; Ostrom et al. 1994; Arnold 1998).

Researchers generally emphasize the costs and benefits that accrue to individuals from group action. If the difference between the costs and benefits of constructing an institution to manage a resource is not positive, no incentive exists for individuals to invest their time, efforts, or money in the enterprise. For example, while a majority of people in a community would stand to gain if a rule about harvesting was in place, the costs of discussing and agreeing on such a rule could be greater than the future stream of benefits to the individual. Or if ethnic tensions exist among members of a community, the costs of constructing an institution to manage a natural resource are greater than in a community with more harmonious relations. In a cost-benefit calculus, the expected net positive benefits of an institution provide incentives for individuals to craft management rules. Such research is, of course, in part a matter for empirical study: Such conditions and factors will be present to varying degrees and interact in different ways over space and time. If enough cases employ similar concepts and agree on units of measurement, comparisons can be made to determine which attributes at what levels are more important than others to promote collective action (see Ostrom and Wertime, 2000).

Instead of offering my own list of the attributes of users and resources most important to institutional creation, I argue that two conditions are necessary for the emergence of self-governing institutions for natural resources. These two conditions—dependence and scarcity—must be present before individuals will incur the costs of establishing and enforcing their own rules.

Dependence and Scarcity

If we assume that individuals generally act when it is in their interest to do so, two conditions are necessary before they will expend the effort to manage a commonly held natural resource (in this study we address forest resources). First, individuals must view themselves as dependent on some forest resource (see Ostrom's attribute A1). The reasoning for this condition is straightforward. Unless a resource provides some benefit, individuals will not incur the costs entailed in constructing an institution to manage it (and such costs can be quite high since, at a minimum, individuals must cope with the processes of decision making, monitoring, and enforcement structures [e.g., Perrings 1995; Ascher 1995]). Note that dependence is not the same as an economist's concept of value. Economists define value by scarcity; dependence does not necessarily imply scarcity. All humans depend on the breathable atmosphere, while for economists, its plenitude obviates its value. Dependence does not need to be defined in terms of pecuniary benefits. Community members may be highly dependent on sacred or recreational forests, and may consider it worth their time and effort to manage them.

Although the dependence condition appears somewhat trivial, it continues to frustrate conservationists as they seek to build projects with the help of local communities. The things that conservationists value (conservation, biodiversity, carbon sinks, intact biomes) may not be the same as those on which local communities depend (Bailey 1996). Locals may not see themselves as dependent on ecosystem-level collective goods. Community members, therefore, must be induced with other benefits (more money, land, or resources, less erosion, cleaner water, and the like) to participate in such schemes. Such projects are fragile because these other benefits generally do not last when the projects end (Carrasco 1993).

Despite its obvious nature, dependence is also quite difficult to measure precisely, especially across cases. As economists have discovered in their attempts to measure the "total economic value" (TEV) of a resource (total economic value includes the benefits of direct use [e.g., timber and nontimber forest products], indirect use [e.g., ecosystem services], option values [e.g., potential revenues from less consumptive enterprises such as tourism], and existence values [e.g., sacred forests or totem animals; Pearce and Moran 1995]), most communities depend on forests for specific products. Dependence on each product, in turn, is affected by conditions such as the availability of substitutes, location of markets, and local household economic strategies. Further, subsets of the community may be dependent on different products, making it difficult to derive any single accurate measure of the dependence of an individual or a community on a forest's resources.

The IFRI protocols used in this study employ a number of measures to determine how individuals depend on a forest, including perceived levels of dependence on the forest for important resources, amounts harvested, availability and cost of substitutes, distribution of dependence within the community for each product, uses for each product, changes in product levels over time, and so on (IFRI Field Manual 1999).

The second condition necessary for the emergence of self-governance is scarcity: Individuals must perceive a resource to be scarce before they will contribute to a collective solution. If individuals view a resource as plentiful, they will not be willing to endure costs to manage it. This condition is also relatively well known to both academics and conservationists. Indeed, anthropologists following Boserup's (1965) thesis of population-induced agricultural intensification argue that without scarcity there are few reasons for people to create and maintain rules about resources (e.g., Harner 1975: 125; Johnson and

Earle 1987: 10–11; Netting 1993: 157–188). Perception is key here. For example, if little land for extensive migration actually exists, but if people perceive that they can use up a forest's resources and move on, they will be less inclined to organize to manage their current actions and resources.

In sum, the conditions of dependence and scarcity must both be present before members of a community will engage in the construction of institutions to manage their natural resources. If individuals do not see themselves as dependent on a resource, they will not organize to manage it whether or not it is scarce. If individuals do not perceive a resource as scarce, they will not organize to manage it whether or not they are dependent on it.

Dependence, Scarcity, and Institutions: The Cases of Morán and Las Cebollas

Although located in different parts of eastern Guatemala, the communities of Morán and Las Cebollas share many characteristics. (See figure 3.1.) The

Figure 3.1. Location of study sites in Guatemala.

members of both communities practice subsistence agriculture. They depend on forest products for fuelwood, timber, and cattle grazing. And they are also largely left alone by national and subnational governments, which have allowed them to craft local institutions regarding their natural resources.

The pattern of institution-crafting we find in Morán and Las Cebollas illustrates the importance of the dependence and scarcity conditions. The residents of both communities have established institutions to manage agricultural land, which is considered valuable and relatively scarce. The communities have approached forest management differently, however. Members of Morán have not constructed many rules about their forest's use. It remains an open-access forest for community members. The Las Cebollas community possesses a similar open-access forest that locals use extensively. But community members have also created and enforced rules that prevent harvesting from a particular forested patch, called the Protective Forest. Because locals in these communities do not view the product streams from most of their forests as scarce, they have no incentive to invest in creating institutions to manage them, even though they are dependent on their products. However, part of the Las Cebollas forest was seen by locals as essential to the production of water for agriculture. This perceived scarcity of water helped to motivate families in Las Cebollas to create the rules for a Protective Forest even as the community ignores the ongoing depletion of other forested areas.

The Settlements of Morán and Las Cebollas

The community of Morán is located at 1,200 m above sea level within the watershed of the Río Santiago, a subwatershed of the Río Motagua in the Sierra de las Minas mountain range (see table 3.1 and fig. 3.2). The community falls inside the political borders of the department of Zacapa and the municipality of Río Hondo. Morán is also located within the buffer zone of the Sierra de las Minas Biosphere Reserve. Morán is composed of sixty-nine households; the people of Morán are campesinos, or subsistence farmers, practicing milpa agriculture traditional to most Central America. The most important crops are maize and black beans. Locals also grow other tropical crops (e.g., coffee, plantains, manioc, yams) and fruit trees (e.g., oranges, mangoes), but these are secondary in importance to maize and beans. Agriculture is almost entirely for direct consumption by households, though small amounts of excess harvests are sold in the regional market. Cattle are also important as a form of wealth and financial security. Fields and pastures are found mostly on steep slopes within the Río Santiago watershed. All households seek additional land, since soils can be exhausted and the amount of land that is flat enough for crops is limited.

Land tenure in Morán is complex, involving several layers of legal demar-

Table 3.1. Characteristics of Study Sites in Eastern Guatemala.

Site	Year Settled	Elevation (meters above sea level)	Number of Households	Area of Forest Community (hectares)	Distance from Market (round-trip minutes walking)
Morán	≈1800	1,200	69	117	400
Las Cebollas	≈1880	1,500	43	867	270
				(protective = 14)	

Source: IFRI data forms.

cations, usufruct rules, and biosphere reserve management policies. According to cadastral maps of the Sierra de las Minas Biosphere Reserve, the majority of the area now utilized by Morán for agriculture, cattle pasture, and extraction of forest resources is municipal or *ejido* land locally called El Sitio. Within El Sitio are located communal agricultural lands (*trabajaderos*) worked and fenced together by community members. Also, smaller usufruct plots, known as *tierras con dueños* ("lands with owners") are found in El Sitio. Rights to work in these plots, though not formally considered legal by the Guatemalan government, are recognized by the community members and can be inherited, sold, and rented. Apart from the municipal lands, mostly in the northern extent of the Río Santiago watershed, are found *tierras privadas,* lands legally demarcated as privately owned. However, just as in the municipal lands, individual or family usufruct plots *con dueño* are scattered across the land demarcated as private. As delimited by the Master Plan of the biosphere reserve, Morán and the majority of lands economically important to its residents fall within the buffer zone of the reserve; within the buffer zone the law allows the sustainable use of resources to better the quality of life of its inhabitants.

The characteristics and practices of the Las Cebollas community are similar to those of Morán. Las Cebollas is located in the municipality of Quezaltepeque, in western Guatemala (see fig. 3.3). The community has claims to approximately 1,850 ha of land, much of it on slopes of about 1,500 m. As in Morán, the residents of the forty-three households that make up the community practice subsistence milpa agriculture (although coffee growing is an increasing practice). The site was settled during the early nineteenth century on land formally belonging to their respective municipalities (*ejidos*). Las Cebollas, like Morán, consists of land parcels belonging to households and unclaimed land operating as a commons. Legally, these lands remain municipality-owned *ejidos* if the original settlers or their descendants never obtained title to the land. However, de facto residents have developed elaborate and well-defined use rights over these lands. Individual parcels are typi-

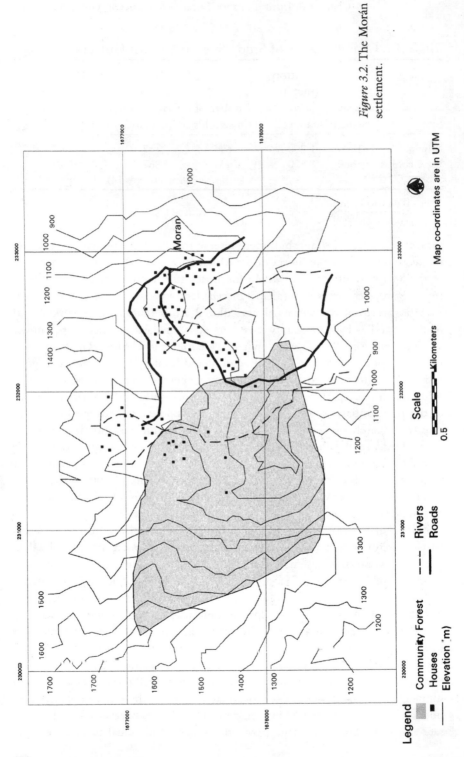

Figure 3.2. The Morán settlement.

Map co-ordinates are in UTM

Scale

0.5 Kilometers

Legend

Community Forest
Houses
Elevation (m)

Rivers
Roads

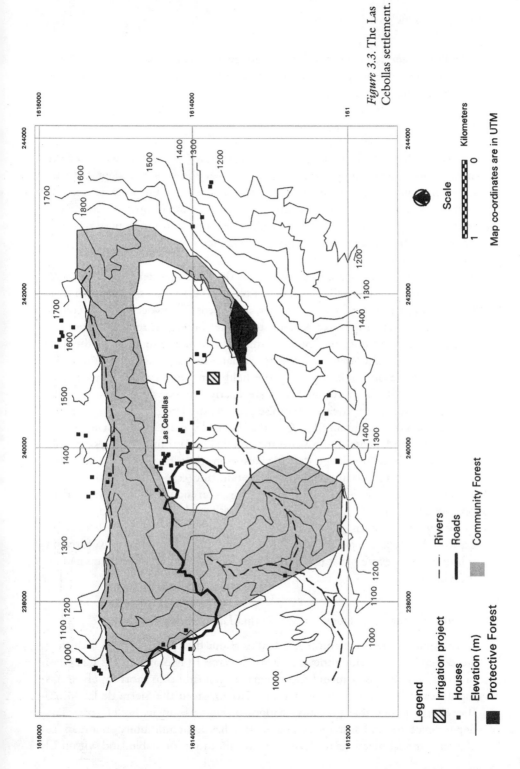

Figure 3.3. The Las Cebollas settlement.

Legend

- Irrigation project
- Houses
- Elevation (m)
- Protective Forest

- Rivers
- Roads
- Community Forest

Scale

0   1

Kilometers

Map co-ordinates are in UTM

Las Cebollas

cally fenced and respected by all local residents. Unlike Morán, Las Cebollas is not near any government-owned nature reserve, nor do large de jure private plots exist within its borders.

The Forests of Morán and Las Cebollas and Their Use

The forests located on the lands of Morán and Las Cebollas are typical of the area: open-canopied pine/hardwood forests that show obvious signs of sustained human use. Locals use these forests for three main purposes: (1) extraction of *ocote,* or resinous pine, for kindling; (2) extraction of firewood, oak varieties being preferred because they produce less smoke (though pine is sometimes used); and (3) pasture areas for cattle that feed on the ground-cover vegetation.

In addition to these three main uses of the forest, residents of both communities enter the forest for a number of other products. Locals cut down trees for the construction of fences, homes, and sheds. They occasionally collect plants for medicinal uses. Rocks and stones are sometimes removed from the forest for building purposes. Some families in Morán also hunt in the surrounding forests, although little wildlife remains in the areas around the communities. Based on the estimates of the field teams that gathered the data in these settlements, both communities are nearly entirely dependent on their community forests for fuelwood, timber, and pastureland.

Members of Morán and Las Cebollas generally perceive the major products of firewood, ocote, and pastureland to be abundant in their forests. While most members acknowledge that it takes more time to walk to gather firewood, or find that certain species are less abundant (especially hardwood varieties of trees) than in years past, they see this as an inconvenience, not a crisis. No doubt the steady out-migration from both settlements, resulting in relatively slow population growth in the two communities, has helped this perception. Also, while some members understand that the amount of pastureland is limited, they express that it is satisfactory for the number of cattle owned by individuals.

Natural Resource Institutions in Morán and Las Cebollas

Both communities have constructed rules about the resources on which they are dependent and which they perceive as scarce. In Morán and Las Cebollas, one such resource is farmland. Good agricultural land is in short supply and is highly valued. This is especially true in Morán, given the Sierra de las Minas Biosphere's policy that prevents changes in land use in its buffer zone. The dependence on and scarcity of arable land has led community members to convene annual meetings to decide on the allocation of arable land within El

Sitio, to negotiate rental and sharecropping contracts regarding plots of farm-land, and to establish and enforce rules regarding the use of fire in clearing fields. The ubiquitous barbed-wire fences around land indicate that commu-nity members also take individual actions to protect this natural resource. In Las Cebollas, community members also have established rules about the use and exchange of land.

Although community members depend heavily on their forests—forest products .are clearly salient to everyone's lives—locals in Morán and Las Cebollas perceive no scarcity in the flow of fuelwood, timber, or pasture. According to the argument proposed here, this means that residents will not create rules to manage these resources.

Qualitative evidence supports this argument that residents of Morán and Las Cebollas have few if any rules about the use of their large community forests: In the dozens of interviews we held with virtually every community member, we could find few formal or informal local rules related to influenc-ing the amount or kinds of forest products harvested by residents. Community members at both sites repeatedly said that if a community member wanted firewood or timber, all he or she had to do was cut or collect it.

Quantitative evidence also supports the hypothesis. If community rules about the use of the forest existed, we would expect that certain patterns of forest use would be reflected in the biological condition of the forest itself. For example, if a community had a prohibition on the cutting of large oak trees, we would expect to find more large oaks than if the community did not have such a rule. Or, if a community prevented cattle from grazing in the forest, we would expect to find more ground cover, shrubs, and saplings. If no rules exist about a forest, on the other hand, we would expect that the pattern of use might be predicted by optimal foraging theory (Stephens and Krebs 1986; Hayden 1981; Smith 1983; MacArthur and Pianka 1966; Winterhalder 1981). In short, in the absence of rules, individuals should harvest the easiest and most rewarding forest products first.

I constructed two regression models to test the hypothesis that residents of Morán and Las Cebollas use their forests in a pattern consistent with optimal foraging theory. Using data gathered from randomly distributed plots in each forest, the models attempt to include both natural and human factors that may affect the forest. I selected pine as an indicator species since locals use it for fuelwood and construction. The forest measure used here, tree density, is com-monly used as an important indicator of forest condition. The biophysical vari-ables employed here as independent variables are also widely used to account for variation in forest conditions (Spurr and Barnes 1992).

The unit of analysis is the forest plot. At each site, plots were randomly dis-tributed over the area of the forest. In the plots of Morán, three concentric cir-cles were established of 10, 3, and 1 m radius. In the 10 m radius circle, all trees with a diameter at breast height (DBH) ≥ 10 cm were measured for their DBH, height, and species name; in the 3 m radius circle, the same information was recorded for all saplings and shrubs 10> DBH > 2.5; the species and percentage of cover was recorded for the 1 m radius circle. In the plots of Las Cebollas, the same information was obtained in square plots of 10, 5, and 1 m. Information from each was scaled based on the square meters of each plot. In addition to the biological survey data, other data were recorded, including slope, slope orientation, elevation, and evidence of livestock, insects, and fire (IFRI Field Manual 1999).

For each site, I tested a tree density model. The form of the model is

$$Y_1 = I + X_1\hat{a}_1 + X_2\hat{a}_2 + X_3\hat{a}_3 + X_4\hat{a}_4 + X_5\hat{a}_5 + X_6\hat{a}_6 + \mathring{a}$$

where

Y_1 = TREE DENSITY, the number of pine tree stems per meter per plot
X_1 = ELEVATION, elevation of plot in meters above sea level
X_2 = SLOPE, percentage of slope of the plot
X_3 = INSECT, dummy variable for observed insect damage to trees in plot
X_4 = DISTANCE TO SETTLEMENT, the shortest distance in meters from a plot to the closest house in the community's settlement
X_5 = DISTANCE TO ROAD, the shortest distance in meters from a plot to the community's road
$\mathring{a}$ = a random disturbance term

In this model, I hypothesized that since pine is an important species to locals—for firewood, *ocote*, and timber—the impact of using pine trees would be captured by the number of tree stems remaining in each plot. Individuals should harvest the most accessible trees first.

The first four independent variables attempt to control for the most important biophysical factors that may affect the size of pine trees (see table 3.2). The independent variable *elevation* is the elevation of the forest plot, measured as meters above sea level. The number of pine trees per plot should decrease with elevation. *Slope* is the steepness of the forest plot, measured as a percentage plot (e.g., 45 degrees = 100 percent slope). The number of trees should decrease with increases in slope since trees on a gradient have more difficulty establishing and maintaining themselves. But this variable might also capture human intervention, as it may be more difficult to access trees on steeper slopes. Higher levels of *insect* damage may also prevent growth or kill trees (Spurr and Barnes 1992).

The last two independent variables attempt to capture the human effects on the number of pine trees in Morán's forest. *Distance to settlement* is the independent variable representing the distance, measured in meters, between forest plots and the closest house in the Morán and Las Cebollas communities. If

Table 3.2. Regression Estimates for Pine Density Models.

Independent Variables	DBH Morán	DBH Las Cebollas	Tree Density Morán	Tree Density Las Cebollas
Intercept	76.67	−22.735	.78	−73.31
	(10.795)	(53.669)	(6.6)	(31.14)
Tree density	−0.983★★★	−0.688		
	(.315)	(0.4)		
Elevation	−0.04★★★	.008	.002	.064★★
	(..011)	(.038)	(.007)	(.019)
Slope	−1.363	14.48	1.2	−18.23★★
	(8.429)	(13.09)	(5.15)	(7.535)
Insect	−3.008	27★★★	−0.563	−4.63
	(3.11)	(8.65)	(1.9)	(5.85)
Distance to settlement	.066★	.00003	.017	.007★★
	(.044)	(.005)	(.027)	(.003)
Distance to road	0.185★	.001	0.2★★★	−.003
	(.121)	(.005)	(.064)	(003)
R²	.66	.54	.57	.58
	(6.987)	(7.37)	(4.2)	(5.11)
F	12.369★★★	2.33★	703★★★	3.62★★
N =	33	19	33	19

★ = significant at the $p < .15$ level

★★ = significant at the $p < .05$ level

★★★ = significant at the $p < .001$ level

community members are trying to maximize their return to effort, then plots closer to settlements should contain fewer pine stems than plots located farther away. *Distance to road* captures the distance, also measured in meters, from the one major road in each community to a forest plot. Because it would be easier for individuals to transport pine products by road to their homes or fields, pine trees would be taken from plots closer to the road. Thus, as distance from road increases, we expect to see an increase in the number of pine stems per forest plot.

The results of the models for Morán and Las Cebollas are presented in table 3.2. Taken together, they provide evidence that in the absence of rules, the residents of the two communities use their forests in an optimal foraging pattern.

The tree density models perform relatively well for both sites ($R^2 = .57$ and .58). In Morán, the model suggests that distance to road is a significant predictor for the number of pines found within a plot. Using the beta coefficient from this independent variable, the model predicts an increase of twenty more pine stems per plot with every 100 m increase in distance from Morán's road. The same model for the Las Cebollas community forest also finds a distance variable significant, distance to settlement: The model predicts an increase of seven pine trees per plot for every 1,000 m of distance from the settlement. The other significant independent variables—elevation and slope—are also in their hypothesized directions.

Taken together, these models provide some support for the hypothesis that in the absence of rules, people follow an optimal foraging theory for gathering resources. Since hauling fuelwood and timber from the forest takes effort, we would expect people to take more and larger products from the closest and easiest locations. Although residents of Morán or Las Cebollas depend on them, these forest products are not considered scarce, and no rules have been created to limit or alter their harvesting. The open-access nature of these community forests is seen in the distribution of pine trees remaining in the forest.

Scarcity and Forest Rules in Las Cebollas

But this is not quite the full story for the Las Cebollas site, because in addition to their open-access community forest the residents in Las Cebollas have established a Protective Forest within which all harvesting of products is disallowed. I argue that the perceived scarcity of a resource they depend on—in this case water—motivated the establishment of the Protective Forest.

Ten of the wealthier families in Las Cebollas obtained a loan from BANDESA (the National Agricultural Development Bank) of Guatemala in 1986 to establish an agricultural scheme designed to augment their incomes. The families used the monies to construct an irrigation system so that they could produce vegetables during the dry season to sell in the nearby markets of Quetzaltepeque and Chiquimula. Through their interactions with development organizations such as PROZACHI (Program for Rural Development: Zacapa–Chiquimula) and PAF-G (Forest Action Plan for Guatemala), the families understood that forests were important to securing water for their irrigation system. They believed that protecting the watershed's vegetation would protect the flow of river water that fed their new system. To this end, the families succeeded in having the community declare a 14 ha area of forest as protective (of the watershed). The residents of Las Cebollas agreed to disallow the harvesting of any forest products, such as firewood or timber, or the grazing of cattle within this area.

These rules are enforced: The families that helped to found this patch of protected forest regularly walk its boundaries, which are clearly marked with a combination of paths and barbed-wire fences. The community is also small enough in membership and size so as to make undetected transgression of these rules difficult. Consistent with these factors, our forest plot teams encountered neither foraging cattle nor community members seeking fuel or timber in this forest patch for more than two weeks.

These rules have had an obvious effect on the condition of the forest. The Protective Forest boasts the most diverse vegetation of all the forested areas studied at Las Cebollas and contains the largest number of different species and the largest trees. Ground cover was also more dense than in other parts of Las Cebollas partly because of the prohibition on cattle grazing. Some of these differences can also be attributed to the microclimatic conditions of the Protective Forest, much of which is located in a moist ravine. Table 3.3 presents some of the stark differences in forest indicators between the Protective Forest and the open-access community forest.

The Protective Forest boasts nearly 50 percent more stems per area and more than twice the average DBH of pine trees than the open-access community forest, as well as almost twice as many saplings. Additionally, in a comparison with its own open-access forest, another nearby community forest, and two privately managed forests, the Protective Forest posted significantly higher measures for tree and sapling density, as well as tree and sapling basal areas (Gibson et al. 1999). These indicators reveal that some community members of Las Cebollas have created rules that have led to a successfully managed forest.

The Morán and Las Cebollas cases help to illustrate the necessity of the dependence and scarcity conditions for institutional creation. The members of each community have created institutions to help manage their agricultural lands, which they perceive as scarce and on which they depend. For the most part, while dependent on products of their forests, residents have not taken the same steps to create rules to govern the use of their forests: The goods they use are not seen as scarce. Because there are no rules, residents use the forests in an optimal foraging pattern. Members of Las Cebollas did, however, create forest institutions when they deemed water to be necessary and scarce.

Table 3.3. **Forest Conditions in Community and Protective Forests of Las Cebollas.**

Forest	Tree Density (stems/m²) (all species)	Sapling Density (stems/m²) (all species)	Average DBH (cm) (pine species)
Community	.062	.101	24.7
Protective	.087	.184	58.5

Moving Beyond the Necessary Conditions of Institutional Creation

To improve outcomes, many contemporary forestry policies in developed and developing countries are seeking to shift some control over forest management to the community level (Arnold 1987). Recognizing that communities may have the ability to monitor and enforce rules about forest use, policymakers have turned to various ways of devolving authority over forests to local people, usually without privatization. These policy moves signal that some governments are beginning to realize that the 500 million people who live in and around the world's forests will greatly determine the success or failure of forest policies (Arnold 1998).

In a fundamental sense, the local governance of forest resources will help determine the success or failure of important international environmental agreements, such as the United Nations Framework Convention on Climate Change and the subsequent Kyoto Protocol. No matter what national elites agree upon, it is behavior at the local level that produces aggregate outcomes. The signing of international environmental treaties by government officials does not automatically result in better policy design or better implementation on the ground. As they have for years, people in rural areas will filter, alter, or ignore a central government's forest policy. They also create their own rules, generating local institutions and patterns of activity that can diverge widely from the expectations of legislators and bureaucrats.

This study examined such local institutions in two sites of eastern Guatemala. I argued that we can expect to find instances of local institutional creation when (1) residents depend on a resource and (2) they perceive it as scarce. As we saw in Las Cebollas, residents successfully constructed their own rules regarding their Protective Forest when they understood that it helped to guarantee the flow of scarce water to their irrigated crops. While this outcome was in a sense aided by state organizations (the National Agricultural Development Bank), it was constituted by the residents themselves. The individuals from Las Cebollas—and not any forestry enforcement agency—protect this section of forest.

Despite the importance of the locals to forest management, neither international bodies nor domestic governments have a good understanding of the role played by local institutions. Policymaking in the absence of good theory and data invites disaster. This chapter is one example of the work being undertaken to fill this knowledge gap and improve forest policy. An increasing number of theoretically driven studies seek to account for the variation in performance of local-level forest management practices (Stork et al. 1997; Gibson et al. 2000). These studies could have a crucial effect on the evolving nature of forest policy.

Three aspects of research on forests and institutions will help determine the magnitude of its influence on contemporary forestry policy. First, such studies require research designs that move beyond single case studies to test hypotheses with larger sample sizes. Case studies are, of course, irreplaceable: They provide the grist for hypotheses on which more general tests can be made. Unless idiosyncratic effects can be isolated from more general trends, however, policymakers will not be able to derive lessons for crafting better policies. Second, future research must also explicitly model the multilevel nature of forest policy. It is clear that under different conditions, the linkages between the international, national, regional, and local levels can be crucial in generating outcomes in the forest. The advent of remotely sensed data coupled with careful institutional analysis on the ground can help scale up the considerable number of extant case studies regarding communities and their forests (e.g., Liverman et al. 1998). Third, research needs to appreciate the impact of political institutions on forest management (e.g., Ames and Keck 1997; Silva 1997; Dauvergne 1997). The best technical plans for resource management are rarely, if ever, adopted without alterations based on political factors. Policymakers act under constraints imposed by political institutions, not just their environmental concerns. Understanding the systematic effects of these political institutions may explain a great deal of the variance in forest conditions observed on the ground.

Acknowledgments

I gratefully acknowledge the financial support of the National Science Foundation (SBR-9521918), the FAO office for the Latin American and Caribbean region, and Indiana University's Research and University Graduate School. I also thank the members of the field research teams who came from Indiana University, CUNORI, Facultad Latinoamericana de Ciencias Sociales–Guatemala, Defensores de la Naturaleza, Universidad de San Carlos, and Universidad del Valle de Guatemala. I also appreciate the useful comments of Joanna Burger, David Dodds, Fabrice Lehoucq, Elinor Ostrom, and Paul Turner on earlier drafts of this work.

References

Agrawal, A., and G. Yadama. 1997. "How Do Local Institutions Mediate Market and Population Pressures on Resources? Forest Panchayats in Kumaon, India." *Development and Change* 28: 435–65.

Ames, Barry, and Keck, M. E. 1997. "The Politics of Sustainable Development: Environmental Policy Making in Four Brazilian States." *Journal of Interamerican Studies & World Affairs* 39 (4):1–40.

Arnold, J. E. M. 1987. "Community Forestry." *Ambio* 16:122–28.

————. 1998. "Devolution of Control of Common Pool Resources to Local Communities: Experiences in Forestry." Paper presented at the meeting of the UNU/WIDER Project on Santiago, Chile, April 26–28.

Ascher, W. 1995. *Communities and Sustainable Forestry in Developing Countries.* San Francisco: ICS Press.

Bailey, R. 1996. "Promoting Biodiversity and Empowering Local People in Central African Forests." In *Tropical Deforestation: The Human Dimension,* edited by L. Sponsel, T. Headlund, and R. Bailey, 316–37. New York: Columbia University Press.

Baland, J. M., and Platteau, J. P. 1996. *Halting Degradation of Natural Resources. Is There a Role for Rural Communities?* Oxford: Clarendon Press.

Boserup, E. 1965. *The Conditions of Agricultural Growth.* Chicago: Aldine.

Bromley, D., ed. 1992. *Making the Commons Work: Theory, Practice and Policy.* San Francisco: Institute for Contemporary Studies Press.

Carrasco, D. A. 1993. "Constraints to Sustainable Soil and Water Conservation: A Dominican Republic Example." *Ambio* 22:347–21.

Dauvergne, P. 1997. *Shadows in the Forest: Japan and the Politics of Timber in Southeast Asia.* Cambridge: MIT Press.

Gibson, C., D. Dodds, and P. Turner. 1998. "How Does an Open-Access Forest Survive? Salience, Scarcity, and Collective Action in Eastern Guatemala." Manuscript, Indiana University, Center for the Study of Institutions, Population, and Environmental Change, Bloomington.

Gibson, C., F. Lehoucq, and J. Williams. 1999. "Does Tenure Type Matter to Natural Resource Management? Property Rights and Forest Conditions in Guatemala." Manuscript, Indiana University, Center for the Study of Institutions, Population, and Environmental Change, Bloomington.

Gibson, C., M. McKean, and E. Ostrom, eds. 2000. *People and Forests: Communities, Institutions, and Governance.* Cambridge MA: MIT Press.

Harner, M. J. 1975. "Scarcity, the Factors of Production, and Social Evolution." In *Population, Ecology, and Social Evolution,* edited by S. Polgar, 123–38. Paris: Mouton Publishers.

Hayden, B. 1981. "Subsistence and Ecological Adaptations of Modern Hunter-Gatherers." In *Omnivorous Primates,* edited by R. S. O. Harding and G. Teleki, 344–421. New York: Columbia University Press.

International Forestry Resources and Institutions. 1999. *Field Manual.* Version 8. Bloomington, IN: Workshop in Political Theory and Policy Analysis, Indiana University.

Johnson, A. W., and T. Earle. 1987. *The Evolution of Human Societies: From Foraging Group to Agrarian State.* Stanford, CA: Stanford University Press.

Libecap, G. D. 1989. *Contracting for Property Rights.* Cambridge, England: Cambridge University Press.

Liverman, D., M. Hanson, B. Brown, et al. 1998. "Global Sustainability—Toward Measurement." *Environmental Management* 12 (2):133–43.

MacArthur, R. H., and E. R. Pianka. 1966. "On Optimal Use of a Patchy Environment." *American Naturalist* 100:603–9.

McKean, M. A. 1992. "Success on the Commons: A Comparative Examination of

Institutions for Common Property Resource Management." *Journal of Theoretical Politics* 4 (3):247–82.

———. 2000. "Common Property: What Is It, What Is It Good For, and What Makes It Work?" In *People and Forests: Communities, Institutions, and Governance,* edited by C. M. Gibson, M. McKean, and E. Ostrom. Cambridge, MA: MIT Press.

Netting, R. M. 1993. *Smallholders, Householders: Farm Families and the Ecology of Intensive, Sustainable Agriculture.* Stanford, CA: Stanford University Press.

Ostrom, E. 1990. *Governing the Commons: The Evolution of Institutions for Collective Action.* New York: Cambridge University Press.

———. 1998. "The International Forestry Resources and Institutions Research Program: A Methodology for Relating Human Incentives and Actions on Forest Cover and Biodiversity." In *Forest Biodiversity in North, Central and South America, and the Caribbean: Research and Monitoring,* edited by F. Dallmeier and J. A. Comiskey. Vol. 22 of *Man and the Biosphere Series.* Carnforth, Lancashire, England: UNESCO and Parthenon.

Ostrom, E., Gardner, R., and Walker, J. M. 1994. *Rules, Games, and Common-Pool Resources.* Ann Arbor: University of Michigan Press.

Ostrom, E., and M. Wertime. 2000. "The IFRI Research Strategy." In *People and Forests: Communities, Institutions, and Governance,* edited by C. M. Gibson, M. McKean, and E. Ostrom. Cambridge, MA: MIT Press.

Pearce, D., and Moran, D. 1995. *The Economic Value of Biodiversity.* London: Earthscan.

Perrings, C. 1995. "Economic Value of Biodiversity." Beijer Reprint Series no. 58. Stockholm: Beijer International Institute of Ecological Economics.

Silva, E. 1997. "The Politics of Sustainable Development: Native Forest Policy in Chile, Venezuela, Costa Rica and Mexico." *Journal of Latin American Studies* 29:457–93.

Smith, E. A. 1983. "Anthropological Applications of Optimal Foraging Theory: A Critical Review." *Current Anthropology* 24 (5):625–52.

Spurr, S. H., and B. M. Barnes. 1992. *Forest Ecology.* Malabar, FL: Krieger.

Stephens, D. W., and J. R. Krebs. 1986. *Foraging Theory.* Princeton, NJ: Princeton University Press.

Stork, N. E., T. J. B. Boyle, V. Dale, H. Eeley, B. Finegan, M. Lawes, N. Manokaran, R. Prabhu, and J. Soberon. 1997. "Criteria and Indicators for Assessing the Sustainability of Forest Management: Conservation of Biodiversity." Working paper no. 17. Bogor, Indonesia: Center for International Forestry Research.

Wade, R. 1994. *Village Republics: Economic Conditions for Collective Action in South India.* San Francisco: ICS Press.

Winterhalder, B. 1981. "Optimal Foraging Strategies and Hunter–Gatherer Research in Anthropology: Theory and Models." In *Hunter-Gatherer Foraging Strategies: Ethnographic and Archaeological Analyses,* edited by B. Winterhalder and E. A. Smith, 13–35. Chicago: University of Chicago Press.

Chapter 4

Wildlife Resources: The Elk of Jackson Hole, Wyoming

TIM W. CLARK

Wildlife is a common property resource in the United States and throughout the world, yet special interests typically make claims on its uses. The world-famous elk (*Cervus elaphus*) herd of Jackson Hole, Wyoming, is no exception. Like all natural resource management, managing elk can be reduced to questions of "How will they be used?" and "Who gets to decide?" Continuing conflict stems from these two issues. Government agencies that dominate the decision-making process seem to employ a "primitive power balancing" strategy in dealings with one another (see Brunner 1994), and while this dynamic plays itself out, elk management is negotiated through technical and legal language about the elk-feeding program, disease prevention, hunting issues, and states' rights versus federalism. The few officials and citizens who want to break this cycle find it difficult to change the politics. The absence of an effective "commons institution" to address wildlife management is evident in this case, as in many others (Burger et al. this volume, Ostrom chapter 1, this volume).

The Jackson Hole herd of 16,000 migratory elk ranges over a million acres in northwestern Wyoming annually. Between 8,000 and 10,000 animals typically winter on the 25,000-acre National Elk Refuge (NER), although officials' goal for some decades has been 7,500. Elk have traditionally been fed hay and cattle pellets in winter, and parts of the refuge are irrigated for hay production to support the artificially high herd size. Most of the remaining elk winter on feed grounds managed by the Wyoming Game and Fish Department (WGF) and located on nearby national forest lands. Conflict over management is most intense about the NER herd segment. Basically, too many elk are concentrated in too small an area in winter on the NER. Cattle grazing on public lands surrounding the refuge diminishes the forage available to migrating elk in the fall, thus encouraging their concentration on the NER. High densities contribute to high incidence of *Brucella abortus,* a disease that attacks the reproductive organs and lymphatic system of its host, causing spontaneous abortion in elk, cattle, and other wildlife. The Jackson Hole elk herd is heavily infected; about 28 percent of elk on the NER tested positive for brucellosis antibodies (Halverson 2000). (East of the Continental Divide, where there are no feed grounds, only about 1 percent test positive.) Although there are no documented cases of wildlife transmitting brucellosis to cattle in the wild, Wyoming fears losing its brucellosis-free federal status necessary for interstate shipment and sales of cattle. The NER herd segment is also vulnerable to catastrophic loss from tuberculosis, which also poses threats to humans and livestock. High densities of elk also degrade plant communities, especially willows (*Salix* spp.), resulting in a loss of biodiversity (Matson 2000). Feeding costs remain high—nearly $500,000 per year. Management responses to date have generally been to disperse the animals on the refuge by distributing feed pellets more widely and constructing irrigation systems at new locations (in both native and introduced vegetation).

These, however, are merely the substantive problems. This setting also contains process or procedural problems—in short, that a large number of participants see various problems in the elk situation, and they have not found an effective means to resolve the difference. Since goals for management of the Jackson Hole elk herd have not been agreed upon and since problems are defined only in relation to goals, different agencies and interest groups see different problems. Debates rage over the number and density of elk, the cost of feeding, the role of hunting, vaccination, irrigation, and other techniques in management, the loss of biodiversity, the role of the refuge in managing other species (specifically bison, *Bison bison*), the quality of the range, the risks of disease, and related issues. The questions generally boil down to these: Should elk be concentrated on winter feed grounds (following an "agricultural model"), or should we secure adequate winter range throughout the region and reduce or close down the feed grounds (following a "wild animal model")? As the participants debate these issues, they must consider whose values are served or harmed by each model and which institutions are advanced or pushed into the background by each. Finally, the leadership is struggling to define these problems practically, to articulate and implement rationally sound, politically feasible, and morally justifiable alternatives, and to transform the seemingly intractable situation into a new process that empowers people and increases problem-solving skills in the common interest.

Halverson (2000) concluded that the substantive problems in the elk case cannot be resolved until procedural problems are at least partially resolved. After identifying the actors in this complex arena, I examine some of the weaknesses in the decision process, analyze the conditions behind these trends, and offer ways to improve the basic policy process. Data for this chapter come from news articles, interviews, analyses since 1973, historic sources (Cromley pers. comm.), and recent studies by Halverson (2000), Cromley (2000), Kahn (2000), and Matson (2000). Research and analysis are guided by the policy analytic theory and literature cited therein (Lindblom 1990; Lasswell and McDougal 1992; Bell 1997). My standpoint as an analyst is to help participants better organize the process through which they interact in search of their common interest in managing elk, especially those who want to participate but are currently excluded.

Problems in Managing the Elk Herd

Problems stem from the participants' contradictory perspectives and values, how they organize themselves to find an acceptable management outcome, and the kind of leadership that has been used.

Participants in Elk Management

Management of elk on the NER is formally the responsibility of the U.S. Fish and Wildlife Service (USFWS), which has managed the refuge since its inception in 1912, and the state of Wyoming, which owns the elk in public trust as a commons resource. But other participants also have a say in management for various reasons—the National Park Service (NPS), the U.S. Forest Service (USFS), the Teton County Commission, and private landowners, outfitters, and environmentalists (see Halverson 2000; Cromley 2000; Kahn 2000).

The NER lies in southern Jackson Hole, a high-elevation valley centered in the 19-million-acre Greater Yellowstone Ecosystem (Clark 1999; Clark et al. 1999). This world-renowned landscape is experiencing dramatic environmental and human changes, and leaders at all levels are struggling to understand the changes and respond appropriately (Clark 1999b; Primm and Clark 1998). Although the NER has been managed for elk by the USFWS, the refuge is broadening its mission in response to the 1997 National Wildlife Refuge System Improvement Act, which calls for the refuge system "to administer a national network of lands and waters for the conservation, management, and where appropriate, restoration of the fish, wildlife and plant resources and their habitats within the United States for the benefit of present and future generations of Americans." This act mandates the USFWS to "develop and implement a process to ensure an opportunity for active public involvement in the preparation and revision of comprehensive conservation plans." The NER's focus is shifting from single-species management to biodiversity conservation. This reflects the national sentiment. Management is changing, as is the context of management, and federal officials generally embrace this change.

The chief state agency involved is the Wyoming Game and Fish Department (WGF), whose mandate is to provide "an adequate and flexible system for the control, propagation, management, protection and regulation of all Wyoming wildlife." WGF's model of elk management is largely an agricultural one in which animals are fed on feedlots, vaccinated, and otherwise intensively managed like cattle in order to maintain the highest possible numbers for hunting, since the sale of hunting licenses brings in millions of dollars annually and keeps its traditional constituents pacified. The Wyoming Department of Agriculture and many ranchers support this management philosophy. Controlled by a commission appointed by the governor, this agency's policies reflect the views of the governor, who espouses states' rights ideology and vehemently opposes the federal government (Thuermer 1995; Testa 1995). Wyoming is very conservative politically and maintains a local focus. The elk case is just one of many wildlife issues over which WGF—indeed many states in the West—contends with the federal government for authority and control.

The U.S. Forest Service, specifically Bridger–Teton National Forest, winters nearly all the elk that are not on the NER. The forest includes 1,460 square miles of the elk herd's annual range and 73 percent of the 120 square miles of essential winter range. The forest operates under the 1976 National Forest Management Act that requires it "to provide for adequate fish and wildlife habitat to maintain viable populations of existing native vertebrate species." The Forest Service is a multiple-use agency, so Bridger–Teton is also used for recreation, logging, mining, and oil and gas drilling—activities that sometimes conflict with elk management. Most hunting of the Jackson Hole herd takes place in the Bridger–Teton Forest.

Grand Teton and Yellowstone National Parks contain 384 square miles of the herd's annual range. The National Park Service's mission is "to conserve the scenery and the natural and historic objects and the wildlife therein." Grand Teton is one of only two national parks that permits hunting. This controversial hunt pushes elk off fall range and onto the NER earlier than otherwise would occur. Park officials and much of the public would like to eliminate hunting in the park.

The Teton County (Wyoming) Commission is responsible for public decisions in the county, which encompasses 2,000 square miles of annual elk range, including 26 square miles of critical elk winter range on private lands. The commissioners tend to favor land development in their decision making, and currently private land development is booming and the human population is growing rapidly. Moreover, the general sentiment is that, since the county is 97 percent federally owned, the county should not have to make special efforts to protect wildlife on the remaining 3 percent of privately owned lands. Nevertheless, the elk herd is recognized as a highly visible and desirable asset to the county.

A number of nongovernmental participants also want a voice in how elk are managed. The Wyoming Outfitters Association and the Jackson Hole Outfitters and Guides Association are active in promoting their own economic and access interests of hunting and backcountry use. Both groups have been critical of the USFWS management on the NER in the past. The Wyoming Wildlife Federation has called for phasing out the elk feedlots both on the refuge and elsewhere but remains strongly in favor of hunting. Numerous organized and unorganized hunters are also responsive to what happens on the NER. Although all these groups promote hunting, they are sometimes at odds over the number of licenses that are allotted to these businesses instead of being open to the general public. The Jackson Hole Conservation Alliance, Greater Yellowstone Coalition, and the Fund for Animals all seek a more comprehensive understanding of elk and other wildlife. The Fund for Animals opposes all hunting. All have been active in refuge management issues in recent years through the National Environmental Policy Act (NEPA) process and (in some cases) through the courts. Other groups, such as Trout Unlimited, also follow elk issues in the valley but are not major players. There is a growing consensus in the broad environmental community behind a new model of elk management that calls for reducing elk dependence on winter feed, restoring wild or historic patterns of elk movement, and making the decision-making process more open and participatory. Numerous businesses and the Jackson Hole Chamber of Commerce are also concerned about elk management, generally in support of the status quo, because of direct and indirect effects on the local economy.

Weaknesses in the Decision Process

Finding common ground has been an elusive goal in elk management and in natural resource policy and management in general (Langston 1995; Ascher 1999). In addition to discouraging trends in the substantive problems introduced above, there are significant problems—both in design and operation—in the process by which participants interact to make decisions and problems in the behavior of leaders and professionals. The decision process should ideally clarify and secure the common interest. This is a legitimate purpose and a requirement of good governance (Kemmis 1990; Dahl 1989, 1994; Ostrom et al. 1999). Most simply understood, the common interest is an interest shared by members of the community (Lasswell and McDougal 1992). A common interest benefits the community as a whole. In contrast, a special interest is incompatible with the common interest and benefits (and is promoted by) only some members of a community at the expense of the whole community.

The decision-making process through which people interact to solve problems of mutual concern can be thought of as a logical three-part sequence of predecision (getting ready to make a decision), decision (prescribing new rules), and postdecision (carrying out the new rules). This process is generally considered to have seven functions: (1) intelligence gathering, (2) debate and promotion about the nature and status of the problems, (3) deciding on a plan to solve the problems (in other words, setting new rules), (4) invoking the new rules in specific cases, (5) applying the rules through administrative activities, (6) appraising progress or lack of it, and finally (7) terminating the rules when they no longer apply (Lasswell 1971; Clark in press). Decision processes can be mapped, understood, and managed for adequacy by participants. This has not yet happened in the elk case, although outside researchers have examined various aspects of the case (Halverson 2000; Cromley 2000; Kahn 2000). A number of weaknesses in the decision process have revealed themselves.

Lawsuits. Weaknesses in the elk decision process itself are becoming more problematic as the agencies and the public continue to rely on a design that has not resolved problems in the past. Several lawsuits have been prosecuted in the 1990s over elk management, caused in part by the design of interagency interactions. Legal claims have been initiated by an animal rights group, a rancher, an association of hunters, a conservation group, and WGF (Halverson 2000). Although the courts settle disputes in an authoritative and controlling manner, settlements are ephemeral. Addressing both substantive and procedural problems in elk management in court is time consuming and financially costly. Judgments are rendered on the basis of evidence submitted by two factions in conflict, usually over narrow issues such as whether to vaccinate or not. Court intervention breeds ill will and distrust, further drawing down the ability of participants to work together in the future. The courts seldom resolve fundamental, underlying problems. As one WGF biologist put it, "You wind up with someone [the judge] who doesn't know anything making decisions about how to handle the herd" (Bohne cited in Halverson 2000: 27).

NEPA. The federal government is required to use NEPA and the preparation of environmental assessments and environmental impact statements (EISs) to address management and involve the public. NEPA has come under intense criticism in recent years because it is a linear process that does not work well to clarify and secure the common interest. As organized groups proliferate in the EIS process, it becomes more difficult to integrate them through politics to secure the common interest. Each interest group tends to focus on narrow demands as a means to best use its limited resources and maximize its effectiveness. An EIS typically mobilizes divergent interest groups to use their scarce resources to promote narrow and inflexible demands and to seek other rigid allies that do not compromise their demands. Opposition groups respond in kind to each other, utilizing their resources to block opponents, creating a power-balancing process (Brunner 1994). In such situations, NEPA serves as a substantive and procedural constraint to clarify and secure common interests. The federal government continues to use the NEPA design almost exclusively to address natural resource problems. The state, however, does not use NEPA, a NEPA-like process, or any other public participatory problem-solving mechanism to address complex management issues.

Goals. The goals sought by the extended community concerned with elk conservation are unclear. The recent spate of lawsuits and divergent values and views expressed in the media are evidence that the decision process in the Jackson Hole elk case has yet to find common ground (see Halverson 2000; Cromley 2000; Kahn 2000). This is nothing new; elk management has been problematic since Jackson Hole was first settled. Olaus Murie, who studied elk on the NER with the U.S. Biological Survey, recounted a prolonged debate among local residents in the 1930s on "what to do about the elk" (Murie and Murie 1966). The citizens insisted that the government feed more hay to solve the problem of having too many elk on private lands each winter. But for Murie and others, supplemental feeding was part of the problem. His solution was to secure additional elk winter habitat against human encroachment. He recorded that "People do not want to provide enough natural range for wildlife. Sportsmen demand bigger and bigger game herds but do not trouble to provide living space for them in the way nature intended. They want to simply stuff the animals with hay, the easy way—and that is supposed to settle all problems. That's what's the trouble with the elk!" (p. 177). The goal and the management means required to achieve it remain troublesome to this day.

Problem Definition. Because participants do not agree on the goals and the means to achieve them, each side faces a different set of problems (which usually includes other participants' perspectives). This situation was succinctly stated by Tom Toman (1996), Wyoming Game and Fish district supervisor, who noted that "the biggest problem that I can identify is that agencies often derive solutions to problems before the problems have been clearly identified or defined." From a substantive standpoint, Halverson (2000) attributed all problems to the winter feeding program on the NER, which concentrates animals at 4,000 per square mile (compared to 15 per square mile on summer range), and which in turn exacerbates diseases, habitat degradation, loss of biodiversity, and consumption of half a million dollars annually. From a procedural or process standpoint, Halverson (2000) detailed issues that have prevented government agencies from resolving the substantive problems, including overreliance on "experts" (biological professionals) to define and address the problems and, as a result, an exclusively technical conception of the problems, bureaucratic orthodoxy, and weak strategic leadership. Other problem definitions in circulation are based largely on utilitarian, economic, or bioethical standpoints, many of which compete with one another. In short, state and federal officials, who are jointly responsible for elk management, and other actors, who seek to influence the process to serve their own interests, are attempting to solve the substantive management problems in divergent ways through a poorly designed decision process (Cromley 2000). According to Barry Reiswig, NER manager (cited in Halverson 2000: 10), elk management has become more problematic because of conflict among agencies and with the public and special-interest groups.

Design. The mechanisms employed to integrate the perspectives and strategies of the two principal agencies, USFWS and WGF (and their constituencies), have frustrated resolution of substantive problems. Halverson (2000) described the historic designs used in interagency relations. The first mechanism, which ran from 1927 to 1935, was the Commission on the Conservation of Elk of Jackson Hole, Wyoming, created by the President's Committee on Outdoor Recreation. It included a diverse set of governmental and nongovernmental participants. During the 1940s and 1950s the agencies discussed elk management in a less formal design. But after years of conflict, the agencies set up a new design, the Jackson Hole Cooperative Elk Studies Group, in 1958. This group, which is still active, seeks to "coordinate plans, programs, and findings of studies, and to provide an exchange of ideas, information, and personnel to study the elk herd and its habitat" (Wilbrecht et al. 1995).

Both USFWS and WGF sources report that the group's effectiveness has been limited in recent years by internal disputes over fundamental policy issues, including who has authority and control over the elk, herd management objectives, and the vaccination program (Halverson 2000). WGF wants to vaccinate more elk against brucellosis, while the USFWS wants clear scientific evidence that vaccination is efficacious before it permits more intensive and costly management intrusion on the NER. The recent lawsuit by WGF against the USFWS to permit the state to vaccinate elk has clouded interagency relations. In addition, no public participation is permitted in the current official program, except through environmental assessments under the 1969 NEPA. This mechanism for decision making about elk follows the bureaucratic model of operation under the assumptions—roundly criticized in recent years—that government can efficiently manage natural resources, that government should direct the process, that the locus of needed work should be the agencies, that discussions should be largely technical, and that natural resource professionals (who believe that, by definition, they serve no special interests) should control the process (Moseley 1999). The Elk Studies Group, involving a mix of groups, diverse forms of reasoning, and contradictory ideologies and goals, has tended to be conventional (rather than functional) in its problem-solving approach (see Miller 1999).

In summary, the elk decision process has produced a highly controversial and tenuous approximation of the common interest at best, and it has been unable to resolve competing claims about how the elk should be managed and who should decide. But rather than appraise and revise it, many key participants continue to use the same design, causing or aggravating problems.

Leadership

The role and effect of leadership in the elk case have been evident over the last twenty-five years. Overall, effective leadership, both in and out of government, has been lacking. However, this is changing, and a few leaders have come to the forefront who are open to understanding and solving interrelated substantive and procedural problems inherent in the elk case. Some of the leaders of the key agencies in past decades tended to be narrowly bounded, technically focused, and authoritarian. Some relied on old models of leadership wherein the technical expert knew best, power was what mattered, and defense of agency position was paramount. Others ignored or avoided actual problems and focused on biological or technical aspects of elk management. A few played hardball power politics. Recruitment of leaders in the past seems to have relied on people moving up the ranks who were selected for their loyalty to agency norms and policy preferences and skill in promoting them. They behaved defensively and seemed to believe that the best defense was an aggressive offense. These older styles of leadership supported and enhanced the centralization, bureaucratization, and professionalization of wildlife management and transacted the government's business in traditional, status quo ways.

Factors That Explain the Current Situation

These several problems can generally be understood in terms of three classes of factors: institutional, contextual, and leadership.

Institutional Factors. Agency perspectives on the elk situation reflect the constituencies and different cultures of each organization as well as the organizational form used to carry out operations. The conflict in the elk decision process is a consequence of the clash of different philosophies (value outlook and cognitive perspective) and operating designs. Much of the controversy in elk management involves one value: power (Cromley 2000). This is not unexpected since the "central myth in the maintenance of any social system is the myth of authority" (MacIver 1947: 42), and that myth is at stake in the elk case. Power struggles abound in situations where authority and control are fragmented, unclear, and in flux—as in the West, where federal agencies have typically managed land while the states manage wildlife, and in the case of migratory species like elk that range across lands under multiple jurisdictions. People who are predisposed to power and its modes of operation are drawn to leadership and professional positions, and people with like perspectives tend to gravitate toward each other and to develop a common, mutually reinforcing cultural outlook based on similar core beliefs. Change, if it comes at all to people and organizations that are motivated by power, is costly and slow and is usually met with resistance and conflict.

With regard to elk in northwestern Wyoming, WGF in particular seems to seek more control. Seeing threats from animal rights groups (Thuermer 1990) and other "outside" forces (including a declining hunting population), WGF has adopted a largely defensive policy stance and is inclined to concede nothing to its perception of opponents. Conflict reached a new level of polarization in a 1998 lawsuit in which the state asked the court to order the USFWS to allow the state to vaccinate elk on the NER against brucellosis. (This case was decided in 1999 in favor of the USFWS.) The USFWS had refused to grant the state's original request for both political and management reasons. In a conservative, bureaucratic organizational system such as WGF, attention to the agency's own underlying assumptions about contextual factors and standard operating procedures is minimal compared to defense of the organization's core philosophic values and demands for more authority and control (Clark 1997). These institutional factors set up an "us-versus-them" mentality, which is predisposed by the states'-rights-versus-federalism conflict dating to the Constitution of our nation and promulgated by many Western state governments and agencies. This outlook can be an obstacle to solving complex societal issues because it promotes a rigid, exclusive, and confrontational mode of interaction. The proliferating lawsuits and continued wrangling over goals, problem definitions, and models of management all indicate institutional rigidities, intractable routines, nonadaptiveness, and failure to bridge or create linkages. Ideally (seldom approximated in practice), all participants in the elk case would be aware of their own outlooks, understand how those outlooks direct their behavior and that of their employing organizations, and take this knowledge into account in their actions.

Context. The context of wildlife conservation in northwestern Wyoming is rapidly changing, as it is throughout the nation (Kellert 1996; Clark 1999b). Contextual changes include changes in peoples' values (Kahn 2000). As new people move into the region, their values and perspectives clash with those held by long-term residents. The NER, for instance, is currently used for hunting, fishing, wildlife observation, a sleigh-ride concession, jogging, and biking, among other uses, but commonly decisions about use that benefit one group deprive another of important values. The decision to end hunting indulges one group but deprives another. Many different values are at stake in the interpersonal and interorganizational interactions surrounding elk management. (Power, wealth, rectitude, respect, well-being, affection, enlightenment, and skill are the eight generalized categories of values [Lasswell 1971].) A number of groups are jockeying for power, and most have at least some financial stake in elk management. But additional values are at play as well, even in such interactions as lawsuits. Individuals and organizations seek respect, they seek to demonstrate the "rightness" of their positions, or they seek to exercise their skills and knowledge in management actions. All these values are open to gains or losses in the elk decision process. Kahn (2000) characterized value dynamics over time, noting that as more diverse people utilize or become interested in elk and the refuge, the interactions and value transactions among these people also increase. His analysis of trends in values showed a decline in community "ownership" of the refuge and increased centralization, bureaucratization, and professionalism in the agencies as the human population increases. Because of these trends, value decisions about elk are difficult to make and often result in conflict. In general, people's values are changing from utilitarian uses of wildlife to more conservation-oriented values, but these shifts are often not reflected in agency management.

Another contextual factor is that the role of the public in management is changing dramatically. Citizens and interest groups are no longer content to be passive bystanders who ratify (or rail against) predetermined agency policies (Berry 1999). They demand a more active role in wildlife conservation. Public involvement in management processes is now a challenge that agency officials must address successfully. But, as Magill (1994: 295) noted, many natural resource professionals and managers are "academically and psychologically ill-prepared to acknowledge the legitimacy of public demands." This is especially difficult when the public—at local, regional, or national scales—strongly asserts values that conflict with agency objectives or with each other.

Leadership. Leadership has always been important in wildlife conservation. In the elk decision process many people have cited the importance of individual personalities and leadership styles (e.g., Bohne, Curlee, Griffin, Harvey, Lichtman, cited in Cromley 2000: 71–72). In response to the historic conflict in the elk case and other factors in society at large, leaders in the agencies, including professional experts, have centralized, bureaucratized, and professionalized elk management (Kahn 2000). Important decisions today about the NER and the Jackson Hole elk herd, in contrast to several decades ago, are made in state-level or regional offices and sometimes even in Washington, D.C., all far removed from the local, place-based community closest to the elk. The federal land management system overall has changed over the years (Moseley 1999). Bureaucratization of state and federal agencies has increased staffs and budgets as well as rules, roles, and regulations. Land managers at all levels have become professionalized and highly trained in their fields, often in a narrow sense. Schneider and Ingram (1997: 172) observed that "where science and professionalism have come to dominate, goals are utilitarian, and no distinction is made between what is good for science and professional groups and what serves the public interest." It is difficult for government agencies to produce leaders with the knowledge and skills to keep their organizations current, adaptable, and effective. Too often, organizations fail to recognize and support good leaders.

Recommendations

If past trends and conditions continue in the elk case, then future decision processes and substantive management will be similar to those of the past. But certain trends that suggest opportunities to improve elk management are discernible. If participants can capitalize on these, it may be possible to institute a more flexible, integrative, and effective approach to elk management in the common interest. First, public interest in the elk and the refuge has risen in recent years, many participants are growing tired of the endless conflict, and there are increasing demands for more inclusive participation and for opening a civic dialogue on management goals. Second, a few leaders are emerging who recognize the need and opportunity for change. Third, the 1997 National Wildlife Refuge System Improvement Act calls for preparation of a long-term management plan. Fourth, the recent decision by the Department of Interior to undertake a multiyear, multimillion-dollar EIS on management of the NER also offers an opportunity for new approaches to improve the decision process and address substantive problems.

Three measures can help improve decision making in the elk case. First, community-based participatory groups can address some problems in the decision process (Cromley 2000; Moseley 1999). Such groups must be inclusive and have a community-wide reputation for honesty. They can help disparate groups to find and clarify shared interests that all participants agree on, beginning, perhaps, with something as fundamental as "the health and sustainability of the elk herd" or "ending the conflict" and then adding more specific and realistic goals and objectives. This would help reduce some of the narrow and rigid demands promoted by the NEPA process and facilitate agreement on goals and problem definitions. Participatory groups are also a way to stay in touch with changing public values. Public inclusion is a process of bringing citizens into the management, science, and decision making of elk conservation. It offers managers a tool and a strategy to understand public values better, to create a constructive management environment, and to develop plans that integrate social and natural conditions (Berry 1999).

One citizens' group is currently organizing itself in the elk case (Hoskins

1999). It operates on the assumption that elk management will best be accomplished through a participatory process that includes people with diverse perspectives and takes into account complex interactions among ecological, social, and economic systems. Such a process does not currently exist. If this citizens' group is to participate successfully, several practical requirements must be met (Moseley 1999). It must build social capital, or a stock of trust, skill, and civic knowledge. High capital is required to create community-based collaborations that can act as governance structures to effect change (Lasswell 1971). It must be a skilled, genuine, problem-solving exercise, not just an interest-based, negotiated (or facilitated) effort. Collaborative norms and habits must come to dominate all interactions. People with varying levels of knowledge, distinct values, roles, perspectives, and skills must be able to come together in meetings to discuss, analyze, and make meaning of complex information. Such groups also need linkages to their larger communities to gain acceptance for their work, to mobilize labor and financial resources, and to undertake collective action. These kinds of groups need the capacity for planning and some implementation, which requires administrative and substantive skills (Moseley 1999). Finally, the harmful effects of government must be minimized. Scott (1998), for instance, argues that governments have a tendency to try to simplify and structure society and nature in an effort to control people and their use of natural resources.

Second, government, which is mandated by law to manage land and wildlife, must design, operate, adjust, and lead a better decision process. This effort might involve changes in the membership, operations, or scope of the Cooperative Elk Studies Group, changes in the NEPA-derived public input process, new cooperation with a citizens' group, a series of civic dialogues, or other mechanisms to achieve more problem-oriented and contextual ways of solving problems. The goal is to help communities identify their common interests and secure rational, politically workable, and morally justifiable decisions. This will require a special kind of skilled, strategic leadership. Because the elk problem is fundamentally one of people and their values, leaders are especially needed who are skilled in creating the kind of intellectual and political environment in which good decisions will be made (Westrum 1994). This requires skills both in technical matters and in "the process skills that promote interdisciplinary teamwork" to serve the common interest (Clark et al. 1994: 427; Clark 2000).

Several agency managers in the elk case appreciate the need for better leadership and are already openly experimenting with new leadership methods and problem-solving approaches, including community-based exercises. This kind of "transformational" leadership, according to Burns (1978), brings more effective modes of interaction and decision making into practice. It engages people in such a way that leaders and followers are raised to greater levels of motivation and morality. The best modern example is Gandhi, who aroused and elevated the hopes and demands of people and in the process enhanced his own life and personality. Leaders in the elk case are leaving behind maintenance of the bureaucracy, perpetuation of the status quo, and "transactional" leadership styles that merely facilitate exchanges of benefits (for example, economic, psychological, political) among people (Burns 1978). These progressive leaders are seeking new knowledge and skills to be more effective problem solvers. Their goal in resource management should be to bring about "ways and means for blending wisdom and science, for balancing free association and intellectual discipline, for expanding and refining information, and for building a problem-solving culture that balances 'permanent' with 'transient' membership, thereby remaining open to new participants and to fresh ideas while retaining the capacity for cumulative learning that refines, clarifies, and simplifies" (Burgess and Slonaker 1978: 1).

If one or more agencies or interest groups maintains a strong power orientation, however, it will remain difficult to create a cooperative climate, focus on the problems at hand, or establish open, inclusive processes. Power can distort the way in which agency leaders or community-based efforts explore new goals, and it can thwart even the best-designed problem-solving structures.

Third, a new goal is needed that moves away from the agricultural model of elk management. This idea needs to be explored by the agencies, the technical experts, the citizenry, and the interest groups as a means to solve the substantive problems caused by the crowding of elk onto winter feed grounds. Hoskins (1999) outlined the goal and management challenges and suggested that the new goal ought to be securing extensive, quality winter habitat off the feed grounds to lower elk population densities by redistributing them. This initiative (or policy innovation), which he called "restoring wild patterns," would seek more protection, acquisition, and conservation of habitat in strategic, novel, more effective ways to sustain wild, free-ranging wildlife. This goal is supported by an unknown percentage of the public. For significant habitat to be conserved, changes in elk management and human land uses must be secured in a manner that is appropriately timed and minimally disruptive ecologically, socially, economically, and politically. One way to begin to test whether the initiative to restore wild patterns has support (from the government and the public) is to decommission one of the smaller, state-operated feed grounds to learn how such an operation can be done in the most logical and least disruptive fashion and to learn how people, institutions, and elk (and other species) respond. If this effort is undertaken using a community-based approach and supported by transformational leadership, much can be gained in terms of building social capital and improving elk management. Such a prototypical effort can then be sustained, expanded, modified, or abandoned in response to what has been learned.

Taken together, these three options constitute key parts of a sound, long-term strategy for improving elk conservation in the common interest (see Brunner and Clark 1997). It will require building social capital, skilled leadership, and a better decision process through which government, experts, special interests, and citizens can learn and interact successfully. These recommendations are consistent with democracy and open-ended problem solving. They constitute adaptive management at its best.

Conclusion

All concerned parties share an interest in the future of the common property resource that is the Jackson Hole elk herd. In practice, though, there is little agreement on how realistically to specify goals, carry out needed management, and, especially, answer basic questions such as who should decide management policy. There are many beneficiaries of the current decision process and the agricultural model of elk management, including the state of Wyoming and WGF, hunters, and outfitters and related businesses. But these interests are being challenged in court and in the media by people who want to modify this model to encourage elk to move freely throughout western Wyoming. These challengers, largely the environmental community, academics, and some nonhunting segments of the public, demand broader conservation goals and more participation in the decision-making process. At the heart of the growing elk management problem is a chronically weak decision process that withholds from many groups the opportunity to participate meaningfully. Reconfiguring the decision process to make it more inclusive, open, and honest; more comprehensive and integrative; more creative, rational, effective, and timely; and nonprovocative and ameliorative—all standards recommended by Lasswell (1971)—offers the best vehicle to address this common property management problem. This can be achieved via a well-structured and operated, community-based, participatory process combined with skilled transformational agency leadership, and the restoration of elk to a free-roaming ecology via an adaptive management approach.

Acknowledgments

Previous fieldwork by Christina Cromley, Anders Halverson, H. Bradley Kahn, and Noah Matson aided this article. Discussions with Robert Hoskins, Barry Reiswig, Meredith Taylor, Tory Taylor, Lloyd Dorsey, Bruce Smith, Michael Schrotz, Jim Griffin, Steve Brock, Bernie Holtz, Franz Camenzind, Garry Brewer, and Joanna Burger are appreciated. The comments of two dozen citizens who participated in a March 1999 civic dialogue on elk management in Jackson, Wyoming, are also greatly appreciated. Denise Casey, Joanna Burger,

Barry Reiswig, and another colleague reviewed the manuscript. I am grateful for support from the Northern Rockies Conservation Cooperative, Catherine Patrick, Gil Orday, the Wiancko Charitable Trust, Fanwood Foundation, Henry P. Kendall Foundation, Denver Zoological Foundation, New-Land Foundation, and Yale University's School of Forestry and Environmental Studies and Institution for Social and Policy Studies.

References

Ascher, W. 1999. *Why Governments Waste Natural Resources: Policy Failures in Developing Countries.* Baltimore: Johns Hopkins University Press.

Bell, W. 1997. *Foundations of Future Studies: Human Science for a New Era.* New Brunswick, NJ: Transaction Publishers.

Berry, J. K. "From Paradigm to Practice: Public Involvement Strategies for America's Forests." Ph.D. diss., Yale University, 1999.

Brunner, R. D. 1994. "Myth and American Politics." *Policy Sciences* 27:1–18.

Brunner, R. D., and T. W. Clark. 1997. "A Practice-Based Approach to Ecosystem Management." *Conservation Biology* 11:48–58.

Burger, J., C. Field, R. B. Norgaard, E. Ostrom, and D. Policansky. 2000. "Introduction." In *Protecting the Commons: A Framework for Resource Management in the Americas,* edited by J. Burger, E. Ostrom, R. B. Norgaard, D. Policansky, and B. D. Goldstein. Washington, DC: Island Press.

Burgess, P. M., and L. L. Slonaker. 1978. "The Decision Seminar: A Strategy for Problem-Solving." Merschon Center Briefing Paper no. 1-1-22. Ohio State University, Merschon Center, Columbus.

Burns, J. M. 1978. *Leadership.* New York: Harper Torchbooks.

Clark, T. W. 1997. *Averting Extinction: Reconstructing Endangered Species Recovery.* New Haven, CT: Yale University Press.

———. 1999a. *The Natural World of Jackson Hole, Wyoming: An Ecological Primer.* 2nd ed. Moose, WY: Grand Teton Natural History Association.

———. 1999b. "Interdisciplinary Problem-Solving: Next Steps in the Greater Yellowstone." *Policy Sciences* 32:393–414.

———. In press. *The Policy Process: A Practical Guide for Natural Resource Managers and Conservationists.* New Haven, CT: Yale University Press.

———. 2000. "Interdisciplinary Problem Solving in Endangered Species Conservation: The Yellowstone Grizzly Bear Case." In *Endangered Animals,* edited by R. P. Reading and B. J. Miller, 285–301. Westport, CT: Greenwood Publications Group.

Clark, T. W., R. P. Reading, and A. L. Clarke. 1994. "Synthesis." In *Endangered Species Recovery: Finding the Lessons, Improving the Process,* edited by T. W. Clark, R. P. Reading, and A. L. Clarke, 417–431. Washington, DC: Island Press.

Clark, T. W., A. H. Harvey, M. B. Rutherford, B. Suttle, and S. Primm. 1999. *Annotated Bibliography on Management of the Greater Yellowstone Ecosystem.* Jackson, WY: Northern Rockies Conservation Cooperative.

Cromley, C. M. 2000. "Developing Sustainable Management Practices: Lessons from the Jackson Hole Bison Management Planning Process." In *Developing Sustainable*

Management Policy for the National Elk Refuge, Wyoming, edited by T. W. Clark, D. Casey, and A. Halverson, 66–100. Bulletin No. 104. New Haven, CT:Yale School of Forestry and Environmental Studies.

Dahl, R. A. 1989. *Democracy and Its Critics.* New Haven, CT:Yale University Press.

———. 1994. *The New American Political (Dis)order.* Berkeley: University of California, Institute of Government Studies Press.

Halverson, A. 2000. "The National Elk Refuge and the Jackson Hole Elk Herd: Management Appraisal and Recommendations." In *Developing Sustainable Management Policy for the National Elk Refuge, Wyoming,* edited by T. W. Clark, D. Casey, and A. Halverson, 23–52. Bulletin No. 104. New Haven, CT:Yale School of Forestry and Environmental Studies.

Hoskins, R. 1999. "A Strategic Opportunity to Re-create Elk and Bison Management in Jackson Hole." *Northern Rockies Conservation News.* Summer 1999 (12):6–7.

Kahn, B. 2000. "Uses and Valuation of the National Elk Refuge, Wyoming." In *Developing Sustainable Management Policy for the National Elk Refuge, Wyoming,* edited by T. W. Clark, D. Casey, and A. Halverson, 139–170. Bulletin No. 104. New Haven, CT: Yale School of Forestry and Environmental Studies.

Kellert, S. R. 1996. *The Value of Life.* Washington, DC: Island Press.

Kemmis, D. 1990. *Community and the Politics of Place.* Norman: University of Oklahoma Press.

Langston, N. 1995. *Forest Dreams, Forest Nightmares.* Seattle: University of Washington Press.

Lasswell, H. D. 1971. *A Pre-view of Policy Sciences.* New York: Elsevier.

Lasswell, H. D., and M. S. McDougal. 1992. *Jurisprudence for a Free Society: Studies in Law Science and Policy.* New Haven, CT: New Haven Press.

Lindblom, C. E. 1990. *Inquiry and Change: The Troubled Attempt to Understand and Shape Society.* New Haven, CT:Yale University Press.

MacIver, R. M. 1947. "The Myth of Authority." In *The Web of Government,* 39–59. New York: Macmillan.

Magill, A. W. 1994: "What People See in Managed Landscapes." *Journal of Forestry* 92 (9):12–16.

Matson, N. 1999. "Biodiversity and its Management on the National Elk Refuge, Wyoming." In *Developing Sustainable Management Policy for the National Elk Refuge, Wyoming,* edited by T. W. Clark, D. Casey, and A. Halverson, 101–138. Bulletin No. 104. New Haven, CT:Yale School of Forestry and Environmental Studies.

Miller, A. 1999. *Environmental Problem Solving: Psychosocial Barriers to Adaptive Change.* New York: Springer.

Moseley, C. 1999. "New Ideas, Old Institutions: Environment, Community, and State in the Pacific Northwest." Ph.D. thesis,Yale University, 1999.

Murie, O. J., and M. Murie. 1966. *Wapti Wilderness.* New York: Knopf.

Ostrom, E. 2000. "Reformulating the Commons." In *Protecting the Commons: A Framework for Resource Management in the Americas,* edited by J. Burger, E. Ostrom, R. B. Norgaard, D. Polincansky, and B. D. Goldstein. Washington, DC: Island Press.

Ostrom, E., J. Burger, C. B. Field, R. B. Norgaard, and D. Policansky. 1999. "Revisiting the Local Commons: Local Lessons, Global Challenges." *Science* 284 (April 9, 1999):278–82.

Primm, S. A., and T. W. Clark. 1998. "The Greater Yellowstone Policy Debate: What Is the Policy Problem?" *Policy Sciences* 29:137–66.

Schneider, A. L., and H. Ingram. 1997. *Policy Design for Democracy*. Lawrence: University Press of Kansas.

Scott, J. C. 1998. *Seeing Like a State: How Certain Schemes to Improve the Human Condition Have Failed*. New Haven, CT: Yale University Press.

Testa, M. 1995. "Shuptrine: Federal Lands Vote 'Disgraced' the State." *Jackson Hole News*, May 24, A13.

Thuermer, A. M., Jr. 1990. "G&F Warns against Animal Rights Groups." *Jackson Hole News*, November 21, 21.

———. 1995. "State Will Not Curtail Feed to Wintering Elk." *Jackson Hole News*, February 1, 9A.

Toman, T. 1996. "Tom Toman's Ramblings." Unpublished manuscript, Totem Studies Group, Northern Rockies Conservation Cooperative, Jackson, WY.

Westrum, R. 1994. "An Organizational Perspective: Designing Organizations from the Inside Out." In *Endangered Species Recovery: Finding the Lessons, Improving the Process*, edited by T. W. Clark, R. P. Reading, and A. L. Clarke, 327–49. Washington, DC: Island Press.

Wilbrecht, J., R. Robbins, and J. Griffin. 1995. "History and Management of the National Elk Refuge." Unpublished document in National Elk Refuge files, Jackson, WY.

Chapter 5

Cooperative and Territorial Resources: Brazilian Artisanal Fisheries

ALPINA BEGOSSI

Human territoriality is a fundamental method to control space and resources. In aquatic habitats, territoriality encompasses competition for water for drinking, fishing, and irrigation (Malmberg 1984). At sea, territorial behavior includes not only the water around land, but also isolated patches of ocean. In the nineteenth century, isolated platforms were defended as private territories for sailors who were off duty (Malmberg 1985).

In ecology, optimality models such as optimal foraging theory have enlightened optimal territory size, time spent in territorial defense, and territory sharing (Lendrem 1986). One of the predictions of the model is that the bigger the territory, the more food is secured. However, because of the cost of defending big territories, the optimal territory size is the result of a trade-off between feeding benefits and defense costs.

Territoriality is very important when dealing with management strategies and property rights. Management of resources includes behaviors associated with a resource type and abundance, interactions among individuals, and the way individuals use resources. Individuals very often have rules concerning the use of resources, and such rules may include delimitation of boundaries. The search for local rules in fisher communities is relatively recent, because fisheries management normally ignored the views of fishers (Berkes 1985; Hviding and Baines 1994).

Local rules involve costs, such as time and effort. Consequently, self-organization is likely to occur only after resource users observe scarcity (Ostrom chapter 1, this volume). A detailed cost-benefit analysis concerning territoriality, or economic defensibility, in relation to features of resources is given by Dyson-Hudson and Smith (1978). These authors predicted that (1) unpre-

109

dictable and abundant resources lead to nomadism, information sharing, and low defensibility; (2) unpredictable and scarce resources lead to dispersion (high nomadism) and low economic defensibility; (3) predictable and abundant resources lead to territoriality and low nomadism, showing high economic defensibility; and (4) predictable and scarce resources lead to low-medium nomadism, showing fairly low economic defensibility. A very unpredictable resource with low abundance is too costly to manage or defend in relation to the expected returns.

The importance of information sharing should be taken into account when dealing with fisheries because locating fish is an important source of uncertainty (Mangel and Clark 1983). Information sharing is found in communities where reciprocity is high, which often occurs with close kin. Recent information where commons have been managed well indicates an important role for cooperation (Burger et al., this volume).

Fisheries include examples of different levels of cooperation (Mangel and Clark 1983). In most small-scale fisheries the crew is composed of closely related kin (brothers, fathers and sons; Nemec 1972), which increases information sharing. Brothers from Búzios Island, Brazil, fish in stable pairs and help each other to find fish schools, provide each other's family with fish when one cannot fish, and experience higher fishing returns (kg/man/hour) compared to men who fish alone (Begossi 1996 a,b). Other communities show a different behavior, and fishing grounds are often maintained in secrecy (Forman 1967). Sea tenure refers to property institutions that limit access in fisheries, influence competition, and conserve fish species (Cordell 1989). Sea tenure involves incipient and informal rules, as well as organized and legalized laws.

Local rules may be informal, formal, or legalized. Informal rules are very common in small communities, ranging from 10 to 100 families, since those rules are usually associated with close kinship relations. Cordell (1985) discussed the importance of local rules in fishing communities of Bahia State (northeastern Brazil) that were maintained through the concept of *respeito* (respect). *Respeito* is linked to reciprocity, which shapes and controls interpersonal relations; fishers can be absent from their territories because people honor each other's claims. Small-scale fishermen in Brazil show different attitudes toward local resources that are worth examining in the light of current management of commons resources.

In this chapter, I analyze the fishery features (technology, species, and market orientation) and the level of sea tenure (access rules, fishing ground ownership) of artisanal Brazilian fisheries from marine and riverine environments. I show that the kind of gear used, demographic density, market demands, and government environmental pressures are variables that lead to different outcomes in terms of territoriality and the ability of local organizations to define access rules. Both marine and riverine artisanal fishers described share the

Table 5.1. Features of the Fishing Communities Studied in Brazil. Type of rule means the observation of any local access rules or rights concerning fishing.

Locale	Community	Main Technology Used	Resource	Tourism	Type of Rule
Coastal					
Grande Island	Aventureiro	Hook and line, set gill nets	Squid and fish	No	Firstcomers' rights
Búzios Island	Porto do Meio	Hook and line, set gill nets	Squid and fish	No	Territorial kinship rights for set gill nets
Puruba Beach		Hook and line, encircling and set gill nets	Fish	Yes	No
Itacuruçá Island (Sepetiba Bay)	Gamboa	Encircling nets	Shrimp and fish	Intense	Territorial conflicts with trawlers
Jaguanum Island (Sepetiba Bay)	Calhaus	Set gill nets	Shrimp and fish	Intense	Territorial conflicts with trawlers
Riverine					
Araguaia River		Hook and line	Fish	Intense	Exclusion of local fishers
Grande River	Icém, Fronteira	Cast net, hook and line, set gill nets and longlines	Fish	Yes	No overlapping between fishers; territorial rights for longlines
Upper Juruá River	Juruá, Tejo, Bagé, S. João, Breu	Cast net, hook and line, and set gill nets	Fish	No	Collective rules

importance of kinship ties in the social and economic organization and an economy based on manioc and fish, except for the inhabitants of the Upper Juruá, Acre State, who also practice rubber-tapping (Begossi 1998a).

Two basic fishing communities are described in this study: Atlantic Forest coast (*caiçaras*) and riverine fishers (*caboclos*) from the southern (Grande River), central (Araguaia River), and northern (Juruá River) portions of Brazil (table 5.1). Fishing in these areas ranges from subsistence activities to commercial (professional) fisheries. The fisheries along the southeastern coast of Brazil were defined by Diegues (1983) as petty-commodity and capitalist production. Petty-commodity fishermen include fisher-farmers who use dugout canoes and sell about 60 percent of their production in adjacent markets, while "artisanal fishers" use motorized canoes or small boats and sell about 90 percent of their production to local markets. Capitalist production includes trawler fishers, who fish along the continental shelf and sell their catches to central markets, and entrepreneurs, who own large boats with electronic gear and who fish at the edge of the continental shelf (Diegues 1983).

Brazilian riverine fisheries include diffuse fisheries and large-scale commercial fisheries. The first are fished by rural and small-town inhabitants, including part-time fishers who sell the high-quality fish and consume fish of low market value. The large-scale commercial fisheries are centralized in Manaus and Belém, major cities of Amazonas and Pará State, and include fleets that travel up to 2,500 km from the cities (Petrere 1989; Ribeiro and Petrere 1990).

Thus there are two major artisanal fisher groups examined in this study (fig. 5.1). The first is composed of small-scale fishers who fish in paddled canoes with hooks and lines for subsistence and for cash (whenever possible).

Figure 5.1. Atlantic Forest sites in southeastern Brazil and riverine-area fishing communities in Brazil.

These fishers usually perform farming activities. The second group consists of professional fishers who use motorized canoes or boats and sell their catches to a local market or to fish buyers. Tourists, sportfishers, and recreational fishers also interact with the artisanal fishers, but in both marine and fresh water they usually fish using hooks and lines. On the Atlantic Forest coast there are *embarcados,* or "boat fishers," who work in commercial trawlers for wages.

Atlantic Forest Fisheries of Southeastern Brazil

Atlantic Forest fisheries include communities of coastal inhabitants who live close to Atlantic Forest remnants, on the northern coast of São Paulo State and the southern coast of Rio de Janeiro State. Fishing grounds used by Atlantic Forest coastal fishers are usually located close to communities (figs. 5.1 and 5.2).

Local inhabitants called *caiçaras,* natives descended from the Indians and Portuguese, live alongside tourism, fishing and cultivating manioc. African and Japanese residents have also been responsible for cultural repertoires and fishing techniques, such as *cêrco* (*kaku-ami,* or floating nets; Mussolini 1980). Japanese families are still responsible for the marketing of coastal fisheries at São Paulo State, as they transfer fish from the fisher to the consumer.

Caiçaras of the Atlantic Forest coast fish for subsistence and for commerce. Some communities are more engaged in commercial fishing than others, although their fishing technology is artisanal. They fish in small canoes (paddled or motorized) or in small boats, using hooks and lines for fish and squid, gill nets for fish, and encircling nets for shrimp.

Behavior of fishers at the macro level was identified by mapping fishing grounds used from 1986 to 1998. The locations of grounds did not change in the communities in which temporal comparisons were possible, such as those of Búzios Island and Sepetiba Bay. Apparently, an informal division of fishing grounds occurs among the *caiçaras,* despite the fact that commercial trawlers also enter waters used by these communities, such as the Bay of Sepetiba.

At the micro level, the management of local marine resources includes different scales of individual or community behavior, from kinship ties to collective rules with claims on fishing grounds. Fishing grounds may be the property of a fisher family or for the exclusive use of artisanal fishers from a particular area. These special cases were detailed by Begossi (1995a, 1996a) and by Castro and Begossi (1995a). In this chapter, I analyze the access rules for fishing grounds employed by the communities of Aventureiro (Ilha Grande), Búzios Island, Puruba, Gamboa, Itacuruçá Island, and Jaguanum Island (table 5.1, fig. 5.2), in terms of fishing, technology, resource, and importance of tourism.

Aventureiro (Ilha Grande): The analysis presented herein is based on 326

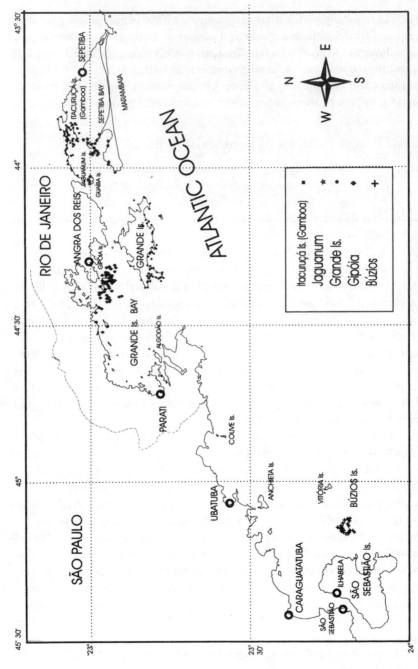

Figure 5.2. Atlantic Forest coastal areas, including fishing grounds used by fishers.

fish landings and thirty interviews conducted in 1995–1996 by Seixas (1997). The Aventureiro community consists of twenty-two families and thirty-nine fishers located in an area protected by the state government of Rio de Janeiro (State Biological Reserve) at Ilha Grande, Rio de Janeiro State (Seixas and Begossi 1998). Fishing grounds were marked in 1998 using the GPS (global positioning system; fig. 5.2; Begossi 1998b). Artisanal fishing in paddled canoes or in small boats is for squid, spottail pinfish, jacks, yellow chub, bluefish, mullets, mackerels, and groupers (table 5.2 gives scientific names), using hooks and lines and set gill nets.

Table 5.2. Common and Scientific Names of Marine Animals Mentioned in Brazilian Studies.

English Name	Local Name	Scientific Name—Family
Marine		
Bluefish	Enchova	*Pomatomus saltatrix*
Bluerunner	Xarelete	*Caranx* spp.
Catfish	Bagre	Family Ariidae (sea) and Pimelodidae (river)
Cutlass fish	Espada	*Trichiurus lepturus*
Grouper	Garoupa	*Epinephelus* spp.
Halfbeak	Panaguaiú	*Hemiramphos balao*
Jack	Carapau	*Caranx* spp.
Kingfish	Imbetara	*Menticirrhus americanus*
Mackerel	Sororoca, cavala, cavalinha	*Scomberomorus* spp., *Scomber* spp.
Mullets	Tainha, paratí	*Mugil* spp.
Sand drum	Corvina	*Micropogonias furnieri*
Shrimp	Camarão	*Penaeus schmitt,* among others
Snook	Robalo	*Centropomus parallelus*
Spottail pinfish	Marimbá	*Diplodus argenteus*
Squid	Lula	*Loligo sanpaulensis*
Weakfish	Pescada	*Cynoscion* spp.
Yellow chub	Piragica	*Kyphosus* spp.
Yellow tail	Olhete	*Seriola lalandi*
Riverine		
—	Barbado	*Pirinampus pirinampu*
—	Bode	Loricariidae
Catfish	Catfish	Pimelodidae
—	Corimba, corimbatá, curimatá	*Prochilodus* spp.
—	Mandí	Pimelodidae
—	Piau	Anostomida

No territories for fishing were observed at Aventureiro (Ilha Grande). The rule of "first come, first served" regulates the use of sites to set gill nets, and fishers share information about fishing grounds. Seixas and Begossi (1998) argued that the lack of territorial behavior may be due to a high unpredictability of local marine resources, relatively high resource abundance, low number of fishers, use of gears with high mobility (hooks and lines), noncommercial fishing, lack of conflict with recreational fishing (tourism is not important there), and strong reciprocity among community members.

Búzios Island (São Paulo State)

Búzios Island shares with Aventureiro the features of relative isolation, no real tourism, strong kinship ties, and difficulties associated with traveling to the coast due to rough seas and coast distance. At Búzios Island, data on 906 fishing trips were obtained in 1986–1997 (Begossi 1996b) and additional information on fishing grounds (using the GPS) was obtained in 1997 (Begossi 1998b). Hooks and lines and set gill nets were the gear used, usually in paddled canoes, and sometimes in motor canoes or small boats for squid, bluefish, halfbeak, bluerunner, weakfish, yellowtail, and groupers (tables 5.1 and 5.2). The Búzios Island community has forty-four families: twenty-three families, including sixteen fishers, were from Porto do Meio, the location studied in detail. No ownership of fishing grounds was observed for hook-and-line fishing, but informal ownership was observed for gill-net fishing, where kinship ties regulated access (Begossi 1995a). The reasons for lack of ownership of fishing grounds for hook-and-line fishing may be the absence of tourist-related conflicts, use of gear with high mobility, and relatively high resource abundance associated with a low number of fishers. The scarcity of fishing grounds to set gill nets may explain the occurrence of informal territories regulated by kinship ties. Gill nets are usually set in rocky parts of the sea or in small bays close to home, so they may be easily controlled by families.

Puruba Beach (São Paulo State)

Puruba Beach is located at the mouth of the Puruba and Quiririm rivers. It is a small community, with about fourteen families connected by close kinship ties. Data on 193 fishing trips undertaken by fifteen fishers were obtained in 1991–1993. Hooks and lines, encircling nets, and set gill nets were used, often from paddled canoes, to catch fresh and marine fish, such as snook, mullets, and catfishes (Begossi 1998c). No one was found to have rights on fishing grounds at Puruba Beach for hook-and-line fishing. There are few data on set gill-net fishing, since 68 percent of trips were performed using hooks and lines, and most of the rest used encircling nets. Apparently the mobility of the gear, low local density, and relatively low density of recreational fishers do not require people to have regulatory mechanisms on fishing grounds.

Sepetiba Bay, Rio de Janeiro

Communities on Itacuruçá Island (Gamboa) and Jaguanum Island (Calhaus), located on Sepetiba Bay, were studied in 1989–1990, when data on 271 fishing trips were obtained. Additional data on fishing grounds were obtained in 1997 using the GPS (Begossi 1998b; fig. 5.2). Sepetiba Bay is used by artisanal, commercial, and recreational fishers. It is an area with intense tourism because it is 60 km from Rio de Janeiro. The island of Itacuruçá includes many tourist houses, except for Gamboa, a community of twenty-six families that includes fishers and personnel involved in tourist activities. Jaguanum Island includes about 100 families. Artisanal fishing on Sepetiba Bay includes encircling nets used especially by Gamboa fishers, and gill nets set by Jaguanum fishers for shrimp, sand drum, mullets, and kingfish.

Over eight years the fishing grounds used by the communities remained the same. However, conflicts over fishing areas were very common, especially between artisanal and trawler fishers, and some local fishers abandoned the use of set gill nets and drifting longlines because of damage caused by trawlers (Begossi 1995a). These conflicts are also related to the fixed gear used at Jaguanum Island, relatively high fisher density caused by the presence of tourists and commercial fishers, and low availability of fishing grounds compared to other Atlantic Forest areas. Fixed gear requires a limited area for some time interval, which is defined by the nature of the technology.

Figure 5.2 illustrates how coastal fishermen partition fishing grounds. Technology may limit how far a fisherman can travel, although this variable is not sufficient to explain the pattern observed. In addition, artisanal fishing sites are disrupted by trawlers, seen as intruders by locals. The temporal stability of artisanal fishing grounds over eight years supports the view that there is an informal division on fishing grounds, making it a key point for management. The fishing areas of artisanal fishers from different artisanal communities do not overlap (fig. 5.2). A macro-scale approach that extends beyond each community to include relations among communities shows how local management must include the whole Atlantic Forest coastal fishing area. The data show clearly that each fishing community usually stays in its own geographic region instead of going to other islands or along the coast.

At Sepetiba Bay there is a clear perception by fishers of trawler intrusion, and residents have claimed the bay as an artisanal fishing area through collective action in meetings, assemblies, and newspaper articles (Begossi

1995a). Despite the conflicts, the division in the use of fishing grounds is considered informal because artisanal fishers do not claim rights to fishing grounds among themselves, although claims are directed toward trawler fishing.

Riverine Fisheries in Brazil

Artisanal fisheries in Brazil are still significant, at least for the subsistence fishing of native populations (Petrere 1989). The artisanal fisheries described in this study include the Grande River in southeastern Brazil, the Araguaia River in central Brazil, and the Juruá River in western Amazônia (fig. 5.1). Local inhabitants, called *caboclos,* participate in subsistence and economic activities based on small-scale agriculture (especially the harvesting of manioc), artisanal fishing, extraction of natural resources, and tourism. These communities have many aspects in common with the *caiçaras* along the Atlantic Forest coast. Both are descendants of Brazilian Indians and Portuguese colonizers, and both have an agriculture that includes beans, sweet potatoes, and especially manioc.

Fishing by *caboclos* is usually performed in paddled or motorized canoes or in small boats, and fishing gear includes a variety of hooks, set gill nets, encircling nets (sea), cast nets (river). Plants are cultivated and collected in the forest for food, housing, handicrafts, and medicine. Finally, both *caiçaras* and *caboclos* have a deep relationship with aquatic and forestry resources (Begossi 1998a; Morán 1990).

The riverine communities studied are located in different Brazilian areas, with different vegetation types and different levels of interaction with the local economy. For example, the Araguaia River community is close to the *cerrado* (Brazilian savanna), where cattle ranching is intense, and tourism involves recreational fishing and activities related to tourist houses along the rivers. Riverine communities along the Juruá River are in the Amazonian rain forest, in the Extractive Reserve of the Upper Juruá. Their activities include rubber extraction and bean and tobacco commerce, as well as fishing and hunting for subsistence.

Araguaia River (Goiás and Mato Grosso States)

Historically the economy of the Tocantins-Araguaia was based on extraction of natural resources, such as nuts and fruits (Ribeiro et al., 1995). With the arrival of the Portuguese in the eighteenth century, settlers exploited nuts, gems, gold, game, and fish, which were transported down the rivers. Capital-intensive agriculture and huge livestock industries are features of the *cerrado* areas of the Araguaia River. Today the Araguaia River seems a very special case because of intense tourism.

The portion of the river from Barra do Garças to Bananal Island was studied in 1997–1998 through interviews with 50 percent of the riverine families (fig. 5.1; Begossi 1998d). We estimated that seventy-two families lived along about 900 km of the riverbanks. Recreational fishing was very intense, especially in July (the dry season), when camping grounds and huts for tourists were set up along the white beaches. Riverine inhabitants engaged in small-scale agriculture, fishing, cattle ranching, and tourist-related jobs (as boat rental agents, fishing guides, and housekeepers). Fishers used hooks and lines to catch mandí and other catfishes, as well as piau.

Rules were imposed by government-funded environmental agencies; conflicts with agency representatives were mentioned by fishers in interviews in São Felix do Araguaia, where artisanal fishing was still found. Other places, such as Luís Alves, abandoned artisanal fishing. Vila Isabel was important in artisanal fishing in the 1970s but now includes many ex-fishers. In the Araguaia River artisanal fishing was relegated to secondary importance, while recreational fishing was promoted. No local rules were observed to be in effect concerning fishing, probably due to the lack of commercial fishing and to regulations imposed by governmental agencies.

Grande River

Riverine communities on the Grande River, Paraná basin, were studied by Castro (1992) in 1988–1989, who sampled seventy-three trips in the wet season (November to March), forty-five trips in transitional months between seasons (April and October), and twenty-three trips in the dry season. Forty-one riverine fishers studied concentrated their activities near the Hydroelectric Plant of Marimbondo and lived at Icém (São Paulo State) and Fronteira (Minas Gerais State, fig. 5.1). Icém was established in the beginning of this century, but Fronteira developed more recently during construction of the hydroelectric plant (Castro and Begossi 1995).

This area of the Grande River included artisanal and recreational fishers who used different fishing grounds and gear to catch different species, avoiding group conflict. However, in transitional months between the wet and dry seasons, group conflicts were observed and territorial fishing rights were claimed for the catch of barbado (Castro and Begossi 1996). These territories included fishing grounds where longlines were used by older fishers, who defended their boundaries verbally or by force (such as cutting lines). The territories are hereditary or subject to trade (Castro and Begossi 1995). Enforcement of local rules at the Grande River shifts seasonally, according to resource availability and fisher density. In the wet season fish resources were abundant (especially corimba) and cast nets were frequently used, whereas in the dry season resources were scarce. In transitional months, territorial rights were asserted because resources were scarce, but people were still fishing. Both artisanal and recreational groups fish intensely in the wet season and do little fishing in the dry season, concentrating in fishing grounds downstream of the hydroelectric plant. In this area, recreational fishing lines often got entangled with local longlines, causing conflicts (Castro and Begossi 1995, 1996).

The Upper Juruá

The Extractive Reserve of the Upper Juruá was legalized in 1990 as a result of collective actions and local organization of rubber tappers (Begossi 1998c). The first meeting of the National Council of Rubber Tappers occurred in 1985, followed by a local meeting at the Upper Juruá in 1986 (Cunha et al. 1992, 1993). The Coordinating Committee of the Reserve developed a Community Economic Development Plan in 1988, including areas for a cooperative, research, social infrastructure, and technical activities (Cunha et al. 1992, 1993). Radio (Verdes Florestas) provided communication among families in a place where transportation is possible only along the rivers, which are difficult to navigate in the summer. The local *caboclos* in the ASAREAJ (Associação dos Seringueiros e Agricultores da Reserva Extrativista do Alto Juruá) organized meetings where strategies for local production and conservation were analyzed and developed, including a management plan, which was legally approved by the IBAMA (Brazilian Federal Environmental Agency) in 1994.

Fishers in Upper Juruá Riverine communities were studied in 1993–1994 and included families living along the banks of the rivers Juruá, Tejo, Bagé, S. João, and Breu (fig. 5.1). Families included rubber tappers and small-scale agriculturists, including subsistence fishers. Interviews were carried out with 143 adults (101 families), but we estimated 500 families lived along these riverbanks (Begossi et al. 1995; Begossi 1998d). Cast nets and hooks and lines were the main gear used to catch bode and mandí in the dry season. In the wet season, hunting activities were important and the fish were relatively scarce.

Conservation rules, organized by local inhabitants along with their associations (CNS and ASAREAJ), are enforced at the Upper Juruá, and the local association recruited grassroots monitors. Local rules associated with fishing included not using set gill nets in the mouths of tributary rivers. This is a case of comanagement of rubbertappers and universities, with the inclusion of the government for legal support. Shared governance or state regulation jointly with user self-management is a viable option (McCay and Acheson 1987; Feeny et al. 1990; Ostrom 1993).

Marine and riverine artisanal fishers in Brazil show a diversity of environments and a gradient scale of market influences, from subsistence (Upper

Juruá) to commercial fishing (Sepetiba Bay). *Caiçaras* and *caboclos* share a high interaction with the environment: They have artisanal fishing technologies, and their levels of organization range from high (as in communities in the north; for example, Conselho Nacional dos Seringueiros, the National Rubber Council) to low or fragile (as in the Atlantic Forest coast; Begossi 1998a).

At Sepetiba Bay, implications of artisanal fishers' territorial behavior in relation to the bay help in local management, since fishers' attitudes are directed toward conservation measures. In other Latin American areas, such as Lake Titicaca, rules regarding communal territories were widely enforced in spite of their informal status and opposition of government officials because community members were willing to share the costs of enforcement (Levieil and Orlove 1990). In the lakes in the Lower Amazon, commercial and local fishers (*ribeirinhos*) exhibited self-organization and local management by creating informal lake reserves (not legally authorized) through closure of the lake to outsiders and establishment of rules for local fishers. Because lakes are enclosed, local fishers may see a direct relationship between fishing pressure and lake productivity (McGrath et al. 1993).

Discussion

Information and its costs, uncertainty in fisheries, and kin ties show connections regarding cooperation or territoriality among fishers. Territorial rights mean to control outsider entrance, which involves costs. Other variables, such as those related to gear, density, competition, market, and legislation, are factors associated with the existence or nonexistence of local rules and rights and to levels of cooperation or territoriality among fishers.

The Role of Information

To evaluate the patterns of local institutions that assign exclusive use rights among the marine and riverine fishers described, it is necessary to analyze features of both the resources and communities. Marine or riverine resources are often unpredictable, and estimates of stock abundance are usually highly uncertain, as are estimates of recruitment, growth, and natural mortality rates (Mangel and Clark 1983; Pálsson 1998). Thus fishing is a risky activity, considering risk as a probabilistic variation (Stephens and Krebs 1986). Sea tenure is an institutional response to uncertainty because cooperative practices and information sharing are risk-spreading responses to hazards and to unpredictable occupations and environments (Cordell 1989). The migratory nature of many fish species (Barthem and Goulding 1997) increases the problems of defining boundaries and excluding users (Feeny et al. 1996). Other aspects are the cascading effects, felt from local to global scales (Burger et al., this volume). For example, when riverine people fish for migratory species, they may affect fisheries downriver, or on river tributaries.

The fisher must decide where to go and which species to fish. However, as environments change rapidly, accurate decisions are difficult to make (Boyd and Richerson 1985). One of the tricky questions in foraging theory is how foragers value information, taking into account the costs of recognition and discrimination of the prey (Stephens and Krebs 1986). Information sharing is very important because it diminishes the cost of individual trials, and kinship ties strengthen the opportunities for cooperation and information sharing among relatives. In figure 5.3 I summarize the relationships among variables,

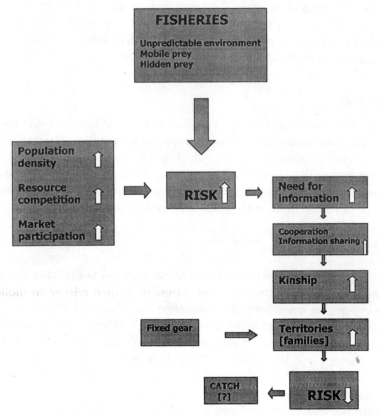

Figure 5.3. Schematic of the relationship among variables, including territorial rights and kinship, that influence risk in fishing communities.

including the unpredictability of fisheries related with risk, information sharing, kinship ties, cooperation, and territoriality. One of the main implications is diminishing risks that may be perceived by fishers through catch increases. I do not have data from *caiçaras* and *caboclos* to test whether increases in the catch are due to territoriality, but cooperation among brothers tends to increase catches at Búzios Island (Begossi 1996b).

The classic study by Acheson (1987, 1972) on the territoriality of the "harbor gang" or lobster fishing villages located in the coast of Maine demonstrated the existence of a persistent rumor that defended areas had larger catches and incomes compared to other areas. The Maine fishers felt that legalizing territories would be beneficial. Their motives were conservation and the right to fish "in their areas," while the costs of enforcement would pass to state wardens (Acheson 1987). Alexander (1977) studied sea tenure among the Mawelle (southern Sri Lanka), where net cycles were employed: A net could be used on the harbor side at any time during the day after the net immediately preceding it in the cycle had been used. Although the system gave equal opportunities to all nets, it did not result in equal returns; in this case it created demographic increase which, in turn, increased the number of nets. The function of the access right was not to limit the number of nets but to ensure that outsiders did not use nets in Mawelle Beach, accelerating a fragmentation process (Alexander 1977). Finally, in the case of fishing at the Grande River, exercise of territorial rights in critical months was shown to minimize competition between local and recreational fishers (Castro and Begossi 1995, 1996).

Analysis of the behavior of Brazilian fishers using optimal foraging models revealed suboptimal behavior in many cases, probably due to difficulties in obtaining information on fisheries. The optimal model used for Atlantic Forest fishers from Búzios Island and from Puruba Beach showed almost no variation in the variables tested. For shrimp fishing at Gamboa (Itacuruçá Island), the model was stronger: $r^2 = 0.38$ for the effect of time spent fishing in patches on catches, and $r^2 = 0.22$ for the effect of travel time on fishing (Begossi 1995b). However, fishers remained for a long time in a patch relative to model prediction (Begossi 1992). Despite the usefulness of optimal foraging theory to analyze fisheries, other studies have pointed out the limitations of the model applied to fisheries (McCay 1981). These conflicting results demonstrate the difficulty of predicting fishing, increasing the importance of cooperation, reciprocity, and information sharing. The importance of the mobility of prey in optimal foraging behavior also demonstrates that the nature of the species hunted is a variable that influences fishers' decision processes, contrary to what Durrenberger and Pálsson (1987) observed in their analyses of access to fishing grounds.

Access Rules and the Capacity to Exclude Outsiders

At Bahia, Cordell (1985) listed the salient features for territorial rights or sea tenure: environmental factors, collective mechanisms and sanctions, social contexts where disputes occur, and problems related to uncontrolled areas of the sea. Ruddle et al. (1992) identified principles for tenure systems in the South Pacific, including social status, use rights, territory definition, control by traditional authorities, occurrence of conservation practices, and existence of sanctions for infringement of regulations. Other factors that explain the different behaviors found among Brazilian fishers include type of gear (fixed or mobile), density of fishers (including tourists), level of resource competition (conflicts), market economic necessity (high when the resource is part of an economic activity), and external laws or interference (the presence of governmental authorities linked to protected areas or to development planning; table 5.3).

Table 5.3. Variables Involved in the Capacity of Fishers. *Main gear* refers to the gear with which some local rule is associated. *Density* refers to the density of fishers, including other categories, such as industrial or recreational fishers. *Competition* refers to conflicts between fisher categories. *Necessity* refers to the importance of the resource as a means of monetary gain. *External laws* refers to the interference of environmental government agencies.

Community	Main Gear	Density	Resource Competition	Necessity	External Laws
Coastal					
Aventureiro (Grande I.)	Mobile	Low	Low	Subsistence	Strong
Porto do Meio (Búzios I.)	Fixed*	Low	Low	Commerce	Weak
Puruba Beach	Mobile	Low	Low	Subsistence and commerce	Strong
Gamboa (Itacuruçá I.)	Mobile	High	High	Commerce	Weak
Calhaus (Jaguanum I.)	Fixed	High	High	Commerce	Weak
Riverine					
Araguaia	Mobile	High	High	Subsistence	Strong
Grande	Fixed	Medium	Medium	Commerce	Weak
Juruá	Mobile	Low	Low	Subsistence	Comanagement

* No rule is associated with hook and line, the gear frequently used.

These variables vary among communities, along with their local rules and actions (table 5.3). Some are important in defining local rules for resource use and who is going to be included or excluded as a resource user. For example, areas where fixed gear is important, such as Búzios Island and Grande River, have local rules concerning the use of such gear. Communities in which there are no commercial fisheries, such as those of Aventureiro (Grande Island) and the Araguaia River, develop fewer rules. These two communities are located in areas with strong law enforcement.

Two communities of high density and conflict showed different outcomes in terms of collective action. On the Araguaia River, tourism is concentrated in recreational fishing, and artisanal fishing lost its way, because many fishers abandoned fishing. In the Araguaia–Tocantins basin, economic interests, along with the lobby of tourist agencies, have worked against fishery management because they want to ensure large fish for recreational fishing (Ribeiro et al. 1995). In this case, conflict and external influences led to a lack of rules and to the exclusion of riverine inhabitants from fishing activity. Recreational fishing pushed the exclusion of artisanal fishing. Bromley and Cernea (1989) pointed out that when local institutional arrangements are destroyed, common property regimes are converted to open access, in which rules of capture drive people to get as much as quickly as possible. There are no data on institutional arrangements before the advent of intensive tourism in the Araguaia River, but the exclusion of local artisanal fishers shows that local arrangements, if they existed, were probably eliminated.

In the case of Sepetiba Bay, where there are conflicts with trawler fishers, I observed three outcomes: (a) gear shifts due to trawler damages; (b) collective action aimed at establishing rules to use the bay, including the demand to exclude trawlers from the bay; and (c) a suboptimal behavior among shrimp fishers, estimated by optimal foraging models (Begossi 1992). In the latter case, fishers spent more time in a fishing ground than was predicted by the optimal foraging model, which led to two hypotheses: (1) fishers have difficulties in evaluating resources in a fishing ground because of high variance in catches and difficulties related to a hidden, submersed prey, or (2) trawlers push fishers to take all the fish they can before they arrive with trawler nets.

Market orientation is also important as a variable in predicting sea tenure or a common regime. Market opportunities may make a common-property resource more valuable because expansion of market opportunities and growing scarcity of the resource result in new arrangements to manage the resource more effectively (Thomson et al. 1992) and to prevent short-term gains (Hanna 1998). Places with territorial rights, such as Búzios, Sepetiba Bay, and Grande River, have artisanal commercial fisheries (table 5.3). At Búzios, choice of fish catch is related to price; fishers search for less bony fish that have higher market prices (Begossi and Richerson 1992).

Size of the fisher group may also be an important variable in predicting sea tenure and self-organization. Small-scale units permit more efficient handling of management issues, sharing of new biological information, and establishment of local rules (Acheson et al. 1998). Similarly, it is easier for small groups to recognize each other, detect rule infractions, and exclude outsiders (Feeny 1992). The literature on reciprocity (Trivers 1971) and cooperation (Alexander 1979; Axelrod 1984, tit-for-tat strategy) analyzes the questions of cooperation and probability of encounter (both of which diminish as group size increases). Group sizes have to show large variations to be important. In the Brazilian communies studied, group sizes do not show large enough variations to be used as a comparative variable.

With the exception of the Upper Juruá Extractive Reserve, where there is comanagement, external rules of government-funded environmental agencies often are not in concordance with the needs of local communities. The existence of external environmental rules does not guarantee maintenance of the resource for natives or for other local users, as illustrated by the Araguaia case. External laws may work against the local population. The experiences of the extractive reserves demonstrates that comanagement is an option that should be developed in Brazil for fisheries. Internal consistency and people's compliance with managers are important determinants of management success (Smith 1990). The future of community-based marine resource management may lie in comanagement with the government (Ruddle 1993). The search for variables that may predict communities' capacities to establish rules and to self-organize is a task that includes local features and global ties (such as market activities).

Conclusion

The variables analyzed here, such as the nature of technology used, the density of fishers and the amount of resource competition, the existence of market demands, and the occurrence of areas controlled by government environmental agencies are helpful in understanding why some areas are prone to self-organization while others show signs of exclusion by outsiders. Uncertainty regarding the fishery, the importance of information sharing to diminish risk, associated pressures on resources, and the use of fixed gear explain why kinship ties are so important in determining access rules to territories. Communities that employ fixed gear and include different types of fishers (trawlers, tourists) develop local territorial rules and the capacity for self-organization. High fisher density and market pressures generate conflicts in the use of resources that can be resolved by developing local rules and institutions. External influences, such as the rules of governmental agencies, are often not helpful to local communities. Comanagement, such as occurred at the Upper

Juruá Extractive Reserve, illustrates that local resources can be managed using a self-organized strategy.

Acknowledgments

I thank the Brazilian Agencies FAPESP for grants in 1992, 1994, 1996, and 1997, and the Conselho Nacional de Desenvolvimento Cientifico e Tecnologico (CNPq) for a research productivity scholarship. The MacArthur Foundation supported the fieldwork at the Upper Juruá, Acre. I am grateful to Joanna Burger and Bonnie J. McCay for their helpful suggestions.

References

Acheson, James. 1972. "Territories of Lobstermen." *Natural History* 81: 60–79.

———. 1987. "The Lobster Fiefs Revisited: Economic and Ecological Effects of Territoriality in Maine Lobster Fishing." In *The Question of the Commons,* edited by Bonnie McCay and J. Acheson, 37–65. Tucson: University of Arizona Press.

Acheson, James, J. A. Wilson, and R. S. Steneck. 1998. "Managing Chaotic Fisheries." In *Linking Social and Cultural Systems for Resilience,* edited by Carl Folke and Fikret Berkes, 390–413. Cambridge, England: Cambridge University Press.

Alexander, Paul. 1977. "Sea Tenure in Sri Lanka." *Ethnology* 16:231–51.

Alexander, Richard. 1979. *Darwinism and Human Affairs.* Seattle: University of Washington Press.

Axelrod, Robert. 1984. *The Evolution of Cooperation.* New York: Basic Books.

Barthem, Ronaldo, and M. Goulding. 1997. *The Catfish Connection.* New York: Columbia University Press.

Begossi, Alpina. 1992. "The Use of Optimal Foraging Theory to Understand Fishing Strategies: A Case from Sepetiba Bay (State of Rio de Janeiro, Brazil)." *Human Ecology* 20 (4):463–75.

———. 1995a. "Fishing Spots and Sea Tenure in Atlantic Forest Coastal Communities: Incipient Forms of Local Management." *Human Ecology* 23 (3): 387–406.

———. 1995b. "The Application of Ecological Theory to Human Behavior: Niche, Diversity and Optimal Foraging." In *Human Ecology: Progress through Integrative Perspectives,* edited by Richard Borden, M. Bubolz, L. Hens, J. Taylor, and T. Webler, 153–61. East Lansing, MI: Society for Human Ecology.

———. 1996a. "The Fishers and Buyers from Búzios Island (Brazil): Kin Ties and Production." *Ciência e Cultura* 48 (3):142–47.

———. 1996b. "Fishing Activities and Strategies at Búzios Island (Brazil)." In *Fisheries Resource Utilization and Policy,* edited by Robert Meyer, C. Zhang, M. L. Windsor, B. J. McCay, L. J. Hushak, and R. Muth, 125–40. Proceedings of the World Fisheries Congress. New Delhi: Oxford and IBH Publishing.

———. 1998a. "Cultural and Ecological Resilience among Caiçaras of the Atlantic Forest and Caboclos of the Amazon, Brazil." In *Linking Social and Cultural Systems for Resilience,* edited by Carl Folke and Fikret Berkes, 129–57. Cambridge, England: Cambridge University Press.

————. 1998b. "Pesqueiros e territórios em comunidades de caiçaras da Mata Atlântica. Report FAPESP." Grant no. 97/6167-0 from FAPESP. Unpublished report.

————. 1998c. "Property Rights for Fisheries at Different Scales: Applications for Conservation in Brazil." *Fisheries Research* 34:269–78.

————. 1998d. "Knowledge on the Use of Natural Resources: Contributions to Local Management." In *Research in Human Ecology: An Interdisciplinary Overview,* edited by Luc Hens, Richard J. Borden, Shosuke Suzuki, and Gianumberto Caravello, 39–52. Proceedings of the symposium organized at the Seventh International Congress of Ecology (INTECOL), Florence, Italy, July 39–25. Brussels: VUB Press.

————. 1999. "Scale of Interactions of Brazilian Populations (Caiçaras and Caboclos) with Resources and Institutions." *Human Ecology Review* 6 (1):1–7.

Begossi, Alpina, B. D. Amaral, and R. A. M. Silvano. 1995. "Reserva Extrativista do Alto Juruá: Aspectos de etnoecologia." In *A questão ambiental: Cenários de pesquisa.* Textos NEPAM, Série Divulgação Acadêmica, Org. Sônia Barbosa, 95–105. Campinas: UNICAMP.

Begossi, Alpina, and P. J. Richerson. 1992. "The Animal Diet of Families from Búzios Island: An Optimal Foraging Approach." *Journal of Human Ecology* 3 (2): 433–58.

Berkes, Fikret. 1985. "Fishermen and the 'Tragedy of the Commons.'" *Environmental Conservation* 12:199–206.

Boyd, Robert, and P. Richerson, 1985. *Culture and the Evolutionary Process.* Chicago: University of Chicago Press.

Bromley, Daniel W., and M. C. Cernea. 1989. "The Management of Common Property Natural Resources." World Bank Discussion Papers no. 57. Washington, DC: The World Bank.

Burger, Joanna, C. Field, R. Norgaard, E. Ostrom, and D. Policansky. 2000. "Common-Pool Resources and Common Institutions: An Overview of the Applicability of the Concept and Approach to Current Environmental Problems." In *Protecting the Commons: A Framework for Resource Management in the Americas,* edited by J. Burger, E. Ostrom, R. B. Norgaard, D. Policansky, and B. D. Goldstein. Washington, DC: Island Press.

Castro, Fábio. 1992. "Aspectos ecológicos da pesca artesanal no Rio Grande, à jusante da Usina Hidrelétrica de Marimbondo." Master's thesis, Campinas, UNICAMP.

Castro, Fábio, and A. Begossi. 1995. "Ecology of Fishing on the Grande River (Brazil): Technology and Territorial Rights." *Fisheries Research* 23:361–73.

————. 1996. "Fishing at Rio Grande: Ecological Niche and Competition." *Human Ecology* 24 (3):401–11.

Cordell, John. 1985. "Sea Tenure in Bahia." Common Property Steering Committee, BOSTID. Washington, DC: National Research Council.

————. 1989. *A Sea of Small Boats.* Cambridge, MA: Cultural Survival

Cunha, Manuela C., K. S. Drown, Jr., and M. W. B. Almeida, coord. 1992. "Can Traditional Forest-Dwellers Self-Manage Conservation Areas? A Probing Experiment in the Juruá Extractive Reserve, Acre, Brazil." Project supported by MacArthur Foundation Grant no. 92-21848.

————. 1993. Annual Report of the Project "Can Traditional Forest-Dwellers Self-Manage Conservation Areas? A Probing Experiment in the Juruá Extractive Reserve, Acre, Brazil."

Diegues, Antonio C. S. 1983. *Pescadores, camponeses etrabalhadores do mar.* São Paulo: Editora Ática.

Durrenberger, E. Paul, and G. Pálsson. 1987. "Ownership at Sea: Fishing Territories and Access to Sea Resources." *American Ethnologist* 14:508–22.

Dyson-Hudson, D., and E. A. Smith. 1978. "Human Territoriality: An Ecological Reassessment." *American Anthropologist* 80:21–41.

Feeny, David. 1992. "Where Do We Go from Here? Implications for the Research Agenda." In *Making the Commons Work,* edited by Daniel W. Bromley, 267–92. San Francisco: Institute for Contemporary Studies Press.

Feeny, David, F. Berkes, B. J. McCay, and J. A. Acheson. 1990. "The Tragedy of the Commons Twenty-Two Years Later." *Human Ecology* 18:1–19.

Feeny, David, S. Hanna, and A. F. McEvoy. 1996. "Questioning the Assumptions of 'The Tragedy of the Commons' Model of Fisheries." *Land Economics* 72:187–205.

Forman, Shepard. 1967. "Cognition and the Catch: The Location of Fishing Spots in a Brazilian Coastal Village." *Ethnology* 6:417–26.

Hanna, Susan S. 1998. "Managing for Human and Ecological Context in the Maine Soft Shell Clam Fishery." In *Linking Social and Cultural Systems for Resilience,* edited by Carl Folke and Fikret Berkes, 190–212. Cambridge, England: Cambridge University Press.

Hviding, Edward, and G. B. K. Baines. 1994. "Community-based Fisheries Management, Tradition and the Challenges of Development in Marovo, Solomon Islands." In *Development and Environment, Sustaining People and Nature,* edited by Dharam Ghai, 13–39. Oxford: Blackwell Publishing.

Lendrem, D. 1986. *Modelling in Behavioural Ecology.* Australia: Croom Helm.

Levieil, Dominique, and B. S. Orlove. 1990. "Local Control of Aquatic Resources: Community and Ecology in Lake Titicaca, Peru." *American Anthropologist* 92: 362–82.

Malmberg, T. 1984. "Water, Rhythm and Territoriality." *Geografiska Annaler* 66B:73–89.

———. 1985. "Teritoriality at Sea: Preliminary Reflections on Marine Behavioral Territories in View of Recent Planning." *Man-Environment Systems* 15: 15–18.

———. 1990. "Human Territoriality: Past-Present-Future." *Studies in Human Ecology* 9:95–100.

———. 1993. "Is Territoriality a Taboo?" Conference of Danish Urban Planning Researchers, November 8–10, University of Odense, Denmark.

Mangel, Marc, and C. W. Clark. 1983. "Uncertainty, Search and Information in Fisheries." *J. Cons. Int. Explor. Mer.* 41:93–103.

McCay, Bonnie J. 1981. "Optimal Foragers or Political Actors? Ecological Analyses of a New Jersey Fishery." *American Ethnologist* 8:356–81.

McCay, Bonnie J., and J. Acheson. 1987. *The Question of the Commons.* Tucson: University of Arizona Press.

McGrath, David G., F. Castro, C. Futemma, B. D. Amaral, and J. Calabria. 1993. "Fisheries and the Evolution of Resource Management on the Lower Amazon Floodplain." *Human Ecology* 21:167–95.

Morán, Emilio F. 1990. *A ecologia humana das populações da Amazônia.* Petrópolis: Editora Vozes.

Morse, D. H. 1980. *Behavioral Mechanisms in Ecology.* Cambridge, MA: Harvard University Press.

Mussolini, Gioconda. 1980. *Ensaios de antropologia indígena e caiçara.* São Paulo: Editora Paz e Terra.

Nemec, T. F. 1972. "I Fish with My Brother: The Structure and Behavior of Agnatic-based Fishing Crews in a Newfoundland Irish Out Port." In *North Atlantic Fishermen,* edited by Raoul Andersen and C. Wadel, 9–34. Toronto: University of Toronto Press.

Ostrom, Elinor. 1993. "The Evolution of Norms, Rules and Rights." Beijer Discussion Papers no. 39. Stockholm: The Beijer Institute of Ecological Economics.

———. 2000. "Reformulating the Commons." In *Protecting the Commons: A Framework for Resource Management in the Americas,* edited by J. Burger, E. Ostrom, R. Norgaard, D. Polincansky, and B. D. Goldstein. Washington, DC: Island Press.

Pálsson, Gísli. 1998. "Learning by Fishing: Practical Engagement and Environmental Concerns." In *Linking Social and Cultural Systems for Resilience,* edited by Carl Folke and Fikret Berkes, 48–66. Cambridge, England: Cambridge University Press.

Petrere, Miguel, Jr. 1989. "River Fisheries in Brazil: A Review." *Regulated Rivers: Research and Management* 4:1–16.

Ribeiro, Mauro C. L. B., and M. Petrere, Jr. 1990. "Fisheries Ecology and Management of the Jaraqui (*Semaprochilodus taeniurus, S. insignis*) in Central Amazonia." *Regulated Rivers: Research and Management* 5:195–215.

Ribeiro, Mauro C. L. B., M. Petrere, Jr., and A. A. Juras. 1995. "Ecological Integrity and Fisheries Ecology of the Araguaia-Tocantins River Basin, Brazil." *Regulated Rivers: Research and Management* 11:325–50.

Ruddle, Kenneth. 1993. "External Forces and Change in Traditional Community-based Fishery Management Systems in the Asia-Pacific Region." *Maritime Anthropological Studies* 6:1–37.

Ruddle, Kenneth, E. Hviding, and E. Johannes. 1992. "Marine Resources Management in the Context of Customary Tenure." *Marine Resource Economics* 7:249–73.

Seixas, Cristiana S. 1997. "Estratégias de pesca e utilização de animais por comunidades pesqueiras da Ilha Grande (Brazil)." Master's thesis, Campinas, UNICAMP.

Seixas, Cristiana S., and A. Begossi. 1998. "Do Fishers Have Territories? The Use of Fishing Grounds at Aventureiro (Ilha Grande, Brazil)." Paper presented at the Seventh Conference of the International Association for the Study of Common Property, Vancouver, June 10–14, 1998.

Smith, M. Estellie. 1990. "Chaos in Fisheries Management." *Maritime Anthropological Studies* 3:1–13.

Stephens, D. W., and J. R. Krebs. 1986. *Foraging Theory.* Princeton, NJ: Princeton University Press.

Thomson, J. T., D. Feeny, and R. Oakerson. 1992. "Institutional Dynamics: The Evolution and Dissolution of Common-Property Resource Management." In *Making the Commons Work,* edited by Daniel W. Bromley, 129–60. San Francisco: ICS Press.

Trivers, Robert. 1971. "The Evolution of Reciprocal Altruism." In *The Sociobiology Debate,* edited by A. L. Caplan, 213–26. New York: Harper & Row.

Part Two

REGIONAL AND CROSS-BOUNDARY COMMONS

Chapter 6

Water Resources:
The Southwestern United States

EDELLA SCHLAGER AND WILLIAM BLOMQUIST

This chapter treats potable water supplies provided by surface streams and underground aquifers in the southwestern United States as a commons. Those supplies have come under tremendous stress in the twentieth century from mining, agriculture, industry, and urban development.

Considerable effort has been devoted to designing, implementing, and modifying institutions and policies to address acute and chronic problems of overuse and degradation. Through the first three-quarters of the twentieth century, a common response to water scarcity in the West was the construction of federally funded dams, reservoirs, and distribution systems to capture and move available water supplies to meet increasing demands. Such large water projects are no longer financially or ecologically feasible.

Numerous western states are turning to conjunctive water management as one means of developing additional water supplies. Conjunctive water management, which requires the coordinated use of surface water systems and groundwater basins, is more cost effective and less environmentally damaging than large-scale surface storage systems.

The extent and form that conjunctive water management takes in western states is strongly conditioned by the states' institutional arrangements for allocating and using water. Those arrangements provide opportunities for and obstacles to conjunctive management.

The states of California and Colorado are used here to illustrate the effects of institutional arrangements on conjunctive water management. California and Colorado were selected because both are located in the relatively arid American Southwest and have experienced significant problems of water supply maldistribution and water quality degradation. Conjunctive use programs

133

have been developed and implemented in some watersheds in both states. Some of those programs are decades old, while others are quite recent. Some are operated on a scale smaller than that of a watershed; others involve huge interwatershed transfer and storage efforts. And both states contain areas in which conjunctive-use programs are physically feasible but have not been developed and implemented.

The institutional arrangements governing water in Colorado and California exhibit critical differences that create radically different conjunctive water management practices. Both states use relatively decentralized approaches for defining and administering rights in both surface water and groundwater. Local water providers and water users exercise substantial authority in developing, monitoring, and enforcing water rights, with very little central direction from state governments. Colorado law, however, recognizes the hydrologic connection between surface water and groundwater tributary to a surface water source, governing both types of water with a single legal doctrine: prior appropriation. Furthermore, Colorado law provides powerful incentives for water users to develop individual private property rights in water. California, by contrast, governs surface and groundwater with multiple legal doctrines that do not recognize the hydrologic connection between the two types of water. And except in special instances, water users are discouraged from pursuing the creation of well-developed property rights in water.

In the following section water in the American Southwest is characterized as a common-pool resource. Next, the multiple dilemmas that face water users in the Southwest are explored. Then the promise of conjunctive management for solving such dilemmas is discussed. Finally, the challenge of realizing conjunctive management in light of existing institutional arrangements is explored using Colorado and California as case studies.

Defining the Commons in Southwestern Water Supplies

Potable water supplies exhibit subtractability, a defining characteristic of the commons. Although the hydrologic cycle of evaporation and precipitation replenishes all surface and underground water resources on Earth, those processes occur gradually and also feature spatial and temporal variability. Water use in any location can exceed the rate of replenishment, for periods of brief or extended duration. Furthermore, some locations have arid climates, regularly receiving less precipitation and experiencing faster rates of evaporation than other areas.

Subtractability: Interactions among User Effects

While water in a stream channel, a lake or sea, or an underground aquifer appears as an undifferentiated mass resource—the quintessential "common pool"—water extracted from the surface or underground body is an alienable quantity. It can be stored, measured, transported, even bought and sold as a commodity, and consumed. A quantity of water captured for consumption by one user is unavailable to another user, at least until it is returned to the body of water from which it was taken.

Defining this commons in terms of potability of water supplies adds another dimension of subtractability. Uses of water, and of overlying or adjacent lands, that degrade the quality of a water supply also effectively reduce the amount available to other users by rendering the supply unsuitable for some purposes. The effect is essentially the same as that of a reduction of supply created by overuse; that is, the demands of all interested users cannot be met because of the actions of some users.

Still other interactions among water users and uses create additional subtraction effects, albeit not immediately related to potability. Users may visit technological externalities upon one another (essentially "crowding" the resource), as when wells placed too closely together interfere with one another's pumping or an upstream diversion device reduces the flow of water passing the next downstream intake. Surface water supplies are especially susceptible to cross-use externalities, as when damming a stream satisfies some purposes (flood control, hydropower generation, recreational uses of the reservoir) but reduces or eliminates the ability to satisfy other values (scenic beauty, recreational uses of the stream itself, migration and spawning activity of anadromous fish). In these and many other instances, interaction effects among users and uses result in what is meant by subtractability: One user's enjoyment of the resource reduces the quantity or quality of what remains to be enjoyed by others.

Difficulty of Exclusion

It is difficult to exclude users from access to surface water streams and underground aquifers in the southwestern United States. Interrelated scale, cultural, legal, and economic factors contribute to that difficulty of exclusion.

Given the importance the British and American systems place on land ownership in determining rights of access and use to natural resources, the simplest means of effecting exclusion would be enclosure of the resource within the confines of landowners' real property. This is essentially impossible in the U.S. Southwest for two reasons. First and more obviously, virtually all surface water systems and groundwater basins extend beyond the real property of any owner. Second, a considerable amount of land in the Southwest is committed to federal reservations for Native American tribes, national parks and monuments, and military installations. The resources appurtenant to them are not available for private enclosure or ownership, and although the federal government has reserved the right to use water to fulfill the purposes of the reservation, it has elected not to use its ownership of the land to exclude others from access to the water resources on or beneath that land.

Historical development and cultural views contributed further to the emergence of alternative legal rules governing access to and use of water supplies in the Southwest. In keeping with a cultural view that water supplies in an arid region were too precious to everyone to allow complete ownership by anyone, the corpus of each water resource—the stream itself, the groundwater basin, and so forth—was in most western states declared to be owned in common by the people of the state. What could be reduced to at least temporary possession was the *use* of the water (Mann 1963; Vranesh 1987).

The systems of usage rights that emerged reflected the economic development of the region at the time it was formed into U.S. territories and then states. Landowners adjacent to or overlying a water source had rights of access and use for their lands, but the development of mining and irrigated agriculture in the West also favored creation of a set of legal rules allowing water to be alienated from its source and transported for use on nearby or even distant lands—a process known as "appropriating" water (Smith 1992; Libecap 1989). Thus, the ownership of the body of water was retained by the people or the state, and individuals' rights to use water could be acquired by one or more legal doctrines.

In the absence of simple rules for enclosure and possession of water resources as part of land ownership, the task of exclusion was daunting. The scale and mobility of surface water, and the scale and relative invisibility of groundwater supplies, raise the transaction costs of excluding individuals from access and use. In all but a few instances (some discussed within), establishing definitions of who is allowed or forbidden to use a water supply and how much they may use and, above all, monitoring a surface water system or an aquifer in order to detect and prevent unauthorized uses have been judged to be uneconomical.

The combination of these cultural, legal, and economic-scale effects has produced a commons situation in potable water supplies in the southwestern United States. The story of twentieth-century institutional development regarding water in the Southwest has largely to do with overcoming difficulties of exclusion and addressing interactions among user effects.

Overuse and the Threats to Water Supply and Quality

The development, distribution, and protection of water resources are among the most important and defining political and public policy issues in the U.S. Southwest. In the region's largest state, California, available water supply is projected to fall short of demand by 2 to 5 million acre-feet by the year 2020

(California Department of Water Resources 1993). In Colorado, many of the rapidly growing cities in the Denver metropolitan region are searching for adequate supplies of water to meet future water demands.

Spatial and Temporal Influences on the Water Supply-Demand Balance

Spatial, temporal, and socioeconomic factors contribute to the imbalance between the demand for and supply of water. Water supplies are sometimes located far from areas of greatest water demand, a set of conditions fostered in part by the legal rules allowing appropriation of water from its source. In California, 75 percent of available water supply occurs in the northern part of the state, while about 75 percent of water demand occurs in the south. Much of Colorado's population and valuable agricultural land are located east of the Rocky Mountains. For instance, over 80 percent of Colorado's population resides in metropolitan areas located primarily on the eastern slopes of the Rockies (U.S. Census Bureau 1999). However, much of the state's water originates on the western slopes of the Rockies, including several major western rivers such as the Colorado, the Rio Grande, the Arkansas, and the South Platte.

Equally important, water demands for agricultural and for urban domestic and industrial purposes are temporally out of phase with the availability of water supplies. In the Southwest as elsewhere in North America, water supplies are most plentiful during the cooler winter and spring months, but peak demands for irrigation, cooling, recreation, drinking water, hydroelectric power, and waste disposal occur in the summer.

Socioeconomic Factors Pressuring the Water Commons

While spatial and temporal factors confound attempts to match demand and supply, water demands continue to skyrocket because of population growth and the recognition and legitimation of environmental values. The Southwest region is experiencing the greatest rates of population growth in the United States. Arizona, California, Colorado, Nevada, and Utah all rank among the ten fastest growing states (U.S. Census Bureau, 1999). In Colorado alone, the population of the Denver metropolitan region grew by 23 percent during the 1990s. Growth rates of counties south and east of the city of Denver exceeded 7 percent in 1998 (Denver Regional Council of Governments 1999).

Water demands have intensified in particular locations within the Southwest, compounding the stress on potable water supplies in those places. Urbanization has concentrated demands for water for human uses while diminishing both the quantity and quality of water returning to surface and underground sources. Higher-intensity agricultural and industrial practices have also increased the concentration of water demands and the contamination of water supplies.

The largest and most established urban areas of the Southwest have hosted industries for nearly a century, many of which combined economic prosperity with approaches to waste disposal that may be described politely as less than stringent. Nearly every major metropolitan area in the region has water supplies affected or threatened by underground contaminant plumes. Military installations, once drawn to the Southwest by large expanses of federally owned land, now are receding in number and economic importance but leaving behind startling amounts of contamination of soil and water resources. Water supplies once thought to be potable in situ now must be subjected to extensive (and expensive) treatment or abandoned altogether.

The rising demand for water for human consumptive uses in the Southwest now confronts a growing recognition and valuation of other water uses. Public preferences over the array of water resource values, and the configuration of organized interest groups concerned with water resource policy, have shifted substantially during the past four decades (Nunn and Ingram 1984).

An increasingly legitimate use of water is to protect and sustain environmental and recreational values. Surface water in all its manifestations—wetlands and estuaries as well as streams and lakes—is now recognized as important not merely for consumptive uses but also as aquatic and riparian habitat. For example, the 1993–94 update to the California Water Plan included, for the first time since the plan's initial appearance in 1957, an estimate of environmental water needs in addition to urban and agricultural needs (California Department of Water Resources 1993). Alleviating ecological losses in the San Francisco Bay/Sacramento–San Joaquin Delta alone will require that hundreds of thousands of acre-feet of water per year be made available on a reliable basis to that area (Natural Heritage Institute 1997).

The replacement of the agrarian society with the affluent society in the western United States has brought greater appreciation of the recreational and aesthetic values of surface water supplies. In the "new West," wild and scenic rivers are valued per se for their aesthetic properties, and both natural and human-made streams and lakes are valued for their ability to refresh the spirit as well as the flesh (Bates et al. 1993). Any new proposal for impounding a surface stream in the West in the 1990s was as likely to meet opposition from weekend whitewater warriors as from irrigators or miners.

Depletion Effects in the Southwestern Water Commons

The combined effects of these pressures on water supplies and threats to water quality are becoming plainly evident in the U.S. Southwest. In California, not only does the state water plan project significant shortfalls in meeting near-term future consumptive and environmental demands, but the groundwater supplies of the state have already been overdrafted by more than 2 million acre-feet. Groundwater overdraft—the persistent withdrawal of groundwater at rates that exceed replacement—throughout the Southwest has led to some-times gradual, sometimes dramatic occurrences of land subsidence through dewatering of the underground soils.

Most surface water streams in urbanized portions of the region are drying up or have been converted to little more than channels for the conveyance of treated wastewater. The region's largest (indeed, defining) river, the Colorado, is in years of normal precipitation exhausted to little more than a trickle of flowing salts and sediments by the time it reaches the Mexican border. Overall, absent the ability to exclude new uses and limit demand, water supplies in the Southwest are showing the subtractability effects of overuse and degradation long associated with the commons.

Responding to Commons Problems, Part One: Working the Supply Side

Through most of the twentieth century in the American Southwest, demands for increased water storage and distribution capacity were met by building vast surface water storage and conveyance systems. But the prospects for meeting additional water demands via additional construction have dimmed.

Even if environmental considerations did not preclude construction of new facilities at a particular site, other considerations would work against such a project. Urbanization and agricultural development have raised land prices, so acquisition of land for dams, reservoirs, aqueducts, and pipelines is far more expensive now. The financial situation of the federal government from the late 1970s through the early 1990s, and of state governments through the 1980s, diminished for a long time federal and state officials' ability and willingness to fund new facilities on the scale needed to meet new demands in the old ways (Nunn and Ingram 1984; Reisner 1994; Shupe et al. 1989).

Southwestern communities and states find themselves in a bind. They face rapidly increasing demands for water without the traditional means of devel-oping water supplies to meet those demands. Alternative approaches that have been considered or implemented include increased water conservation, increased reuse of treated water supplies, and (at least for California) desalina-tion of ocean water. Conservation has progressed significantly in the Southwest, but the other alternatives have not been embraced on a large scale because of political and economic considerations: Desalting remains more expensive than most other options (Speigler and El-Sayed 1994), and some efforts to expand water reuse have been stymied by public reluctance or reg-ulatory constraints (National Academy of Sciences 1998).

Conjunctive Water Management: The Promise

A number of communities have turned to the conjunctive use of surface and underground water resources, also known as conjunctive management, as a means of increasing water supply reliability without building large surface storage and distribution systems (Burges and Marnoon 1975; Gleason 1976; Lampe 1987; Mann 1968; Thorson 1978; U.S. ACIR 1990). Conjunctive management involves the coordination of surface water supplies and storage capacity with groundwater supplies and underground water storage capacity in ways that use the strengths of each commons to help overcome the weaknesses of the other (see box 6.1).

The purposes of conjunctive management are to maximize water availability, protect water quality, and sustain ecological needs and aesthetic and recreational values. Among the other potential benefits promoted by advocates of greater conjunctive use are reduced exposure to and effects of drought, faster recovery of surface and underground supplies after drought occurrences, reduced reliance on costly and environmentally disruptive sur-

---

Box 6.1 Conjunctive Water Management: Definition, Purposes, and Methods

Conjunctive management is the deliberate coordinated use of surface water supplies and facilities (streams, lakes or reservoirs, dams, and pipelines) with groundwater supplies and the aquifers that store and transmit them to maximize the reliability and economical use of both resources and take advantage of the interactions between them.

Purposes that can be served by conjunctive management include
- Meeting peak water demands with a minimum of facilities
- Reducing vulnerability to drought
- Supplementing surface water flows with pumped groundwater
- Reducing overdraft in groundwater basins by returning water to storage

Methods of accomplishing conjunctive management include
- Using surface facilities such as dams to capture surplus flows for controlled release and percolation into underground soils
- Storing water supplies underground so surface facilities can be emptied for flood control
- Drawing groundwater supplies down to maintain or augment surface stream flows
- Encouraging water users to substitute surface or groundwater supplies according to their relative scarcity

face water impoundments and distribution systems to meet peak water demands, and enhanced protection of aquatic life and habitat (Todd and Priestaf 1997).

In general, conjunctive water management is intended to achieve these purposes by using groundwater basins as a regulatory storage medium helping to smooth out the variations in water demands and surface water supplies. Surface water storage and underground water storage are treated as components of a single system (that is, operated conjunctively), and water needs are met by shifting mixes of surface and groundwater supplies determined by their relative availability.

Surface and groundwater resources may be complementary, and if found in proximity to one another create the potential for an effective conjunctive management program. Streambeds can be used as naturally occurring distribution systems, delivering surplus surface water to a basin for recharge or delivering water recovered from a recharge site to water users. Furthermore, stream and lakebeds can be used as recharge areas, where surface water percolates to underground storage. Conversely, groundwater basins allow relatively long-term storage of surplus water and in some locations support the flow of surface streams.

Recognition of this complementarity has drawn greater attention to the economic value of groundwater basins as reservoirs for water storage. Underground water storage has become a financially, as well as environmentally, attractive alternative to new dams and reservoirs. The value of a groundwater basin can even be measured in terms of the avoided cost of an equivalent quantity of surface storage capacity (e.g., Blomquist 1992), and those avoided costs are greatest with respect to storage capacity to meet occasional peak or emergency demands. In a 1995 review of options for implementing the provisions of the Central Valley Project Improvement Act, the U.S. Bureau of Reclamation identified increased conjunctive management as the least-cost alternative. Estimates of the cost of water yielded through conjunctive-use operations were in the range of $60 to $120 per acre-foot, compared with a range of $300 to nearly $3,000 per acre-foot from the construction of additional surface storage facilities. A similar finding resulted from a study done around the same time for a large urban water district, the San Francisco Bay Area's East Bay Municipal Utility District (Fisher et al. 1995).

Conjunctive Water Management: The Challenge

Numerous physical impediments may preclude conjunctive management. A groundwater basin may be relatively small with very little storage capacity or be covered by a layer of clay soils that makes recharge difficult, or it may be so closely connected to a surface water source that it does not retain water well enough. Besides ill-structured groundwater basins, conjunctive management may be impossible because "no water supply is available, water that is available cannot be transported or conveyed to the area for storage, water in storage cannot be transported to the point of prospective sale" (Hauge 1992: 25–27).

There are numerous sites in the West that *are* well suited to conjunctive management, but it is important to make the point that demands, surface supplies, underground capacity, and a desirable amount of surface-ground interaction are not automatically found together. The physical logistics of moving surface water supplies to groundwater basins, storing them until needed, and retrieving and delivering them when and where needed can be a significant impediment to the implementation of a conjunctive management program, even when the successful effort would yield substantial benefits.

In addition to physical impediments, conflicts among multiple uses made of streams and rivers and groundwater basins may limit conjunctive use. Conjunctive management does not occur in settings in which no previous use has been made of the underground and surface water systems. Instead, it is a new set of uses layered on top of existing uses. Existing users may attempt to thwart conjunctive-use programs that violate or substantially infringe on such uses. For instance, groundwater basins were first and foremost valued for their ability to produce water, and not for their storage potential. Well owners intent on protecting the productivity of their wells do not welcome the wide swings in water table levels that occur when basins are drawn down during drought years to supplement surface supplies and replenished during wet years with surplus surface flows (Guy and Cordua 1998).

Conflicts also emerge between groundwater users and surface water users in settings where groundwater basins and surface water sources are hydrologically connected. Well pumping lowers a basin's water table, which can in turn draw water down from an overlying surface stream. The surface water users find that their water source is reduced or dried up (see illustration B in figure 6.1). Conversely, maintaining underground water tables to support stream flows precludes full use of the storage capabilities of an aquifer. Thus, conjunctive management may conflict with existing uses made of ground water and surface water sources.

By far, however, the major obstacles to conjunctive management are the property rights and administrative systems states have devised to allocate and manage water resources. In some states, distinct property rights systems were developed and adopted for surface water and groundwater. In California, separate organizational arrangements even developed for establishing use rights to waters from each source, with surface water rights acquired by permits issued by the State Water Resources Control Board and groundwater rights usually determined though adjudication in the courts (Blomquist 1992). The presence of separate systems defining and governing water rights contributed substan-

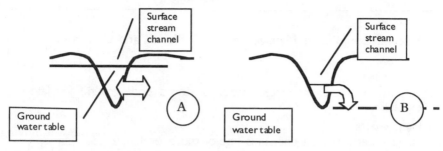

Figure 6.1. Groundwater–surface water interactions.

tially to uncertainty among water users about the security of their rights in a conjunctive-use operation that combines water sources and in a number of instances has made water users unwilling to implement conjunctive management even where physical circumstances were favorable.

In other instances, such as Colorado, well-defined property rights and systems for administering those rights were initially developed for surface waters. Later attempts to incorporate groundwater into a system best fitted for surface water have proved difficult and fraught with conflict. Conflict between groundwater pumpers and surface water appropriators in Colorado created an approach to conjunctive management unlike that found in other western states. There, conjunctive management is not used for the long-term underground storage of surplus surface water. Instead, conjunctive management is used to maintain surface stream flows and protect the property rights of senior surface water appropriators.

Responding to Commons Problems, Part Two:
Establishing and Limiting Rights of Access and Use

Problems of supply-demand imbalance and resulting depletion and degradation can be addressed partially by trying to enhance supplies. Much of the arid Southwest sustained its rapid and remarkable development through the twentieth century by employing these supply development strategies. But the supply-side approach circumvents only temporarily the subtractability and nonexclusion factors that contribute to the commons problems attending potable water supplies there. Most of the remainder of our discussion focuses on the institutional development efforts that have been designed to address those factors in California and Colorado, both with respect to controlling water use and to allowing or promoting conjunctive management. (See box 6.2)

Box 6.2 Conjunctive Management in California and Colorado

CALIFORNIA

TYPICAL PROJECT
Surplus surface or imported water is stored underground for later extraction

PARTICIPANTS
Large water project agency, plus one or more local water districts

SCALE
Typically large (10,000 acre-feet or more per year)

COLORADO

TYPICAL PROJECT
Groundwater pumping or storage rights in upstream reservoirs are used to guarantee stream flow for downstream appropriators

PARTICIPANTS
Water users associations, developers, municipalities

SCALE
Typically small (500 acre-feet or less per year)

The Water Rights System in Colorado

In Colorado, native surface water is allocated according to the prior-appropriation doctrine. Prior appropriation allocates water on the basis of first in time, first in right. The person making the first appropriation of water from a stream holds rights to a portion of the water senior to all subsequent appropriators. The next person in time to appropriate water from that same stream holds rights to a portion of the water senior to all subsequent appropriators but not to the first appropriator. Under such an allocation rule, if water is scarce, appropriators do not equally share in reductions; instead, the rights of senior appropriators are satisfied and junior appropriators are foreclosed. The justification for this is that in times of shortage, if all were to share equally in reductions no one would receive sufficient water to serve his or her purposes. Instead, it is better that at least some be served (Vranesh 1987: 71). Rights can be transferred, and point of diversion and type of use can change, as long as junior appropriators are not injured.

Administration of Water Rights in Colorado

While the prior-appropriation doctrine is recognized and practiced in all western states, only in Colorado is the doctrine primarily defined, challenged, revised, administered, and monitored at the local level by water users within the context of water courts. In all other western states, a state administrator or state agency defines, administers, and enforces water rights according to the prior-appropriation doctrine.

In Colorado, when an appropriator chooses to seek a decree, he or she files an application with the water clerk in the water court within whose jurisdiction the appropriation occurs (Vranesh 1987: 442). The application is turned over to a water referee. Referees investigate the claims made in the applications and protests. Often, referees conduct unstructured hearings to discuss the issues with the applicants and any objectors. If the issue is relatively simple and free of conflict the referees ask the applicants to draft the appropriate decree (Vranesh 1987: 444).

The findings of fact or law of the referee do not bind the water judge. Thus, if a referee's ruling is appealed, de novo hearings are held before the water judge. Such hearings are more formal than those before the referee; however, the rules of civil procedure are not guiding. Applicants bear the burden of proof demonstrating the absence of injury to other water appropriators. The courts generally allow the parties to the case an opportunity to propose terms and conditions that would prevent injury, and the judges themselves may suggest such terms and conditions (Vranesh 1987: 446–47). The Colorado Supreme Court has exclusive appellate jurisdiction over water cases, and appeals are allowed only with respect to matters that were protested in the water court proceeding.

Once a decree is entered, it must be administered, monitored, and enforced. Appropriators along with water commissioners administer and monitor water rights. Appropriators monitor one another's water diversions; however, they rely on water commissioners to engage in the day-to-day activities of measuring and recording water diversions to ensure that appropriators take only the amounts of water to which they are rightfully entitled and to shut down junior appropriators in the proper order until senior appropriators' water rights are satisfied (Vranesh 1987: 468). An appropriator will turn to a water commissioner if the appropriator believes that his or her water rights are being violated. It is up to the water commission to investigate and settle such issues.

A single water commissioner serves each water district in Colorado, of which there are eighty. Water commissioners are employees of the State Engineer's Office. Division engineers, of which there are seven—one for each major watershed—coordinate the activities of all water commissioners within a single watershed. The state and division engineers play the roles of coordinator and information gatherer and disseminator. The division engineers maintain and update lists of appropriation rights and priorities in each division. They determine the accuracy of statements made in water applications and protests. They measure water flows, determine who is in priority, and order junior appropriators shut down. They inspect and monitor diversion works, reservoirs, and dams, ensuring safety and accurate measurement of diversions (Vranesh 1987: 509). The state and division engineers provide the information and technical resources to appropriators, courts, and the state legislature, allowing these actors to define, revise, administer, monitor, and enforce water rights.

Conjunctive Management in Colorado

The South Platte River is hydrologically connected to a groundwater aquifer that is estimated to contain approximately 8 million acre-feet of water (MacDonnell 1988: 585). Most of that water is inaccessible, not because of technological hurdles but because of the prior-appropriation doctrine.

The prior-appropriation doctrine is not well suited for governing groundwater. Drawing upon groundwater necessarily lowers the water table. As noted earlier, lowering the groundwater table in an area of groundwater–surface water interaction reduces surface water flows, which can injure senior holders of surface water rights. Actively using the groundwater basin by drawing heavily on it during times of drought and refilling it during times of abundance can completely deny holders of surface water rights their constitutionally protected rights in surface water flows. The trade-off is clear. Protecting holders of surface water rights forecloses access to much of the water in the aquifer. Actively using the aquifer decimates the rights of surface water appropriators.

Colorado suffered a sustained drought in the 1950s. Farmers drilled wells and pumped groundwater to irrigate their crops. For instance, in 1940, in the Arkansas River basin in the southeastern portion of the state, an estimated forty irrigation wells were in operation. By 1972, 1,477 wells pumped 208,000 acre-feet of water (McDonnell 1988: 582). Noticeable effects on surface water flows appeared in the 1960s. Colorado courts had long recognized that tributary groundwater—groundwater hydrologically connected to a stream or river—was governed by the prior-appropriation system. Thus, the answer to the problem of pumping tributary groundwater seemed obvious. Since most rights in tributary groundwater were junior to most surface water rights, wells should be shut down.

The concept of the futile call made it difficult to shut down well pumping. A futile call occurs when a senior appropriator's rights would not be satisfied even if appropriations junior to it were shut down (Vranesh 1987). In such a case, junior appropriators are allowed to continue to divert water. Shutting down wells to satisfy senior surface water calls is often futile because of a time lag between groundwater pumping and surface water flows. In most cases, shutting down wells will not have an appreciable effect on surface water flows for weeks or months.

In 1965, the Colorado legislature granted the state engineer rule-making authority and directed the engineer to use such authority to resolve the increasingly intense conflict between groundwater pumpers and holders of surface water rights (Radosevich et al. 1976: 138). In the summer of 1966, the engineer exercised his new authority and ordered thirty-nine wells that were junior to surface water appropriations in the Arkansas River Valley shut down (Radosevich et al. 1976: 139). This action triggered three decades of conflict. After several attempted rule makings, numerous lawsuits filed by well owners against the state engineer, threats by senior surface water appropriators to abandon the prior appropriation doctrine if junior well pumpers were not regulated, the passage of the 1969 Colorado Water Rights and Determination Act, and a U.S. Supreme Court case between Kansas and Colorado, agreement was reached on rules for incorporating tributary groundwater into the prior-appropriation system in the South Platte River Valley and eventually in the Arkansas River Valley (Radosevich et al. 1976: 148–149). These rules were hammered out among surface water and groundwater appropriators and the State Engineer's Office, in the context of the water courts that served appropriators in the two river basins. Conjunctive management played a central role in the rules (Radosevich et al. 1976; Vranesh 1987).

The rules adopted for the South Platte River basin are conceptually quite simple. First, the rules defined a timetable for phasing out all well pumping. Second, wells covered by a court-decreed plan of augmentation or a temporary plan of augmentation could continue to operate.

Augmentation plans were created in the Water Rights Determination Act of 1969. Augmentation is Colorado's version of conjunctive management. Junior appropriators, whether of surface water or of tributary groundwater, can protect their diversions from being shut down by senior appropriators by augmenting stream flow. A plan of augmentation for a well, or series of wells, involves determining the out-of-priority depletions to stream flows, or injury to the river, caused by well pumping, and identifying a source of water that will be made available to the river at the time and place of injury to senior appropriators.

Augmentation can take a variety of forms. In the South Platte River Valley, well owners purchase surface water rights and make the water from those rights available to senior surface water appropriators when it is needed. In other words, the water is placed in the river at the time and place senior appropriators require it. Well owners also directly recharge surplus surface water into the groundwater basin. Because the basin is hydrologically connected to the river, the recharged water migrates back to the river, supplementing river flows. For instance, the Fort Morgan Irrigation Company, located in the northeastern part of the state, uses its irrigation canal, several stretches of a dry creek bed adjoining the canal, and numerous ponds located adjacent to or at the end of the canal as recharge areas. During the nonirrigation season (October–March) when water in the river is generally plentiful, the Fort Morgan Irrigation Company diverts water from the South Platte River and runs it in its canal, the creek bed, and the ponds. The water seeps underground, slowly flows back to the river, and enhances the stream flow of the river primarily during the summer peak demand. Members' wells can continue to operate, even though they are drawing out-of-priority water, because of the replacement water to the South Platte River provided by the augmentation structures.

In the Arkansas River basin, augmentation is performed for the same purposes as in the South Platte watershed but is executed in an entirely different manner. These differences are driven partly by physical and partly by institutional circumstances. Well owners in the Arkansas River Valley managed to avoid the incorporation of their wells into the prior-appropriation system until the 1990s. In the mid-1980s, the state of Kansas filed suit against Colorado, claiming that Colorado did not maintain adequate Arkansas River flows across the stateline into Kansas, in violation of the Arkansas River Compact. The special master, appointed by the U.S. Supreme Court, sided with Kansas. Among other things, Colorado was directed to regulate well pumping in the Arkansas River basin in accordance with the prior-appropriation system. The state of Colorado acted quickly to bring Arkansas River Valley wells within the prior-appropriation system so as to minimize the penalties the state will owe Kansas. Similar to what transpired in the South Platte River basin two decades before, the state and division engineers, the state attorney general, and the water appropriators, within the context of the water court, devised a set of rules to regulate well pumping.

All well owners in the Arkansas River Valley belong to well-owner associations. Each year, the well associations provide a list of wells by river reach; the amount of water each well expects to pump; and the actual water, by river reach, that the well-owner association will make available to the division engineer to cover out-of-priority depletions to the river. The Engineer's Office collects monthly data on well pumping, stream depletions, and stream replacements. Each month the engineer, the well-owner associations, and a representative of the State of Kansas review the accounts to ensure that the out-of-priority stream depletions have been covered.

The replacement plans developed by the well-owner associations are in-lieu recharge programs. Instead of directly recharging water into the aquifer, as do their counterparts in the South Platte basin, they purchase or lease rights to surface water. The surface water is released to the stream over the course of the irrigation season so as to replace the water taken out of priority by well pumping. Sources of replacement water are surface storage and distribution projects developed by the Southeastern Colorado Water Conservancy District, the Cities of Pueblo and Colorado Springs, and the Bureau of Reclamation.

Well-owner associations along the Arkansas River have chosen to develop in-lieu recharge programs because of the circumstances in which they find themselves. First, the tributary aquifer of the Arkansas River is narrower than that of the South Platte, and water tables are higher. There is very little room to recharge into the aquifer. Second, the Arkansas River is overappropriated. Only rarely would a very junior augmentation decree be in priority so that water could be drawn from the river and placed in recharge ponds. Third, cities located upstream of the well owners have developed surface storage systems whose volume currently exceeds their water needs. Cities have, and probably will have for the next fifty years, surplus surface water to lease.

Augmentation plans and replacement plans have softened the harshest edges of the prior-appropriation doctrine. The prior-appropriation doctrine, based on first in time, first in right, protects the earliest appropriations, forcing the burden of scarcity on to later appropriations. Augmentation plans allow junior appropriators to confront scarcity, not by shutting down their appropriations but by developing and using additional sources of water to satisfy the water rights of senior appropriators. These plans have been particularly crucial in allowing for the greater use of groundwater resources than would have otherwise been the case if the prior-appropriation doctrine had been strictly enforced.

In Colorado, conjunctive management has been used as a mechanism for incorporating tributary groundwater into the prior-appropriation system. While conjunctive management has reduced conflict among well owners and surface water appropriators, sources of tension remain.

Some augmentation and replacement plans, while allowing for extensive use of groundwater, are fragile. They are fragile because they have not been fully incorporated within the prior-appropriation doctrine, leaving those who rely on them vulnerable, especially during times of water shortage. For instance, some replacement plans in the Arkansas River basin and some temporary plans of augmentation in the South Platte River basin are based exclusively on leased surplus surface water. During drought, surplus water may not be available, requiring the cessation of many wells and the agriculture dependent on them.

Trying to coordinate across two interconnected but differently structured resources—groundwater and surface water—continues to generate conflict in Colorado. Forcing tributary groundwater into the prior-appropriation system forecloses access to substantial amounts of groundwater. To gain access to that groundwater would require substantial modifications to the prior-appropriation system. Appropriators, the Colorado Supreme Court, the Colorado legislature, and the state engineer have wrestled with this issue for more than three decades, achieving fragile solutions that allow existing pumpers to continue to access groundwater. Once a sustained drought occurs, however, such fragile agreements are likely to crumble as senior rights holders fight to protect their rights and as junior rights holders fight to gain access to large but largely untapped sources of water, the tributary aquifers of the South Platte and Arkansas River basins.

The Surface Water Rights System in California

In California, as in Colorado, the doctrine of prior appropriation is followed with respect to surface water supplies and their uses. Surface water users apply to the State Water Resources Control Board to receive permits to divert and use specific quantities of water per year. Applicants must show a beneficial use for the water and show that their diversion and use will not interfere with the rights of senior appropriators or transgress regulatory protections of species, habitat, or other public values.

Four notable exceptions or limitations in California's implementation of the prior-appropriation system have had major implications for conjunctive management. First and most important, three of the largest surface water systems in California—the Sacramento, San Joaquin, and Colorado Rivers—have been allocated differently because their flows are controlled by large-scale water projects, and the operators of those projects deliver water to contractors in their service areas. The California Department of Water Resources operates the State Water Project, which transmits water from the Sacramento River watershed to contractors in the central and southern portions of the state via the California Aqueduct. The U.S. Bureau of Reclamation operates the federal Central Valley Project, which supplies water along the San Joaquin River to contractors in the central portion of the state. The Metropolitan Water District of Southern California (a local special-purpose water district, but one with an enormous territory and population) operates the Colorado River Aqueduct, which supplies water to member agencies in Southern California.

The water supplied by those systems comprises much, indeed probably most, of the surplus water stored in conjunctive-use projects in California. The contractual basis of water allocation from these major projects has important implications for conjunctive management in California. Each system operator—the state, the U.S. Bureau of Reclamation, and Metropolitan—has an incentive to sell surplus water in wet years, to maintain revenues but also to move water through the system to free up capacity in case the next season is wet, too. The contractual relationships with local entities also mean that each system operator has an incentive to try to find ways of making good on water delivery commitments during dry years. These incentives have encouraged each system operator to explore possibilities for storing surplus water for recapture during shortages, resulting in several instances in additional contracts for underground water storage in areas with available capacity.

The second and third limitations on the appropriative-rights system in California are the public trust doctrine and the common law of public nuisance. Both have been employed against the appropriation by the Los Angeles Department of Water and Power (LADWP) of water from the Owens Valley and from streams feeding Mono Lake. The public trust doctrine potentially limits appropriations that threaten harm to publicly held values, and in the Mono Lake case the doctrine was applied in a lawsuit to find LADWP liable for negative effects on Mono Lake resulting from diversion of the streams that fed it. The common law doctrine of public nuisance was employed in a lawsuit over the Owens Valley, charging that LADWP's appropriation of water has caused a variety of harms to the local residents, including adverse health effects resulting from a significant increase in blowing dirt and silt from the dried-up Owens lakebed. Since LADWP used water conveyed from Owens Valley and Mono Lake to supply its conjunctive management program in the San Fernando Valley, reduced appropriations resulting from the settlement of these lawsuits have had substantial ramifications for that program.

The fourth notable exception to the appropriative-rights system is the often-litigated but rarely recognized doctrine of pueblo water rights. Settlements established as pueblos during Spanish colonization of California were granted under Spanish law a right to use as much water as needed for the residents of the pueblo. The validity of this right was carried over into Mexican law after independence from Spain and was subsequently recognized by treaty as a valid property claim when California passed to the United States. A pueblo water right (thus far recognized only for the cities of Los Angeles, San Diego, and San Francisco as successors to their respective pueblos or presidios) is superior to all appropriative-rights claims and may even be recognized as dedicating the complete flow of a stream (for example, the Los Angeles River) to the pueblo successor. Los Angeles's pueblo right was an important element in the development of the LADWP's use of the groundwater basin underlying the San Fernando Valley for storage and recovery of groundwater that was part of the Los Angeles River system.

The Groundwater Rights System in California

Rights to the use of underground water supplies in California are recognized and allocated by a multifaceted (and sometimes overlapping) set of rules that can euphemistically be called complex. We begin with the legal distinction between underground water that is regarded as surface water and underground water that is regarded as groundwater.

Underground water *may* be a hydrologically continuous portion of the flow of a stream, and California law recognizes this connection. In the Southwest, a stream may seem to disappear into the earth, showing just a dry bed for hundreds of feet or even for several miles, then reappearing at the surface farther along. In between, the stream still exists and moves underground. In California water rights law, underground water moving in a recognizable "channel" and flowing along a definite path is treated as if it were surface water. It is under the prior-appropriation system, falling within the jurisdiction of the State Water Resources Control Board (or it may be treated as part of the "pueblo right" of a pueblo successor since the underground water is part of the stream to which the successor has complete rights).

Otherwise, underground water is regarded as "percolating water," that is, groundwater per se. The rules regarding allocation of groundwater are quite different, not least in the fact that they are not within the jurisdiction of any state agency but instead present something like a body of common law, made and enforced primarily in the courts. That applies even to the threshold question of whether an individual is pumping groundwater per se, or "underground surface water." To determine which system of rights governs one's pumping, it is necessary to establish what kind of groundwater one is pumping, and this often occurs in a court.

For groundwater, all of the following possibilities for acquiring and defending rights of use apply in California:

1. Overlying landowners enjoy nonquantified rights to pump groundwater for beneficial use on their overlying land. Shortages arising from the commons problem this system encourages are allocated according to the doctrine of correlative rights, which means that overlying owners are entitled to a proportion of the aquifer's sustainable yield that corresponds to their proportions of the overlying land.
2. If overlying owners' uses do not exhaust the aquifer's sustainable yield, there remains some amount of surplus groundwater left for capture. Individuals may appropriate this surplus groundwater by pumping it and delivering it to nonoverlying lands or to lands they do not own (municipalities that supply water to their residents are typical appropriators in this regard). Such an appropriator may apply to the State Water Resources Control Board for a permit to extract a specific quantity of groundwater, although such a permit will always be contingent on the factual question of whether groundwater remains available in surplus. Decreases in the surplus result in elimination of appropriators in reverse order of seniority, and ultimately of all appropriators, to ensure supplies for overlying owners.
3. Overlying owners and senior appropriators cannot sleep on their rights,

however, because an appropriation of nonsurplus groundwater exercised notoriously and continuously without objection during a period of shortage may ripen into a superior prescriptive right.

4. Individuals or organizations that import water into a watershed for use on the land also have a right to pump and use the return flows of their imports.

5. Pumping rights may also be (and in several cases have been) acquired by adjudication. These quantified rights may derive from a stipulation among the parties or from a determination by the court based on any combination of the preceding doctrines.

It is especially important to note for purposes of contemplating conjunctive management that all of these are methods of determining rights only to the yield or "flow" of a groundwater basin. There is *no* system in California water law for determining rights to the storage capacity of a groundwater basin.

In California, the normal case (that is, not in adjudicated basins) is that water in underground storage is treated as a common resource available to all overlying landowners, with no specific user rights assigned. Water in surface water storage is treated differently.

Having different systems for surface and groundwater rights in California, not to mention having complicated systems for each, has not provided incentives for creation of conjunctive management programs. Conjunctive use requires that surface and underground water supplies be treated—at least in fact if not in law—as more or less interchangeable. California law not only treats groundwater and surface water differently but treats some underground water as if it were surface water and other underground water as if it were not.

Administration of Water Rights in California

California water and water rights are developed, allocated, administered, monitored, and enforced by a combination of state and local entities. The State Water Resources Control Board (which includes a system of Regional Water Quality Control Boards) and the California Department of Water Resources are the two prominent state agencies concerned with the allocation and management of water *supplies.*

All other water supply management organizations in California are local. California contains an immense number of water districts and other local water supply agencies. There are general-act water districts, special-act water districts, some municipal water utilities, and private water companies. Some water districts and municipal utilities have authority to manage groundwater extractions, but most do not, and none of the private companies do. Very few local agencies have had authority to manage groundwater in storage.

The institutional structure of groundwater management in California therefore also has not contributed to the development of conjunctive management programs. In 1992, in an effort to promote groundwater management within the state while retaining the tradition of local control, the California legislature enacted Assembly Bill (AB) 3030. Under AB 3030, the authority to engage in a wide variety of groundwater management activities is conferred on any type of local water district, as long as it undertakes an extensive process of consultation and planning with all other water agencies and general-purpose governments overlying a basin.

AB 3030 is understood to have opened a door to the development of conjunctive management programs almost anywhere in the state, as long as one or more local water districts takes the lead in initiating and completing the consensus-building and plan-development processes created by the law. On the other hand, AB 3030 was enacted only eight years ago, and most locations in which the process has begun are still in the plan-development stages.

Conjunctive Management in California

Because of the composition of water management organizations in California, almost any large-scale conjunctive management project will involve multiple entities. At least one major water project operator (the California Department of Water Resources, the U.S. Bureau of Reclamation, the Metropolitan Water District of Southern California, or the Los Angeles Department of Water and Power) will be involved in supplying the large quantities of surplus surface water when it is available. One or more contractors that receive deliveries from such a project (for instance, State Water Project contractors, Central Valley Project contractors, MWD member agencies) will be involved, since only they have legal rights to receive the water. One or more (usually many more) of the "retail-level" local water suppliers or users will be involved, since they must adjust their operations to employ surface water or groundwater supplies as well as cooperate in any financial arrangements involved with those adjustments. And where applicable, a local agency responsible for management of the groundwater basin itself will be involved.

This multiorganizational approach has provided some benefits in California, operating like an industry with wholesalers, retailers, and multiple incentives to develop the "best deal" for one's constituents or customers (U.S. ACIR 1990). On the other hand, there is no gainsaying that it imposes substantial transaction costs on the development and implementation of conjunctive water management in the state.

Conjunctive management projects in California tend to be in high-demand urban areas underlain by large groundwater basins. These conditions appear to be associated with benefits from conjunctive management that are large enough to exceed the costs of assembling and maintaining the interorganizational coordination needed to accomplish conjunctive management in California. The institutional arrangements governing water resource management in California have probably discouraged smaller-scale projects in areas of lesser water demand, but they have allowed conjunctive management to occur where the stakes have been high enough for organizational participants to sustain the endeavor.

California's institutional arrangements provide protection of multiple interests, and virtually ensure that no conjunctive water management programs will be implemented unless each of those multiple interests has been accommodated. The benefits of such an approach can be substantial and include noteworthy long-term stability for conjunctive water management programs that are implemented. Some of the conjunctive-use operations we have studied are now sixty or more years old and continuing to operate in much the same fashion as when they were initiated. The stability of these programs has in many instances helped to keep their operating costs low and economic efficiency high.

Those institutional arrangements also, however, contribute to a project-by-project, deal-by-deal approach to the development and implementation of conjunctive-use programs. The number of parties involved tends to be larger than would be the case in a state with a more centralized water policy and management structure, and almost every party to a potential deal wields a veto. Accordingly, the transaction costs associated with the development and initial implementation of conjunctive-use programs are very high in California.

The opportunity costs imposed by these arrangements may also be substantial. The institutional barriers contribute to the underutilization of many hydrogeologically well-suited basins, overreliance on surface storage facilities, and avoidable overdrafting of groundwater supplies in several areas. Finally, the project-by-project approach tends to produce conjunctive-use programs that are highly basin-specific, with few or no cross-locality arrangements. As a consequence, California may never realize the more optimistic forecasts of the potential of conjunctive management to narrow the state's overall water budget deficit, since those estimates assumed considerable ability to extract and transfer stored water across locations.

Still, with dry-year yield of the state's major surface water projects diminishing and water demands continuing to rise, the pressure is on at the U.S. Bureau of Reclamation, the California Department of Water Resources, and the Metropolitan Water District of Southern California to develop groundwater storage arrangements in the Central Valley and Southern California. Each agency understands that conjunctive management is vital to meeting dry-year water needs without additional harmful impacts to the environment. And their local-level colleagues have recently formed an Association of Ground Water

Agencies (AGWA) that has shown an active interest in promoting development of conjunctive use throughout the state.

Conclusions

Users of the water commons in California and Colorado have enjoyed some important advantages as they have attempted to address the problems of depletion and degradation associated with subtractability of use and difficulty of exclusion. One important advantage inheres in the nature of water itself, compared with biological common-pool resources. Water may be "fugitive," but its movements and variations are far more easily observed, measured, and predicted than is the case with many biological resources. Furthermore, water can be stored indefinitely, which creates the very possibility of arranging to use surpluses in one period as a hedge against shortages in the future. A resource that is storable and easily and accurately measurable is certainly more readily amenable to management efforts than one for which those characteristics are diminished or absent.

Other crucial advantages have accompanied the high level of economic development that occurred in the region during the twentieth century. The prosperity of the most highly developed urban and agricultural areas within the region—a prosperity built in no small measure on the depletion of water resources, by the way—provided the financial wherewithal to support efforts to improve water resource utilization and overcome difficulty of exclusion. The water resources of the region have been studied extensively and intensively and repeatedly, at an accumulated cost that now undoubtedly runs to the billions of dollars. Such data are widely available, and for the most part easily shared, providing an information base on which new institutional arrangements can be built and against which resulting changes in water conditions can be measured.

The economic development of the Southwest has been paralleled also in the development of social, economic, political, and legal institutions that constitute social capital to be drawn upon for the resolution of conflicts and the construction of joint enterprises. Although the descriptions of Colorado and California provided above may leave the impression of something like "institutional overkill" or at least an embarrassment of riches in this regard, the presence of relatively reliable and well-established institutions such as state constitutions and statutes, state and local government agencies and courts and the bodies of regulatory and judicial law they produce, water-users' associations, and an array of consulting firms and individuals who accumulate experiences with the resolution of local problems and carry that experience to other localities represents a valuable (albeit sometimes conflictual) set of capacities. Defining and limiting rights of access and use, and coordinating the management of surface and underground resources, are far from easy but are surely easier with such capacities than without them.

On the other side of the same coin, the disadvantages encountered by water users as they have tried to ameliorate problems in the water commons of the U.S. Southwest have had to do primarily with the pace of development and the complexity of the institutional setting. Although economic development provided the financial base to support certain kinds of actions to try to resolve the region's commons dilemmas, there is no gainsaying that the development of irrigated agriculture, mining, and other industries, combined with the enormous influx of residents and their concentration in a relatively small number of immense metropolitan areas, also served to create the water problems of this arid region in the first place and exacerbate them later.

While the availability of institutional mechanisms and forums with which to address and resolve disputes has been essential to achieving any kind of control over water resource access and use in the Southwest, there are signs that the accumulated complexity of those institutions is itself becoming a burden on the ability to develop cooperative and innovative solutions to shared water problems. Federal, state, and local rules and organizations on the public-sector side are intensely articulated with land-use development and water-use decisions driven largely by private-sector concerns. An accumulated body of constitutional, statutory, regulatory, and judge-made law is nearing the point where the rules governing water and related resources can provide a means for almost anyone to block almost anyone else's actions (see, e.g., Blomquist 1998). And as efforts to resolve the problems of the southwestern water commons aggregate from the stream or groundwater basin up to the watershed and river-basin scales, the number of water organizations involved expands geometrically, not arithmetically.

If it ever was possible to cast the water commons of the Southwest in the metaphorical terms of a few farmers grazing on the same town commons, that time passed quite a while ago. The challenges of allocating and protecting water supplies and water quality are now bound up with every complex aspect of the present and future of one of the most dynamic regions within the Americas.

References

Association of Ground Water Agencies. 1998. "Conjunctive Use Issues." Unpublished paper prepared by AGWA.

Bates, S., D. Getches, L. MacDonnell, and C. Wilkinson. 1993. *Searching Out the Headwaters: Change and Rediscovery in Western Water Policy.* Washington, DC: Island Press.

Blomquist, W. 1992. *Dividing the Waters: Governing Groundwater in Southern California.* San Francisco: ICS Press.

————. 1998. *Water Security and Future Development in the San Juan Basin: The Role of the San Juan Basin Authority.* Fountain Valley, CA: National Water Research Institute.

Burges, S. J., and R. Marnoon. 1975. *A Systematic Examination of Issues in Conjunctive Use of Ground and Surface Waters.* Water Resources Information System Technical Bulletin no. 7. Olympia: State of Washington Department of Ecology.

California Department of Water Resources. 1993. *The California Water Plan Update.* Bulletin no. 160-93. Sacramento: California Department of Water Resources.

Denver Regional Council of Governments. 1999. "Regional Data Bank." Available at www.drcog.org/

Fisher, A., D. Fullerton, N. Hatch, and P. Reinelt. 1995. "Alternatives for Managing Drought: A Comparative Cost Analysis." *Journal of Environmental Economics and Management* 29 (3) (November):304–20.

Gleason, V. E. 1976. "Water Projects Go Underground." *Ecology Law Quarterly* 5 (4): 625–68.

Guy, David J., and Jennifer Cordua. 1998. "Conjunctive Use from the Ground Up: The Need to Protect Landowners' Rights to Groundwater." In *Ground Water and Future Supply,* 139–47. Proceedings of the Twenty-first Biennial Conference on Ground Water, Report no. 95. Davis: University of California Water Resources Center.

Hauge, C. J. 1992. "The Importance of Ground Water in California." In *Changing Practices in Ground Water Management—The Pros and Cons of Regulation,* 15–30. Proceedings of the Eighteenth Biennial Conference on Ground Water, Report no. 77. Riverside: University of California Water Resources Center.

Johnson, N. K., and C. T. DuMars. 1989. "A Survey of the Evolution of Western Water Law in Response to Changing Economic and Public Interest Demands." *Natural Resources Journal* 29 (2) (Spring):347–87.

Lampe, L. K. 1987. "Recharge Saves Water for a Not-So-Rainy Day." *American City and County* 102 (6) (June):40–46.

Libecap, G. 1989. *Contracting for Property Rights.* Cambridge, England: Cambridge University Press.

MacDonnell, L. 1988. "Colorado's Law of 'Underground Water': A Look at the South Platte Basin and Beyond." *University of Colorado Law Review* 59 (3):579–625.

Mann, D. E. 1963. *The Politics of Water in Arizona.* Tucson: University of Arizona Press.

Mann, J. F., Jr. 1968. "Concepts in Ground Water Management." *American Water Works Association Journal* 60 (12) (December):1336–44.

Metropolitan Water District of Southern California. 1995. *Integrated Water Resources Plan.* Executive Summary. Los Angeles: Metropolitan Water District of Southern California.

Muir, Frederick, and Kevin Roderick. 1990. "L.A. Agrees to Shut Owens Valley Pumps." *Los Angeles Times,* April 4, B-1.

National Academy of Sciences, Committee to Evaluate the Viability of Augmenting Potable Water Supplies with Reclaimed Water. 1998. *Issues in Potable Reuse: The Viability of Augmenting Drinking Water Supplies with Reclaimed Water.* Washington, DC: National Academy Press.

Natural Heritage Institute. 1997. *Feasibility Study of a Maximal Groundwater Banking Program for California.* Working draft.

Nunn, S. C., and H. M. Ingram. 1984. *America's Water: Current Trends and Emerging Issues.* Washington, DC: The Conservation Foundation.

Radosevich, G. E., K. C. Nobe, D. Allardice, and C. Kirkwood. 1976. *Evolution and Administration of Colorado Water Law: 1876–1976.* Fort Collins, CO: Water Resources Publications.

Reisner, M. 1994. "Deconstruction in the Arid West: Close of the Age of Dams." *West-Northwest* 1 (1) (Spring):1–11.

Schlager, E., W. Blomquist, and S. Y. Tang. 1994. "Mobile Flows, Storage, and Self-Organizing Institutions for Governing Common Pool Resources." *Land Economics* 70 (3) (August):294–317.

Shuit, Douglas P. 1999. "Water Conservation Efforts Begin to Pay Off in Southland." *Los Angeles Times,* June 15, A-1+.

Shupe, S. J., G. D. Weatherford, and E. Checchio. 1989. "Western Water Rights: The Era of Reallocation." *Natural Resources Journal* 29 (2) (Spring):413–34.

Smith, D. 1992. *Rocky Mountain West: Colorado, Wyoming and Montana 1859–1915.* Albuquerque: University of New Mexico Press.

Speigler, K. S., and Y. M. El-Sayed. 1994. *A Desalination Primer.* Philadelphia: Balaban Publishers.

Tarlock, A. D., J. N. Corbridge, Jr., and D. H. Getches 1993. *Water Resource Management: A Casebook in Law and Public Policy.* 4th ed. Westbury, NY: The Foundation Press.

Thorson, N. W. 1978. "Storing Water Underground: What's the Aqui-fer?" *Nebraska Law Review* 57 (3):581–632.

Todd, D. K., and I. Priestaf. 1997. "Role of Conjunctive Use in Groundwater Management." In *Conjunctive Use of Water Resources: Aquifer Storage and Recovery,* 139–45. Herndon, VA: American Water Resources Association.

Trelease, F. J. 1965. "Policies for Water Law: Property Rights, Economic Forces, and Public Regulation." *Natural Resources Journal* 5 (1) (May):1–48.

U.S. Advisory Commission on Intergovernmental Relations. 1990. *Coordinating Water Resources in the Federal System: The Groundwater–Surface Water Connection.* Washington, DC: U.S. Advisory Commission on Intergovernmental Relations.

U.S. Census Bureau. 1999. *Statistical Abstract of the U.S.* Available at www.census.gov.

Vranesh, George. 1987. *Colorado Water Law.* 3 vols. Boulder, CO: Natural Resources Law Center.

Chapter 7

Recreational and Commercial Fisheries

DAVID POLICANSKY

Fishing, an old human activity, involves typical common-pool resources. Its attendant management problems have been well studied (e.g., NRC 1999a, b; Begossi chapter 5, this volume; McCay chapter 8, this volume). The commons resource is the fish; if an individual subtracts one fish, one less fish is available to others. However, because fish reproduce and grow, the resources are renewable, which sometimes leads people to conclude mistakenly that they are inexhaustible (NRC 1999a). As commons resources, fish are somewhat different from many other commons resources because they move around and they are hard or impossible to count accurately. As a result, property rights to fish, especially marine fish, are usually poorly defined. Indeed, wildlife and fish cannot be owned in their natural state until they have been caught because of public trust doctrine (Bader 1998). Because property rights to fish are ill defined, establishing management regimes has been complicated (e.g., Gordon 1954; Hannesson 1997); because fish move around in an opaque medium and thus are hard to count accurately, monitoring their populations and developing biologically sound management regimes have been even more difficult. These obstacles have led to a problematic combination of incentives and disincentives, including a reluctance to share information at times, that have affected the organization and efficiency of fishing and fishery management (OECD 1997; NRC 1999a, b).

In general, fisheries (that is, systems of fish and fishing activities, including associated institutions) began with the resources—the fish and access to the water that contains them—treated as public goods with no limits. As fishing activity increased and the availability of the resources diminished, limits in the form of resource depletion and management regulations increased as well. But only relatively recently has the theory of property rights been applied to fisheries (Gordon 1954; Graham 1935; Hannesson 1997) and consideration been given to the difficulties of assigning property rights to a mobile, temporally and spatially variable resource whose precise amount is extremely difficult to assess. Here I briefly consider the general problems of fisheries as common-pool resources with poorly defined property rights and discuss some general solutions to those problems (Begossi and McCay discuss some specific aspects of the matter and detail some specific solutions in chapters 5 and 8, respectively). Then I discuss recreational fisheries, which are usually excluded from such considerations and which differ in several important and some subtle ways from commercial fisheries but are good examples of common-pool resources. My focus is on North America.

Attributes of the Resource

Industrial-scale ocean fisheries have typically been characterized by poorly defined property rights and open access, although some local fisheries do have well-developed territorial controls (for example, surf clams in nearshore waters of the U.S. East Coast and an inshore codfish fishery in Newfoundland [McCay chapter 8, this volume] and a marine gastropod in Chile [Castilla and Fernandez 1998]). Inland (freshwater) fisheries more often have well-defined property rights. Open access, although common, is not nearly as universal as it was until recently in ocean fisheries, largely because property rights are better defined. For example, rivers usually have well-defined and recognized ownership of their banks. Although some U.S. states, such as Montana, provide for public access at or below the high-water mark, private ownership effectively excludes public access in many places. Ocean fisheries vary from extremely local ones, such as sea-horse fisheries in some Pacific Islands (Russ and Alcala 1994) and artisanal fisheries in Brazil (Begossi chapter 5, this volume), to ones that cover large areas of the global oceans, such as fisheries for large pelagic species like tunas. The latter can be complicated to manage, especially when several countries' Exclusive Economic Zones (EEZs) are involved (e.g., Schurman 1998). Many fisheries, including some of the most economically significant ones, occur over millions of square kilometers of ocean.

The greatest portions of marine fisheries are in coastal areas, and thus most are within the EEZs of one or two nations. Access to coastal fisheries and those in adjacent international waters has been contentious at times. Access to a nation's EEZ is often limited to its own fishers and some from other countries by treaty, and foreign commercial fishing is not currently permitted in the United States' EEZ (NRC 1999a). Thus, the establishment of EEZs by most fishing nations has reduced contention over international access in some cases, but it has not reduced disputes about allocation among groups of fishers within a single country. The exclusion of foreign fishers from the U.S. EEZ represents a limitation of access, although by itself it has not reduced fishing effort (NRC 1999a).

Except for very large lakes, most freshwater fisheries are local because the geography of freshwaters usually results in populations that are fairly isolated from each other (see Begossi chapter 5, this volume, for a discussion of the relevance of this to managing commons resources in Brazil). Of course, many commercially important species of North American and European freshwater and anadromous fishes depend on artificial enhancement (stocking), which makes them very different from most marine fisheries, although they still are commons resources. Also, freshwater fisheries in the United States are primarily recreational (again with the exception of the Great Lakes) or include a complex mix of recreational and commercial activities, while commercial fisheries dominate the landings of most marine species.

Excluding everyone from a particular marine fishery is possible, although it is difficult to avoid all poaching, but excluding only some people while allowing others to fish can be more problematic (NRC 1999b). In most commercial fisheries, the problem is manageable, especially in single-species fisheries (NRC 1999b), but in public recreational fisheries, there are few examples of the exclusion of some people but not others from access to what is widely perceived as a public resource, and cases where exclusion is selective in any way are even rarer.

It is important to distinguish between licensing and selective exclusion of some but not all potential participants from a recreational fishery. A license requirement is applied equally to all participants (in the United States, most or all states charge more for nonresident than for resident licenses, but none that I am aware of prohibits nonresident recreational fishing). Indeed, it is difficult to establish a legal basis for selectively excluding even all nonresidents of a particular state, although higher charges for nonresident than for resident licenses appear to have a sound legal basis (Bader 1998). Selective exclusion would allow members of a preselected group to fish, as do individual transferable quotes (ITQs) in marine commercial fisheries, but nonmembers would not be allowed to fish. Private landowners, of course, can selectively restrict access.

The scale of the fishery in space and its technological sophistication have a large effect on the array of management options, as do the abundance and distribution of the fish resource and its predictability in space and time; the local culture and traditions; and the attitudes and resources of local, regional, and national governments. Begossi and McCay (chapter 5 and 8, respectively, this volume) both discuss some of these kinds of variations in detail. The proximity and economic status of other industries, such as tourism, extractive industries, commercial and residential developments, recreational fishing, other kinds of commercial fishing, fish farming, and so on, also influence the availability of options for management and their likely outcomes. For example, Begossi (chapter 5, this volume) describes how the economic power of tourism and recreational fishing adversely affected the management of artisanal fishing in the Araguaia River in Brazil.

Approaches to Solutions: Commercial Fishing

The simplest way that fishery resources have been protected from overexploitation has been through limitation of the total catch allowed. This is the basis for the management of many commercial and recreational fisheries. However, simply limiting the total catch, while it may well protect the resource, often results in social disruption and economic waste. The often described case of Pacific halibut (Buck 1995; Pennoyer 1997; NRC 1999a, b) is an excellent example. Although the resource was protected by catch limits for many decades, competition among fishers to catch their share of the total allowable catch resulted in a large excess of fishing capacity and a derby-type fishing season that lasted only one or two days per year. If the weather was bad on one of those days, the risk of getting no share of the fish often outweighed the risk of fishing accidents (NPFMC 1991). Some of the fishing accidents were fatal.

In general, protecting common-pool resources from overexploitation in an economically and socially rational way requires finding a way to limit access to the fishery (that is, to exclude many or even most potential users) and creating incentives for users to invest in the fishery instead of overexploiting it (Ostrom et al. 1999). An increasingly widely used, although controversial, method of creating incentives for users to invest in a fishery is the establishment of individual fishing quotas (see NRC 1999b for an extensive discussion). These management regimes provide individuals (or firms) specified shares of a total allowable catch of a fishery. The idea is that these individuals no longer need to compete for shares of the catch and hence are not rewarded by overcapitalization (NRC 1999a). Often the individual quotas are transferable according to established rules, and hence they often are referred to as individual transferable quotas (ITQs).

The individual quota programs for Alaska halibut and sablefish have improved the availability and quality of fresh fish, eliminated or reduced the race for fish (derby fishing), eliminated or reduced the tendency of fishers to operate in dangerous weather, reduced the number of participants in the fisheries (as intended), and increased profits for those who hold quota shares (Smith 1997; NRC 1999b). However, the ITQ is not a panacea and is not without problems. For example, concerns remain about ITQs' tendency to reduce the number of participants in fisheries (that is, through loss of jobs), the fairness or unfairness of initial allocations of shares, the degree to which shares represent ownership of the fish before they are caught, concentration of shares in the hands of a few individuals or firms, and the appropriateness of giving away a public resource (McCay 1995; NRC 1999a, b). Many of these difficulties are not yet resolved (NRC 1999b), and even some of the legal aspects of ownership of and access to fishery resources continue to evolve (Bader 1998).

Another approach to quota-based fishery management is the community development quota (CDQ) program, established by the U.S. North Pacific Regional Fishery Management Council to address economic and social problems in isolated communities. The program allocates a portion of the total allowable catch of various commercial species to rural coastal communities in Alaska. Like ITQs, CDQs restrict access to a commons resource, but unlike ITQs, only a portion of the catch is allocated by the program. The CDQ program's strengths and weaknesses were recently reviewed in detail by the National Research Council (NRC 1999c).

Not all problems related to commercial fishing are commons problems, of course. The National Research Council (NRC 1999a) recently reviewed fishery management problems and possible solutions, but here I want to describe an interesting experiment to determine whether eliminating issues related to property rights (and hence commons problems) would result in better fishery management. Moxnes (1998) asked eighty-three subjects to manage a simulated virgin fish stock. The subjects were drawn from fishery-related activities in Norway, including commercial fishermen, researchers, and advisers. Each subject was granted exclusive property rights to the stock, thus eliminating the commons problem. Despite their having perfect property rights, subjects consistently overinvested in capital to exploit the fishery to an average of 60 percent. Moxnes concluded that the most likely explanation of this behavior was misperception of biological and economic feedback, which results from the stock nature of the resource (that is, the time lag between fishing and effects on recruits). This time lag makes it more difficult to assess the effects of fishing on the fish population and on fishers' profits or losses. Moxnes concluded further that this problem needs to be considered in fishery management along with (not instead of) the commons problem.

Approaches to Solutions: Recreational Fishing

In many respects, recreational fishing is like commercial fishing. Larkin (1972) described recreational fishers as commercial fishers who are independently wealthy. Distinguishing recreational from commercial fisheries is often complicated because many activities that involve recreation also involve important market transactions involving the provision of guides, boats, and fishing opportunities. Indeed, chartering and guiding operations appear to be growing in popularity and economic significance. In addition, some recreational anglers and charter-boat captains sell some or most of their catches.

However, especially recently, many recreational fishers release their catches alive, and in those cases, resource management differs significantly from commercial fishery management. In addition, many species of recreational importance, especially inland species, are maintained by extensive stocking programs. The fish themselves often do not have all the attributes of common-pool resources, such as genetic and species diversity. Thus protecting the resource from overexploitation often has additional complications. These issues can be present in commercial fisheries, especially when artificial enhancement is important. Extensive private hatchery operations can be supported by an association of commercial fishermen (such as the Prince William Sound Aquaculture Corporation), who then have a shared interest in the hatchery fish. But the hatchery fish mix with wild fish, a different commons resource, and management and planning are quite complicated, with many agencies and interest groups and some continuing conflicts (Kron 1995).

Yet even in cases where overexploitation of fish populations is not an issue, recreational angling presents common-pool resource problems: As in the situation described by Burger (chapter 9, this volume) involving personal watercraft (PWC), the limited common-pool resource for anglers is space, or is at least related to space. Although Burger describes many ways that PWCs adversely affect the physical and biological environments, such as by creating waves that cause shoreline erosion or creating noise that, along with the waves, disturbs or disrupts the nesting of birds, PWCs also affect the enjoyment of many environments simply by occupying the same space. The same is true of many uses of the environment, including powerboating, flying, and even such nonmechanized activities as hiking. And this brings us to the space problem in managing recreational fishing: Anglers often interfere with the enjoyment of other anglers.

Interestingly, this common-pool resource problem is seldom considered by recreational fishery managers in the United States. As an example, in a recent survey that asked the heads of freshwater fishery–management agencies to list important management issues, space and angler crowding were not mentioned (Ross and Loomis 1999). Yet crowding is clearly a problem, and it is sometimes recognized as such. Merritt and Criddle (1993) studied the very crowded and sometime contentious chinook salmon fishery on Alaska's Kenai River, and they recorded crowding as a significant problem. On North Carolina's Outer Banks, the beaches are crowded with off-road vehicles in the fall. In some places there are three rows of vehicles for hundreds of yards along the beach. Fishing magazines and electronic bulletin boards, especially those devoted to fly-fishing, have frequent discussions about the overcrowding of popular or publicized waters. If the total intensity of recreational angling (number of anglers multiplied by mean time spent fishing) continues to increase, and if accessible fishing habitat continues to decrease, the crowding problem will escalate.

Two major solutions for commons problems have long been used by private individuals or groups for angling: They band together and form an angling club, then buy the land containing the fishable water. This allows them to limit access and vests them in the property, so they have an interest in protecting (investing in) the resource.

How can a public management agency achieve this? In the United States, limiting access to publicly owned land and persuading people to invest in it are problematic. I briefly review some of the difficulties involved and then discuss in some detail a Canadian approach to the problem. The aim is to provide a basis for thoughtful consideration of methods of addressing angler overcrowding (and the resultant adverse environmental effects), not to recommend adoption of the Canadian or any other particular plan.

Apparently there is no legal basis in the United States for a state to exclude only the residents of other states from access to its fishing waters, although it is permissible to charge nonresidents more for the access (Bader 1998). In addition, license fees are a major source of funding for state fishery programs, averaging 41 percent of the budget in the forty-seven states that responded to a recent survey (Ross and Loomis 1999). Because the states do not have to do more to obtain the higher nonresident angling-license fee than to obtain the resident angling-license fee, there is a financial incentive to encourage nonresident angling. In addition, many short-term economic benefits accrue to states through fishing activities; consequently there are additional reasons not to discourage any—including nonresident—angling.

In the United States, direct limitation of access to public angling waters is very uncommon. Access to some national parks with good angling is reduced by limiting the number of cars that can enter, and some public rivers have limits on the numbers of boats or rafts that can be on the river at any given time. Permits are required for some wilderness areas, and they are limited in number. Limits on entry to public waters for recreational angling, to maintain or improve the quality of the angling itself, is very uncommon. For example, Colorado's 1999 fishing regulations explicitly provide for limiting access of anglers to some waters, but only when there is damage to the riparian environment caused by too many people or in case of dangerous water conditions.

A few exceptions involve streams in the southeastern United States. Some streams in Stone Mountain Park in North Carolina have a "beat" system: Permits are issued on a daily basis until a limit is reached, and thereafter no additional anglers are allowed on the streams for the specified period (North Carolina Department of Parks and Recreation, n.d.). Dukes Creek and its tributaries within the state-owned Smithgall Woods–Dukes Creek Conservation Area in Georgia are open to fishing year-round under a permit system according to Georgia's 1999 fishing regulations. A limited number of permits can be obtained by advanced registration. However, I know of no other plan for limiting entry that is as well developed as British Columbia's Bulkley River Angler Use Plan (BRAUP). That plan is embedded in a broader fishery policy for the whole province (MELP 1996).

The BRAUP was adopted in December 1998 (see MELP 1998, 1999). The basis for the plan was a report from the Fisheries Branch of the British Columbia Ministry of Environment, Lands and Parks (MELP 1996). That report concluded, "Angler crowding on rivers is the greatest concern of anglers and angler groups. It is most common on the premier steelhead rivers because the choice places to fish are limited. Thus, it became necessary to classify waters to maintain a measure of quality angling and to reduce crowding." The basis for the BRAUP is explicitly to reduce angler crowding and enhance the quality of the angling experience. MELP developed the plan based on more than eighteen months of effort and subsequent recommendations by a volunteer stakeholder committee. The BRAUP was slated to be reevaluated periodically, beginning at the end of 1999 (MELP 1998).

The plan recommends that the Bulkley River be managed to meet four objectives: (1) to provide a quality angling experience for all anglers, especially British Columbia residents; (2) to protect opportunities for British Columbia residents to participate in the fishery; (3) to provide for a stable and economically sound guiding industry; and (4) to contribute to the economic diversification of local communities, including Houston, Telkwa, Smithers, Moricetown, and Hazelton, British Columbia, by enhancing tourism and business opportunities.

This remarkably candid and clear statement of objectives distinguishes the BRAUP from many other planning documents. The plan recognizes that meeting some of the four objectives might make meeting others more difficult but does not discuss this problem in detail, and the fourth objective receives less explicit attention than the other three. The plan recommends management of the river such that the total number of rod-days (that is, one angler fishing for one day) is limited to 10,500. Of those rod-days, 1,504 should be guided and 8,996 unguided. The number of guides would be limited to seven, with no restriction on who their clients may be. The plan recommends that 7,056 (68 percent) of the nonguided days be allocated to British Columbia residents, 540 (6 percent) to residents of other parts of Canada, and 1,400 (26 percent) to residents of other countries. The plan further recommends that only Canadians or guided non-Canadians be allowed to fish the Bulkley River on weekends during the peak fishing season (September 1 through October 31). No changes in fishing regulations were planned for the 1999 fishing season. Finally, the plan provides a working definition of a quality angling experience: "an experience whereby the angler has a reasonable expectation of catching a fish during the course of an angling day plus a reasonable opportunity during the course of that day to arrive at a section of water which is not already occupied by another angler" (MELP 1998). That definition provides an objective measure for the success of the plan, even if it is not quantitative.

Despite the thoughtfulness and candor of the plan and its explicit attention to the space problem in recreational fishing, some interesting questions arise about it, and its success (or failure) bears close attention. How is this plan to be achieved? The plan acknowledges that "the best way to ensure compliance with the proposed allocation of rod-days is to implement a limited entry system for all classes of anglers (including both residents and non-residents of British Columbia)." But there is no mechanism currently available to limit entry (Reid White, Skeena Region Fish and Wildlife Manager, pers. comm. 1999). This might not be an immediate problem because the recommended total number of rod-days (10,500) exceeds the average annual number of rod-days over the past thirty years (7,602) by 38 percent and exceeds the 1997 number of rod-days (3,983) by 163 percent. (The highest recorded number of rod-days was 15,919 in 1986.) Nonetheless, it seems that many political and legal issues will have to be addressed before the plan can be the basis for restrictive regulations.

Another question concerns the very high rod limits in the plan described above, higher than those experienced in recent years. With such high limits, it would seem that no regulations will be needed for some time. If this is true, then the problem of angler overcrowding that was the basis for the plan will not be fully solved by the plan because its proposals do not become active until the overcrowding becomes much worse than it currently is. Perhaps this issue reflects a common problem associated with stakeholder groups, namely the difficulty they can have in arriving at difficult solutions. Too often, in trying to provide something for every group, they fail to provide a solution that benefits the greater whole in the long run. This is in itself a manifestation of the commons problem. The plan does call for periodic reevaluation, however, and so the possibility remains that the recommended rod-day limits will be lowered. The more charitable interpretation—that a mechanism for lowering the rod-day limits was built into the plan with the intention of using it—may be even more accurate.

The Dean River in British Columbia is also managed under the broad auspices of British Columbia's angling guide policies. It has an interesting limit on entry. Canadian residents with valid fishing licenses can fish it during the season, and the limited number of guides can fill their rod allocations with whoever pays them to fish. Non-Canadians must apply through a lottery system for access to fish the river, and fewer permits are granted than the number of applicants. Thus the river has a limited-entry system for non-Canadians. This is in accordance with the objective in the Bulkley River plan of "adopting strategies which ensure that BC residents are the last group of anglers to be restricted in the event that restrictions become necessary in order to meet the objective of preserving a quality angling experience on the Bulkley River" (MELP 1998).

Additional questions arise in considering these plans as models for use elsewhere. It is not clear that in the United States it would be politically palatable or legally permissible to exclude nonresidents of a state from fishing, or even limit their activity, although even Canada has not implemented a system that discriminates against nonresidents of a province. A smaller proportion of anglers in the United States come from abroad than in Canada (where many come from the United States), and so restricting non-U.S. citizens from recreational angling in the United States holds less promise for reducing crowding than excluding non-Canadians might in Canada. Finally, it is not clear how willingly the U.S. angling public would accept being excluded from fishing that is supported by their own taxes, and so it is not clear how successful or widespread limited-entry schemes for recreational angling could become. Nonetheless, the space problem in recreational angling is increasingly important, and everything is to be gained by considering it thoughtfully, whatever the regulatory outcome might be.

Conclusions

Commercial fishing represents an archetypal commons-pool resource-management problem. Approaches to resolving the problem that treat it as a commons issue by limiting access and providing incentives for users to invest in the resource hold promise and are becoming more widely used. However, there is more to fishery management than solving the commons problem, and a broad view is needed.

Like commercial fishing, recreational fishing is an important activity, especially in the United States, involving millions of people and billions of dollars. Although it has many features in common with commercial fishing, recent changes in people's economic status, lifestyles, and perceptions of the environment have led to significant changes. Two of the largest changes are the increases in catch-and-release fishing and in crowding (or perception of crowding). Most fishery-management agencies in the United States do not appear to be spending a lot of effort on the crowding problem, which is difficult to solve. However, resource managers in British Columbia have addressed the crowding issue directly over the past decade. Similar consideration by managers in the United States would certainly be instructive and probably productive.

Acknowledgments

I thank R. Norgaard and an anonymous reviewer for many constructive comments, and especially for reminding me how hard it often is to distinguish between commercial and recreational fishing.

References

Bader, H. 1998. "Who Has the Legal Right to Fish? Constitutional and Common Law in Alaska Fisheries Management." Marine Advisory Bulletin no. 49. Fairbanks: University of Alaska Sea Grant College Program.

Begossi, A. 2000. "Cooperative and Territorial Resources: Brazilian Artisanal Fisheries." In *Protecting the Commons: A Framework for Resource Management in the Americas,* edited by J. Burger, E. Ostrom, R. B. Norgaard, D. Policansky, and B. D. Goldstein. Washington, DC: Island Press.

Buck, E. 1995. "Overcapitalization in the U.S. Commercial Fishing Industry." Congressional Research Service Report for Congress, 95-296-ENR. Washington, DC: Congressional Research Service.

Burger, J. 2000. "Multiuse Coastal Commons: Personal Watercraft, Conflicts, and Resolutions." In *Protecting the Commons: A Framework for Resource Management in the Americas,* edited by J. Burger, E. Ostrom, R. B. Norgaard, D. Policansky, and B. D. Goldstein. Washington, DC: Island Press.

Castilla, J. C., and M. Fernandez. 1998. "Small-Scale Benthic Fisheries in Chile: On Co-management and Sustainable Use of Benthic Invertebrates." *Ecological Applications* 8 (1) Supplement: S124–S132.

Gordon, H. S. 1954. "The Economic Theory of Common Property Resources: The Fishery." *Journal of Political Economy* 62:124–42.

Graham, M. 1935. "Modern Theory of Exploiting a Fishery, and Its Application to North Sea Trawling." *Journal du Conseil* 13:264–74.

Hannesson, R. 1997. "The Political Economy of ITQs." In *Global Trends: Fisheries Management,* edited by E. K. Pikitch, D. D. Huppert, and M. P. Sissenwine, 237–45. Bethesda, MD: American Fisheries Society.

Kron, T. 1995. "Prince William Sound Salmon Enhancement Programs and Considerations Relative to Wild Stocks." In *Interactions between Cultured Species and Naturally Occurring Species in the Environment,* edited by M. R. Collie and J. P. McVey, 49–53. Proceedings of the Twenty-second U.S.–Japan Aquaculture Panel Symposium, Homer, Alaska, August 21–22, 1993. Report AK-SG-95-03. Fairbanks: University of Alaska Sea Grant College Program.

Larkin, P. A. 1972. "A Confidential Memorandum on Fishery Science." In *World Fishery Policy: Multidisciplinary Views,* edited by B. Rothschild, 189–97. Seattle: University of Washington Press.

McCay, B. J. 2000 "Community-based and Cooperative Fisheries: Solutions to Fishermen's Problems." In *Protecting the Commons: A Framework for Resource Management in the Americas,* edited by J. Burger, E. Ostrom, R. B. Norgaard, D. Policansky, and B. D. Goldstein, Washington, DC: Island Press.

MELP (British Columbia Ministry of Environment, Lands and Parks). 1996. *Angling Guide Report and Policy Review Implementation: Working towards Improvement.* Victoria: British Columbia Ministry of Environment, Lands and Parks, Fisheries Branch.

———. 1998. *Angling Use Plan Bulkley River: Approval. December 1998.* Smithers, British Columbia: Skeena Region, Ministry of Environment, Lands and Parks. Available at http://www.elp.gov.bc.ca/ske/bulk_aup/bul_aup.html.

———. 1999. *Angling Use Plan Letter to Stakeholders, February 10, 1999.* Smithers, British Columbia: Skeena Region, Ministry of Environment, Lands and Parks. Available at http://www.elp.gov.bc.ca/ske/bulk_aup/rdletter.html.

Merritt, M. F., and K. R. Criddle. 1993. "Evaluation of the Analytic Hierarchy Process for Aiding Management Decisions in Recreational Fisheries: A Case Study of the Chinook Salmon Fishery in the Kenai River, Alaska." In *Proceedings of the International Symposium on Management Strategies for Exploited Fish Populations,* edited by G. Kruse, D. M. Eggers, R. J. Marasco, C. Pautzke, and T. J. Quinn II, 683–703. Report 93-02. Fairbanks: University of Alaska Sea Grant College Program.

Moxnes, E. 1998. "Not Only the Tragedy of the Commons: Misperceptions of Bioeconomics." *Management Science* 44:1234–48.

National Research Council (NRC). 1999a. *Sustaining Marine Fisheries.* Washington, DC: National Academy Press.

———. 1999b. *Sharing the Fish: Toward a National Policy on Individual Fishing Quotas.* Washington, DC: National Academy Press.

———. 1999c. *The Community Development Quota Program in Alaska.* Washington, DC: National Academy Press.

North Carolina Division of Parks & Recreation. *Stone Mountain State Park.* Durham: North Carolina Department of Environment and Natural Resources, Division of Parks and Recreation.

North Pacific Fisheries Management Council (NPFMC). 1991. *Environmental Impact Statement, Regulatory Impact Review, Regulatory Flexibility Analysis for the Proposed Individual Fishing Quota Management Alternatives for the Halibut Fisheries in the Gulf of Alaska and Bering Sea/Aleutian Islands.* Anchorage, AK: North Pacific Fishery Management Council.

Organisation for Economic Co-operation and Development (OECD). 1997. *Towards Sustainable Fisheries: Economic Aspects of the Management of Living Marine Resources.* Paris, France: OECD Publications.

Ostrom, E., J. Burger, C. B. Field, R. Norgaard, and D. Policansky. 1999. "Revisiting the Commons: Local Lessons, Global Challenges." *Science* 284:278–82.

Pennoyer, S. 1997. "Bycatch Management in Alaska Groundfish Fisheries." In *Global Trends in Fisheries Management,* edited by E. Pikitch, D. D. Huppert, and M. Sissenwine, 141–50. American Fisheries Society Symposium 20. Bethesda, MD: American Fisheries Society.

Ross, M. R., and D. K. Loomis. 1999. "State Management of Freshwater Fisheries

Resources: Its Organizational Structure, Funding, and Programmatic Emphases." *Fisheries* 24 (7):8–14.

Russ, G. R., and A. C. Alcala. 1994. "Sumilon Island Reserve: 20 Years of Hopes and Frustrations." *NAGA, the ICLARM Quarterly* 7 (3):8–12.

Schurman, R. A. 1998. "Tuna Dreams: Resource Nationalism and the Pacific Islands Tuna Industry." *Development and Change* 29:107–36.

Smith, S. 1997. "Giving IFQs Their Due." Editorial. *The National Fisherman,* June 7, 1997.

Chapter 8

Community-based and Cooperative Fisheries: Solutions to Fishermen's Problems

BONNIE J. McCAY

The commons dilemma can be called "the fisherman's problem" (McEvoy 1986) because marine fisheries provide persuasive cases for the conventional theory of the tragedy of the commons. Marine fisheries share practical, legal, and cultural obstacles to exclusion, particularly in the Americas, where they are often perceived as highly cherished frontier economies, underscored by concepts such as the public trust (McCay 1998). The harvesters, or in more general terms the appropriators (Schlager and Ostrom 1992), tend to be in competitive relationships with each other (Crutchfield and Pontecorvo 1969); although often fiercely independent, they are also interdependent because they are appropriating from the same common-pool resource or related resources within an ecosystem. They usually experience high levels of both risk and uncertainty (Hilborn 1997), the effects of which permeate the entire system, including family relationships, the structure of crews, attitudes toward safety precautions, strategies of investment and of finding the fish, and the regulatory process (Acheson 1981; Smith 1988).

What, then, can be said about prospects for sustainable development of marine fisheries? Can resource users participate in effective management of fisheries commons or must it be forced on them? How do scale, homogeneity, culture, markets, and their embeddedness within larger systems affect the answers to these questions (McCay and Jentoft 1998)? Do the conditions of open access, competition, and uncertainty overwhelm attempts by resource appropriators, and even their representatives in government, to come to terms with each other and the rather unruly, elusive, and unknowable resources on which they depend?

I address these questions by providing overviews of some of the international and national fisheries institutions of the Americas, followed by examples of self-regulation by fishers or cooperative management between resource users and government agencies in the United States and Canada.

Institutions for International Fisheries Commons

Truly "open-access" fisheries remain in the high seas, beyond national boundaries of extended jurisdiction (since the late 1970s, these are in most cases 200 nautical miles or 370 km from coastal baselines). These include fisheries for highly migratory species such as the tunas (*Thunnus* spp.) and swordfish (*Xiphias gladius*) but also for many other species. The high-seas fisheries provide the worst cases of how open access and regulatory failures can lead to "tragedies of the commons." International environmental management is particularly challenging. There is no central authority; the system is technically one of anarchy, and thus monitoring and enforcement are very problematic, depending as they do on the voluntary participation of member governments, which have no jurisdiction over the activities of vessels belonging to other governments, especially those of nonsignatory countries (Peterson 1993).

Nonetheless, management regimes for many of the high-seas fisheries have developed under the aegis of the United Nations; they are based on regional and international treaties and the work of dedicated individuals, scientific institutions, and governments. Important examples for the Americas are the International Convention on the Conservation of Atlantic Tunas (ICCAT), the Northwest Atlantic Fisheries Organization (NAFO), the International Pacific Halibut Commission, the International Fur Seal Treaty, and the International Whaling Commission. Another significant organization is ICES (International Council for Exploration of the Sea), which was founded in the late nineteenth century. The ICES brings together scientists from governments with interest in the North Atlantic and provides scientific advice for some of the European fisheries.

The design principles elucidated by Ostrom (1990; Ostrom chapter 1, this volume) are as relevant to international fisheries regimes as they are to small-scale ones, as shown by Noonan (1998) in his comparison of reasons for the relative success of the South Pacific Fisheries Agency (FFA) and the relative failure of the European Union (EU) in managing their fisheries commons. Among those reasons is the fact that the FFA has done better than the EU in providing arenas for conflict resolution and incentives for monitoring and enforcement by the member nations (Noonan 1998). Hall's (1998) comparative analysis of six international fisheries regimes, using Ostrom's design principles, showed that in five cases the fishing nations involved have cooperated to create and maintain robust institutions for certain issues, namely access rights and resource allocation, which are politically effective. But this does not necessarily mean conservation effectiveness.

A major challenge concerns "straddling stocks," fish stocks such as walleye pollock (*Theragra chalcogramma*) in the North Pacific and cod (*Gadus morhua*) and other groundfish off Newfoundland, which are found in both national and high-seas domains, such that national sovereignty applies to part of the stock and open access to the other (Burke 1997; Munro 1996). The United Nations has helped reduce the third-order collective-action problem—of incentives to work toward some kind of agreement when "free-riding," or relying on others to do it, may provide benefits available to all—by providing information and infrastructure for deliberation on this as on other problems, but is hamstrung by the traditions of national sovereignty and flag-state enforcement.

Resource appropriators (e.g., owners and workers on fishing vessels, owners of processing and marketing firms) usually work through their national governments, but as in the case of ICCAT, they may participate as part of a team of national representatives to the negotiations. Seeing the uncertainties and costs of relying on international politics to protect their interests, some representatives of coastal communities, small-scale fisheries, cooperatives, and fish workers have developed their own networks and meetings. Notable examples are the International Collective of Fish-Workers, based in India, which publishes an international publication, *Samudra,* and the National Fishworkers' Forum in India, which used its international connections to help it force the government to cancel licenses issued to joint ventures that were fishing indiscriminately in Indian waters (Kurien 1998). The Indian organizations share information and support with similar organizations in places as distant as Chile (the National Confederation of Artisanal Fishworkers of Chile) and Canada (the Maritime Fishermen's Union, based in Nova Scotia).

National Fisheries Institutions

With extended national jurisdiction over fisheries in the late 1970s—a key part of the United Nations Law of the Sea negotiations that led to the 1982 Convention on the Law of the Sea (Sanger 1987)—the governments of coastal nations gained new powers and responsibilities for fisheries management. The South American nations of Chile, Ecuador, and Peru had much earlier claimed "patrimonial" rights to 200 miles of ocean and hence to the tunas and other fishes found off their shores. Canada also had a major stake in expanding its jurisdiction, particularly on its Atlantic coast, which had become the focus of a major international fishery for cod and other groundfish during the 1960s and 1970s, seriously depleting fish stocks of the region (Parsons 1993). The

United States had a more ambivalent position because some of its fishing fleets depended on ready access to fish stocks off the shores of other countries (especially the South American ones mentioned above), while others were experiencing distress from foreign fishing off their shores (especially those of the eastern seaboard) or saw opportunities in the rich foreign fisheries that had developed off their coasts (e.g., the Bering Sea fisheries for pollock off of Alaska).

How have national governments managed their newly enlarged commons? Appraisals for the United States and Canada are not positive despite the wealth and scientific expertise of both nations. This discussion focuses mostly on Canada and the United States. I do not, however, see any reason for optimism for Central and South America, where resources for fisheries science, monitoring, and enforcement are even more limited and where oceanic and climatic phenomena such as El Niño play such a direct and often devastating role (Lagos and Buizer 1992).

Canada

Anticipating and closely following extended jurisdiction, Canada quickly developed a combination of science-based management and limited entry into most marine fisheries. By 1990 there was virtually no open-access fishery of consequence left in Canada, but still its fisheries were in trouble because of errors in the science used (Finlayson 1994), misuses of science in the policy process (Hutchings et al. 1997), and unknown ecological factors (Hutchings 1996). The great cod fisheries of Newfoundland collapsed, leading to a closure of those and other fisheries in 1992, which continues into the early years of the twenty-first century. Some of the salmon stocks of British Columbia are now in serious trouble as well (e.g., Pacific Salmon Commission 1999).

In Canada, decisions about marine fisheries reside in a cabinet-level appointment, the minister of fisheries, who uses a complex system of technical and political advice from the regions but retains singular decision-making authority (Apostle et al. 1998). This appears to enable rapid decision making about controversial measures such as shutting down entire fisheries or imposing individual transferable quotas (an attempt to use quasi-private property in managing the fisheries). Fisher involvement has been limited to a complex "consultative management" scheme in which the Department of Fisheries and Oceans (DFO) retains control over the nature and extent of input that industry can provide (Apostle and Mikalsen 1995). Recognizing that Canada's fisheries continue to be plagued by biological and economic instability (Parsons and Beckett 1997), policy appears to be moving in several directions.

One trend is to remove allocation decisions from the agency by giving them to markets, as in individual transferable quotas (ITQs), or placing them in advisory bodies (a proposal not yet implemented). Another is to find ways to reduce capacity, including the numbers of people and vessels in the fishery, through buy-out and retirement programs, and increase the professionalism of fishers through training and licensing. A third is to delegate more responsibility and authority to user groups. The government has offered the notion of "partnerships" between groups of fishers and the fisheries agency in a new fisheries bill and in the meantime has developed a system whereby groups of fishers must prepare conservation harvesting plans before fishing, a step toward contractual comanagement (see Rieser 1997).

Partnership-based management is controversial, at least in Atlantic Canada, because it allegedly marginalizes coastal communities, as distinct from fish harvesters. Coastal community representatives are striving for community-based management as an alternative to both ITQs and "partnerships." One case of community quotas was a 1995 agreement to allocate part of the total allowable catch (TAC) for a particular area to the fishers of the community of Sambro, Nova Scotia, who could decide themselves how to allocate it rather than have it assigned as ITQs (Apostle et al. 1998). Subsequent grassroots efforts and civil disobedience expanded the principle of community-based management to the "fixed-gear" sector in the Bay of Fundy region (Kearney et al. 1998). The DFO informally agreed to allocate quotas to two "community management boards," based on the collective catch history of the fishers they represent. The boards then develop management plans through a participatory, consensus-based process. The boards have no formal legislative capacity to enforce these plans; instead they use contract law. Fishers who wish to participate sign a contract agreeing to follow the plan and accept designated penalties for violation. If they decline, they may participate in a government-run competitive fishery. The boards are intended to become the basis for fishers' participation in scientific research and an overarching council for the bay as a whole.

The United States

There is much more political resistance to limited entry in the United States than in Canada and most other places where limited entry has been proposed, but by the late 1990s most of the important commercial fisheries required licenses based on prior involvement in the fishery or other criteria. This was partly in response to evidence that other management measures had not protected most fish stocks and an agency analysis that open access was a major cause of the problems (Sissenwine and Rosenberg 1993). It was also the result of protectionist moves of particular industries in response to competition from newcomers and outsiders. However, there is still strong resistance to limited entry into major fisheries, such as shrimp, and expectation within fishing communities that some reopening of entry will occur in currently restricted ones, such as the New England groundfisheries.

In the United States, fisheries management is delegated to the states within 3 nautical miles of the coast; beyond that it is federal government responsibility but has been delegated by Congress to regional management councils. The councils prepare fishery management plans that must be approved and implemented by the federal government (through the federal Department of Commerce, National Marine Fisheries Service). Their delegated powers are limited by national standards and other laws established by Congress. The councils are designed to allow for considerable user-group and public participation in the process; voting members are not only representatives of state and federal fisheries agencies but also people who represent fishing interests, commercial or recreational, as well as academics and environmentalists. They are under repeated attack for being captured by special fishing interests (e.g., World Wildlife Fund 1995) but they are very diverse in structure and function as well as in the problems they face.

New directions in U.S. policy include stronger representation of environmentalists on fishery management councils and in legislative decision making, as well as the—so far incomplete—incorporation into policy and practice of ideas such as biodiversity, the precautionary principle, and reliance on marine reserves. In contrast with Canada and other northern countries, the United States has seen a more cautious approach to individual transferable quotas in management, on the one hand, but on the other far less interest in delegating management roles to local-level groups and communities. Nonetheless, reviews of problems and solutions appear to recognize the values of both market-based management tools and improved user participation and attempts to better match the scale and scope of management regimes and natural systems (NRC 1994, 1996, 1999a, 1999b). Concerted attempts to match scale and scope are being made in the state of Maine. The legislature and fishing constituency of that state have committed themselves to a management system for lobster (*Homarus americanus*) and sea urchins (*Arbacia punctulata*) whereby decisions about controls on effort are devolved to regional democratic committees (Acheson and Steneck 1997).

Management by Resource Users

Policy emphasis on local-level, community-based, and cooperative fisheries management is divided and wavering. Nonetheless, such forms of management are significant. The following section reports on "self-regulating" management regimes I have studied in relation to ideas about the nature of the resource and the size and heterogeneity of the resource users, as well as other variables that affect the success and failure of collective action for sustainable resource use (Ostrom 1990; Ostrom chapter 1, this volume; McKean 1992; Miles 1989; Felt et al. 1997).

According to recent reviews of an extensive literature (Schlager 1994; Acheson and Wilson 1996), small-scale fishers are most likely to regulate access to valued fishing sites (Begossi chapter 5, this volume), open and closed areas and seasons, the technology used, and special areas thought to be essential for fish reproduction. Much rarer, but evident as I shall show, is user group restriction of how much fish or shellfish they catch, which is what most contemporary fisheries science accounts mean by "management."

The Pacific Whiting Cooperative: How Small Size and Homogeneity Can Work

A recent case of self-regulation in marine fisheries involves very large, expensive catcher-processor vessels in the fishery for Pacific whiting (*Merluccius productus*) in the cold waters of the Bering Sea in the North Pacific (NRC 1999a:128–129). It highlights how small size and homogeneity can help realize working agreements for managing a common-pool resource.

In the North Pacific, the annual TAC of whiting is divided among various sectors, including the catcher-processor vessels, which hold 34 percent of the 1997–2001 TAC. In the past, they competed for their quota in the familiar process that creates incentives for overcapitalization as well as wasteful practices such as taking and discarding other species (bycatch) and hurried processing leading to lower than optimal yields of product from harvested fish. In April 1997, the four companies involved agreed to eliminate this "fishing derby" and its side effects by allocating the quota among themselves, forming a cooperative for the purpose. To avoid possible antitrust prosecution, a significant barrier to user-based management agreements in the United States, members submitted their proposal to the Department of Justice, which approved it. This meant that the companies could use fewer vessels; the companies announced that the remaining portion of the 1997 fishery yield from on-board processing had improved by nearly 20 percent, and there were significant reductions in bycatch.

The whiting cooperative continues. It may have had one of the negative effects of any limited entry system: deflecting effort to other fisheries that might already be fully capitalized or overcapitalized. But the companies did succeed in developing a more rational system for their own fishery. Their success seems to have been helped by the small number of actors involved, all of whom knew each other very well and who were fairly homogeneous in terms of investments. It was also increased by the fact that there was little uncertainty about the quota itself, and no other groups were immediately hurt by the decision: The cooperative allocated a known quota that had already been allocated to the at-sea processing vessels. In the spring of 1999 five catcher-processor vessels in the offshore pollock fishery formed a similar cooperative, facilitated by an October 1998 change in the American Fisheries Act (S.1221) establishing protocols for fishing cooperatives (Chambers 1999). Very similar arrangements are found in Canada under the rubric of "enterprise alloca-tions," precursors to ITQs. The difference is that in the Canadian cases, for off-shore groundfish and lobsters, the government, not the companies, made the allocations among the companies involved in the fisheries (Crowley and Palsson 1992). However, it is arguably the same: Only a handful of companies are involved, and they are working with a portion of the overall allowable catch that has been allocated to their sector of a larger fishery. The representa-tives of those companies work very closely with government decision makers such that it is difficult to determine where the rule-making initiative and deci-sion-making power reside, unlike the U.S. Pacific whiting cooperative case, where initiative and decisions originated with the companies.

The Virtues of Staying Put and Local

Self-regulation is particularly apt for sedentary species such as shellfish and for stationary fishing gear such as fish traps. It is far easier to create and maintain boundaries when the resource or the capture technology does not move than when it does, particularly when both are close to land and hence readily mon-itored.

The history of fisheries for bay clams (*Mercenaria mercenaria* and *Mya are-naria*) and oysters (*Crassostrea virginica*), highly sedentary nearshore species, includes many instances of local regulation by the users or by local govern-ments, such as the townships of Cape Cod, Massachusetts, or counties in New Jersey or Maryland. In the United States, even where state governments have claimed exclusive rights to manage fisheries on behalf of the "public trust," management rights and responsibilities are often delegated to the local level, such that the management systems become examples of comanagement (McCay 1998; Pinkerton 1994). Similarly, the successful cases of comanage-ment for sustainable use of small-scale fisheries in Chile involve relatively sedentary animals such as conchs and sea urchins (Castilla and Fernandez 1998). Crabs and lobsters are more mobile but are often found within an area sufficiently well defined that the fishers find it worth their while to defend exclusive territories and, in some cases, impose catch limits (Acheson 1988).

Fishers are also likely to manage sites of *access* to mobile resources to reduce the costly and dangerous effects of conflict and competition and achieve soci-etal norms such as fairness and equality. On Fogo Island, Newfoundland, access to inshore sites for placing large netted-twine cod traps was regulated in locally distinct ways (McCay 1978) until the inshore fishery declined in the late 1980s. Along the rocky shores near the communities of Joe Batt's Arm and Tilting, on the northeastern and eastern sides of the island, no one could set a trap in a "berth" or favored site until a certain day in June, and then only after a gun was fired, allowing all of the crews to leave for the berths they wished to use. If two or more crews converged on the same berth, the local fisheries officer drew straws to determine the proper claimant. On the other side of the island, particularly around the port of Seldom-Come-By, the regulatory system was different: The best trap berths were allocated according to inherited rights, the rest on a first-come-first-served basis. The system of Joe Batt's Arm and Tilting was devised around 1907 as a way of handling conflicts arising from increased demand on the trap berths, due to increased human population and to attempts by fish merchants to expand the use of traps. The situation had also become dangerous and costly: Crews sometimes staked their claims early in the season, when high seas and ice were still likely. The new system addressed this with the opening gunshot.

Other rules in Fogo Island's fishery included restrictions on how close fishing gears could be placed to each other, particularly competing technologies (for example, gillnets and cod traps) and whether baitless fish lures called jiggers could be used on certain more distant fishing grounds. The jigger rule was partly protectionist: Local fishers could more easily get bait for fishing on those grounds, so an anti-jigger rule kept others away. It was also conservationist: The hooks on jiggers strike the fish on any part of the body, ripping them open but not always bringing them to the surface. This rule was particularly important at places and times when very large female cod were expected; these were referred to as "mother fish," that is, fish to be protected for the future.

As Ostrom (chapter 1, this volume) argues, a supportive legal structure is often important to local-level systems of common-pool resource management. The Newfoundland regulations described above were developed locally but written into the law of Newfoundland—as local rules—and enforced by the government's paid fisheries officer (see also Martin 1979; Andersen and Stiles 1973). When Newfoundland became part of Canada in 1949, and the fisheries became subject to federal management, the local rules were no longer legitimized at higher levels, but local observance of most of the rules continued, supported by the federal fishery officers (Matthews and Phyne 1988).

The scope and intent of the regulations described were, of course, inadequate to the task of conserving the fish stocks, which were migratory and covered huge areas, subject to predation by large offshore fishing fleets. Nonetheless, when the Canadian government abandoned the local rules, particularly after the 200-mile limit of 1977 allowed it to take a major role in managing the fish stocks, it also abandoned social and ecological lessons about the local scale (Matthews 1993). Only today, and only in a very halting way, are fisheries scientists in Canada—and the United States—recognizing the importance of highly localized phenomena, such as breeding grounds and overwintering grounds, for the viability of fish stocks otherwise defined at large scale, and of locally derived knowledge about such stocks (Neis 1992).

New Jersey Cooperatives: Managing Heterogeneity and Free-Riding

Local regulation of how many fish are caught and landed is very rare (Schlager 1994), particularly for highly migratory species found over a large area. However, it was evident during the late 1970s and 1980s at two fish-marketing cooperatives in New Jersey (McCay 1980, 1987, 1989). The cooperatives not only regulated members' catches but also found ways to handle heterogeneity. The cooperatives each had eighteen to twenty-two vessel owners as members. Becoming a member was difficult. Making it worthwhile to try were attractions such as the cooperatives' control over a critical scarce resource: waterfront space for offloading and tying up boats. There were other benefits as well, including help in marketing catches and the possibility of annual "patronage refunds" of the profits.

The Point Pleasant cooperative was studied in some detail (McCay 1980). Entry was limited by the amount of dock space available and members' notions of who could be relied on to be "highliners" or very productive fishermen and willing to go along with the informal and formal rules of the cooperative. This in effect imposed limits on entry into the fishery in the region, because of the scarcity of dock space and fish-packing houses.

The fisheries are diverse and wide ranging, but during the winter months most members specialized in fishing for a species known regionally as whiting or silver hake (*Merluccius bilinearis*). Although the cooperative sold to the large fish markets of the Atlantic seaboard, such as Fulton Market in New York City, demand for whiting was limited. Market gluts—when so many fish were offered for sale that the price plummeted—were very common and problematic: The price could vacillate by a factor of ten or more (for example, from 10 cents to $1.50).

The Point Pleasant and Belford fishing cooperatives developed systems of imposing catch limits on members' boats when the market had the potential of being glutted. A sign was posted (e.g., "40 boxes today"). It made sense to do this even though the fresh-fish urban markets were served by fishing fleets around the globe because the winter whiting fishery was virtually theirs alone. At this time, during the cold-weather months the fish were found fairly close to the New Jersey ports, in the warmer waters of a deep submarine canyon emanating from the Hudson River system. The fish were less available to New England fishers, who fished for them in the summer months instead. Accordingly, the New Jersey ports, as well as some in New York, had a near monopoly on the domestic part of this fishery during the winter months (far-offshore foreign fishing boats targeted whiting as well, but rarely for the fresh-fish markets). This helped keep the prices reasonably high, but gluts were still a problem. It was to this problem that self-regulation was directed.

At Point Pleasant, the catch limits were implemented in ways that dealt with the problems of rewarding high performance while punishing those who violated the rules. During the early part of the fishing week, captains who came in over the limit were given credit for the catches by the manager, but later in the week, closer to the critical marketing period of Thursday and Friday, payment for anything they brought in over the limit was redistributed equally among the rest of the members. In these ways the cooperative was able to recognize the heterogeneity of its members while keeping free-riding to a manageable level.

"Free-riding," the *bête-noire* of collective action (Olson 1965), was a far more serious problem at the regional level: Other whiting fishers benefited from the market price effects of the catch limits imposed by the New Jersey coopera-tives. From time to time, in the 1960s and 1970s, leaders of the cooperatives tried to persuade people in the New York ports to adopt a similar system. This did not work, but they were able to organize several regional "tie-ups" to protest low market prices. Even with free-riding the cooperatives persisted, with members aware that their "sacrifices" benefited others but convinced that without the catch limits, the prices would plummet, hurting everyone.

This institutional arrangement was suspended throughout most of the 1990s. Free-riding was rampant and the resource itself declined as many new boats entered the fishery in response to sharp declines in TACs in the tradi-tional groundfish fisheries of New England. Whiting were scarcer on the inshore grounds for which New Jersey boats had such an advantage. Accordingly the limits on entry created by the cooperative's control over scarce dock space were inadequate to the task. It became an open-access fish-ery, and self-regulation no longer made any sense. Members of the coopera-tives had to find other fisheries, such as squid, and redirect their regulatory efforts to the workings of the regional fishery management councils, includ-ing attempts to use limited entry to protect their positions.

The Surf-Clam Fishery: Heterogeneity in a Participatory Setting

One of the constraints to self-regulation of common-pool resources in the United States and other capitalist economies is that it can be interpreted as anticompetitive behavior, coming up against antitrust laws. The cooperatives described above were absolved from this by special congressional acts, includ-ing a federal law protecting registered agricultural cooperatives from antitrust challenges. Participants in another important fishery of the eastern seaboard of the Atlantic Coast, for surf clams (*Spisula solidissima*) and ocean quahogs (*Arctica islandica*), confronted this problem and turned their commons dilemma over to one of the regional management councils, the Mid-Atlantic Fishery Management Council, showing yet another way that the embeddedness of locally devised systems can make a difference.

By the 1960s and early 1970s participants in the relatively new surf-clam fishery recognized that they had created an open-access monster. The surf-clam fishery began in the late 1940s, when a hydraulic method was invented to help dredge up the clams; the clams quickly replaced bay clams in the important clam chowder market and other markets. By the early 1970s more and more vessels, ever larger and more powerful, were entering the unregulated fishery. The clams, immobile and hence easily harvested once located, were quickly depleted. The fleets moved from patch to patch, from Long Island, New York, to Virginia. There were discussions of industry-based regulation of catches or gear, but antitrust issues loomed large. Nothing was done until the regional fishery management council system was created in 1977; the surf-clam fishery was the first to be regulated under the new U.S. system for managing fisheries in waters from 3 to 200 nm offshore; it was also the first to be put under limited entry. The council created a moratorium on new vessels, an overall TAC, and a system limiting how much time each vessel could spend fishing for clams, to spread the fishery out over the year on behalf of the processors.

The industry was ready and eager to use the management system to accomplish goals it could not legally accomplish by itself. The new council system provided the institutional solution to the industry's commons problem of how to get everyone to agree to a set of restrictions that would affect and benefit them all. It is probable that the industry could not have come to agreement anyway, given the large number of participants (more than 180 boats at the peak) and their economic heterogeneity (a few very large vertically integrated firms and many "independents"; some owner-operator vessels but other firms made up of large fleets of vessels; plus of course geographic, personal, and ethnic differences).

The obstacle posed by heterogeneity was very evident in the new system. Between 1978 and 1989, the industry had some comanagement powers vis-à-vis the Mid-Atlantic Fisheries Management Council (MAFMC), which at times asked the industry to come up with its own plans for adjusting the system (see Turgeon 1985). The heterogeneity depicted, and the very real differences in power and interest it suggests, made it extremely difficult to reach consensus on important issues, namely how to correct distortions created by the limited-entry system. As fishing capacity increased and certain year-classes of clams grew enough to be fished, the amount of time each vessel could fish had to be ratcheted back to spread the quota over the year. By 1986 surf clammers could fish only six hours every two or three weeks. From as early as 1980, there seemed to be agreement that some kind of allocation of the quota to individual vessels would be necessary, but agreement on exactly how that would be done was elusive. The size and heterogeneity—the power structure, really—of the industry played a major role in causing an eleven-year delay in the decision to make a major institutional change: ITQs (McCay and Creed 1990). This is a market-based system of management with the potential of changing conditions that led to overcapitalization and dangers at sea (that is, the race to fish against limited time or quotas).

ITQs went into effect in 1990, the first instance of this method of fisheries management in the United States and one of the few in the world. In this case, ITQs rapidly led to fleet downsizing and intensified existing patterns that concentrated ownership and control in relatively few firms (McCay and Creed 1994; NRC 1999a). Nonetheless, the surf-clam management regime remains a commons institution because setting the annual TAC and other conditions of the fishery remain responsibilities of the regional fishery management council, on behalf of the public trust, which remains in the clam resources themselves. The ITQ holders must continue to interact with each other, government regulators, and other members of the public as part of a management community.

Size, Homogeneity, and Comanagement in a Canadian Setting

When we compared the surf-clam management regime with a Canadian ITQ fishery for groundfish (McCay et al. 1995; McCay et al. 1998), several points emerged. One was that size and heterogeneity did matter, but not that much. The Canadian fishery, a small-dragger fishery for cod, haddock (*Melanogrammus aeglefinus*), and pollock (*Pollachius virens*), mostly in Nova Scotia, experienced the dramatic institutional change of ITQs very quickly, within a year after the possibility was announced, even though the size of the affected group was much larger. There were more than 440 licenseholders in the Canadian fishery, compared with fewer than 60 vessel owners (about 120 vessels) in the U.S. surf-clam fishery before ITQs. The Canadian fishers were scattered over a huge area, in dozens of small and large fishing ports. The U.S. fishers in this fishery worked out of only about four ports.

On the other hand, the Canadian fishers were more homogeneous in economic terms: Few were vertically integrated into processing firms, and the goal and spirit of egalitarianism was supported by the rule that the owner had to be a vessel operator. But the main point, for the decision to make the change in property rights, was that the decision in Canada was not made by members of the industry; it was made by the minister of fisheries. The more democratic, participatory process of deciding on ITQs in the United States set up a situation where strong differences within the industry could result in a long delay.

A major policy question is whether ITQs represent changes in property rights; in the United States the government has explicitly denied that they are property rights. Rather, ITQs are privileges. Similar language is used in Canada but not in Iceland, where they are clearly property rights. From an academic perspective, they represent claims of ownership that are similar to private property claims, particularly rights to decide how to use the property and to transfer it to someone else.

A second point was that whereas in the U.S. case the industry played a very strong role in deliberations about the institutional change that led to ITQs, in the Canadian case, also begun in 1990, the industry emerged as a strong player in the next phase of management, deciding on and implementing the actual details of the ITQ-based management system. A comanagement arrangement was created once the major decision was made, and representatives of the industry worked closely with government officials, and those they represented, to design the details of the new system. This resulted in a system (like the ITQ system that went into effect in Alaska more recently, in 1995 [NRC 1999a]) designed to prevent the rapid downsizing and consolidation of property and power that occurred in the surf-clam case. Holders of ITQs had to be vessel operators as well as owners (although exceptions were grandfathered in), there were upper limits on how much ITQ anyone could own, and, at first, there were strict limits on transferability, which was allowed only within the fishing season, not permanently. Another significant feature of the Canadian system is that in exchange for gaining exclusive rights to shares of the overall total allowable catch, the ITQ holders had to pay for, and help design and implement, a system of dockside monitoring. This was another focus for the comanaging group (called the IQ Group) that emerged and continues to meet regularly (Apostle et al. 1998).

Whereas the ITQ system applies to the entire U.S. surf-clam fishery, the Canadian ITQ system is embedded within a larger management regime for the groundfish species. People with other claims of rights and property are vying for the same fish, leading to a highly conflictual situation. The overall TAC is allocated between offshore vessels (belonging to a few vertically integrated companies, under an enterprise allocation system) and a fairly large set of nearshore and inshore vessels, by fisheries area and by species. An important distinction is mobile gear (such as draggers) and fixed gear (such as gill nets and lines). Government efforts to expand the ITQ system (and user fees for monitoring and enforcement) are resisted by the fixed-gear fleet, as mentioned earlier in the discussion of efforts to develop community-based management.

Conclusion

All fisheries regimes, from international to local, must deal with similar problems, namely how to manage access to and use of a common-pool resource without depleting both the resource itself and the coffers of those involved beyond the point of no return. To date, governments have accomplished little for the international, high-seas fisheries, largely because of the persistence of the rule of flag-state sovereignty and right to enforcement, but even there opportunities for change are more evident than before (Burke 1997). Within their own jurisdictions, national governments also experience difficulties using their powers and abilities to support scientific research to make marine fisheries sustainable. In some places, this is because of the persistence of open access as an ideological position or the de facto outcome of difficulties enforcing restrictions. Open access, combined with attempts to conserve fish by setting TACs, sets up conditions for overcapitalization, which in turn creates immense pressures on management organizations to up the ante (Ludwig et al. 1993). In these and other places the problem is also due to the uncertainties of knowledge, scientific and otherwise, and social barriers to effective utilization of the knowledge of people actually working on the water.

Both Canada and the United States are grappling with these and related problems. Among the somewhat disparate directions that policy is taking in both countries is interest in delegating and devolving some management authority to groups of resource users or local communities. Qualifications of local communities and groups of resource users as resource managers are mixed, affected in part by size, heterogeneity, and other variables identified in academic studies. The cases reviewed show realized potentials for user-based resource management within the play of such factors as the nature of the resource, the size and heterogeneity of the resource-using group, and the political economy within which they are embedded.

I close with a commentary on an expanded notion of "community-based management," another way of talking about self-regulation by appropriators and local-level management.

A recent National Research Council report (1999b) focused on "virtual communities," groups of resource users who may or may not be from the same geographic or cultural communities but share past, present, and anticipated future involvement in a particular fishery. The suggestion came initially from the experiences and thinking of people such as Nat Bingham, a former fisher and major coordinator of cooperation among fishers, landowners, and conservationists in protecting salmon, and journalist Brad Matsen, well aware and appreciative of such efforts as well as the interactions among offshore fishers. I wish to build on it by extending it to "epistemic" communities. Epistemic communities are defined by their relationships to information and knowledge, rather than to place, occupation, or kinship. The definition of *epistemic commu-*

nity found in the international environmental policy literature (e.g., Young 1982; Haas 1990) presupposes a much greater degree of agreement on values than is likely or possible in many fishing communities. Nonetheless, people who interact with each other, whether in collaboration or in competition, can have very different "epistemes" but become part of the same community and compete similarly for privileged status as sources of information and advice. This concept would broaden the notion of "virtual community" (NRC 1999b) to include not only the owners, skippers, and crew of fishing vessels but also regulators, enforcers, academic observers, and others who have over the years vested themselves in the issues at hand.

There are intriguing congruences between the epistemic communities of the individuals, institutions, and governments that sometimes form around international regimes and the communities that form around national/regional government-based fisheries management issues. In both the U.S. surf-clam and the Canada small-dragger ITQ cases, epistemic communities evolved over the years. They include scientists, agency officials, paid representatives of the industries, industry members, and even journalists and academic observers. Like the international epistemic communities, the effects of the diversity of backgrounds and interests present are modified by shared focus on tasks at hand, some consensus on values or at least understanding of differences in values and objectives, and a history of interaction. People come to know each other, share information and ideas with each other, predict each other, and trust each other, with or without expectations that they will all come to consensus. This, too, might be considered community-based resource management.

References

Acheson, J. M. 1981. "Anthropology of Fishing." *Annual Review of Anthropology* 10:275–316.

————. 1989. "Where Have All the Exploiters Gone? Co-management of the Maine Lobster Industry." In *Common Property Resources,* edited by Fikret Berkes, 199–217. London: Belhaven Press.

Acheson, J. M., and J. A. Wilson. 1996. "Order out of Chaos: The Case for Parametric Fisheries Management." *American Anthropologist* 98 (3):579–94.

Andersen, R., and G. Stiles. 1973. "Resource Management and Spatial Competition in Newfoundland Fishing: An Exploratory Essay." In *Seafarer and Community: Towards a Social Understanding of Seafaring,* edited by P. H. Fricke, 44–66. London: Croom Helm.

Apostle, R., G. Barrett, P. Holm, S. Jentoft, L. Mazany, B. McCay, and K. Mikalsen. 1998. *Community, Market and State on the North Atlantic Rim: Challenges to Modernity in the Fisheries.* Toronto: University of Toronto Press.

Apostle, R., and K. Mikalsen. 1995. "Lessons from the Abyss: Reflections on Recent Fisheries Crises in Atlantic Canada and North Norway." *Dalhousie Law Journal* 18 (1):96–115.

Begossi, A. 2000. "Cooperative and Territorial Resources: Brazilian Artisanal Fisheries." In *Protecting the Commons: A Framework for Resource Management in the Americas,* edited by J. Burger, E. Ostrom, R. B. Norgaard, D. Polincansky, and B. D. Goldstein. Washington, DC: Island Press.

Burke, W. T. 1997. "Trends in International Law for High-Seas Fisheries Management." In *Global Trends: Fisheries Management,* edited by E. K. Pikitch, D. D. Huppert, and M. P. Sissenwine, 50–60. Bethesda, MD: American Fisheries Society.

Castilla, J. C., and M. Fernandez. 1998. "Small-Scale Benthic Fisheries in Chile: On Co-management and Sustainable Use of Benthic Invertebrates." *Ecological Applications* 8 (1), Supplement:S125–S132.

Chambers, S. 1999. "Whiting Co-op Blazes Trail." *Pacific Fishing* 20 (8) (August):22–25.

Crowley, R. W., and H. Palsson. 1992. "Rights Based Fisheries Management in Canada." *Marine Resource Economics* 7 (2):1–21.

Crutchfield, J. A., and G. Pontecorvo. 1969. *The Pacific Salmon Fisheries: A Study of Irrational Conservation.* Baltimore: Johns Hopkins Press.

Felt, L., B. Neis, and B. McCay. 1997. "Co-management." In *Northwest Atlantic Groundfish: Perspectives on a Fishery Collapse,* edited by J. Boreman, B. S. Nakashima, J. A. Wilson, and R. L. Kendall, 185–94. Bethesda, MD: American Fisheries Society.

Finlayson, A. C. 1994. *Fishing for Truth: A Sociological Analysis of Northern Cod Stock Assessments from 1977–1990.* St. Johns': Memorial University of Newfoundland, Institute of Social and Economic Research.

Haas, P. M. 1990. *Saving the Mediterranean: The Politics of International Environmental Cooperation.* New York: Columbia University Press.

Hall, C. 1998. "Institutional Solutions for Governing the Global Commons: Design Factors and Effectiveness." *Journal of Environmental & Development* 7(2):86–114.

Hilborn, R. 1997. "Uncertainty, Risk, and the Precautionary Principle." In *Global Trends: Fisheries Management,* edited by E. K. Pikitch, D. D. Huppert, and M. P. Sissenwine, 100–106. Bethesda, MD: American Fisheries Society.

Hutchings, J. A. 1996. "Spatial and Temporal Variation in the Density of Northern Cod and a Review of Hypotheses for the Stock's Collapse." *Canadian Journal of Fisheries and Aquatic Sciences* 53:943–62.

Hutchings, J. A., C. Walters, and R. L. Haedrich. 1997. "Is Scientific Inquiry Incompatible with Government Information Control?" *Canadian Journal of Fisheries and Aquatic Sciences* 54:1198–1210.

Kearney, J., A. Bull, M. Recchia, M. Desroches, L. Langille, and G. Cunningham. 1998. "Resistance to Privatisation: Community-based Fisheries Management in an Industrialised Nation." Paper presented at International Workshop on Community-based Natural Resource Management, The World Bank, Washington, D.C., May 10–14.

Kurien, J. 1998. "Traditional Ecological Knowledge and Ecosystem Sustainability: New Meaning to Asian Coastal Proverbs." *Ecological Applications* 8 (1) Supplement:S2–S5.

Lagos, P., and J. Buizer. 1992. "El Niño and Peru: A Nation's Response to Interannual Climate Variability." In *Natural and Technical Disasters: Causes, Effects and Preventive Measures,* edited by S. K. Majumdar, G. S. Forbes, E. W. Miller, and R. F. Schmalz, 223–38. Philadelphia: Philadelpha Academy of Science.

Ludwig, D., R. Hilborn, and C. Walters. 1993. "Uncertainty, Resource Exploitation, and Conservation: Lessons from History." *Science* 260 (2 April):17, 36.

Martin, K. O. 1979. "Play by the Rules or Don't Play at All: Space Division and Resource Allocation in a Rural Newfoundland Fishing Community." In *North Atlantic Maritime Adaptations,* edited by R. Andersen. The Hague: Mouton.

Matthews, D. R. 1993. *Controlling Common Property: Regulating Canada's East Coast Fishery.* Toronto: University of Toronto Press.

Matthews, D. R., and J. Phyne. 1988. "Regulating the Newfoundland Inshore Fishery: Traditional Values versus State Control in the Regulation of a Common Property Resource." *Revue d'études canadiennes* 23 (1–2):158–76.

McCay, B. J. 1978. "Systems Ecology, People Ecology, and the Anthropology of Fishing Communities." *Human Ecology* 6 (4):397–422.

———. 1980. "A Fishermen's Cooperative, Limited: Indigenous Resource Management in a Complex Society." *Anthropological Quarterly* 53:29–38.

———. 1987. "The Culture of the Commoners: Historical Observations on Old and New World Fisheries." In *The Question of the Commons,* edited by B. McCay and J. Acheson, 195–216. Tucson: University of Arizona Press.

———. 1989. "Sea Tenure and the Culture of the Commoners." In *A Sea of Small Boats,* edited by John Cordell, 203–26. Cambridge, MA: Cultural Survival.

———. 1995. "Common and Private Concerns." *Advances in Human Ecology* 4:89–116.

———. 1998. *Oyster Wars and the Public Trust: Property, Law and Ecology in New Jersey History.* Tucson: University of Arizona Press.

McCay, B. J., R. Apostle, and C. Creed. 1998. "ITQs, Comanagement, and Community; Reflections from Nova Scotia." *Fisheries* 23 (4):20–23.

McCay, B. J., R. Apostle, C. Creed, A. Finlayson, and K. Mikalsen. 1995. "Individual Transferable Quotas (ITQs) in Canadian and US Fisheries." *Ocean and Coastal Management* 28 (1–3):85–116.

McCay, B. J., and C. F. Creed. 1990. "Social Structure and Debates on Fisheries Management in the Mid-Atlantic Surf Clam Fishery." *Ocean & Shoreline Management* 13:199–229.

———. 1994. *Social Impacts of ITQs in the Sea Clam Fishery.* Final Report to the New Jersey Sea Grant College Program, New Jersey Marine Sciences Consortium, February 1994.

McCay, B. J., and S. Jentoft. 1998. "Market or Community Failure? Critical Perspectives on Common Property Research." *Human Organization* 57 (1):21–29.

McEvoy, A. 1986. *The Fisherman's Problem: Ecology and Law in the California Fisheries, 1850–1980.* Cambridge, England: Cambridge University Press.

McKean, Margaret A. 1992. "Success on the Commons: A Comparative Examination of Institutions for Common Property Resource Management." *Journal of Theoretical Politics* 4(3):247–81.

Miles, E. L., ed. 1989. *Management of World Fisheries: Implications of Extended Coastal State Jurisdiction.* Seattle: University of Washington Press.

Munro, Gordon R. 1996. "The Management of Transboundary Fishery Resources and Property Rights." In *Taking Ownership: Property Rights and Fishery Management on the Atlantic Coast,* edited by Brian Lee Crowley, 253–86. Halifax, Nova Scotia: Atlantic Institute for Market Studies.

National Research Council. 1994. *Improving the Management of U.S. Marine Fisheries.* Washington, DC: National Academy Press.

———. 1996. *Upstream: Salmon and Society in the Pacific Northwest.* Washington, DC: National Academy Press.

———. 1999a. *Sharing the Fish: Toward a National Policy on Individual Fishing Quotas.* Washington, DC: National Academy Press.

———. 1999b. *Sustaining Marine Fisheries.* Washington, DC: National Academy Press.

Neis, B. 1992. "Fishers' Ecological Knowledge and Stock Assessment in Newfoundland." *Newfoundland Studies* 8 (2):155–78.

Noonan, D. S. 1998. "International Fisheries Management Institutions: Europe and the South Pacific." In *Managing the Commons,* 2nd ed., edited by J. A. Baden and D. S. Noonan, 165–77. Bloomington: Indiana University Press.

Olson, Mancur. 1965. *The Logic of Collective Action.* Cambridge, MA: Harvard University Press.

Ostrom, E. 1990. "Reformulating the Commons." In *Protecting the Commons: A Framework for Resource Management in the Americas,* edited by J. Burger, E. Ostrom, R. B. Norgaard, D. Policansky, and B. D. Goldstein. Washington, DC: Island Press.

Pacific Salmon Commission. 1999. "Fraser River Sockeye Salmon Runs Collapse." News Release no. 7, August 6, 1999. E-mail transmission from *Dave's Fishery Report,* davidellis@lightspeed.bc.ca, August 8, 1999.

Parsons, L. S. 1993. *Management of Marine Fisheries in Canada.* Canadian Bulletin of Fisheries and Aquatic Sciences no. 225. Ottawa: National Research Council of Canada and Department of Fisheries and Oceans.

Parsons, L. S., and J. S. Beckett. 1997. "Fisheries Management in Canada: The Case of Atlantic Groundfish." In *Global Trends: Fisheries Management,* edited by E. K. Pikitch, D. D. Huppert, and M. P. Sissenwine, 73–79. Bethesda, MD: American Fisheries Society.

Peterson, M. J. 1993. "International Fisheries Management." In *Institutions for the Earth,* edited by P. M. Haas, R. O. Keohane, and M. A. Levy, 249–305. Cambridge, MA: MIT Press.

Pinkerton, E. 1994. "Local Fisheries Co-management: A Review of International Experiences and Their Implications for Salmon Management in British Columbia." *Canadian Journal of Fisheries and Aquatic Sciences* 51:1–17.

Rieser, A. 1997. "Property Rights and Ecosystem Management in U.S. Fisheries: Contracting for the Commons?" *Ecology Law Quarterly* 24 (4):813–32.

Sanger, C. 1987. *Ordering the Oceans: The Making of the Law of the Sea.* Toronto: University of Toronto Press.

Schlager, E. 1994. "Fishers' Institutional Responses to Common Pool Resource Dilemmas." In *Rules, Games, and Common-Pool Resources,* edited by E. Ostrom, R. Gardner, and J. Walker, 247–65. Ann Arbor: University of Michigan Press.

Schlager, E., and E. Ostrom. 1992. "Property Rights Regimes and Natural Resources: A Conceptual Analysis." *Land Economics* 68 (3):249–62.

Sissenwine, M. P., and A. A. Rosenberg. 1993. "Marine Fisheries at a Critical Juncture." *Fisheries* 18 (10):6–14.

Smith, M. E. 1988. "Fisheries Risk in the Modern Context." *MAST (Marine Anthropological Studies)* 1 (1):29–48.

Turgeon, D. D. 1985. "Fishery Regulation; Its Use under the Magnuson Act and Reaganomics." *Marine Policy* 9 (April):126–33.

World Wildlife Fund. 1995. *Managing U.S. Fisheries: Public Interest or Conflict of Interest?* Washington, DC: U.S. Land and Wildlife Program, World Wildlife Fund.

Young, O. R. 1982. *Resource Regimes: Natural Resources and Social Institutions.* Berkeley: University of California Press.

Chapter 9

Multiuse Coastal Commons: Personal Watercraft, Conflicts, and Resolutions

JOANNA BURGER

Coastal Commons

In 1968, Garrett Hardin predicted that with increasing population, the eventual fate of all resources held in common was overexploitation and degradation (Hardin 1968). Others, such as Lloyd (1968), Gordon (1954), and Scott (1955, 1993) also made the same point, although with less impact. In the interim we have witnessed the potency of technological progress in partially meeting the needs of ever-expanding populations. Per capita consumption has increased at a faster rate than population in many regions of the world, and technological change and trade have respectively amplified and extended the human footprint on the globe to an unprecedented extent. Hardin's concerns ultimately focused people's attention on the relationship between individual behavior and resource sustainability and between technology and overconsumption by some segments of the population.

Much of the discussion about commons issues has dealt with fisheries, forests, irrigation systems, groundwater basins, and rangelands from a local or regional perspective (see Alexander 1982; NRC 1986; Berkes 1986, 1989; McCay and Acheson 1987; Benjamin et al. 1994; McCay 1995; Blomquist 1996; McKean 1996). While many of these traditional commons involve use of a renewable but depletable resource (fish, trees, water, grass), other commons are emerging that involve resources that are even more difficult to bound and are more elusive (air quality, water quality; Burger et al. this volume). Moreover, we are realizing that many traditional commons are far more complex than we initially imagined. For example, irrigation systems not only

involve quantities of water extracted by traditional users but include considerations of contamination, multiple uses, and ecosystem health.

One of the commons resources that Hardin (1968) mentioned in his classic paper has received little attention: recreational use of waterways and public
lands. In this chapter I suggest that coastal regions are a commons containing
many different common-pool resources that can be extracted or exploited, are
renewable, and can benefit from considerations of the rights and responsibilities of the "commoners." I use the recent intrusion of personal watercraft as an
example of one type of user extracting from the commons to the detriment
of other commoners. While commons issues in the oceans have received considerable attention (Costanza et al. 1998), the coastal commons has been largely ignored (but see McCay chapter 8, this volume).

Overall, the majority of people in the world live within 100 km of bays
and estuaries, making the wise use of these commons resources essential
(Norse 1993; NRC 1995). While commercial fisheries have been the primary
and traditional commons resource of concern in estuarine and coastal environments, there are many other common-pool resources involved. These
include fish and shellfish for recreationists, estuarine land for development,
noise-free air, and disturbance-free water and shorelines. The intersection of
these resources results in conflicts among commoners using various resources
in coastal environments for aesthetic, recreational, or commercial purposes
(fig. 9.1).

While the conflicts between fishers, homeowners, business owners, recre-

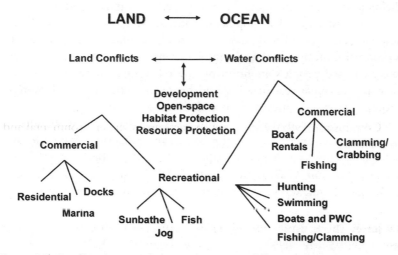

Figure 9.1. Conflicts in coastal commons among different commoners or users.

ationists, and natural-resource managers have been clear for many decades, rapid growth of the use of personal watercraft (PWCs) in the last decade has put an additional strain on both the commons resources and the institutions that would normally deal with this new intrusion. Some of the objectives of this chapter are to examine the effect of PWCs on natural resources, to describe their specific effects on avian resources, and to provide possible solutions. The urgency for resolution results from the magnitude of harm that PWCs can cause to natural resources in a very short period of time, as well as to their increase in numbers.

The importance and generality of examining coastal commons issues is clear from the fact that increasingly urban populations are concentrating along the coasts, and land-use patterns in coastal regions have shifted from farming and fishing to a variety of transportation, recreational, and residential uses (Margavio and Forsyth 1996). Remarkably, recreational commons have been largely ignored, and such issues will continue to grow in importance as recreational use in coastal regions increases.

In this chapter I delineate commons issues in the coastal zone of New Jersey, describe the conflicts of PWCs with other coastal resources and human uses, place PWC use within a commons framework, and examine institutional solutions for resolving conflicts and consensus building regarding the appropriate use of PWCs. Finally I discuss the lessons to be learned from these conflicts in coastal commons.

New Jersey as a Microcosm for Coastal Commons Issues

New Jersey is a microcosm for examining coastal commons issues because it is the most densely populated state in the nation, it is one of the most highly industrialized states, it is mostly coastal, coastal tourism is one of its primary business sectors, and yet it boasts significant natural resources (Cunningham 1978; Stansfield 1983; Burger 1991, 1996; DiIonno 1997), including important fisheries (MacKenzie 1992). For example, the value of commercial fish landings in New Jersey was more than $95 million in 1995 (Atlantic States Marine Fisheries Commission 1997). With these characteristics, the environmental and commons problems in New Jersey often foreshadow problems other states and countries will soon face as their own development, demographic changes, and land-use changes follow. As more people move to the coasts to live and to recreate, the commons problems will increase as the complexity of the common-pool resource use increases.

New Jersey shares with most other Western Hemisphere coastal areas a relatively recent history of exploitation, compared to Asia, Europe, and northern Africa, where coastal regions have been developed for many cen-

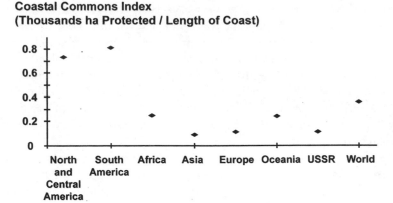

Figure 9.2. Relative amount of marine and coastal area protected by region.

turies or millennia. The use of coastal regions in the Americas as shipping ports dates back only a few centuries, while seaports in other regions of the world have existed for several millennia. The fortunate accident that the Americas had a relatively low population density for most of human history has resulted in more land being available for protection. For example, the Americas have far more hectares of land protected per length of coastline than any other region of the world (figure 9.2, after Hammond 1990 and Roberts 1996). The degree to which such lands are protected from use by different user groups is itself a commons issue but not one dealt with in this chapter. Although the degree of protection each area receives can be disputed, this land remains in public ownership. Another indication of the uniqueness of the coastal commons in the Americas is the relatively low number of urban cities (population of more than 500,000); the Americas have one large coastal city for every 4,208 km of coastline, while the rest of the world has one for every 2,845 km of coastline (computed from Hammond 1990).

While coastal regions in the Americas were always used by American Indians, their use was sporadic, low, and seasonal; they avoided the coasts at some times of the year because of the hordes of insect pests (Worth 1972). The rapid development of the New Jersey shore, and elsewhere along the Atlantic Coast, occurred after World War I, when public works programs allowed the draining of the marshes to control insects. This was followed by another period of intensive growth after World War II when widespread development and use of insecticides reduced mosquito and fly populations. This growth trend continues today along most of the Atlantic Coast.

Personal Watercraft and Coastal Commons: The Players and Spatial Limits

Resource and land-use conflicts among fishers, landowners, businessmen, recreationists, and natural-resource managers proceeded slowly as each group developed and relevant laws and rules were promulgated. The legal process for managing common-pool coastal resources began with the initiation of migratory bird treaties at the turn of the century and proceeded with fisheries laws and regulations, marine mammal protection acts and CITES laws (Convention on International Trade in Endangered Species of Wild Flora and Fauna), land-use laws and regulations, and boating laws and conventions. In most cases, problems with coastal common-pool resources develop slowly, as in the case of exploitation of certain fish stocks, and there is ample time to develop institutions to deal with overexploitation, although such problems are not always solved rapidly enough to prevent massive declines of some fish species (Safina 1993, 1994).

The advent of PWCs has been rapid and ubiquitous (Burger 1998a). Over the past ten years, annual sales of PWCs in the United States have increased—from about 30,000 in 1987 to more than 150,000 in 1997 (fig 9.3). PWCs can travel as fast as, or faster than, conventional boats in extremely shallow water and because of shallow drafts can go many places that motorboats cannot (Burger 1997; National Park Service 1998). Personal watercraft are relatively small boats (usually less than 16 feet long) that are powered by an internal combustion engine with a water jet pump as the primary source of power. They are fast, maneuverable, and noisy and have access to shallow aquatic environments that other boats cannot enter; this increases the potential for resource damages.

Coastal commons resources are particularly difficult to manage because

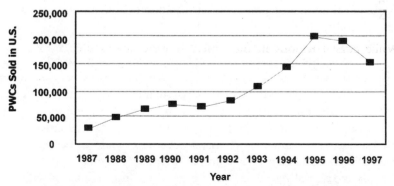

Figure 9.3. Sales of personal watercraft in the United States, 1987–1997.

there are so many players, including landowners, fishers, other business owners and operators, recreationists, and natural-resource managers. Each group contains many diverse subgroups: (1) landowners include public and private owners; (2) fishers include commercial and recreational anglers; (3) business owners and operators include those who sell or rent personal watercraft, owners of marinas and other businesses, and motel operators; (4) recreationists include PWC operators, other boaters, fishers, clammers, bird-watchers, and beach users; and (5) natural-resource managers include those interested in specific resources as well as ecosystem health, such as conservationists and wildlife biologists. Many users value the aesthetics of their activities as much as the resources they extract. Each player may use one or several of the common-pool resources along the coast, thus placing them in conflict with other users and with other natural resources.

Winners and Losers

Ultimately, the management of common-pool resources (*sensu* Ostrom 1990; Ostrom chapter 1, this volume; Ostrom et al. 1994) comes down to access limitations (who will be excluded from what, and how), subtractability (how much does the taking by one person impinge on the taking by another), and enforceable rules. Restriction or exclusion of commons resources is difficult (Berkes et al. 1989). It is often in the individual's best interest to take as much as possible as soon as possible because the individual derives the entire advantage while paying only part of the cost. Hardin used the example of a herder placing one more animal on the common grazing lands. The herder gains the entire advantage of that animal while bearing only a small part of the cost of depletion of the grazing lands. Thus, it is always in the herder's interest to add one more cow. The solution, in Hardin's view, was to impose some form of government or private ownership from the outside (Hardin 1968, 1998). His solution, however, admits no other land ownership types and ignores the possibility that institutional or group actions can address the questions of access and subtractability (Feeny et al. 1990).

While Hardin was discussing traditional common-pool resources, such as grazing lands and fishing rights, our complex modern society has added many other resources that are, in fact commons resources. The use of personal watercraft is a commons resource in that the use of such craft by some detracts from the value of the resource (coastal waterways) to others. At its simplest level, the use of personal watercraft has the potential to make the coastal environment (or other aquatic environments for that matter) less usable and appealing for other commoners. The damage is both physical and aesthetic.

The common-pool resources that are involved in the conflict with personal watercraft include (1) the water surface; (2) water quality (through grease and oil pollution); (3) fish, shellfish, seagrass beds, and other below-surface natural resources; (4) air quality (through noise pollution); and (5) shoreline resources (through wave disturbance). While the water surface itself has seldom been considered a common-pool resource, disruption of the water surface by PWCs can cause problems for other boaters, commercial and recreational fishermen, homeowners, and natural resource managers (table 9.1). The uncontrolled use of PWCs at high speeds disrupts the behavior and foraging of wildlife, the ability to fish, clam, or crab by recreational and commercial fishers, and the tranquility of the environment for a wide variety of commoners.

Moreover, PWCs pose a direct human safety hazard. Although they account for only 11 percent of all registered boats, they are responsible for 35 percent of all accidents and 44 percent of all personal injuries (Shattuck 1997; National Park Service 1998). The noise created by PWCs has proved to be an important factor detracting from the quality of the coastal experience for many commoners. This led many parks and reserves to ban or severely limit PWC use, and the National Park Service has published its intent to severely restrict PWC use within the park system (National Park Service 1996, 1997, 1998; Whiteman 1997). While such policies may deal adequately with the immediate problem of personal watercraft, they do not address the larger question of the wise use of commons resources by all, including people who operate personal watercraft. The wise solution may involve integrating personal watercraft use into coastal environments in such a manner as to preserve ecological resources and human values.

Severe conflicts occur in coastal regions between PWC operators and recreational and commercial fishers (Burger 1998a; R. Munson, pers. comm.). PWCs disturb fishers while they are pulling nets or traps and disrupt their gear while it is set. Moreover, a wide range of residents living in coastal regions rank PWCs as the most severe environmental problem in the estuaries, above other problems such as chemical pollution, "junk or debris," overfishing, and boat oil (Burger 1998b).

The universality of concern about PWCs in coastal commons is remarkable. To understand how the public and elected officials rank the problems associated with PWCs relative to other environmental problems in Barnegat Bay, three groups of people were interviewed: public officials, people fishing along the bay, and shopkeepers in the vicinity of the bay. Our interviews included 66 public officials of the municipalities adjacent to Barnegat Bay, 515 people fishing or crabbing in Barnegat Bay, and 189 people owning or managing businesses along Barnegat Bay (after Burger et al. 1999). For all three groups, PWCs were ranked as the greatest concern (fig. 9.4). Some issues were of low concern to all three groups (small boats, sailboats, windsurfing, and birds), while others were considered to be of intermediate concern (pollution,

Table 9.1. Characteristics of Different Types of Commoners Using the Water Surface Commons in New Jersey.

Characteristic	Land Owners	Resource Managers	General Businesses	PWC Vendors	PWC Operators	Other Recreationists	Fishers
Time horizon	Long-term	Long-term	Variable	Medium	Short	Short	Medium to long
Dependency on resource	High	Very high	Medium	Very high	High	High	High
Trust of PWCs	Low	Low	Low	Medium	—	Low	Low
Law-making ability	High	Very high	Medium	Low	Low	Low	Medium
Rule-making ability	Low	Very high	Very low	High	Low	Low	Medium
Knowledge of natural resource	Medium	Very high	Low	Low	Low	Medium	Medium
Organizational experience	Medium	High	Medium	Medium	Low	Medium	High
Repeatability of interaction	High	High	High	Medium	Low	Low	High
Interest in solutions	High	High	Medium	High	Medium	Medium	High
Payoff of solutions	High	High	Medium	High	High	High	High

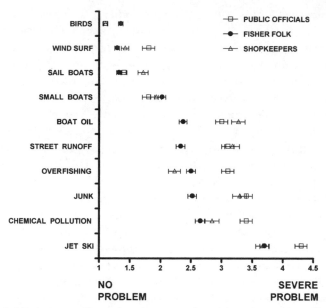

Figure 9.4. Relative ranking of environmental problems by public officials, fishers, and business owners and operators for Barnegat Bay, New Jersey.

debris, overfishing). All groups ranked PWCs as the issue of greatest concern. The relative ranking of PWCs as the environmental issue of greatest concern was also made by 291 people who lived throughout New Jersey and were visiting the shore for the day (Burger 1998b). These data indicate widespread concern for the problems created by PWCs, by residents, business owners and operators, and by elected officials living around the bay, as well as by people residing in other regions of New Jersey.

The Case for Resource Damages

Personal watercraft have the potential for disturbing, disrupting, and destroying a wide range of natural resources, including spawning fish, fish and shellfish nurseries, and nesting birds (National Park Service 1997, 1998). Since PWCs have a shallow draft, they can penetrate into areas that are not available to conventional boats, increasing the damage to bottom muds, aquatic vegetation, and wildlife. The disturbances are many and include disruption of bottom-dwelling fish and invertebrates, interruption of normal activities and behavior of all aquatic organisms and those using these habitats to forage (such as birds), interference with courtship and breeding activities, direct mortality, and changes in community structure. The threat is amplified partially because

PWCs can enter shallow areas of the bay where other boats cannot. Thus, areas of estuarine and coastal environments previously protected from disturbances from other boats are now exposed to disturbances from PWCs.

As with the beginning of any new intrusion or use of natural resources, data on such disturbances are often anecdotal or are reported in the popular press (Williams 1998). However, long-term data sets on common-pool resources provide an opportunity to collect data on effects of specific users. From 1976 until the present I have been monitoring population dynamics and reproductive success of common terns (*Sterna hirundo*) and black skimmers (*Rynchops niger*) in Barnegat Bay (Burger and Gochfeld 1991). Both species usually return to the same islands to breed each year, shifting colony sites only when the habitat becomes unsuitable or they suffer repeated reproductive losses. An island that is exposed to predators repeatedly ceases to be optimal for nesting, and the whole colony moves elsewhere. Over time, the birds have selected the most suitable islands for nesting, those that are high enough to avoid frequent tidal flooding during the breeding season but are low enough to have tidal washovers during the winter that eliminate predators. Additionally, the terns must avoid nesting on islands with herring gulls (*Larus argentatus*), which compete with them for nest sites and prey on their eggs and chicks (Burger and Gochfeld 1991). Remarkably, there are more than 250 salt-marsh islands in Barnegat Bay, and although they may look the same to the casual observer, the terns and skimmers have nested on only 35 of them over twenty-five years of study. The other islands are either too high or too low in elevation, are too close to human habitation, or have no suitable nesting vegetation. Thus, for the terns and skimmers, few suitable nesting islands exist that are not already used (Burger and Lesser 1978). Maintaining stable populations of both species thus requires protecting their current nesting islands because there are not many alternatives.

Since the early 1990s, Little Mike's Island in Barnegat Bay (fig. 9.5) has contained one of the largest nesting colonies of common terns in Barnegat Bay. Before 1996 the colony of 250 to 500 nesting common tern pairs was highly successful (fledging over one young per nest; Burger 1991a). In 1996 there was a sharp increase in PWCs in the vicinity; common terns nesting on Mike's Island were frequently disturbed and fledged no young. In 1997 we initiated a study of the effects of boats (motorboats and PWCs) on behavior of common terns. Since black skimmers (a state-listed endangered species) always nest with common terns and always leave the colony whenever common terns do, we chose to study the more abundant common terns.

The temporal pattern of use by people in motorboats and PWCs was similar; both were most active around noon and again in the late afternoon (fig. 9.6). The results from 1997 were disturbing: PWCs moved all around the bird-nesting island, and they usually moved at fast speeds. PWCs often raced out-

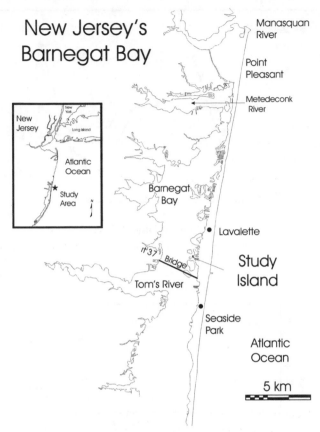

New Jersey's
Barnegat Bay

Manasquan
River

Point
Pleasant

New York

New
Jersey

Long Island

Metedeconk
River

Atlantic
Ocean

Study
Area

Barnegat
Bay

Lavalette

Bridge

Study
Island

Tom's River

Seaside
Park

Atlantic
Ocean

5 km

Figure 9.5. Location of Little Mike's Island in Barnegat Bay, New Jersey, where common terns nest and the water commons was studied.

side the established channel and were closer to the nesting colonies, eliciting stronger responses than those that remained in the channel (Burger 1998a). Motorboats remained in the channel to avoid running aground. Not only did fast-moving PWCs elicit the strongest response from the birds, but the response persisted for two or three minutes following the disturbance (fig. 9.7). In 1997 the 500-pair colony of common terns failed to raise any chicks for the second year in a row.

These results were sufficient to galvanize local conservationists, scientists, resource managers, the state police, and a wide variety of citizens to initiate action to decrease the effect of PWCs on birds and other resources in the bay. Critical for solution of the problem was the inclusion of scientists who could identify and study the effects of personal watercraft, and other commoners

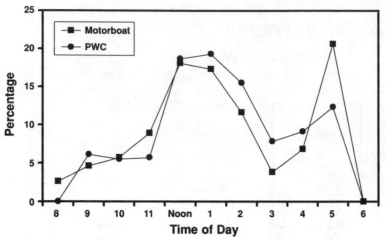

Figure 9.6. Temporal pattern of motorboat and personal watercraft use around Mike's Island, New Jersey.

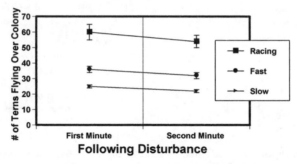

Figure 9.7. Responses of common terns to disturbance as a function of the speed of the boat.

who could galvanize attention and responses. These actions, described in the next section, were sufficient to greatly reduce the effects of PWCs on the terns nesting on Mike's Island in 1998. Fewer PWCs went by the nesting island, they traveled more slowly, and for the most part they remained in the boat channel (Fig. 9.8). The change in speed and route around the nesting island resulted in a significant decrease in the terns' responses (fig. 9.9). Moreover, the terns were successful and raised more than one chick per pair.

Institutional Solutions

It is clear that PWCs can cause damage to several natural resources. Each may need to be treated differently in searching for a solution, although the institu-

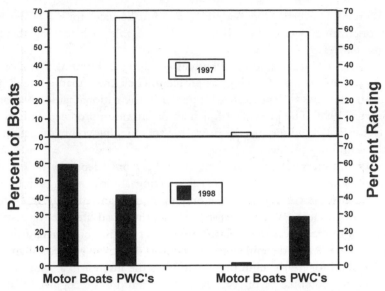

Figure 9.8. Change in behavior of boats and personal watercraft before (1997) and after (1998) agreed-upon rules for reducing disturbances to common terns.

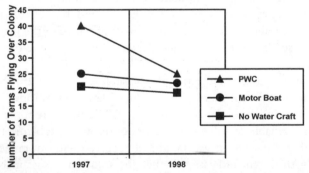

Figure 9.9. Change in response of common terns to boats and personal watercraft as a function of voluntary changes in path and speed of craft moving past the nesting island.

tional mechanisms available may be similar. In this section I discuss potential solutions with respect to the avian nesting colonies, largely because the severity of the effects of PWCs was so clear as to serve as a catalyst. Two aspects were critical for rapid response to the threat to the coastal commons posed by personal watercraft: Scientists were considered commoners who had valuable information to provide other commoners, and environmentalists and educators (from Rutgers University Cooperative Extension Service) took a leadership role in organizing open public forums and were able to bring together all interested parties.

Even the PWC Association and businesses selling and renting PWCs recognized the importance of solving the problem. They knew that failure might result in stricter laws or bans, as has happened in the national parks (National Park Service 1998). The presence of such an organization provided an institutional factor that could serve as the driver for encouraging voluntary action to solve the commons problem.

The commoners differed in their time horizons, dependence on the resource, knowledge of the resource, rule-making ability, and organizational ability. That is, some commoners were only infrequent and short-term visitors to the bay (e.g., some PWC operators), while others had lifetime interests in the health of the resources of the bay (homeowners, most commercial fishers). Similarly, the degree of dependence on the resources of the bay varied among commoners. Yet for nearly all of the commoners the interest in a solution was high, as was the potential payoff. Nearly all the commoners recognized that (1) colonial-nesting endangered species (black skimmers) or species of special concern were involved (common terns), (2) there were clear negative effects from PWC disturbance, (3) laws were available to protect endangered species against harassment, and (4) the public at large was interested in protecting the birds and reducing noise levels and wakes around houses. While everyone agreed on the preferred outcome (no more disturbance of the birds, improved reproductive success of the birds, and decreased noise), the resolution was less clear at the outset.

Several institutional methods were available to address the conflicts that resulted among different users. These included laws, regulations, licenses, education, posting, and enforcement (table 9.2). While these are some of the usual mechanisms available to solve common-pool resource problems, this case was unique in that the solution was rapid and occurred without rancor. Although clearly only time will indicate whether the solution is sustainable, this case study does indicate that solutions can be found quickly when the stakes are high enough.

New Jersey considered laws regulating the use of PWCs, as have been implemented in some other places (National Park Service 1998), as well as licensing, but these procedures are time consuming and cumbersome to adopt. Attempts to impose mandatory licensing met with loud objections from the industry, and although licensing was signed into law, it was halted before the start of the PWC season. Clearly the birds needed immediate protection. The most available methods seemed to be education, posting, enforcement of existing laws regarding operation of boats and harassment of migratory birds, and reliance on consensus building among the commoners.

Table 9.2. Institutional Solutions to Personal Watercraft Conflicts in Coastal Commons in Barnegat Bay, New Jersey.

Type	Used in New Jersey	Possible Outcome
Laws limiting spatial use		Limit access to certain socially or ecologically sensitive regions
Laws limiting temporal use		Restrict use to daylight hours or sensitive periods
Laws limiting age		Limit age at which one can operate PWCs
Licensing		Require all operators to have licenses
Regulations	X	Limit rentals to those operating within a certain area
Required education course	X	Require all operators to take a three-hour course on safe operation of PWCs and impacts to natural resources
Informal workshops	X	Provide information to all commoners on effects of PWCs
Leaflets and brochures	X	Reach rental agencies and other businesses
Posting in sensitive areas	X	Place signs in relevant areas and post buoys to indicate off-limits areas around nesting colonies or other sensitive resources
Enforcement	X	Deploy conservation officers and marine police to provide information and to issue citations

Consensus Building

Consensus building was facilitated by leadership from environmentalists and educators who had enough long-term standing within the community to facilitate public meetings. Organizations such as the Izaak Walton League and the Rutgers Cooperative Extension Service had worked for many years with important marine and coastal issues and were sufficiently respected within the community to be able to bring people with different perspectives to the table.

Consensus building involved several meetings among different interest groups, including PWC associations, PWC operators, and PWC businesses (sales and rentals). These background meetings were essential to introduce everyone to the magnitude of the problem with the resource (nesting birds and water-surface use). A preliminary meeting among the same group of users (listed in table 9.1) had taken place in the spring of 1997 before the start of the breeding season. However, at that time people representing the PWC users clearly stated that there were no available data to show any ill effects on natural resources and that the response was simply due to inconvenience and noise complaints. This meeting stimulated the work in 1997 and 1998 on the common terns.

The consensus-building process culminated in 1998 in a public meeting to which all the relevant commoners were invited. Presentations were made by representatives of each type (landowners, resource managers, scientists, the general public, PWC sales and rental agents, PWC operators, fishers, and other recreationists). The order of presentation was critical: Data on resource damages had to come first, to set the stage for later discussions. Consequently, it was important that all parties had trust in the validity of the data and in the credibility of the scientists involved, and that all agreed that damages to the resource were not acceptable. Further, the potential threat of regulatory action played a role in encouraging discussion.

Employing environmental science to shape policy decisions is clearly a social process (Norgaard 1992), and attention to the issue of trust is critical. While trust among the PWC factions was initially low, two elements essential to consensus building were present: mutual trust in the scientific data and willingness to sit down and discuss the problem. To some extent the data on resource damage were sufficiently strong to allow people who were only concerned about noise and wakes to back away from these concerns to focus on an overriding concern for endangered and threatened species.

The public meeting was followed by an extensive public education campaign including further meetings, newspaper articles about the meetings (listing all the players attending) and the effects on the terns, newsletters summarizing the data, and leaflets about the effects on wildlife. Everyone cooperated in the dissemination of information. Leaflets were made available to all PWC sales and rental offices, as well as other businesses. Many PWC sales and rental managers made it a point to mention the problem of birds and eelgrass beds to PWC operators, particularly to renters.

Since goodwill in avoiding disturbance is effective only if people can clearly identify nesting colonies, personnel from the state's Endangered and Nongame Species Program and the marine police put out additional buoys around Mike's Island and other nesting islands to indicate appropriate routes for boats. For the most part our observations indicate that these routes were respected, and boats did not go close to the nesting islands. The ability to monitor and evaluate the success of such measures on nesting terns was critical to the measure's long-term success. Further public forums will be conducted to report on the efficacy of the actions, which should foster even better compliance in the future.

Conclusion

While future equitable use of water surfaces by the various users in Barnegat Bay is not ensured, this case study clearly indicates that it is possible to achieve action when all relevant parties are included and protection of a particular common-pool resource (migratory birds) is essential. Several lessons can be learned from this case.

1. The existence of many commoners adds to the complexity of the issue, and everyone has to be included in the discussions from the start.
2. It is wise to begin by tackling a problem on which consensus exists (damage to a particular resource) rather than the overall problem of PWCs.
3. Data on damage to the common-pool resource are essential. They must be data that everyone considers important. The credibility of the data and scientist(s) are likewise key. (The role of the scientist is critical; in this case I was recognized as having worked with the birds in Barnegat Bay for more than twenty-five years.)
4. The problem should be able to be circumscribed, with limits to the solution (for instance, stay a certain distance from a nesting island and slowly go past it).
5. Willingness to solve the problem has to be high, backed by severe penalties for not cooperating. (In this case, penalties consisted of the threat of severe legal restrictions on the use of PWCs throughout the bay.)
6. Cooperation and action follows when the solution is in everyone's best interest; finding the common interest is essential.
7. Ability to monitor the success of the agreed-upon actions is essential.

Three factors bear comment: the critical importance of agreeing on what data can address the problem, achieving consensus among diverse viewpoints, and maintaining cooperation (Burger et al., this volume; Ostrom chapter 1, this volume). Recognizing the changing nature of resources and resource use is vital to dealing with complex issues, such as PWCs (see Burger et al., this volume). Resolution of the immediate problem of disturbance to the birds nesting on salt-marsh islands in Barnegat Bay came partly from the initial meetings in which all relevant parties agreed on the need for specific studies to determine whether the birds (or other natural resources) were adversely affected by PWCs. As Clark and Majone (1985) point out, it is essential to agree what knowledge is needed for any policy decision. While rancor existed among the different parties in the absence of any data, this largely disappeared when data clearly showed that the birds were adversely affected. Having scientists with a long history of involvement with Barnegat Bay undoubtedly helped, as did introducing a long-term data set on the reproductive success of the birds.

The linkages between different common-pool resources, which are increasingly important in resource issues of the twenty-first century (Burger et al., this volume), are obvious in estuarine and coastal habitats that serve as the interface between the land and ocean. In this zone, policy decisions will be necessary to shape resource use and to support the decisions of a diverse group of users (Ostrom chapter 1, this volume). The present study provides an example in which the users are diverse, rather than homogeneous, yet they still arrived at a common solution. People with heterogenous views were able to arrive at a common understanding partially because credible and important data showed a clear adverse effect on a valued resource (nesting birds).

The role of cooperation in this case cannot be emphasized enough. Without the cooperation of all participants it would not have been possible to reach a solution. From the time when the initial results on the nesting failures were available until the next breeding season, all of the relevant interests were discussing the problem and its solution. While cooperation was essential, the subtle threat of the use of migratory bird treaty laws (which protect migratory birds from harassment) and maritime law (boats are supposed to remain a certain distance from mean low tide) provided added incentive. Furthermore, it was clear to everyone that more stringent laws pertaining to PWCs alone were being considered.

The use of PWCs in Barnegat Bay is indicative of the larger issue of PWCs in public waters throughout the Americas and can serve as an example of ways to resolve conflicts over shared resources when the users have different objectives and worldviews (see Ostrom chapter 1, this volume). The presence of two types of users (residents and short-term or day users) increases the potential for misunderstanding and decreases the likelihood of trust. While the spatial problem is bounded by the aquatic environment, some aspects, such as noise, are not. Further, it is likely that there will be an expanding temporal scale to the problem because use of watercraft is increasing at the same time as coastal development. The framework for understanding common-pool resource use, as laid down by Ostrom (chapter 1, this volume), was clearly useful both in providing a paradigm for solving this problem and in evaluating the institutions and rules to govern the use of estuarine waters by diverse commoners, including PWCs.

Acknowledgments

The author gratefully acknowledge the editorial comments of M. Gochfeld, B. D. Goldstein, B. McCay, and E. Ostrom; the graphics assistance of R. Ramos;

and the technical assistance of J. Leonard, M. McMahon, and C. Dixon. I especially thank Sharon Rinaldi and R. Moriarty, who graciously allowed observations from their boat docks, thus eliminating any effect we might have had on tern behavior. I also thank Ellen Paul for forwarding to me the proposed ruling of the National Park Service. This research was partially funded by the Littoral Society of America and the Consortium for Risk Evaluation with Stakeholder Participation (CRESP) through the U.S. Department of Energy (AI no. DE-FC01-95EW55084, DE-FG-26-OONT-40938).

References

Alexander, P. 1982. *Sri Lankan Fishermen: Rural Capitalism and Peasant Society.* Canberra: Australian National University.

Atlantic States Marine Fisheries Commission. 1997. "Atlantic Coastal Wetlands Losses and the Economic Value of Fisheries." *Habitat Hotline Atlantic Issue* 21:1–5.

Benjamin, P., W. F. Lam, E. Ostrom, and G. Shivakoti. 1994. "Institutions, Incentives, and Irrigation in Nepal." Decentralization: Finance & Management Project Report. Burlington, VT: Associates in Rural Development.

Berkes, F. 1986. "Local-Level Management and the Commons Problem: A Comparative Study of Turkish Coastal Fisheries." *Marine Policy* 10:215–29.

Berkes, F., ed. 1989. *Common Property Resources: Ecology and Community-based Sustainable Development.* London: Belhaven Press.

Berkes, F., D. Feeny, B. J. McCay, and J. M. Acheson. 1989. "The Benefits of the Commons." *Nature* 340:91–93.

Blomquist, A. 1996. *Food and Fashion. Water Management and Collective Action among Irrigation Farmers and Textile Industrialists in South India.* Linköping, Sweden: The Institute of Tema Research, Department of Water and Environmental Studies.

Burger, J. 1991. "Coastal Landscapes, Coastal Colonies and Seabirds." *Aquatic Reviews* 4:23–43.

Burger, J. 1996. *A Naturalist along the Jersey Shore.* New Brunswick, NJ: Rutgers University Press.

Burger, J. 1997. "Avian Studies in Barnegat Bay." In *The State of Barnegat Bay,* 345–50. New York: EPA, Region II, Barnegat Bay Scientific Advisory Committee.

Burger, J. 1998a. "Effects of Motorboats and Personal Watercraft on Flight Behavior over a Colony of Common Terns." *Condor* 100:528–34.

Burger, J. 1998b. "Attitudes about Recreation, Environmental Problems, and Estuarine Health along the New Jersey Shore, USA." *Environmental Management* 22:869–76.

Burger, J., C. Field, R. Norgaard, E. Ostrom, and D. Policansky. 2000. "Common-Pool Resources and Commons Institutions: An Overview of the Applicability of the Concept and Approach to Current Environmental Problems." In *Protecting the Commons: A Framework for Resource Management in the Americas,* edited by J. Burger, E. Ostrom, R. B. Norgaard, D. Policansky, and B. D. Goldstein. Washington DC: Island Press.

Burger, J., and M. Gochfeld. 1991. *Common Tern: Its Breeding Biology and Social Behavior.* New York: Columbia University Press.

Burger, J., and F. Lesser. 1978. "Colony and Nest Site Selection in Common Terns." *Ibis* 120:443–49.

Burger, J., J. Sanchez, J. Leonard, R. Ramos, and M. Gochfeld. 1999. "Resources and Estuarine Health: Perceptions of Public Officials and the Public." *Journal of Toxicology and Environmental Health* 58:245–60.

Clark, W. C., and G. Majone. 1985. "The Critical Appraisal of Scientific Inquiries with Policy Implications." *Science, Technology and Human Values* 10:6–19.

Costanza, R., F. Andrade, P. Antunnes, et al. 1998. "Principles for Sustainable Governance of the Oceans." *Science* 281:198–99.

Cunningham, J. T. 1978. *This Is New Jersey.* New Brunswick, NJ: Rutgers University Press.

DiIonno, M. 1997. *New Jersey's Coastal Heritage.* New Brunswick, NJ: Rutgers University Press.

Feeny, D., F. Berkes, B. J. McCay, and J. M. Acheson. 1990. "The Tragedy of the Commons: Twenty-Two Years Later." *Human Ecology* 18:1–19.

Gordon, J. S. 1954. "The Economic Theory of a Common-Property Resource: The Fishery." *Journal of Political Economy* 62:124–42.

Hammond, A. L., ed. 1990. *World Resources (1990–91).* Oxford: Oxford University Press.

Hardin, G. 1968. "The Tragedy of the Commons." *Science* 162:1243–48.

———. 1998. "Extensions of 'The Tragedy of the Commons.'" *Science* 280:687–88.

Lloyd, W. F. 1968. "Lectures on Population, Value, Poor-Laws, and Rent. Delivered in the University of Oxford during the Years 1832, 1833, 1834, 1835, and 1836." Reprints of Economic Classics. New York: A. M. Kelley.

MacKenzie, C. L., Jr. 1992. *The Fisheries of Raritan Bay.* New Brunswick, NJ: Rutgers University Press.

Margavio, A. V., and C. J. Forsyth. 1996. *Caught in the Nest: The Conflict between Shrimpers and Conservationists.* College Station: Texas A&M University Press.

McCay, B. J. 1995. "The Ocean Commons and Community." *Dalhousie Review* 74:1–29.

———. 2000. "Community-based and Cooperative Fisheries: Solutions to Fishermen's Problems." In *Protecting the Commons: A Framework for Resource Management in the Americas,* edited by J. Burger, E. Ostrom, R. B. Norgaard, D. Polincansky, and B. D. Goldstein. Washington, DC: Island Press.

McCay, B. J., and J. M. Acheson, eds. 1987. *The Question of the Commons: The Culture and Ecology of Communal Resources.* Tucson: University of Arizona Press.

McKean, M. A. 1996. "Common Property: What Is It, What Is It Good For, and What Makes It Work?" Working paper, Food and Agriculture Organization of the United Nations, Forests, Trees and People Programme, Phase II, Rome, Italy.

National Park Service. 1996. "Use of Personal Watercraft Banned." *National Parks* 70:25–25.

———. 1997. "PWCs out of Place in Parks." *National Parks* 71:17–18.

National Park Service. 1998. "Personal Watercraft Use within the NPS System." *Federal Register* 63 (178):49312–17.

National Research Council. 1986. *Proceedings of the Conference on Common Property Resource Management.* Washington, DC: National Academy Press.

————. 1995. *Understanding Marine Biodiversity.* Washington, DC: National Academy Press.

Norgaard, R. B. 1992. "Environmental Science as a Social Process." *Environmental Monitoring and Assessment* 20:95–110.

Norse, E. A., ed. 1993. *Global Marine Biological Diversity Strategy: Building Conservation into Decision Making.* Washington, DC: Center for Marine Conservation.

Ostrom, E. 1990. *Governing the Commons: The Evolution of Institutions for Collective Action.* New York: Cambridge University Press.

————. 2000. "Reformulating the Commons." In *Protecting the Commons: A Framework for Resource Management in the Americas,* edited by J. Burger, E. Ostrom, R. B. Norgaard, D. Policansky, and B. D. Goldstein. Washington, DC: Island Press.

Ostrom, E., R. Gardner, and J. M. Walker. 1994. *Rules, Games, and Common-Pool Resources.* Ann Arbor: University of Michigan Press.

Roberts, L., ed. 1996. *World Resources (1996–97).* Oxford: Oxford University Press.

Safina, C. 1993. "Bluefin Tuna in the West Atlantic: Negligent Management and the Making of an Endangered Species." *Conservation Biology* 7:229–34.

————. 1994. "Where Have All the Fishes Gone?" *Issues in Science and Technology* (Spring) 11:37–43.

Scott, A. D. 1955. The Fishery: The Objectives of Sole Ownership. *Journal of Political Economy* 63:116–24.

————. 1993. "Obstacles to Fishery Self-Government." *Marine Resource Economics* 8:187–99.

Shattuck, B. 1997. "1996 Boating Accidents." *South Dakota Conservation Digest* (May/June) 23:8–10.

Stansfield, C. A., Jr. 1983. *New Jersey.* Boulder, CO: Westview Press.

Whiteman, L. 1997. "Making Waves." *National Parks* 71:22–25.

Williams, T. 1998. "The Jet Set." *Audubon* (July–August 1998) 100:34–38.

Worth, C. B. 1972. *Of Mosquitos, Moths and Mice.* New York: Norton & Company, Inc.

Part Three

GLOBAL COMMONS

Chapter 10

The Atmospheric Commons

JOHN HARRISON AND PAMELA MATSON

"For the first time in my life I saw the horizon as a curved line. It was accentuated by a thin seam of dark blue light—our atmosphere. Obviously this was not the ocean of air I had been told it was so many times in my life. I was terrified by its fragile appearance."

Ulf Merbold, German astronaut

In satellite images taken from the dark side of Earth, the atmosphere appears as a paper-thin, blue-violet arc stretching along the boundary between the surface of our planet and outer space. Because the atmosphere is this finite, thin skin over Earth, rather than an infinite "ocean of air," it is susceptible to human alteration of its chemistry and function. With increasing frequency and severity over the past century, human activities have reduced the atmosphere's capacity to supply the atmospheric services upon which humans and the rest of the biosphere intimately depend. Protection of atmospheric quality has required, and will continue to require, cooperation of the global community, and such cooperation can be informed by our experience with commons resources.

Localized episodes of air pollution due to natural fires and prehistoric, fire-aided hunting and land clearing have occurred for millennia, but until recently, these local activities had little impact on the global atmosphere. With twentieth-century population increases and technological advances, however, local activities have fundamentally and globally altered the atmosphere's composition and function (box 10.1). During the 1950s and 1960s, nuclear testing by superpowers threatened the atmosphere's capacity to provide clean air and water by creating and dispersing dangerous radioactive fallout (Soroos 1997). In the second half of the twentieth century, chlorofluorocarbons (CFCs) eroded Earth's protective stratospheric ozone layer (box 10.2) while other forms of air pollution have harmed human health and acidified and polluted ecosystems of the industrialized world (box 10.3; Benedick 1991; Hornung and Skeffington 1993). In the 1990s the scientific community warned that human emissions of greenhouse gases (GHGs) have altered and will continue to alter global climate (box 10.4), with potentially devastating effects (IPCC 1990, 1994). Today, increasing industrialization and land-use change, especially in tropical and subtropical regions, are altering the global atmosphere in ways that are poorly understood but certain to be very important (e.g., Keller et al. 1991; Duxbury 1994; Sanhueza 1997; Obrien 1996). In each of these cases, individuals, corporations, or nations acting in their own self-interest have inadvertently threatened the well-being of a larger community by harming the atmosphere's ability to provide its services.

This scenario brings to mind Garrett Hardin's classic article "The Tragedy of the Commons" (Hardin 1968): Herdsmen, acting in their own short-term interest, inadvertently diminish the long-term communal value of a common

---

Box 10.1. The Atmosphere: A Brief Primer

The atmosphere is both a space and a substance. The spatial component of the atmosphere can be divided into layers like onionskins. These layers are called the troposphere (0–10 km), the stratosphere (10–50 km), the mesosphere (50–80 km), and the exosphere (80+ km).[1] The substance of the atmosphere, air, can be divided into components as well: nitrogen (78.08%), oxygen (20.95%), argon (0.93%), carbon dioxide (0.03%), water vapor (0–4% depending on local conditions), and numerous trace gases (Anthes 1992). Some of these gases, such as carbon dioxide, nitrous oxide, and chlorofluorocarbons, do not react immediately and thus are well mixed throughout the global troposphere. Others, such as nitric oxide and carbon monoxide, are very chemically reactive, and thus they and their reaction products are variable over space and time. This mix of gases is both dynamic and mobile, with a mixing time on the order of months, so local changes in atmospheric composition can have regional or global impacts.

[1] Although traces of the atmosphere have been found as far as 60,000 miles from Earth, 99.99% of the atmosphere lies within 80 km of Earth's surface.

Table 10.1. Categories of Goods Relating to Atmospheric Commons.

Exclusion	Subtractability	
	High	Low
Easy	Private goods (e.g., an apple)	Toll goods (e.g., a bridge)
Difficult	Common-pool resources★ (e.g., an oil field)	Public goods★ (e.g., stratospheric ozone)

★Denotes commons resources.

pasture by overgrazing it. In Hardin's example, each herdsman perceives his personal gain from adding one more animal to a common pasture as greater than his personal loss in terms of pasture degradation. This means that the reasonable herdsman will continue to add animals, even past the level that the common pasture can withstand. The eventual result of this activity is pasture degradation and the financial ruin of all herdsmen who depend on the health of the commons. Like the degradation of Hardin's pasture, the degradation of the atmosphere also results from an incompatibility between individual motives and the greater good. This similarity has prompted some to suggest that it is useful to view the atmosphere as a regional or global commons and manage it as such (Soroos 1997; McGinnis and Ostrom 1992). This view has merit, but there are also important distinctions between the atmosphere and Hardin's common pasture. These distinctions are crucial because they bear on our approach to atmospheric protection.

Commons resources[1] are generally nonexcludable (table 10.1; Ostrom chapter 1, this volume), meaning that it is impractical or impossible to keep users from using the resource in question. With the possible exception of airspace, it is almost impossible to exclude users from atmospheric resources.[2] Commons resources can be further divided into subtractable and nonsubtractable commons resources, which are called common-pool resources and public goods, respectively. The Hardinian pasture is a common-pool resource because it is by definition nonexcludable (i.e., all the village herdsmen have access to it) and because it is subtractable (use by one herdsman diminishes the possible use by others). Other examples of common-pool resources include oil reserves, freshwater aquifers, and fisheries, some of which are discussed in other chapters of this book. Public goods, on the other hand, are nonexcludable and nonsubtractable, meaning that it is not possible to exclude users but that use by one does not preclude use by another. Examples of public goods include air quality, water quality, biodiversity, and scenic beauty.

Arguments to treat the atmosphere as a common-pool resource emphasize the role of the atmosphere as a sink resource, a receptacle for gaseous and particulate industrial waste for which the polluter does not incur cost. The argument goes that because one polluter's activity lowers the potential for the atmosphere to act as a sink for the gaseous and particulate waste of others, the atmosphere is a subtractable resource (Soroos 1997). Though this is a seductive argument, atmospheric capacity to absorb pollution is not truly a subtractable resource like a fishery, an oil reservoir, or Garrett Hardin's common pasture. Depletion of atmospheric absorptive capacity is reflected not in resource scarcity and consequent price increases (unless a permit system has been implemented and is effective) but rather in its negative impacts on other resources and quality of life.

The atmosphere is more accurately considered a public good (e.g., Heal 2000; Barrett 2000) and atmospheric degradation a problem of unaccounted externalities (Buck 1998). If one looks at past threats to atmospheric integrity such as stratospheric ozone depletion, regional air pollution, and GHG-induced warming, one sees that all of the major anthropogenic threats have been to atmospheric public goods rather than to atmospheric common-pool resources.

Technically, however, neither designation (public good nor common-pool resource) is adequate by itself because the atmosphere is composed of both subtractable and nonsubtractable resources and therefore has elements of both a common-pool resource and a public good. The space that the atmosphere occupies and the biologically important gases of which it is composed (primarily oxygen for animal respiration, carbon dioxide for plant photosynthesis, and nitrogen plants and animals require to build proteins and nucleic acids) are largely subtractable.[3] However, the services that the atmosphere provides (such as air purification, water purification, water transport, maintenance of Earth's radiative balance, and shielding of the biosphere from both harmful ultraviolet [UV] radiation and meteor impacts) are generally nonsubtractable.

Regardless of how we define the atmosphere's resource type, the atmosphere is subject to a tragedy of the commons in that unregulated individual activities will degrade both common-pool resources and public goods. Current population and technological trends threaten global atmospheric integrity and will do so increasingly in the future. This means that the international community is left with little alternative but to develop the laws and institutions necessary to deal effectively with these threats in a cooperative fashion. To determine the most effective way to do this, it is instructive to examine past international atmospheric protocols[4] and regimes.[5] The successes and failures of these past attempts to address global atmospheric threats illustrate what is likely to be required of commons institutions charged with maintaining the health of the global atmosphere.

Case Studies in Managing the Atmospheric Commons

In the following section, we present three specific cases in which threats to the atmosphere have been addressed by international regulatory and scientific efforts. These case studies—stratospheric ozone depletion, long-range transboundary air pollution, and greenhouse gases—are particularly well-chronicled, high-profile atmospheric commons issues, and they demonstrate the wide range of challenges facing regulators in their attempts to deal with regional and global atmospheric threats.

The Stratospheric Ozone Problem

Stratospheric ozone[6] (O_3) shields the biosphere from the sun's carcinogenic and mutagenic UV radiation. By producing CFCs and other ozone-depleting chemicals, humans have diminished the ozone layer's capacity to serve its pro-

---

Box 10.2. Chlorofluorocarbons and Stratospheric Ozone

Before they were outlawed by the Montreal Protocol, chlorofluorocarbons (CFCs) were widely used in homes and businesses as refrigerants, solvents, aerosol propellants, fire retardants, and cleaning agents. Over time, it became clear that CFCs were responsible for the breakdown of stratospheric ozone (O_3) because they were a source of chlorine free radicals, which could convert O_3 to O_2 via the following reaction sequence:

$Cl + O_3 \rightarrow ClO + O_2$ (chlorine and ozone produce chloride oxide and oxygen)

$ClO + O \rightarrow Cl + O_2$ (chloride oxide and free oxygen produce chlorine and oxygen)

$ClO + O_3 \rightarrow ClO_2 + O_2$ (chloride oxide and ozone produce chlorine dioxide and oxygen) (NOAA 1991)

Via this mechanism, a single chlorine atom can destroy more than 100,000 O_3 molecules.[1] Because CFCs are stable, inert molecules, they generally have an atmospheric lifetime on the order of decades to centuries. Other halogen radicals such as fluoride and bromide ions can initiate a similar reaction sequence. There is no natural source of CFCs.

[1] For more detailed discussion of the mechanism whereby chlorine, fluorine, and bromine compounds can break down stratospheric ozone, see chapter 4 of National Oceanic and Atmospheric Administration 1991, *Scientific Assessment of Ozone Depletion: 1991*. World Meteorological Organization Global Ozone Research and Monitoring Project, Report no. 25.

tective function (box 10.2). In the 1980s, evidence from ground-based Dobson meters in Antarctica and images from the Total Ozone Mapping System (TOMS) satellite indicated that ozone concentrations above the South Pole were declining by 50% during the Southern Hemisphere spring and that ozone thickness had decreased significantly (~13–20%; Makhijani et al. 1995) over northern temperate latitudes and the Arctic as well (NOAA 1991).

The rise in surface levels of UV radiation accompanying ozone depletion has had and will continue to have important damaging effects on human health and the function of the biosphere (Albritton et al. 1992). Scientists have estimated a 0.5% increase in cataract occurrence and a 2% increase in non-melanoma skin cancer for each 1% decrease in stratospheric ozone (Longstreth 1995). Increased UV can also fundamentally alter ecosystems by harming certain organisms more than others or by decreasing overall ecosystem productivity. For example, scientists have attributed an observed 6–12% decrease in southern ocean phytoplankton production to increased levels of UV radiation (Smith et al. 1992), and have blamed increased UV radiation for a global decline of amphibians (Licht and Grant 1997), although this link is still far from certain.

Although stratospheric ozone depletion was first reported in the 1980s, predictions and debate about it stemmed from the previous decade. In 1974, Mario Molina and F. Sherwood Rowland proposed a mechanism whereby chlorine and fluorine ions from CFCs could catalyze the breakdown of stratospheric ozone (Molina and Rowland 1974). International concern, fueled by scientific discovery, culminated in the 1985 Vienna Convention, the 1987 Montreal Protocol, and subsequent strengthening revisions (table 10.2). Although it was initially hotly contested, the Montreal Protocol was eventually ratified by 155 countries. Ratifying developed nations agreed to eliminate halon consumption entirely by 1994 and CFC consumption by 1996. Developing countries were given a grace period but must complete their phaseouts by 2010.

The path to a ban on ozone-depleting chemicals has been a complex one. Before it became apparent that CFCs were responsible for the breakdown of stratospheric ozone they were ubiquitous in the industrialized world. So when CFCs were implicated as agents of stratospheric ozone depletion, industry argued that a move away from them would be a prohibitively costly and extremely slow process. In the end, however, industry was prompted by public pressure to develop alternatives and did so faster and more easily than anyone had imagined possible (Soroos 1997).

The international community's response to the global threat of stratospheric ozone depletion has been widely heralded as one of the great success stories in international atmospheric policy efforts (e.g., Buck 1998; Soroos 1997; Vogler 1995). Indeed, emissions reductions negotiated at the Montreal Protocol and subsequent conventions were substantial, leading some to proj-

Table 10.2. Chronology of Major Atmospheric Treaties.

Issue	Treaty
Long-range Transboundary Air Pollution (LRTAP)	1979—LRTAP Convention
	1985—Sulfur Protocol
	1988—Nitrogen Protocol
	1991—VOC Protocol
	1994—Revised Sulfur Protocol
Stratospheric ozone depletion	1985—Convention for the Protection of the Ozone Layer
	1987—Montreal Protocol
	1990—London Amendments
	1992—Copenhagen Amendments
	1995—Vienna Amendments
Climate change	1992—Rio Framework Convention on Climate Change
	1995—Conference of Parties 1 (Berlin Mandate)
	1996—Conference of Parties 2 (Geneva)
	1997—Conference of Parties 3 (Kyoto Protocol)
	1998—Conference of Parties 4 (Buenos Aires)

ect a "healing" of the ozone hole as early as 2050 (NOAA 1991). With stratospheric ozone, a public good (protection from UV radiation) was threatened by individual actions (the production and use of CFCs). In this case the international community was able to organize effectively to address the global threat. According to Richard Benedick, the chief U.S. negotiator of the Montreal Protocol (Benedick 1991), the treaty succeeded because of (1) the participation of science and scientists; (2) a well-informed public; (3) the activities of the United Nations Environment Programme (UNEP), a multilateral institution; (4) individual nations' policies and leadership (in this case, the United States, far and away the largest producer and consumer of CFCs, was the first to take regulatory action while Canada, Norway, West Germany, and many others also played major roles); (5) participation of industry and citizen groups (often on opposing sides[7]); and finally (6) the fact that the protocol was designed as a flexible, dynamic instrument, which could be adapted as information improved, as it was in the treaties following the Montreal Protocol.

Despite the widespread good feeling surrounding the regime of policies addressing stratospheric ozone depletion, there is still reason for concern regarding stratospheric ozone. The long residence time of CFCs in the atmosphere (more than fifty years in many cases [IPCC 1990]) and the fact that it takes several years for CFCs to get into the stratosphere once they are emitted mean that stratospheric ozone levels will continue to decline before the ozone layer begins to repair itself (*Chem. & Eng. News* 1994). Furthermore, an unexpectedly rapid rise in CFC use by developing countries (where CFCs are still legal) and illegal trade between these countries and the developed world will delay that process (Kelner 1998). It has also recently been discovered that unregulated, ozone-depleting compounds such as halon-1202 and other bromine-containing compounds are increasing their atmospheric concentrations by up to 17% per year ("We Missed That One" 1998).

The stratospheric ozone regime is an example of an international attempt to protect a global public good from destruction by individual local actions. Although there is still reason for concern and vigilance, this regime has been quite successful in attaining its objectives, namely a substantial reduction of ozone-depleting substances.

Long-Range Transboundary Air Pollution

Long-range transboundary air pollution (LRTAP) provides another example of a threat to an atmospheric public good that has been addressed by the international community. *LRTAP* is an umbrella term referring to the suite of regionally important pollutants (box 10.3) that have damaged human health, degraded natural ecosystems, corroded human-made structures, contributed to smog, and caused the formation of harmful tropospheric ozone[8] (Mohnen 1988). These impacts have been particularly severe in industrialized regions of Europe, North America, and East Asia.

One impact of LRTAP emissions, acid rain, has caused widespread forest decline and fish death in Europe and North America (Mohnen 1988). Acid rain has also caused skin and eye irritation around urban areas where emissions of acid precursors are high (Ayers 1991). In addition to acidifying ecosystems, the nitrogen component of LRTAP can change ecosystem function via nitrogen fertilization. This nitrogen enrichment can harm ecosystems by altering key ecosystem processes and reducing biodiversity (Aber et al. 1989, 1998; Tilman 1993).

Formed as a by-product of LRTAP emissions, tropospheric (ground-level) ozone can be as harmful as acid deposition. In addition to harming human health by irritating the respiratory tract and impairing lung function, tropospheric ozone also damages plants by damaging the photosynthetic apparatus, and experts have estimated that ozone damage could decrease productivity in up to 35% of global cereal crops (Friedman et al. 1988; Chameides et al. 1994). The Office of Technology Assessment (OTA) has estimated that high ozone levels cost the United States $1–5 billion in annual crop losses and human health problems (Freidman et al. 1988). Tropospheric ozone and sulfate aerosols, both major components of smog, also reduce air clarity, thereby obstructing views. The severity of this problem has caused the U.S. National Park Service and other government agen-

---

Box 10.3 Long-Range Transboundary Air Pollution, Acid Deposition, and Tropospheric Ozone

Long-range transboundary (LRTAP) results primarily from intensive fossil-fuel use and consists of the suite of sulfur oxides (SO_x), nitrogen oxides (NO_x), and volatile organic compounds (VOCs) that are collectively responsible for the formation of acid rain and tropospheric ozone. LRTAP substances generally have atmospheric residence times such that they can be dispersed regionally but do not mix with the entire global atmosphere.

The precursors to acid deposition are primarily sulfur dioxide (SO_2) and nitrogen oxides (NO_x). Both are products of fossil-fuel combustion and both are oxidized in the atmosphere to sulfuric acid (H_2SO_4) and nitric acid (HNO_3). These strong acids then fall to Earth, with important, sometimes devastating effects on the ecosystems into which they fall. Acid deposition can acidify systems, causing lakes with low buffering capacity to become too acidic to support fish and causing soils to lose important plant nutrients and leach poisonous aluminum into freshwater ecosystems. Deposition of nitric acid can inadvertently fertilize natural systems, thereby altering species composition, ecosystem structure, and ecosystem function. Through corrosion, acid deposition has also irreparably damaged countless cultural relics and monuments.

Whereas ozone in the stratosphere (box 10.1) helps protect organisms from harmful ultraviolet radiation, ozone that occurs in the troposphere, the lowest layer of atmosphere, can be detrimental. Tropospheric ozone is a major component of photochemical smog and is formed when NO_x from fuel combustion reacts with VOCs from fossil fuel, as well as other anthropogenic and natural sources, in the presence of ultraviolet radiation at high temperature: $VOC + NO_x \rightarrow O_3$.

---

cies to launch a major effort to save views of national parks by reducing tropospheric aerosols and ozone.

Although there were individual cases of LRTAP pollution as early as the end of the nineteenth century,[9] LRTAP was not truly addressed by the international community until the 1979 Geneva LRTAP convention. Spurred by the disappearance of fish from Scandinavian lakes, forest death in Central Europe, and monitoring data showing transboundary transport of nitrogen and sulfur oxides, this convention established the institutions to deal with acid deposition, provided for technical cooperation and monitoring, and helped develop the political will to reduce sulfur oxides (SO_x), nitrogen oxides (NO_x), and volatile organic compound (VOC) emissions via subsequent protocols (see table 10.2).

The 1985 Sulfur Protocol called for 30% or greater reductions in SO_2 emissions, and the 1988 Nitrogen Protocol called for a freeze in NO_x emissions at 1987 levels. In addition to the Sulfur and Nitrogen Protocols, there was also a protocol to reduce VOCs (for importance of VOCs, see box 10.3). The 1991 VOC Protocol was unique in allowing signing nations to choose to reduce emissions by 30% either for their whole territories or only in designated Tropospheric Ozone Management Areas (TOMAs), regions of a country that contribute significantly to tropospheric ozone in another nation.

As the initial Sulfur and Nitrogen Protocols were ratified and implemented, it became clear that across-the-board emissions reductions were not the most efficient or effective method to prevent the LRTAP-induced damage. The initial Sulfur and Nitrogen Protocols did not account for the fact that certain areas and ecosystems are more sensitive to LRTAP deposition than others (Hornung and Skeffington 1993). Incorporation of this fact into regulatory efforts caused policy efforts to shift from all-inclusive reductions to the development and implementation of an effects-based approach. The "critical loads"[10] concept was incorporated into the 1994 Revised Sulfur Protocol. A Revised Nitrogen Protocol, which will use a similar effects-based approach, is currently in preparation.

Although the bulk of negotiation regarding LRTAP has occurred in Europe, there is also a significant LRTAP problem in industrialized regions of North America. The United States was a participant in the Economic Commission for Europe (ECE) LRTAP negotiations but did not actually ratify any of the LRTAP protocols. The United States and Canada have chosen instead to address their LRTAP problems with weak bilateral agreements (Soroos 1997). Most of the progress that has been made on the North American LRTAP issue has resulted from domestic programs within the United States and Canada rather than from international cooperation.

With help from fortuitous developments such as the discovery of natural gas reserves in the North Sea, an occurrence that reduced European dependence on sulfur-rich coal, the LRTAP regime has been largely successful in accomplishing many of its sulfur-reduction goals (Soroos 1997). Several European countries initially pledged to reduce SO_2 emissions by 30% in the 1985 Sulfur Protocol but ended up reducing their emissions by as much as 80%. This is reflected in the 37% overall reduction in SO_2 emissions for the European region between 1985 and 1994 (*Acid News* 1994). Reduction of nitrogen oxide emissions, the other major component of acid deposition, has been less successful, with many ratifying countries failing to meet their emission-reduction goals. The success or failure of the VOC Protocol remains to be seen.

The LRTAP regime has been less successful than the stratospheric ozone regime in addressing its atmospheric threat. Although LRTAP negotiations have succeeded in reducing LRTAP below business–as–usual projections, acid–ification remains a problem in Europe and in North America, and nitrogen deposition remains a significant threat to ecosystem health in these regions. With increasing energy needs, fossil-fuel consumption, and biomass burning, LRTAP is also rapidly becoming a problem in East Asia (Galloway et al. 1987; Ayers 1991) and is likely to become a problem throughout much of the developing world.

Despite the LRTAP regime's shortcomings, it has still been useful. In addition to instituting new strategies for reducing air pollution such as flat percentage reductions for all countries involved (subsequently incorporated into efforts to protect the ozone layer), the LRTAP regime has also served as incubator for more sophisticated, cost-effective, and effects-based approaches to regulating air pollution such as the concept of critical loads and the TOMA option in the VOC Protocol. The LRTAP regime has also internationalized air quality monitoring and scientific research efforts, an advance that will facilitate future efforts to address international atmospheric threats.

In attempting to address the LRTAP issue, the international community has tried to maintain air quality, a regional public good. The LRTAP regime has been less successful in achieving its goals than the stratospheric ozone regime but has still made progress toward changing harmful practices.

Greenhouse Gases

In addition to addressing stratospheric ozone depletion and LRTAP, the international community has begun to deal with GHG emissions. One of the major common goods that the atmosphere provides is the maintenance of Earth's radiative balance. According to some estimates, if it were not for the atmosphere and, more specifically, the greenhouse gases it contains, Earth's surface would be 33°C colder on average, uninhabitable by life as we know it (Alexander et al. 1997). Conversely, increases in atmospheric GHG concentrations can significantly warm Earth's lower atmosphere above present levels, with potentially devastating effects. Human activities such as fossil-fuel burning, biomass burning, and chemical fertilizer application currently contribute to observed increases in global atmospheric GHG concentrations (box 10.4).

The Intergovernmental Panel on Climate Change (IPCC), a consortium of more than 2,500 scientists organized by UNEP, states that "the balance of evidence suggests a discernible human influence on global climate" (IPCC 1996). Also according to the IPCC, GHG emissions have increased global average temperatures by about 1°F during the past century, a temperature change faster than any observed in the last 10,000 years, and will continue to alter climate further as concentrations continue to increase (IPCC 1990).

The IPCC also warns that likely outcomes of GHG-induced climate

Box 10.4 Greenhouse Gases and the Greenhouse Effect

Certain gases absorb and reradiate infrared radiation, delaying its journey from Earth's surface to space, thereby warming Earth's surface and lower atmosphere. Radioactively important gases include carbon dioxide (CO_2), methane (CH_4), nitrous oxide (N_2O), water vapor, and CFCs, among others.

Most of these gases have natural origins, but it is clear that humans have greatly increased their atmospheric concentrations in the past century. CO_2, a product of fossil-fuel combustion, biomass burning, and land-use change, has increased more than 30% since the beginning of the Industrial Revolution. Current and projected CO_2 concentrations are significantly higher than any observed over the past 160,000 years. Atmospheric concentrations of methane, which emanates from flooded agricultural fields, have increased by more than 100% since the Industrial Revolution. Nitrous oxide sources include tropical land clearance, fossil-fuel combustion, and fertilization of agricultural fields (Matson and Vitousek 1990). Nitrous oxide concentrations have increased by more than 15% since the preindustrial era and are increasing faster now than ever before (IPCC 1990). Although CFCs have been banned by the Montreal Protocol, they have a long atmospheric residence time (decades to centuries) and therefore will continue to exert an influence on the global climate for decades to centuries to come.

change include a projected increase in global average temperature of 1.8–6.3°F, a sea-level rise of 15–90 cm by the year 2100, increased frequency of floods and droughts, and more extreme temperatures. Such changes are likely to affect human health, agricultural productivity, forest distribution and composition, water availability, and ecosystem health and function and inundate important coastal areas and islands (IPCC 1996). Best estimates place the economic impact of GHG-induced climate change at anywhere from slight economic benefit to trillion–dollar losses (Alexander et al. 1997). The Clinton administration has estimated that greenhouse warming will cost the United States approximately 1.1% of annual U.S. GDP, or $89 billion per year in 1998 dollars (Clinton Administration 1998). The IPCC states that "with the growth in atmospheric concentration of greenhouse gases, interference with the climate system will grow in magnitude, and the likelihood of adverse impacts from climate change that could be judged dangerous will become greater" (IPCC 1996).

With the potentially devastating impacts of greenhouse warming in mind, the global community has begun to address the issue of climate change through a series of international conventions. These conventions began in earnest with the 1992 Rio Framework Convention on Climate Change (FCCC) and have culminated most recently in the 1998 Buenos Aires Conference of Parties. In the 1997 Kyoto Protocol (which as of January 13, 2000, has been signed by eighty-four countries but ratified by only twenty-two), developed nations agree to reduce their total GHG emissions (a package of six gases) to 5–8% below 1990 levels by the 2008–2012 budgetary cycle. Although this appears to be a substantial reduction, it is virtually meaningless in the long term without the participation of developing countries. It is essential that developing nations (now largely uncommitted to GHG reductions) participate meaningfully because if present trends continue, developing-nation emissions increases will shortly swamp out emissions reductions proposed by developed nations.

To lower the cost of compliance, the Kyoto Protocol provides what has been dubbed "when, what, and where flexibility." "When" flexibility is evident in the multiyear commitment period and the allowance for "banking" emissions reductions. "What" flexibility is provided by the inclusion of multiple gases in the protocol and the inclusion of sinks such as aforestation that remove carbon from the atmosphere. And "where" flexibility is embodied by emissions trading and joint implementation among countries that take on binding targets (Clinton Administration 1998). A "clean development mechanism," by which developing nations receive credit for developing with reduced GHG emissions, has also been included in the most recent version of the climate-change treaty (COP 4 Summary 1998).

The Kyoto Protocol and Buenos Aires agreement have brought climate-change issues to the attention of policymakers and the public, but they are only first steps. Participating nations have yet to ratify the treaty, and once they do, compliance is not assured. One major shortcoming of the current treaty is that it does not contain binding targets for GHG emissions in developing nations. This omission seriously lowers the potential for future decreases in GHG emissions and, because the U.S. Senate has stipulated that it will not ratify a treaty without such binding commitments, significantly reduces the probability of meaningful U.S. participation. As the United States is responsible for a disproportionately large percentage of global CO_2 emissions, it is essential that the United States ratify the Kyoto Protocol if it is to succeed.

Although these conditions do not bode well, there are reasons to hope that the GHG regime will succeed in reducing GHG emissions. Strong European leadership and international posturing indicate that certain nations are already committed to reducing GHG emissions. These leader nations may speed GHG-emission reductions by spurring the development of GHG-reducing technology (much as DuPont developed CFC alternatives when pressed by U.S. domestic policies in the 1980s). The development of this technology could substantially lower the cost of emission reductions, and leapfrogging technology to developing nations could help the rest of the world reduce emissions more quickly than would otherwise be possible.

The maintenance of Earth's radiative balance is an atmospheric public good that is endangered by human emissions of GHGs. Because the FCCC has set a research and policy agenda and subsequent international negotiation has determined emission-reduction goals, the success of international efforts to address GHG-induced climate change now depends primarily on the effectiveness of implementation.

Managing the Atmospheric Commons: Options and Obstacles

Drawing on the case studies of stratospheric ozone, LRTAP, and GHG emissions as well as commons theory, we now can examine several options for managing the atmospheric commons. Three approaches that have been proposed for managing commons resources are third-party regulation, privatization, and self-regulation. Third-party regulation is not feasible in the case of global or regional atmospheric threats because there are no disinterested third parties. Even if these parties existed, the scarcity and uneven distribution of resources for monitoring and enforcement of command-and-control legislation render such an approach ineffective.[11]

Another potential remedy to a tragedy of the atmospheric commons would be to privatize the atmosphere, or to make each potential polluter responsible for his or her own parcel of atmosphere. Unfortunately, such an attempt to internalize externalities is not likely to work because of the atmosphere's mobility and rapid mixing rate (box 10.1). These conditions make harmful emissions difficult to trace, thereby complicating the enforcement of ownership and responsibility. This is an important obstacle for international emissions trading, which has been proposed as a solution to LRTAP and GHG emissions.

Given that command-and-control regulation and privatization are largely infeasible, the only type of approach with a reasonable chance for success is one where local concern supports the development and maintenance of regional or global commons institutions. Although this is the best option available, there are several reasons that this approach will be difficult to employ effectively.

One difficulty is the "free-rider" problem, wherein commons members are tempted to cheat on their obligations in order to reap benefits provided by the restraint of others and avoid costs of regulatory compliance. The current illegal trade in freon between Mexico and the United States by the so-called *frio banditos* is a good example of free-riding in action. The free-rider problem is not as paralyzing as it might seem, however. Free-riding nations must interact broadly and repeatedly with other commons members in a context that includes the potential for economic and diplomatic sanctions. This means that free-riding is not as tempting as it is in the typically considered Prisoner's Dilemma games on which conventional commons theory is often based (see Heal in press).

Global atmospheric regulations must be implemented, monitored, and enforced at the local level, and doing all this requires voluntary local compliance. This means that factors dampening local concern for atmospheric quality constitute significant obstacles to successful atmospheric management. Such factors include the stealth of atmospheric threats and lack of public understanding of relevant atmospheric processes. Experience with stratospheric ozone, LRTAP, and greenhouse warming shows that changes in atmospheric quality are often gradual and observable only by scientists with special equipment, meaning that successful communication between the scientific community, policymakers, and the public is absolutely essential to the sound management of the atmospheric commons.[12] In addition, the general public's lack of awareness and understanding of atmospheric processes reduces concern for the atmosphere directly and leaves the public vulnerable to manipulation by special-interest propaganda (e.g., Robinson et al. 1998). Both of these obstacles can be overcome by increased investment in public environmental and science education.

Even if local concern is sufficient to motivate public action, other factors such as unexpected atmospheric complexity or a breakdown in negotiations at the international level can confound regulatory efforts. One case in which insufficient understanding has inhibited effective policy implementation is that of tropospheric ozone. Despite massive efforts to reduce tropospheric ozone, many urban areas still do not meet U.S. EPA standards because, until recently, regulating agencies have been regulating the wrong thing. The effort to reduce VOCs has been substantial (especially VOCs from point sources), but the production of ozone is regulated in many areas by NO_x, not VOCs (box 10.3). Increasingly, and correctly, the focus is turning to the coregulation of VOC and NO_x emissions from vehicles, but the fact that the source of tropospheric ozone was misunderstood for so long showcases the complexity of the atmosphere and demonstrates the need for continuing atmospheric research as well as flexible management schemes.

International diplomatic breakdowns as well as scientific misunderstanding or disagreement can also prevent effective implementation of atmospheric regulation. Although nations have succeeded in developing some trust and reciprocity via the measured success of the ozone and LRTAP regimes, these relationships are complicated by the differential impacts of atmospheric degradation on different nations. With LRTAP, stratospheric ozone, and greenhouse warming, local impacts affect different nations to differing degrees. LRTAP emissions from heavily emitting nations have a disproportionate impact on downwind nations that don't produce as much LRTAP. In the case of stratospheric ozone depletion, resultant impacts are greatest in polar regions and northern temperate latitudes. In the case of global warming, projected sea-level rise is likely to inundate certain small island states, whereas countries in northern temperate latitudes may well experience increased rates of agricultural productivity as a result of warming and increased CO_2 concentrations (IPCC 1996). Admittedly, differential impacts of atmospheric degradation may open opportunities for profitable trade, but net effects are likely to be negative. Differing cultural and legal systems can also complicate progress toward a common understanding and cooperation.

Historic international conflict can amplify the difficulties arising from differential impacts and thereby prevent international cooperation to address threats to atmospheric quality and function. An example of this is the LRTAP negotiation currently under way in East Asia, where historical conflicts between pollution producers (in this case primarily mainland China) and pollution recipients (e.g., Japan, Korea, and Taiwan) have complicated international negotiations and cooperation to reduce transboundary pollution (Arndt and Charmichael 1995).

Moreover, even if educational efforts succeed in generating high levels of local concern, local responses may be adaptive rather than preventive in nature. For example, people might respond to increased climate variability with higher dams and increased GHG-induced temperatures with heat-resistant crops or beach tourism in Newfoundland. Unfortunately, although this type of local response would decrease short-term loss, it would do little to assuage long-term vulnerability to atmospheric changes.

The highly mobile nature of the atmosphere, the breadth and diversity of atmospheric uses and users, the stealth and complexity of atmospheric threats, and the resultant lack of public concern, as well as gaps in scientific understanding and international diplomatic tensions, are all obstacles that must be addressed if the atmosphere is to be protected against future threats to its goods and services. Given these obstacles, managing the global atmosphere is a daunting prospect. And yet, in order to protect the atmosphere for future generations it will be necessary to create a framework for preservation of atmospheric integrity. Any successful future attempt to maintain the health of the global atmosphere will require that regulators address the following issues.

First, local activities can have regional and global consequences, so monitoring, research, synthesis, and regulation must be regional or global, not local, in scope. Conversely, regulation must take local norms and customs into consideration and be implemented at the local scale in order to be effective. Encouragement of local participation in the decision-making process, at least regarding methods of goal attainment, can be instrumental in ensuring eventual regulatory success. Increased investment in environmental education and communication of scientific results to the broader community can also help.

Second, current activities will have lasting effects because of the durable nature of anthropogenic pollutants, and certain threats are more pressing than others. These conditions mean that the time dimension of particular atmospheric threats must be taken into account in the regulatory process. Imminent problems should be addressed swiftly, but if there is time to warn the private sector, as there was with stratospheric ozone, then there should be an effort to do so. Framework conventions are particularly helpful in this regard.

Finally, the complexity of the atmosphere and our incomplete understanding of atmospheric processes must be taken into account in the regulatory process. Atmospheric problems are often more complicated than people originally think, and therefore the incorporation of research and flexibility into regulatory efforts is an important precursor to regulatory success.

Acknowledgments

Thanks to Geoff Heal for insightful conversation, to the National Science Foundation for financial support of Harrison, and to Chris Field, Joanna Burger, and an anonymous reviewer for helpful comments on this manuscript.

Notes

1. Here *resource* is defined as "anything that is used to meet the needs of an organism" (Buck 1998).
2. The atmosphere's legal property status is generally considered *res nullis* (open access), meaning that it is difficult to exclude users from the atmosphere and that the atmosphere can therefore usually be treated as a common-pool resource or a public good (table 10.1). However, under certain circumstances (e.g. when the space rather than the substance or function of the atmosphere is considered, or when emissions caps are enforced), the atmosphere is more correctly treated as *res publica* (public property), and under those circumstances it may function as a toll good (table 10.1).
3. However, feedback interactions between the atmosphere and biosphere complicate this interaction.
4. A protocol is a binding, written agreement between two or more nations, usually an addition to an existing treaty and often specifying technical standards for the treaty. Protocols must be ratified separately. They may also be called treaties or conventions.
5. A regime is a set of implicit or explicit principles, norms, rules, and decision-making procedures around which actors' expectations converge in a given area of international relations. *Principles* are beliefs of fact, causation, and rectitude. *Norms* are standards of behavior defined in terms of rights and obligations. *Rules* are spe-

cific prescriptions or proscriptions for action. *Decision-making procedures* are prevailing practices for making and implementing collective choice (Krasner 1983, quoted in Vogler 1995).

6. The stratosphere, the layer of atmosphere between 10 and 50 km above Earth's surface, contains about 90% of atmospheric ozone.

7. Although the chemical industry initially fought CFC-reducing legislation, in 1986 DuPont Chemical, the company responsible for about 50% of U.S. CFC production, saw an opportunity to market CFC substitutes and shifted its position regarding CFC regulation (Soroos 1997; Benedick 1991). This shift was instrumental in the success of the stratospheric ozone regime.

8. Unlike stratospheric ozone, which occurs several kilometers above Earth's surface and serves a vital function by protecting us from the sun's harmful ultraviolet radiation, tropospheric ozone occurs at ground level and is harmful both to humans and the rest of the biosphere.

9. Built in Trail, British Columbia, in 1896, the Trail Lead and Zinc Smelter produced a plume of pollution that reached south over the U.S.–Canadian border into Washington state, where it damaged local orchards. After decades of negotiation, an international panel eventually ruled that "no state has the right to use or permit the use of its territory in such a manner as to cause injury by fumes in or to the territory of another or the properties or persons therein, when the case is of serious consequence and the injury is established by clear and convincing evidence."

10. A critical load is "the maximum deposition of a given compound which will not cause long-term, harmful effects on ecosystem structure and function, according to present knowledge" (Hornung and Skeffington 1993).

11. The lack of resources for atmospheric management is somewhat surprising considering that the cost of replacement for atmospheric goods and services would be astronomically high. The amount of attention, money, and time currently devoted to maintaining this vital resource is disproportionately low.

12. When earth-system scientists have made discoveries, they have been quite good at communicating their understanding to both the public and the policy community. In fact without the integral participation of scientists, the stratospheric ozone, LRTAP, and GHG regimes would not be nearly as successful. The seeds for future research and monitoring efforts exist in such bodies as the IPCC, LRTAP's Cooperative Program for the Monitoring and Evaluation of the Long-Range Transmission of Air Pollution in Europe (EMEP), the World Meteorological Organization's (WMO's) Background Air Pollution Monitoring Network (BAPMoN), and the International Geosphere–Biosphere Program (IGBP). These and other monitoring networks should be capitalized on by future attempts to address atmospheric threats.

References

Aber, J., W. McDowell, K. Nadelhoffer, A. Magill, G. Berntson, M. Kamakea, S. McNulty, W. Currie, L. Rustad, and I. Fernandez. 1998. "Nitrogen Saturation in Temperate Forest Ecosystems: Hypotheses Revisited." *Bioscience* 48 (11): 921–34.

Aber, J., J. Nadelhoffer, P. Steudler, and J. Melillo. 1989. "Nitrogen Saturation in Northern Forest Ecosystems: Hypotheses and Implications." *Bioscience* 39, 378–86.

Acid News, October 1994, 10–11.

Albritton, D. L., R. Monastersky, J. Eddy, J. M. Hall, and E. Shea. 1992. *Reports to the Nation on Our Changing Planet: Our Ozone Shield.* Fall 1992, no. 2. University Corporation for Atmospheric Research and the National Oceanic and Atmospheric Administration.

Alexander, S. E., S. H. Schneider, and K. Lagerquist. 1997. "The Interaction of Climate and Life." In *Nature's Services: Societal Dependence on Natural Ecosystems,* edited by Gretchen Daily. Washington DC: Island Press.

Anthes, Richard A. 1992. *Meteorology.* 6th ed. New York: Macmillan.

Arndt, R. L., and G. R. Carmichael. 1995. "Long-Range Transport and Deposition of Sulfur in Asia." *Water, Air and Soil Pollution* 85:2283–88.

Ayers, G. P. 1991. "Atmospheric Acidification in the Asian Region." *Environmental Monitoring and Assessment* 19:225–50.

Barrett, S. 2000. "Montreal v. Kyoto: International Cooperation and the Global Environment." In *Global Public Goods: International Cooperation in the 21st Century.* Oxford: Oxford University Press. In press.

Benedick, R. E. 1991. *Ozone Diplomacy: New Directions in Safeguarding the Planet.* Cambridge, MA: Harvard University Press.

Buck, S. J. 1998. *The Global Commons, an Introduction.* Washington, DC: Island Press.

Chameides, W. L., P. S. Kasibhatla, J. Yienger, and H. Levy II. 1994. "Growth of Continental-Scale Metro-Agroplexes, Regional Ozone Pollution and World Food Production." *Science* 264:74–77.

Chemical & Engineering News, September 11, 1994, 5.

Conference of Parties 4 (COP4). "Preliminary Version of COP 4 Decisions and Resolutions." November 27, 1998. Available at official COP4 Web site (http://www.cop4.org/).

Duxbury, J. M. 1994. "The Significance of Agricultural Sources of Greenhouse Gases." *Fertilizer Research* 38 (2): 151–63.

Freidman, R. M, J. M. Milford, R. Rapoport, N. Szabo, K. Harrison, S. Van Aller, and R. W. Niblock. 1988. "Urban Ozone and the Clean Air Act: Problems and Proposals for Change." Washington, DC: U.S. Congress, Office of Technology Assessment (OTA), Oceans and Environment Program.

Galloway, J. N., D. W. Zhao, J. L. Xiong, and G. E. Likens. 1987. "Acid Rain: China, United States, and a Remote Area." *Science* 236 (4808): 1559–62.

Hardin, G. 1968. "The Tragedy of the Commons." *Science* 162:1243–48.

Heal, G. 2000. "Environmental Public Goods." In *Global Public Goods: A New Approach to International Cooperation.* In press.

Hornung, M., and R. A. Skeffington. 1993. Introduction in *Critical Loads: Concept and Application.* London: HMSO.

Intergovernmental Panel on Climate Change (IPCC). 1990. "Policymakers' Summary of the Potential Impacts of Climate Change: Report from Working Group II to IPCC." Cambridge, England: Cambridge University Press.

———. 1994. "Radiative Forcing of Climate Change: The 1994 Report of the

Scientific Assessment Working Group of IPCC: Summary for Policymakers."
Cambridge, England: Cambridge University Press.

———. 1996. "Climate Change 1995." In *Impacts, Adaptations, and Mitigation of Climate Change: Scientific-Technical Analysis: Contribution of Working Group II to the Second Assessment Report of the Intergovernmental Panel on Climate Change,* edited by R. T. Watson, M. C. Zinyowere, and R. H. Moss. Cambridge, England: Cambridge University Press.

Keller, M., D. J. Jacob, S. C. Wofsy, and R. C. Harriss. 1991. "Effects of Tropical Deforestation on Global and Regional Atmospheric Chemistry." *Climatic Change* 19 (1–2):139–58.

Kelner, T. 1998. "Cool Operators." *The Sciences* (September/October):19–23.

"Kyoto Protocol and the President's Policies to Address Climate Change." *Administration Economic Analysis* (July 1998).

Licht, L. E., and K. P. Grant. 1997. "The Effects of Ultraviolet-Radiation on the Biology of Amphibians." *American Zoologist* 37 (2):137–45.

Longstreth, J. D., F. R. Degruijl, M. L. Kripke, Y. Takizawa, and J. C. Vanderleun. 1995. "Effects of Increased Solar Ultraviolet-Radiation on Human Health." *Ambio* 24 (3):153–65.

Makhijani, A., and K. Gurney. 1995. *Mending the Ozone Hole: Science, Technology, and Policy.* Cambridge, MA: MIT Press.

Matson, P. A., and P. M. Vitousek. 1990. "Ecosystem Approach to a Global Nitrous Oxide Budget." *Bioscience* 40 (9):667–72.

McGinnis, M., and E. Ostrom. 1992. "Institutional Analysis and Global Climate Change: Design Principles for Robust International Regimes." In *Global Climate Change: Social and Economic Research Issues.* Chicago: Midwest Consortium of International Security Studies and Argonne National Laboratory.

Mohnen, V. 1988. "The Challenge of Acid Rain." *Scientific American* 259:30–38.

Molina, M. J., and F. S. Rowland. 1974. "Stratospheric Sink for Chlorofluoromethanes: Chlorine Atom–Catalyzed Destruction of Ozone." *Nature* 249:810–12.

National Oceanic and Atmospheric Administration (NOAA). 1991. *Scientific Assessment of Ozone Depletion: 1991.* World Meteorological Organization Global Ozone Research and Monitoring Project, Report no. 25. Washington, DC.

Obrien, K. L. 1996. "Tropical Deforestation and Climate-Change." *Progress in Physical Geography* 20 (3):311–35.

Ostrom, E. "Reformulating the Commons." In *Protecting the Commons: A Framework for Resource Management in the Americas,* edited by J. Burger, E. Ostrom, R. B. Norgaard, D. Policansky and B. D. Goldstein. Washington, DC: Island Press.

Robinson, B. R., S. L. Baliunas, W. Soon, and Z. W. Robinson. 1998. *Environmental Effects of Increased Atmospheric Carbon Dioxide.* Cave Junction, OR: Oregon Institute of Science and Medicine.

Sanhueza, F. 1997. "Impact of Human Activity on NO Soil Fluxes." *Nutrient Cycling in Agroecosystems* 48 (1–2): 61–68.

Smith, R. C., B. B. Prezelin, K. S. Baker, R. R. Bidigare, N. P. Boucher, T. Coley, D. Karentz, S. MacIntyre, H. A. Matlick, D. Menzies, M. Ondrusek, and Z. Wan. 1992. "Ozone Depletion: Ultraviolet-Radiation and Phytoplankton Biology in Antarctic Waters." *Science* 255 (5047): 952–59.

Soroos, Marvin. 1997. *Endangered Atmosphere*. Columbia: University of South Carolina Press.

Tilman, D. 1993. "Species Richness of Experimental Productivity Gradients: How Important Is Colonization Limitation?" *Ecology* 74 (8):2179–91.

Vitousek, P., J. Aber, R. Howarth, G. Likens, P. Matson, D. Schindler, W. Schlesinger, and G. Tilman. 1997. "Human Alteration of the Global Nitrogen Cycle: Causes and Consequences." *Ecological Applications* 7 (3):737–50.

Vogler, John. 1995. *The Global Commons: A Regime Analysis*. Chichester, England: Wiley.

"We Missed That One." *New Scientist* (September 12, 1998).

Chapter 11

Arctic Contaminants and Human Health

JOHN P. MIDDAUGH

The Arctic has been viewed romantically as a harsh, desolate, and remote environment—a vast pristine area spared from the unsavory consequences of human technologic and industrial exploitations and achievements. During the past two decades, an increasing number of environmental investigations have documented that the Arctic has not been unscathed by global transportation of anthropogenic pollutants from mid-latitudes to the Arctic and episodes of local anthropogenic pollution (Stonehouse 1986; Molnia and Taylor 1994; Arctic Monitoring and Assessment Programme [AMAP] 1997, 1998; Rey and Stonehouse 1982). Reports of catastrophic environmental damage in the former Soviet Union have raised concerns because of the threat that river systems and atmospheric pathways may transport large quantities of human-made pollutants from Russia into the Arctic ("Proceedings of Study Group" 1995). Discovery of the widespread presence of heavy metals (mercury, cadmium), persistent organic hydrocarbons (polychlorinated biphenyls [PCBs], dioxins, pesticides), and radionuclides in the Arctic has been heavily felt. Even if direct toxic effects on humans appear to have been trivial, overall health impacts are not. People living in the Arctic are very concerned by these findings and are afraid for their health and for the future of their environment.

Monitoring human-made chemicals in the Arctic has provided a new, important opportunity to measure the extent of global pollution. Documentation of global contribution to Arctic pollution illustrates fundamental tensions inherent in commons issues. Oil and natural resource development provide great economic and health benefits but at the same time harm social and cultural institutions and values. Measurable improvements in overall health status of the Arctic population have been accompanied by new epidemics of alcohol abuse, domestic violence, suicide, and cancer (Middaugh

241

et al. 1991; Young 1994; Alaska Department of Health and Social Services 1994).

The presence of human-made chemicals throughout the Arctic challenges our principles of social and environmental justice. Because atmospheric transportation of pollutants crosses international boundaries, solutions are even more difficult and, of necessity, lie outside the Arctic. Identification of Arctic pollutants serves as one important sentinel indicator of pollution of the global commons. Protection of the global commons will require a broader understanding of Garrett Hardin's "recognition of necessity" (Hardin 1968). Hardin's concept of commons has enabled increased understanding of common-pool resources and forces acting on efforts to manage common-pool resources to ensure their sustainability. Ultimately, "the management of common-pool resources seems to function best where there are sanctions that everyone agrees to and that can be enforced and where the benefits of management are widely recognized" (Burger and Gochfeld 1998).

History of Arctic Contamination

Arctic experiences with resource exploitation and environmental pollution illustrate many of the principles enumerated by the "Tragedy of the Commons" and may provide insight into solutions involving sustainability of resources and principles of social justice. Beginning in the mid-1700s, Russian traders descended upon Alaska in pursuit of furs. For the next 100 years, Russian rule was characterized by exploitation of the fur trade and brutal domination of local indigenous people. Overharvesting of marine mammals and otters led to imposition of furbearer conservation measures as early as 1828 (Black 1988). After Alaska was purchased by the United States in 1867, unrestrained private enterprise brought the sea otter to the verge of extinction by the 1880s. Similarly, the success of whalers led to the collapse of commercial whaling and was responsible for a great famine that reduced the population of Alaska Natives north of the Arctic Circle to fewer than 1,000 by the 1890s (Black 1988).

The 1890s saw the further exploitation of Alaska's natural resources with the famous Klondike gold rush, followed by the Nome gold rush in 1909. Alaska's "boom or bust" existence continued with bonanza years of salmon canneries in the 1920s and 1930s, followed by collapse of the industry, caused by overfishing.

Since the 1960s, Alaska has been heavily dependent on the oil and gas industry. The development of the Prudhoe Bay Oil Fields led to an unprecedented wave of economic development and prosperity. Underlying much of Alaska's experience with resource exploitation has been the reality that until recently most of the benefits from Arctic resources did not accrue to Alaska's indigenous people.

In 1986, high levels of mercury and arsenic were discovered in a localized area of a playground in the midst of Nome, Alaska. The source of these metals was a gold smelter built and operated in the late 1890s and early 1900s during the Nome gold rush. Gold mining almost a century earlier left an unrecognized hazard in the heart of the community. Warnings were posted and widespread media coverage raised alarms before there was consultation with local health officials or the local community. Nome residents, as well as local and state health officials, awoke to find "moonsuited" U.S. Environmental Protection Agency technicians taking soil samples from the playground. Newspaper headlines warned that residents faced a higher-than-normal lifetime risk of cancer and other illnesses because of exposure to these metals. The ensuing health assessment found no evidence that residents were at any increased health risk from the levels that were present (Middaugh et al. 1986a).

Soon afterwards, monitoring of heavy metals in marine mammals from the Aleutian Islands to the Arctic Circle found high levels of mercury and cadmium (Middaugh et al. 1986b). Based on quantitative risk assessment calculations extrapolated from studies of occupationally exposed workers, regulators advised Alaska Natives to cease consumption of walrus and seal because levels of mercury and cadmium exceeded those of regulatory guidelines. A more comprehensive health risk assessment by the Centers for Disease Control and Prevention, Indian Health Service, and State of Alaska Department of Health and Social Services found that the heavy metals discovered were not absorbed by humans consuming these foods and that significant beneficial health effects accrue from eating marine mammals (Middaugh et al. 1986b). Findings were discussed with villagers. After many meetings and widespread controversy, things returned to normal until 1993, when the entire chain of events was repeated.

During this time of increasing awareness of potential threats from heavy metals, reports of potential contamination of Alaska salmon and marine mammals with PCBs and dioxins added to growing concerns over environmental contaminants. First came a major alarm over potential adverse effects of contamination from pulp mills in southeastern Alaska (EPA 1991). Soon afterwards, *Consumer Reports* magazine published a report, widely covered by the news media, about seafood quality ("Is Our Fish Fit to Eat?" 1992). Although subsequent studies established that PCB concentrations in Alaska seafood were below those thought to be associated with adverse human health effects, the news media did not provide widespread coverage of this more reassuring message to the public (EPA 1991; Birnbaum 1994). Documentation of the presence of these human-made chemicals throughout the Arctic ecosystem was a shock to many.

Worldwide attention focused on Alaska after the *Exxon-Valdez* ran aground on Bligh Reef in Prince William Sound on March 24, 1989, spilling 38 million liters of crude oil and creating an 82-square-kilometer oil slick. Eventually more than 1,200 coastline kilometers were affected by the spreading oil. Among the many serious challenges in mounting a response to the spill were issues of safety and health for workers involved in cleanup activities, potential adverse impacts on commercial fisheries, short- and long-term impacts on subsistence food safety, and communication of public health risk information to local communities directly affected by the oil spill. We soon learned that conflicting information on the toxicity of crude oil seriously undermined credibility. The Western sciences of chemistry, toxicology, and risk assessment meant little to local individuals who saw the sweeping devastation of their immediate environment. Further, perceptions that more stringent standards were adopted for commercial seafood compared to locally harvested subsistence seafood further damaged trust in government.

In addition to the widespread publicity given to these acute episodes of pollution in the Arctic, the presence and bioaccumulation of low levels of heavy metals and persistent organic pollutants in the Arctic food chain originating from human-made sources at low latitude has generated concerns regarding the potential long-term risk to the ecosystem and to human health. Unlike exposure scenarios related to a local industrial site, distribution of pollutants in the Arctic appears to be widespread, and people in the Arctic are primarily exposed through their diet, which entails subsistence harvest of local resources (Egeland et al. 1998).

The element mercury (Hg) occurs naturally in the earth's crust, but human activities—for example, coal burning, trash incineration, and production of industrial emissions—increase its release into the environment. Mercury is methylated by organisms in fresh water and marine water and concentrated through the food chain in the tissues of fish and marine mammals. Methylmercury (MeHg) can cause neurological and developmental disorders in humans (EPA 1996).

There is good evidence that heavy metals (mercury [Hg], cadmium [Cd], selenium [Se], and arsenic [As]) were present in the Arctic prior to industrialization and large-scale production of waste. The discovery of extremely well-preserved mummies that are 500 years old in Greenland provided an opportunity to measure levels of heavy metals in animal and human remains predating the Industrial Revolution. Several heavy metals were measured in hair from the human bodies and from the seal-skin garments. Cadmium and selenium levels were similar to those found today. Mercury levels were lower than found today but were still high. As expected, lead levels showed the greatest increase in the last 500 years. Interestingly, although many believe that cancer did not exist in Arctic indigenous people before the 1950s, one of the bodies showed evidence of cancer, most probably a nasopharyngeal carcinoma (Hart Hansen and Gullov 1989; Hart Hansen et al. 1991).

In contrast to heavy metals that occur naturally throughout the globe and are also generated by industrial activity, polyhalogenated diaromatic hydrocarbons (PHDHs) such as PCBs, dibenzo-*p*-dioxins (PCDDs), and dibenzofurans (PCDFs) are lipophilic, persistent, human-made chemicals. Because of their environmental persistence, PHDHs have become distributed in small quantities throughout the world. PHDHs have been transported from temperate regions to the Arctic through the atmosphere and the marine food chain (AMAP 1997, 1998; Egeland et al. 1998).

Effects in Indigenous Peoples

In Alaska, indigenous peoples who consume large quantities of subsistence foods from the sea may be exposed to potentially toxic chemicals. The risks to human health that are of the most concern in subsistence foods in Alaska are chronic, long-term or subtle effects that may occur at very low PHDH dose levels. In particular, widespread publicity that toxic chemicals in subsistence foods might cause cancer, immunotoxicity, reproductive toxicity, and developmental or neurobehavioral toxicity has resulted in great concern about possible exposure (Egeland et al. 1998).

Because fish is a healthful and readily available food item that is high in protein, low in saturated fat, and rich in omega-3 fatty acids and antioxidants such as selenium and vitamin E, the potential risk of exposure to MeHg coexists with health benefits (Egeland et al. 1998; EPA 1996; Bolger 1998; Kinsella 1987; Bauernfeind 1980; National Institutes of Health 1995; Egeland and Middaugh 1997). Further, selenium and vitamin E may protect against the effects of low-level MeHg exposures. Severely limiting the consumption of fish or marine mammals will reduce health benefits and may have unintended or unforeseen negative health consequences (Bolger 1998; Egeland and Middaugh 1997). Thus, evaluation of food safety and the development of food consumption advice must occur within a multidisciplinary public health framework. It is essential that we learn more about these metals and chemical contaminants in the Arctic. There also is a unique opportunity for research, for it is of great interest to know the comparable levels of heavy metals and organic hydrocarbons in birds and marine mammals in the Antarctic.

Managing the Arctic commons becomes even more difficult because of the need to balance benefits, not just to measure differences in costs. In spite of many costs and potential future adverse effects, there have been many substantial benefits to Arctic people.

Public Health Issues in Alaska

Extraordinary changes have taken place in Alaska and in the Arctic in the past fifty years (see table 11.1). In 2000, the health of Alaskans has never been better. Life-threatening infectious diseases such as tuberculosis, polio, diphtheria, rheumatic fever, whooping cough, and meningitis have almost disappeared. The infant mortality rate and the overall death rate have fallen to an all-time low, and life expectancy of an Alaskan has never been higher (Middaugh et al. 1991; Young 1994; Alaska Department of Health and Social Services 1994).

In the 1950s, the life expectancy of an Alaska Native was only forty-seven years—similar to that in Ethiopia or Bangladesh today. A special medical team sent to Alaska in 1950 by the U.S. Congress to assess the health status of Alaska Natives reported that the situation in Alaska was a national disgrace and that Alaska was "unfinished business" (Parran 1954). Until recently, public health and medical efforts in Alaska were focused almost entirely on control of infectious diseases such as polio, measles, diphtheria, whooping cough, streptococcal disease, rheumatic fever, botulism, bacterial meningitis, otitis media, and especially tuberculosis. Just fifty years ago, tuberculosis caused 43 percent of all deaths among Alaska Natives (Middaugh et al. 1991).

As a consequence of the tremendous improvements in overall health status, new disease patterns have emerged. Chronic diseases such as diabetes, heart disease, and cancer, seen infrequently or not at all just fifty years ago, now are common. Arctic residents, particularly Alaska Natives, are experiencing an epidemic of tobacco-caused cancer. In 1950 there were 6 deaths in Alaska from lung cancer; in 1988 there were 143. In 1950, only one Alaska Native died from lung cancer; from 1980 to 1989, twenty-four died each year. In 1950 the death rate from lung cancer was 5.6/100,000; it is now 89/100,000 (Middaugh et al. 1991).

Table 11.1. Health Status Indicators, Alaska, 1950 and 1996.

	1950	1996
Infant Mortality (deaths per 1,000 live births)		
Alaska Native	101	11.0
Alaska all races	24	7.9
Total Mortality (deaths per 100,000)		
Alaska Native	1,742	73
Alaska whites	717	462
Life Expectancy (years)		
Alaska Native	47	69
Alaska whites	66	75

Because there is no scientific consensus about the potential for adverse effects on human health from exposure to mercury and PHDHs at the low levels found in the Alaskan Arctic, especially to the developing fetus, Arctic residents are given conflicting advice about the safety of continuing subsistence food consumption. Discoveries of potential site-related environmental exposures are increasing with identification of past or present exposures to a long list of metals, pesticides, and other human-made chemicals.

At the same time, Arctic indigenous people observe with dismay the increasing frequency of cancer diagnoses among their families, friends, and loved ones. As a result, great concern and fear have arisen about the potential threat of environmental contaminants to human health and the ecosystem.

Government Efforts

Providing public health expertise and capacity to evaluate environmental health problems is a fundamental duty of government. The scope of environmental public health activities is broad, ranging from assurance of the quality and integrity of public food, water, and waste-disposal systems to protecting the environment from human-made pollutants.

Many basic environmental health activities involve regulation and enforcement. In the 1970s, U.S. efforts focused on controlling industrial chemical wastes and discharges and on reducing widespread adverse effects of human-made pollutants on the ecosystem. To do so, the Environmental Protection Agency was established, and numerous powerful and sweeping federal laws were passed to protect the environment.

During the past two decades, significant progress has been achieved nationally and in Alaska in cleaning up our environment and reducing anthropogenic pollutants. However, during this time, program requirements to achieve environmental regulatory standards have become increasingly rigid and inflexible (Presidential/Congressional Commission on Risk Assessment and Risk Management 1997).

Some current environmental regulatory requirements rest on a very weak base of inconclusive or controversial scientific evidence. As we strive to achieve an ever-cleaner environment, ever-increasing costs are required to provide smaller marginal reductions in pollutants. In some instances, activities to meet a tighter standard in one area of environmental regulation may cause serious harm to another area of public health. For example, under the Clean Air Act, the EPA required Alaska to use oxygenated fuels to reduce auto emissions; the additives are believed to have caused widespread illness (Moolenaar et al. 1994).

More effective future policies will require broader integration of public health expertise into environmental regulations (Anderson and Wiener 1995;

Presidential/Congressional Commission 1997). Risk management and public health advice must separate the possible from the probable. Benefits and risks must both be weighed, and trade-offs fully considered. To respond to documentation of the presence of pollutants in the Arctic environment, we need to involve fully the expertise of the public health community and, in turn, Arctic people.

The U.S. government will need to take seriously its obligations under the Arctic Research Policy Act of 1984 and become more actively involved in Arctic research. The United States will need to increase resources and commit scientific expertise to evaluate the implications of Arctic environmental contaminants for human health and the environment. We will also need to involve local residents and communities in this effort. To do so will require funding to enable meaningful participation. We will need to improve communication, particularly to enhance listening skills of scientists and researchers. Through a sustained commitment, we can strive to build participation and establish trust.

Although we have much to learn, and our scientific knowledge is incomplete, many studies have provided information that can be used to provide public health advice with considerable confidence. Our ability to communicate effectively information about cancer, environmental threats, and chemical contaminants is very poor (Anderson and Wiener 1995). For example, a cluster of ten cancer cases occurred in a remote Alaskan village from 1983 to 1986. The village was small, with only 207 residents. Of the seven residents who were diagnosed with lung cancer, all had significant exposure to cigarettes—up to seventy-four pack-years. Although 74 percent of villagers believed cigarettes were an important cause of cancer, many strongly believed that the cancers that occurred were due to other environmental causes. Villagers cited chemical contamination of drinking water from fluoride and chlorine, radioactive fallout from atmospheric weapons testing, the change from a traditional to a Western diet, indoor air pollution from radon, and depletion of the ozone layer as causes of the cancer cluster (Sprott 1988).

We need to learn how to educate and communicate information about science and about environmental threats. We must increase our ability to communicate, especially with different cultures. This will not be easy. The Inuit language has more than sixty words to describe snow; it has no words for "cancer."

Benefits and risks must both be weighed with additional consideration of who actually benefits and who is at risk. Risk-management decisions and risk communication require the careful guidance of public health and the leadership of indigenous peoples. Indigenous leadership is needed to ensure that individuals and agencies with different backgrounds and expertise come together in a constructive process so that the appropriate questions get answered, the appropriate messages get communicated, and the best interests of the people are promoted. Through a holistic approach, public health information can empower individuals to make informed choices.

That levels of anthropogenic contaminants and naturally occurring trace metals in the Arctic are low is gratifying news for immediate public health concerns. But this is not a reason for complacency. We need much more research to enable us to prevent or ameliorate adverse effects on the fragile Arctic ecosystem and Arctic environment. We must have adequate data to monitor trends. And we must prevent further contamination.

Conclusion

Subsistence foods provide important cultural, spiritual, nutritional, and medicinal benefits to Arctic people. At the Tenth International Congress on Circumpolar Health, held in Anchorage in May 1996, Native elders called for a balanced approach to evaluating the risks and weighing the benefits of subsistence foods to ensure the preservation of their cultural identity and total health and well-being (Egeland et al. 1998). Elders expressed their belief that the fear associated with the contaminants may cause greater harm than the actual presence of the contaminants themselves and that health warnings regarding food consumption should be made only when there is strong evidence that the risks outweigh the benefits (Egeland et al. 1998; Wheatley 1994; Shkilnyk 1985; Usher et al. 1995).

The Arctic Assessment and Monitoring Program (AMAP), a component of the Arctic Environmental Protection Strategy, provides a superb opportunity for research (Graham and Wiener 1995; Presidential/Congressional Commission 1997). Essential to its success is the meaningful involvement of Arctic indigenous people in all aspects of the monitoring program and the restoration of trust between agencies, researchers, and local people (AMAP 1997, 1998).

Underlying principles that are essential to enlightened management of Arctic common-pool resources include the following:

- We should affirm the intrinsic integrity and value of the environment and our duty to protect it for its own sake.
- We should be realistic about the immediate potential benefits to human health in the Arctic from results of monitoring these environmental pollutants, although the long-term benefits will be great.
- We need to develop an effective partnership with local people to interpret results of environmental monitoring programs in a way meaningful to local residents.
- We must plan now for a process that will empower Arctic people to make informed choices and to be in command of their lives.

Respect for and recognition of traditional knowledge of Arctic indigenous people are essential to successful management of the Arctic commons. Lessons from two centuries of Arctic exploration provide ample evidence of the value of the Arctic experience:"Here was a nation obsessed by science, whose explorers were charged with collecting everything from skins of the arctic tern to the shells that lay on the beaches. Here were men of intelligence with a mania for figures, charts, and statistics, recording everything from the water temperatures to the magnetic forces that surround the Pole. Yet few thought it necessary to inquire into the reasons why another set of fellow humans could survive, year after year, winter after winter, in an environment that taxed and often broke the white man's spirit" (Berton 1988).

There is great need for a sustained and viable international environmental monitoring program. Results will help us to focus health programs on the major threats to human health and to focus all our programs on the need to protect the Arctic commons for ourselves and future generations.

Local and regional commons issues in the Arctic illustrate the importance of the global commons. Potential threats from environmental contaminants to the Arctic commons from human activities conducted thousands of miles away at low latitudes cannot be solved by local or regional action. Preservation of Arctic cultural and spiritual values is intimately linked to preservation and stewardship of the global environment. Global resource management provides hope for environmental justice and preservation of the Arctic and global commons.

References

Alaska Department of Health and Social Services. 1994. *Healthy Alaskans 2000.* February, Alaska: Department of Health and Social Services, Division of Administrative Services, Planning Section, 20–21.

Anderson, P. D., and J. B. Wiener. 1995. "Eating Fish." In *Risk vs. Risk: Tradeoffs in Health and Environmental Protection,* edited by J. D. Graham and J. B. Wiener, 104–23. Cambridge, MA: Harvard University Press.

Arctic Monitoring and Assessment Programme (AMAP). 1997. *Arctic Pollution Issues: A State of the Arctic Environment Report.* Oslo, Norway: AMAP.

———. 1998. *AMAP Assessment Report Arctic Pollution Issues.* Oslo, Norway: AMAP.

Bauernfeind, J. 1980. "Tocopherols in Foods." In *Vitamin E, a Comprehensive Treatise,* edited by L. J. Machlin, 99–168. New York: Marcel Dekker.

Berton, P. 1988. *The Arctic Grail: The Quest for the North West Passage and the North Pole, 1818–1909.* New York: Viking Penguin.

Birnbaum, L. S. 1994. "Endocrine Effects of Prenatal Exposure to PCBs, Dioxins, and Other Xenobiotics: Implications for Policy and Future Research." *Environmental Health Perspectives* 102:676–79.

Black, L. 1988. "The Story of Russian America." In *Crossroads of Continents. Cultures of*

Siberia and Alaska, edited by W. Fitzhugh and A. Crowell, 70–82. Washington, DC: Smithsonian Institution.

Bolger, M. 1998. "Methylmercury and Fish: Risks and Benefits." *Health and Environment Digest* 12:37–39.

Burger, J., and M. Gochfeld. 1998. "The Tragedy of the Commons Thirty Years Later." *Environment* 40:4–13, 27–28.

Egeland, G., and J. P. Middaugh. 1997. "Balancing Fish Consumption Benefits with Mercury Exposure." *Science* 278:1904–05.

Egeland, G. M., L. A. Feyk, and J. P. Middaugh. 1998. "Use of Traditional Foods in a Healthy Diet in Alaska: Risks in Perspective." *Epidemiology Bulletin. Recommendations and Reports* 2 (1):1–140. Anchorage: Alaska Department of Health and Social Services.

Environmental Protection Agency (EPA). 1991. *Environmental Evaluation of Pollutants in Sitka, Alaska. Final Report.* Seattle: EPA.

––––––. 1996. "Mercury Study Report of Congress: Characterization of Human Health and Wildlife Risks from Anthropogenic Mercury Emissions in the United States." SAB review draft. EPA-452/R-96-001f.

Graham, J. D., and F. B. Wiener. 1995. *Risk versus Risk. Tradeoffs in Protecting Health and the Environment.* Cambridge, MA: Harvard University Press.

Hardin, G. 1968. "The Tragedy of the Commons." *Science* 162:1243–48.

Hart Hansen, J. P., and H. C. Gullov, eds. 1989. *The Mummies from Qilakitsoq: Eskimos in the 15th Century. Meddelelser om Gronland, Man and Society.* Odense, Denmark: Commission for Scientific Research in Greenland.

Hart Hansen, J. P., J. Meldgaard, and J. Nordquist, eds. 1991. *The Greenland Mummies.* London: British Museum Press.

"Is Our Fish Fit to Eat?" Anonymous. 1992. *Consumer Reports* 103–114 (February).

Kinsella, J. E. 1987. *Seafoods and Fish Oils in Human Health and Disease.* New York: Marcel Dekker.

Middaugh, J. P., W. G. Hlady, and S. A. Jenkerson. 1986a. *Nome. Arsenic and Mercury Health Hazard and Risk Assessment.* Anchorage: State of Alaska, Department of Health and Social Services, Section of Epidemiology, Division of Public Health.

––––––. 1986b. *Cadmium in Walrus. Health Hazard and Risk Assessment. St. Lawrence Island.* Anchorage: State of Alaska, Department of Health and Social Services, Section of Epidemiology, Division of Public Health.

Middaugh, J. P., J. Miller, C. E. Dunaway, S. A. Jenkerson, T. Kelly, D. Ingle, K. Perham, D. Fridley, W. G. Hlady, and V. Hendrickson. 1991. *Causes of Death in Alaska. 1950, 1980–1989. An Analysis of the Causes of Death, Years of Potential Life Lost, and Life Expectancy.* Anchorage: State of Alaska, Department of Health and Social Services, Section of Epidemiology, Division of Public Health.

Molnia, B. F., and K. B. Taylor, eds. 1994. "Proceedings of the Interagency Arctic Research Policy Committee, Workshop on Arctic Contamination, May 2–7, 1993, Anchorage, Alaska." *Arctic Research of the United States* 8:1–34.

Moolenaar, R. L., B. J. Hefflin, D. L. Ashley, J. P. Middaugh, and R. A. Etzel. 1994. "Methyl Tertiary Butyl Ether in Human Blood after Exposure to Oxygenated Fuel in Fairbanks, Alaska." *Archives of Environmental Health* 49:402–9.

National Institutes of Health (NIH). 1995. *Effects of Fish Oils and Polyunsaturated Omega-3 Fatty Acids in Health and Disease.* Bethesda, MD: NIH.

Parran, T. 1954. *Alaska's Health: A Survey Report to the United States Department of the Interior by the Alaska Health Survey Team,* edited by W. Q. Elder. Pittsburgh: University of Pittsburgh.

Presidential/Congressional Commission on Risk Assessment and Risk Management. 1997. *Framework for Environmental Health Risk Management. Final Report.* Vol. 1. Washington, DC: Presidential/Congressional Commission on Risk Assessment and Risk Management.

"Proceedings of the Japan-Russia-United States Study Group on Dumped Nuclear Waste in the Sea of Japan, Sea of Okhotsk, and the North Pacific Ocean." 1995. *Arctic Research of the United States* 9:57–146.

Rey, L., and B. Stonehouse, eds. 1982. *The Arctic Ocean. The Hydrographic Environment and the Fate of Pollutants.* New York: Wiley.

Shkilnyk, A. M. 1985. *A Poison Stronger Than Love: The Destruction of an Ojibwa Community.* New York: Yale University Press.

Sprott, J. E. 1988. "Cancer Causation Beliefs in an Alaska Village." *Alaska Medicine* 30:155–58.

Stonehouse, B., ed. 1986. *Arctic Air Pollution.* Cambridge, England: Cambridge University Press.

Usher, P. J., M. Baikie, M. Demmer, D. Nakashima, M. G. Stevenson, M. Stiles. 1995. *Communicating about Contaminants in Country Food: The Experience in Aboriginal Communities.* Ottawa, Ontario: Inuit Tapirisat of Canada.

Wheatley, B. 1994. "A New Approach to Assessing the Effects of Environmental Contaminants on Aboriginal Peoples." *Arctic Medical Research* 53 (Suppl. 2):386–90.

Young, T. K. 1994. *The Health of Native Americans. Toward a Biocultural Epidemiology.* New York: Oxford University Press.

Chapter 12

Medical Care as a Commons

MICHAEL GOCHFELD, JOANNA BURGER,
AND BERNARD D. GOLDSTEIN

The framework of a "commons" and common-pool resource has been used to analyze many situations, from traditional spatially bounded commons such as fisheries and forests to more esoteric and widely distributed resources such as the Internet. Here we apply a commons analysis to medical care in the United States. The quality and availability of medical care are a global problem, and disparities in care from region to region or class to class are great. Angell (1999) considered the United States medical care system to be the most expensive, most inadequate, and most complicated in the developed world. In this chapter we suggest that analyzing medical care as a commons provides clearer perspectives for future management that will enhance access to high-quality care at a socially acceptable cost. In many cases (cited in other chapters in this volume) the challenge is how to limit access to the resource, whereas in medical care the challenge is to expand access equitably while sustaining quality.

Background on Commons

The concept of a commons applies when a resource is available to a group of people who benefit individually from increased personal access while their use of the resource potentially reduces its availability to other users (Berkes 1989; Berkes et al. 1989; Feeney et al. 1990). These hallmarks of a commons resource are referred to as "access" and "subtractibility" (Burger and Gochfeld 1998; Ostrom et al. 1999).

Synthesis: A Commons Approach to Medical Care

Characterizing medical care as a commons requires the following:
1. Identifying the resource(s) in question
2. Defining access and who controls access
3. Describing subtractibility
4. Improving predictability and using it in evaluation
5. Defining and sustaining quality

Participants in the Medical Commons

The traditional commons has three participants: the resource, the users, and the regulators. In medical care we recognize five parties: the resources (providers of medical care), users (patients or potential patients), users' employers, payors (usually insurance companies of some kind), and regulators. We will examine how they distribute control over the medical care resource and access to it (table 12.1). We must emphasize that other analysts might bring a different perspective to the commons (table 12.2). Thus payors or managed care companies might assume that employer dollars are the critical resource and that their task is to fish for these dollars using their list of approved providers or employee choice as the fishing gear. Likewise, employers, who are often the purchasers, are likely to consider themselves users as well, even if they never actually meet a provider. Confusion over the resource has definitely hampered clear understanding of medical care.

Goal for Managing a Commons

The goals for managing a common-pool resource should be maximizing the benefit to the users of the resource, maintaining quality of life and equity, and sustaining the resource. This can be seen most clearly in the management of local fisheries (McCay chapter 8, this volume), where sustainability of the fish stock and future quality of life may require quotas on use or restrictions of access. Success depends on being able to measure the resource and predict its future and on being able to enforce the access restrictions equitably (Ostrom et al. 1999). Likewise a medical care system should enhance the quality of life for users by maintaining their equitable access to adequate, high-quality care. The recent approach to "managing" medical care has included restrictions of access, with a focus on the health care dollar as the limited resource (Koch 1993). We offer an alternative commons analysis in which the user is the patient and the resource is medical care (with provider time as a surrogate for the limited resource).

Table 12.1. Interactions between the Five Parties Governing Patient Access to Providers in the Medical Care Commons. Each party exerts some control on almost every other party and is in turn subject to some degree of control or influence by every party. The cells along the diagonal identify forces involved in self-regulation of each of the parties. (MCP = managed care plan, QA = quality assurance)

	Control by Employer	Control by MCP	Control by Provider	Control by Patient	Control by Regulator
Employer controlled by	(1) Willingness to pay for health benefits (2) Competitiveness	Limits number of providers	Good management of illness and injury reduces absenteeism	(1) Collective bargaining (2) Complaints (3) Poor management of illness or injury leads to absenteeism	Required to offer HMO to employees
MCP controlled by	Employer can refuse to use if cost or reputation unfavorable	Internal QA and limited quest for certification	Ultimate responsibility for referrals	Patient may jump ship or file grievance if dissatisfied	Statutes and regulations restrict or require certain practices to protect patients
Provider controlled by	No direct link	(1) Reimbursement levels (2) Disincentives for referrals (3) Credential check (4) Gag clause	Professional societies' codes of ethics	(1) Patient must trust providers, may select new providers (2) Malpractice suits possible (3) Can seek second opinion	(1) State agencies regulate licensure (2) Can require acceptance of certain compensation plans (e.g., "assignment") (3) Can punish fraud

(continues)

Table 12.1. Continued

Patient controlled by	(1) May discourage use of medical services or reporting of conditions (2) Sets copayments (3) May require employee contribution	(1) Limited list of providers (2) Gag clause on providers (3) Services may be rationed	(1) Provider decides on diagnostic tests and treatment plan (2) Controls medical knowledge	(1) Potential for subtractibility if some patients overuse (2) Limited provider resource	Not much direct link, but can punish fraud
Regulator controlled by	Legal injunctions against enforcement of regulations	Political pressure from insurance industry	Opportunity for political pressure by professional organizations	Political pressure of patient as voter	Political priorities preclude effective regulation

Table 12.2. The Medical Care Commons from Different
Perspectives and a Comparison with a Fishery.

Fishers	Medical Providers	Managed Care Plans	Patients
Boats and nets	Insurers: MCPs and employers	Providers	Employers and MCPs
Fish	Patients	Employers and patients	Providers
Income	Income	Profit	Medical care

Lessons from the Commons

We believe the primary issues of access and subtractability and the secondary issues of quality and sustainability qualify medical care as a commons resource. However, the more significant question is whether it is useful to examine it as a commons and whether lessons learned about other successfully managed commons can inform discussions about the medical care system of the future. We will examine how different forms of access control can increase or decrease equitable access to necessary services that maximize medical care for the largest number of people. We argue that focusing future discussion on the issues of access and subtractibility in general, rather than on the macro issue of total health care budget or the present micro issue of rationing specific medical services (e.g., whether to pay for certain drugs or services), will facilitate decisions governing the nation's overall health care.

Subtractibility or Surplus

Subtractibility exists when the use of medical services by one person prevents (or more realistically for health care, delays) use by another or when it subtracts from the overall quality of the resource. Determining whether subtraction has occurred or will occur requires data on both the current use and the past and future availability of the resource. Long delays for medical appointments or elective surgery are one metric. At any one time the number of providers is fixed, although over time the pool of providers is elastic and can expand or shrink in response to the service needs of the nation (Lewis 1933; Light 1986). There are reported surpluses of physicians in certain disciplines or geographic areas, and in the mid-1990s several authorities argued vociferously that the health care cost problem could be attributed to a surplus of physicians who generate their own need for services (Pew 1995; Reinhardt 1997).

If there is truly a surplus of physicians (Light 1986; Pew 1995), then subtractibility should not pose a problem. Moreover, increased productivity requirements—whether self-imposed or imposed by managed care plans (MCPs)—appear to mitigate subtractibility. Less time with each patient means more patients per hour, hence no delay in scheduling appointments, hence little evidence of subtractability. However, a reduction in quality can be part of subtractibility, as exemplified by the smaller fish or inferior species captured by fishers in areas of uncontrolled overfishing.

In medical care, as in any commons, subtractibility and reduction in quality depend on the structure of the system and its incentives (Grumbach et al. 1998) and on whether the "commoners," in this case patients, have an adequate voice in apportioning access or whether they acquiesce in accepting diminished resource quantity or quality, as fishing families must when quotas are imposed by outside regulators or when overfishing removes the most desired fish.

Quality and Sustainability

Quality of medical care is elusive, and several approaches are being developed to measure it (Naylor 1998). The provision of services, whether plumbing, auto repair, or medical care, requires that providers have adequate knowledge and experience and spend the necessary amount of time with the pipes, vehicles, or patients that they service. The quality of care, in terms of both clinician care and new technologies, has created a great sense of optimism and expectation in the public. Although sound epidemiologic research (sometimes labeled outcome research) is necessary to determine the link between technologic innovations and favorable outcomes, the public (stimulated by enthusiastic media coverage) is likely to equate quality with availability of new technology, even when the outcome has not been measured.

As the productivity demand on medical care increases, each clinician-patient encounter is shortened (Kassirer 1997; Grumbach et al. 1998), reducing the quality of the care (and increasing the need for subsequent visits). René Dubos emphasized that health requires far more than the application of scientific knowledge (Dubos 1959), and providers must influence the belief systems and practices, as well as the medications of their patients, all of which requires precious time.

Many physicians have written that patient care is compromised by the denial of services deemed desirable for the patient's benefit, and this is reflected in the higher satisfaction of patients in traditional versus managed care plans (Rubin et al. 1993). In 1999 the situation because dynamic as Congress moved to make MCPs accountable and MCPs introduced policies whereby medical decisions are made solely by physicians. Because patients in MCPs often believe that decisions are made by clerks or managers, it sounds good to have medical decisions assigned to physicians, but only time will tell whether this improves decision making for MCPs because physicians employed by MCPs are likely to have a conflict of interest in making these decisions. However, in 1999 and 2000 Congress did not enact the patients' bill of rights, balking at allowing patients to sue their MCPs.

The Marketplace and Provider Surplus

Just as fisheries are subject to "management," so is the medical care resource: the number, specialties, and distributions of clinicians (Reinhardt 1994). Many authors have discussed how the production of physicians (the basic resource) should be responsive to the needs of society (e.g., Reinhardt 1997; Wilensky 1997). Hardin (1968) emphasized that overpopulation inevitably strains any common-pool resource to a point at which open access is no longer tenable. In medical care, great demand comes from the elderly population, in which chronic and serious ailments accumulate with age. The rapid increase in the relative number of elderly represents overpopulation of a particular population segment, which greatly challenges the medical care system.

Estimates of the physician supply relative to need have waxed and waned (Lewis 1933; GMENAC 1980; Light 1986; Wilensky 1997). In the 1960s Congress decided that the United States needed more physicians, and it subsidized medical education, resulting in both new schools and larger classes (Light 1986). The Pew Commission (1995) argues that a change in the pattern of government support would encourage or allow the physician supply to respond more realistically to the marketplace, and it recommended limiting medical school capacity. Weiner (1994) predicted that if 60 percent of Americans were in MCPs by 2000 there would be a surplus of 140,000 medical specialists and 29,000 generalists, or about 30 percent of the total number of patient care physicians. This embodies the tacit assumption that quality of care would not be compromised to enhance profitability. We observed that since the mid-1980s physicians were eager to sign up with as many MCPs as possible, even in the face of reduced remuneration and autonomy. This suggests that physicians perceived a doctor surplus or at least a patient shortage.

Access to Medical Care

Control of access to the resource is an important feature of commons analysis. In a fishing community, the members of the community form the first level of access regulation. In medical care, limited access can negatively affect both individual and public health. Access is an intrinsic feature of national health policy, and Canada, for example, maintains universal access, whereas Australia has abandoned that principle (Gray 1998). Under the evolving "managed insurance" system, the access of members is governed by the insurance plan(s) made available to them through their employers, each of which has a network of primary care providers (PCPs) who have decision authority over various treatment options and referrals.

Current Access Rules and Institutions

Each of the five participants in the medical care commons has a role in influencing access (table 12.3). Currently, MCPs market their services to employers, including government agencies. The employer selects one or more MCPs to offer its employees, and the selected MCPs market their services to employees. The employer then pays each MCP for each person it enrolls. Table 12.1 illustrates some of the asymmetries in relationships between the players. There are many modifiers embodied in the negotiation between employer and MCP and the negotiations between MCPs and providers. The PCPs can also choose not to participate in certain MCPs depending on ethical or remuneration issues. Large MCPs can force providers to lower charges, even to the point at which providers refuse to accept patients from certain MCPs.

The MCP controls patient access by selecting PCPs in its approved provider network, and these PCPs in turn control access to specialists and specialized services, influenced by the MCP's incentive policies. The oft-heard

Table 12.3. Control of Access in the Medical Commons.

Parties	Role in Governing Access
Patient's employer	Selection of MCPs offered to employees, with incentives to select one plan over another; imposition of copayments
Managed care plan	List of PCPs and specialists offered to the insured Incentives to PCPs to reduce referrals and costly treatments; gag clauses to limit information to patients regarding options
Patient	Choice of PCP from list and willingness to switch MCPs or PCPs; decisions regarding need for care at any time; willingness to make copayments or to pay for out-of-network service
Provider	Decisions regarding referrals influenced by risk aversion and incentives/disincentives; choice of which MCPs in which to participate
Regulator	Superimposes requirements for minimum stays; outlaws gag clauses; debating patients' bill of rights

complaint, "my insurance won't cover it" indicates that limited coverage effectively curtails access.

Many MCPs further limited access through so-called gag rules imposed on their physicians. Gag clauses are among the most insidious means of restricting access, prohibiting providers from telling their patients about all treatment options, especially out-of-network ones. Woolhandler and Himmelstein (1995) published the gag clause in their contract, which read in part, "Physician shall keep the proprietary information [payment rates, utilization review procedures, etc.] and this agreement strictly confidential."

Through statutes or regulations, the regulators can govern how the MCP operates. The federal government recently issued policies that forbade gag rules and prohibited HMOs from paying bonuses to limit services under Medicare and Medicaid. Some states have made such clauses illegal and have imposed minimum hospital stays, but a comprehensive patient's bill of rights is still pending at the federal level. Among other rights, this would give patients the right for full disclosure of treatment options (Annas 1998). However, as one of the largest employers, controlling employee health as well as Medicare and Medicaid benefits, government has a serious conflict of interest in regulating the managed insurance industry. Mechanic (1996) points out that "not-for-profit plans are converting to for-profit status at an alarming rate" and that despite public outrage, governments are subsidizing this switch by contracting with these same companies for their employee plans and by switching Medicaid patients into these plans.

A patient has some initial control over which MCP and PCP he or she selects (albeit in the absence of outcome or satisfaction data). The patient can also present grievances to the employer, the MCP, and the regulator (see table 12.1). The freedom of the patient to switch from one plan to another varies from state to state and depends on the employer. Switching from traditional coverage to an MCP is strongly encouraged with large financial incentives, and the reverse switch may be costly or forbidden. A dissatisfied patient or one whose need for specialized services is denied by Plan A may switch to Plan B. Rather than punishing Plan A, this may be viewed with a sigh of relief—another costly "covered life" off the books.

Referrals Govern Access to Specialists

Rosenbaum et al. (1999) discuss who should control access to specialists. Should access be restricted to personal physicians, PCPs, or MCP employees (whether MDs or not)? Thus the patient who needs medical services really has little leverage. PCPs who control access to specialists also face a conflict of interest because their compensation is based in part on the number and cost of specialist referrals (General Accounting Office 1988). This abrogates the condition of trust between provider and patient (Mechanic 1996) because patients suspect that their doctors are being well paid for not offering them optimum treatment.

The most egregious example of a disincentive is the risk-sharing approach described by Moore (1979). Under that concept the PCP gatekeeper is paid directly by the plan, and from that personal account pays the specialists and other providers, including hospitals to which patients are referred. At the end of the year, after the PCP has received basic compensation, the PCP retains 50 percent of the surplus (amount not expended on referrals). This provides a powerful incentive to restrict referrals, even in the face of quality reviews and patients' ability to switch PCPs within the same plan.

Ethical Issues Governing Incentives and Access

One cannot separate the medical care commons from some ethical questions that are closer to the surface in medicine than in the management of fisheries, grasslands, or the Internet. However, even with fisheries, for example, value judgments are made, including the intrinsic benefit of maintaining the lifestyle of a fisher family. Many physicians and others express grave concerns over the ethics of for-profit managed care: "The incentives to limit treatment under managed care are generally more problematic than the incentives to provide excessive care intrinsic in the fee-for-service system" (Bergen 1996; Mechanic 1996; Lawrence et al. 1997; Frankford and Konrad 1998).

For example, under the patient-payor and insurance-payor system the practice known as "fee splitting" was universally regarded as unethical. Physicians were not allowed to accept kickbacks from the specialists to whom they referred patients. We agree with Pearson et al. (1998) that the current system amounts to reversed fee splitting.

The Role of Subtractibility in Medical Care

A century ago, George Bernard Shaw's (1906) diatribe against the condition and motivations of physicians (*The Doctor's Dilemma*) included an explicit account of subtractability: Taking on one patient precluded treating another. Determining subtractability in modern medical care is more complicated, even when the focus is on cost rather than service. The time frame for evaluating the resource is important. For fisheries, fish stocks grow and decline, depending on biologic factors (fecundity, carrying capacity) and social factors (exploitation, pollution). The availability of medical care may be limited in the short run but not necessarily in the long run. New physicians are educated, trained in specialties, and deployed to various practice settings. In the short run we can measure the availability of medical care by examining what happens to waiting lists for appointments and elective surgery. Subtractibility on the individual level can be measured in various ways, which include delays in care and diminished quality of care. On the national scale it can be measured in the withholding of care from one segment of the population (e.g., the elderly; Hamel et al. 1999) to make limited resources available to others.

Patterns and Predictability

Central to the successful management of a commons is the ability to predict the future availability of the resource (that is, fish or medical care). This requires sound data on past and future use (harvest rates or service use) as well as on the resource base itself (fish stocks or medical providers) and the system for obtaining it (boats or referrals). Although various parties gather abundant data on medical care, these data are seldom made available in a form that can help employers and employees make appropriate choices. Moreover, the MCPs are the main source of such data. For regulators, information on patterns of use and outcomes is becoming available slowly (e.g., Riley et al. 1999). Rapid expansion in informatics and outcome research should facilitate the collection of data needed to inform all parties as to the quality of the resource. However, data must come from unbiased sources.

Roles in the Current System

How can a commons analysis help in managing the medical care system? Each of the players has many, and sometimes conflicting, roles in medical care. Here we mention a few roles that derive from our commons approach.

Roles for the Commoners

An important feature of a sustainable commons is that the commoners who use the resource play a major or even dominant role in evaluating its quality and developing institutions or procedures for governing access to it. For medical care, this requires that patients play more a more active role in their own care and in influencing the system by the choices they make, grievances or legal actions they initiate, or politicians they elect. Of all participants, the user or patient party is the most numerous and has a strong interest, though not currently a strong voice, in sustaining the resource. Patients may also become more skillful in managing their own health, thereby reducing their demand for medical services.

Roles for Employers

Managed care has gained ascendancy largely through its promise to reduce medical care costs to employers without reducing quality. However, employers receive data only on costs, not on quality. Private employers and the government can influence medical care through their purchasing power (Bergthold 1990), influencing both quality and access (Bodenheimer and Sullivan 1998). If employers made comprehensive cost decisions, they would include outcome data such as absenteeism and reduced employee turnover, not just payment to MCPs. Alternatively, a single-payer plan might exclude employers entirely.

Roles for Managed Care Plans

Neither commoners nor providers are particularly sympathetic to the fact that managed insurance corporations have fiduciary responsibility to their investors, which transcends other responsibilities. This is one reason that critics find the for-profit model inimical to a successful system (Lawrence et al. 1997) or at least a significant handicap (Mechanic and Schlesinger 1996; Kuttner 1998). The media focuses on the role of MCPs in reducing access and restricting coverage (e.g., Kilborn 1998). However, MCPs have the potential for improving access and quality. Grumbach et al. (1998) showed that provider satisfaction was higher in MCPs that based incentives on quality measures and patient satisfaction than in those that provided incentives based on productivity or restricted referrals.

Many MCPs invest extensively in marketing to prospective employers, patients, and providers. An equivalent investment in support of publicly available, independent quality reviews would be a major social benefit to all parties, including the MCPs, because directors of MCPs reportedly place a high value on physician expertise in health services and outcome research and in quality assurance and improvement (Halbert et al. 1998).

Roles for Providers

The main role for providers is to act as gatekeepers (for PCPs) or to accept referrals (as specialists). The ascendancy of managed care required the acquiescence of providers and their willingness to join provider networks. Providers also can exert control through collective action in negotiating with health care plans (Findlay 1997) or through professional societies. The MCP industry has taken legal action with initial success to curtail physician organizing activity, but such activity remains a major force for changing how medical care services are provided.

Roles for Regulators

In the fishery analogy, federal and state agencies can set quotas, close areas, and enforce other limitations. Government regulation can both restrict and liberalize access to medical care. Before 1990 the regulations affecting MCPs were mainly those requiring employers to offer HMOs to their employees and in some states requiring physicians to accept "assignment." Therefore, many MCP practices were not regulated. This situation is gradually changing. The relationships between MCPs and employers, MCPs and providers, and MCPs and patients offer fertile ground for statutes and regulations (see table 12.1).

However, as previously mentioned, government, particularly the federal government, has a conflict of interest because it also one of the largest employer-purchasers of medical services and is also responsible for Medicaid and Medicare payments. The U.S. government also has extensive experience with the largest staff-model HMO, the U.S. military medical service. In addition, the federal government provides partial subsidization for private employers who provide health insurance.

Although control of access is currently shared directly among patients, providers, and MCPs, the disproportionate role of MCPs creates an unstable situation, and regulators are slowly taking steps to restore more equitable control. If formal efforts are made to reduce the resource, by decreasing the number of clinicians, the impact of subtractibility will be manifest in delayed visits, shorter visits, and increased reliance on other professionals (or even nonprofessionals).

Regulators have played an increasing role, as evidenced by regulations to curb excesses such as gag rules and one-day hospitalizations for obstetrical care, and proposed legislation that would open MCPs to liability suits. The plans themselves undergo bankruptcy and mergers to improve profitability (three out of eight plans that corresponded with Michael Gochfeld in 1998 reported a change in ownership in 1997–1998, and one was declared bankrupt). Increased regulation will reduce the profitability of some plans, leading them to leave the marketplace, and we predict that there will be fewer and larger payers. Thus MCPs may come to resemble traditional insurance plans.

Alternative Medical Care Systems

We view the current medical care situation as unstable. What, then, are some ways of supplanting the current medical system in the coming decade? We see several: (1) expansion of MCPs under increasing regulation, (2) a return to the insurance-payer phase with uncontrolled access, (3) a return to the patient-payer phase, (4) establishment of patient cooperatives, and (5) implementation of some variant of a single-payer system. Each of these alternatives has strengths and limitations. Although the first seems to be the current trend, we anticipate progressive disenchantment by users, providers, and regulators, and we predict its decline or demise. This disaffection is already leading to an increased interest in a single-payer system. National health insurance is not a new concept (Shvarts et al. 1999). A single-payer system, however organized, controlled, or funded, would most likely improve access and equity but would not automatically ensure improved quality of care. Universal coverage (Light 1999) is one essential feature of any new system, and a focus on prevention (Needleman 1998) and improved public health is obviously another (Mechanic 1998; Schauffler and Scutchfield 1998).

However, establishment of such a system might include rationing certain procedures. For example, if a decision were made to restrict access to coronary artery bypass grafts for people over a given age (say seventy-five), this might penalize a health-conscious person who practices good health behaviors and develops significant coronary artery disease after age seventy-five, relative to a less health-conscious person who develops the same degree of disease at age sixty.

A unified system, aimed at equity, able to focus on quality and sustainability, would embrace those currently uninsured or underinsured. Cost efficiency would be a goal and would be intensely scrutinized. The balance between providers and demand could be improved by incentives that shifted providers between specialties or geographic areas. The plan itself would have the incentive to manage the resource (providers) as well as the services they provide, aiming for a balance between provider supply and user demand. This information would feed back quickly into the training arena.

Conclusion: Medical Care in the Twenty-First Century

What will the medical care commons look like in the new century? A commons analysis focuses our attention on maintaining access and quality and on ameliorating subtractability. The system or a mixture of systems should provide high-quality (scientifically validated) care at a cost that the nation is willing to accept. The impact of technological advancements and information availability will inevitably increase, and their benefits should be accessible to those who need them.

The seesaw between incentives for excessive use and incentives for inadequate use should come to an equilibrium with incentives for appropriate use, guided by unbiased outcome research. This requires the educational system to enhance the training of practitioners with increased emphasis on prevention, informatics, and self-assessment. This in turn requires unbiased, publicly available data.

Sustainability of a high-quality medical care system must involve its users, the patients, in determining issues of access and quality. The system must provide all parties with adequate data on service use and health outcomes, which will facilitate sound choices. Medical care is an immensely personal resource, and the profitability of such a system should go to sustain the system. Commoners, providers, employers, and even insurers stand to benefit from a system that promotes equitable access to medical care.

Acknowledgments

Over the years we have benefited from discussions with many friends and colleagues regarding the science, economics, and ethics of medical care. These include Anne Sommers, Donald Light, David Mechanic, Howard Kipen, Sandra Mohr, and Carol Diamond. We appreciate the critical reading by Michael Greenberg, Elinor Ostrom, Elaine Leventhal, and Barry Friedlander. Our work was supported in part by the Consortium for Risk Evaluation with Stakeholder Participation (CRESP) under a Department of Energy cooperative agreement (AI no. DE-FC01-95EW-55084). Tables used with permission from the Environmental and Occupational Health Sciences Institute.

References

Angell, M. 1999. "The American Health Care System Revisited: A New Series." *New England Journal of Medicine* 340:48.

Annas, G. J. 1998. "A National Bill of Patients' Rights." *New England Journal of Medicine* 338:695–99.

Bergen, S. S. 1996. "Ethical Issues in Managed Care." *UMDNJ Environmental Scan* (May 1996):1–4.

Bergthold, L. 1990. *Purchasing Power in Health.* New Brunswick, NJ: Rutgers Press.

Berkes, F., ed. 1989. *Common Property Resources: Ecology and Community-based Sustainable Development.* London: Belhaven Press.

Berkes, F., D. Feeny, B. J. McCay, and J. M. Acheson. 1989. "The Benefits of the Commons." *Nature* 340:91–93.

Bodenheimer, T., and K. Sullivan. 1998. "How Large Employers Are Shaping the Health Care Marketplace." First of two parts. *New England Journal of Medicine* 333:1003–07.

Burger, J., and M. Gochfeld. 1998. "The Tragedy of the Commons: Thirty Years Later." *Environment* 40 (10):4–13, 26–27.

Dubos, R. 1959. *Mirage of Health: Utopias, Progress and Biological Change.* New Brunswick, NJ: Rutgers University Press, 1987.

Feeney, D., F. Berkes, B. J. McCay, and J. M. Acheson. 1990. "The Tragedy of the Commons: Twenty-Two Years Later." *Human Ecology* 8:1–19.

Findlay, S. 1997. "Doctors' Hope for Their Ills: Unions." *USA Today,* April 15, 1997, 3A.

Frankford, D. M., and T. R. Konrad. 1998. "Responsive Medical Professionalism: Integrating Practice, Education, and Community in a Market-driven Era." *Academic Medicine* 73:138–45.

General Accounting Office. 1988. *Medicare: Physician Incentive Payments by Prepaid Health Plans Could Lower Quality of Care*. GAO/HRD-89-29. Washington, DC: Government Printing Office.

GMENAC. 1980. *Report to the Secretary*. U.S. Department of Health and Human Services Graduate Medical Education National Advisory Committee. Washington, DC: Government Printing Office.

Gray, G. 1998. "Access to Medical Care Under Strain: New Pressures in Canada and Australia." *Journal of Health Policy and Law* 23:905–48.

Grumbach, K., D. Osmond, K. Vranitzan, D. Jaffe, and A. B. Bindman. 1998. "Primary Care Physicians' Experience of Financial Incentives in Managed-Care Systems." *New England Journal of Medicine* 339:1516–21.

Halbert, R. J., A. Bokor, R. Castrence-Nazareno, M. D. Parkinson, and C. E. Lewis. 1998. "Competencies for Population-based Clinical Managers." *American Journal of Preventive Medicine* 15:65–70.

Hamel, M. B., J. M. Teno, L. Goldman, J. Lynn, R. B. Davis, A. N. Galanos, N. Desbiens, A. F. Connors Jr., N. Wenger, and R. S. Phillips. 1999. "Patient Age and Decisions to Withhold Life-sustaining Treatments from Seriously Ill, Hospitalized Adults." *Annals of Internal Medicine* 130:116–25.

Hardin, G. 1968. "The Tragedy of the Commons." *Science* 162:1243–48.

Kassirer, J. P. 1997. "Managing Managed Care's Tarnished Image." *New England Journal of Medicine* 337:338–39.

Kilborn, P. T. 1998. "Largest HMOs Cutting the Poor and the Elderly." *New York Times,* July 6, 1998, A1.

Koch, A. L. 1993. "Financing Health Services." In *Introduction to Health Services,* 5th ed., edited by S. J. Williams and P. R. Torrens, 113–50. Albany, NY: Delmar Press.

Kuttner, R. 1998. "Must Good HMOs Go Bad?" *New England Journal of Medicine* 338:1558–63, 1635–39.

Lawrence, D. M., P. H. Mattingly, and J. M. Ludden. 1997. "Trusting in the Future: The Distinct Advantage of Nonprofit HMOs." *Milbank Quarterly* 75 (1):5–10.

Lewis, D. 1933. "The Place of the Clinic in Medical Practice." *JAMA* 100:1905–10.

Light, D. 1986. "Surplus Versus Cost Containment: The Changing Context for Health Providers." In *Applications of Social Science to Clinical Medicine and Health Policy,* edited by L. H. Aiken and D. Mechanic, 519–42. New Brunswick, NJ: Rutgers University Press.

———. 1999. "Good Managed Care Needs Universal Health Insurance." *Annals of Internal Medicine* 130:686–89.

McCay, B. 2000. "Community-based and Cooperative Fisheries: Solutions to Fishermen's Problems." In *Protecting the Commons: A Framework for Resource Management in the Americas,* edited by J. Burger, E. Ostrom, R. B. Norgaard, D. Polincansky, and B. D. Goldstein. Washington, DC: Island Press.

Mechanic, D. 1996. "Changing Medical Organization and the Erosion of Trust." *Milbank Quarterly* 74:171–89.

———. 1998. "Topics for Our Times: Managed Care and Public Health Opportunities." *American Journal of Public Health* 88 (6):874–75.

Mechanic, D., and M. Schlesinger. 1996 "The Impact of Managed Care on Patients' Trust in Medical Care and Their Physicians." *JAMA* 275:1693–97.

Moore, S. 1979. "Cost Containment through Risk-Sharing by Primary Care Physicians." *New England Journal of Medicine* 300:1359–62.

Naylor, C. D. 1998. "What Is Appropriate Care?" *New England Journal of Medicine* 338: 1918–19.

Needleman, H. L. 1998. "Childhood Lead Poisoning: The Promise and Abandonment of Primary Prevention." *American Journal of Public Health* 88:1871–77.

Ostrom, E., J. Burger, C. B. Field, R. B. Norgaard, and D. Polincansky. 1996. "Revisiting the Commons: Local Lessons: Global Changes." *Science* 284:278–282.

Pearson, S. D., J. E. Sabin, and E. J. Emanuel. 1998. "Ethical Guidelines for Physician Compensation Based on Capitation." *New England Journal of Medicine* 339:689–93.

Pew Health Professions Commission. 1995. "Critical Challenges: Revitalizing the Health Professions for the 21st Century." San Francisco: University of California Center for the Health Professions.

Quinn, J. B. 1997. "Is Your HMO OK—or Not?" *Newsweek* (February 10, 1997): 52.

Reinhardt, U. E. 1994. "Planning the Nation's Health Workforce: Let the Market In." *Inquiry* 31:250–63.

———. 1997. "The Impending Physician Surplus: Is It Time to Quit?" *JAMA* 277:69.

Riley, G. F., A. L. Potosky, C. N. Klabunde, J. L. Warren, and R. Ballard-Barbash. 1999. "Stage at Diagnosis and Treatment Patterns Among Older Women with Breast Cancer: An HMO and Fee for Service Comparison." JAMA 281:720–26.

Rosenbaum, S., D. M. Frankford, B. Moore, and P. Borzi. 1999. "Who Should Determine When Health Care Is Medically Necessary." *New England Journal of Medicine* 340:229–32.

Rubin, H. W., B. Gandek, E. H. Rogers, M. Kosinski, C. A. McHorney, and J. E. Ware Jr. 1993. "Ratings of Outpatient Visits in Different Practice Settings. Results from the Medical Outcomes Study." *JAMA* 270:835–840.

Schauffler, H. H., and F. D. Scutchfield. 1998. "Managed Care and Public Health." *American Journal of Preventive Medicine* 14:240–41.

Seifer, S. D., B. Trocepin, and G. D. Rubenfeld. 1996. "Changes in Marketplace Demand for Physicians: A Study of Medical Journal Recruitment Advertisements." *JAMA* 276:695–99.

Shaw, G. B. 1906. *The Doctor's Dilemma.* New York: Brentano. 1911.

Shvarts, S., D. L. A. de Leeuw, S. Granit, and J. Benbassat. 1999. "Public Health Then and Now." *American Journal of Public Health* 89:248–53.

Weiner, J. P. 1994. "Forecasting the Effects of Health Reform on US Physician Workforce Requirement: Evidence from HMO Staffing Patterns." *JAMA* 272:222–30.

Wilensky, G. R. 1997. "Alleviating the Physician Glut: What's the Government's Role." *JAMA* 277:73.

Woolhandler, S., and D. U. Himmelstein. 1995. Editorial. "Extreme Risk: The New Corporate Proposition for Physicians." *New England Journal of Medicine* 333 (25):1706–07.

Part Four

DECISION-MAKING TOOLS

Chapter 13

Spatial Techniques for Understanding Commons Issues

JEFFREY E. RICHEY

The ancient civilizations of Mesopotamia, in the Fertile Crescent made possible by the Tigris and Euphrates Rivers, were among the first cultures to explore the advantages and discover the costs of using watershed–based common pool resources (*sensu* Ostrom and Ostrom 1977). They produced bountiful crops with irrigation and plowing and in the process discovered water scarcity, salinization, and soil loss. In the generations since, access to water has been a key determinant in the evolution of human society. The cost has been that the cumulative impact of human use has altered Earth's freshwater ecosystems profoundly, to a greater extent than terrestrial ecosystems (Vitousek et al. 1997).

Of all of the environmental security issues facing nations, an adequate supply of clean water is one of the most important. In developed economies, the water supply business has traditionally been very stable, but in the last two decades dramatic changes have occurred and supplies have become more difficult to obtain (Beard 1996). In developing economies, the task of providing adequate water supplies is almost overwhelming. Increases in resource demand rise directly with increases in population (fig. 13.1). Conflicts arising from the global use of water will be exacerbated in the years ahead, with a growing human population and the stresses that global changes will impose on water quality and availability.

Future management and optimization of water (and other common–pool resources) must emphasize demand management, efficiency improvements, and conservation. This will require increasingly sophisticated information on the functioning of the underlying physical and biological systems and how they are affected by socioeconomic and political institutions. Because these

273

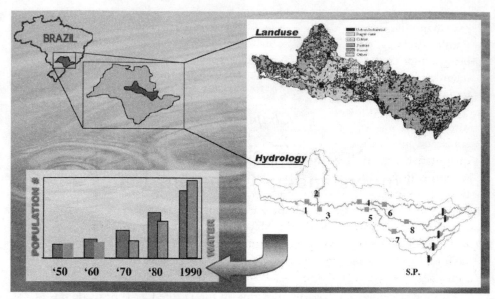

Figure 13.1. Increase in water use accompanying increase in population in the Piracicaba River basin, São Paulo, Brazil.

resources are frequently distributed across multiple physical and political boundaries, it is imperative that a suitable paradigm be developed that can guide their more sustained use.

Hardin (1998) may have laid a foundation for that paradigm. He observed that "in the language of twentieth century commentators traditional thinking was magnificently verbal and deplorably nonnumerate." A consequence is that contemporary policy and laws are sparse on quantitative criteria with which complex trade-offs can be evaluated. Hardin continued, "One of today's cardinal tasks is to marry the philosopher's literate ethics with the scientist's commitment to numerate analysis." Such a marriage would produce what might be called a *numerate ethics.*

The underlying assumption for a numerate ethics is that, in the face of inevitable pressures on the environment, resources can be allocated and used with a higher degree of precision than is currently possible. Although it must be recognized that resource decisions will be made regardless of the depth of supporting information, the question here is whether a numerate ethics can rigorously contribute to that decision support process. A template allowing decision makers to consider rigorous scenarios of alternative futures could play an important role in making complex environmental decisions. Design of such a template will require a robust numerate analysis of the systematic dynamics of the landscape with sufficient detail to be relevant on a broad geographic base. Contemporary earth system sciences, with their emerging capabilities in spatial and dynamic modeling coupled to such sophisticated observation systems as satellites, are now poised to provide the basis for numerate analysis. To bring ethics to the numerate analysis, the process must involve not only the scientists building the models but the policymakers and the citizenry of the region who use the analysis.

At least three problems must be resolved. The first is to understand and capture the characteristic dynamics and scales at which water moves across the landscape and into the ocean, under both intrinsic and human influences, into quantitative structures, or models, that can provide the basis for analysis. The second is to examine the key issues for a specific region (including recognition of the policy realities of cross-jurisdictional boundaries and ultimately politics at which resource decisions are typically made) and adapt the models to focus on these issues. The third problem is how to perceive and present the reality of the extremely complex information that would be derived through such a process. For another analysis of how water can be managed as a commons, see Schlager and Blomquist (chapter 6, this volume).

Capturing the Spatial and Temporal Dynamics of Watersheds

A watershed, as the landscape through which all waters flow from their highest source before draining naturally to the sea, can be considered a fundamental organizing unit of the land surface and its population (fig. 13.1). A watershed is defined by landforms, which do not necessarily correspond to political boundaries. Their edges are the ridges and hilltops that direct water into a stream or river, and their surfaces are the landscapes where communities grow. Rain or snow falls to the land surface. Some of this precipitation is returned to the atmosphere (through evapotranspiration), some is stored in the soil (as soil moisture), and the balance drains into stream networks (where it provides river flow, or discharge). As streams descend, tributaries and groundwaters add to their volume, creating ever-larger rivers.

As rivers leave the highlands, they slow and start to meander and braid. In the lower stretches of unmanaged rivers, water moves between the river's mainstream and its floodplain, modifying the flow regime and creating critical ecological niches. River and floodplain ecosystems are closely adapted to a river's flooding cycle. The diversity of a river lies not only in the various types of land surfaces (or land uses) it flows through but also in the changing seasons and the differences between wet and dry years.

Disruption of the linkages between the landscape and rivers and between rivers and their floodplains through human intervention fundamentally alters the nature of riverine ecosystems. Waterways have always been, and will continue to be, used for irrigation, transport, flood control, industrial and domestic consumption, and dilution of chemical wastes. The most disruptive influence on watersheds has been dams. Starting about fifty years ago, large dams were seen as a solution of water resource issues, including flood control, hydroelectric power generation, and irrigation. Now some 40,000 large dams obstruct the world's rivers. In the United States, only 2 percent of the rivers run unimpeded, and 5,500 large dams make it the second most dammed country in the world (Vitousek et al. 1997). But the time when large dams constitute a realistic answer to solving water problems probably is over.

The overall balance of energy over a watershed affects how water is partitioned between the atmosphere, soil, and river channel. Globally, human beings now use about a quarter of total terrestrial evapotranspiration and more than half of the runoff water that is fresh and reasonably accessible (with about 70 percent used in agriculture). Local or regional climate change may alter rainfall patterns. Irrigation increases atmospheric humidity in semiarid areas, often increasing precipitation and thunderstorm frequency. Changes in the landscape also have significant impact on watersheds and river flow. Converting a forest to a field or parking lot will change the flow pathways from rain to the river. Land transformation from forest to agriculture or pasture increases albedo and decreases surface roughness, which has the net regional effect of increasing temperature and decreasing precipitation.

Intrinsic Spatial and Temporal Scales of Watersheds

In terms of management, individual small stream segments are often the unit of concern to a local agency and are often observed by simply "walking the stream." But the hydrology of that stream is determined by the larger watershed that stream is nested in, which probably has its headwaters in an another county or even country. Impacts of land-use change on an entire river basin cannot be defined simply by summing up the impacts observed on individual streams; extrapolations based on scaling must be made. Overall, we must recognize the spatial and temporal relationships between dynamic ecosystems within river basins, where a landscape is composed of ever-changing elements, according to how the system is observed.

So what are the scales at which watersheds and their models can realistically be represented? Ultimately, this is a trade-off between how finely individual processes can be described, the data that are actually available, and the ability of computers to make calculations. Theoretically, there is a continuous range of scales represented in a watershed. In practice, the nature of how observations can even be made imposes some serious constraints. For example, an observer flying over a section of the Amazon floodplain will see a series of discrete and recognizable landscape patches, made up of streams, main river, pastures and forest, and open and closed lake environments (fig. 13.2). The

Figure 13.2. What the environment looks like at different scales: the Amazon floodplain (top, bottom left), Rio Xingu (upper right), and Taiwan (lower right).

processes occurring in each patch can be readily be measured directly. A landscape of this scale can best be described by satellites of the LANDSAT Thematic Mapper (TM) type, which can "see" up to 180 km in extent. But the distinction of what can be observed is reduced to 30-m homogeneous patches (pixels) in fewer spectral bands than the eye itself will observe, resulting in a more blurred view of the landscape. When we move to larger scales yet, which is necessary to characterize regions, our ability to observe distinct features is degraded further. For example, the Advanced Very High Resolution Radiometer (AVHRR) satellite can "see" for hundreds of kilometers but with no better than 1-km pixels, in fewer bands yet. As a result, for example, the Rio Xingu in the Brazilian Amazon is barely distinguished, never mind details of the floodplain. In moving from the AVHRR-scale view to the global scale, pixels of 1° latitude/longitude (about 100 km on a side in low to midlatitudes) render large regions essentially uniform (for instance, Taiwan becomes 2 pixels). At these larger scales, specific objects in space are less important than the general "pulse" between longer temporal patterns and larger spatial extents. Time and magnitude of spatial variance are perhaps the most important variables at these scales. Issues of data aggregation and temporal phasing drive the modeling requirements.

The temporal scales of watersheds cover as much range as do the spatial scales. Although the shape of the landscape itself (hills, valleys) will evolve (on geological time scales), these changes occur much more slowly than the seasonal and yearly evolution of the land cover and land use. These seasonal changes in turn occur much more slowly than a rainstorm, whose characteristic time scale is on the order of minutes to hours. The processes with which we are concerned, such as the translation of rainfall into runoff across different types of landscapes, are themselves described differently at different space scales. The overall ensemble of these landscape features, which we can observe at multiple scales, can be thought of as the physical template on which the more rapidly dynamic processes can operate.

Toward a Spatially Explicit Model of the Landscape

To bring this multiscaled physical template into a computational environment, the template can be thought of as being made up of a series of multiple elements (called grid cells or drainage basin elements), each of which has uniform attributes that can be characterized (fig. 13.3). These attributes (themselves spatial models) must include representations of the landscape that subsequent dynamic models require (such as the hydraulic properties of soil imparted by soil texture). A region is then made up of multiple grid cells, according to the resolution desired and what data it is feasible to acquire. The ensemble of these

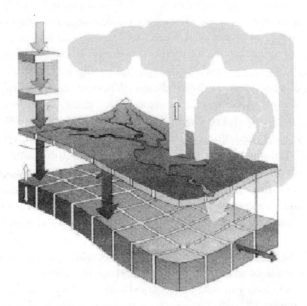

Figure 13.3. Schematic of the physical template basis for a geographic information system (GIS) representation of the land surface and climate.

attributes can be represented in a computer format with which calculations can be made. The emergence of geographic information system (GIS) computer software allows such an organization of information.

The physical template is more than a GIS database of thematic layers. It is the explicit geographically referenced statement of the relationship between these data layers over both space and time. The template captures the multiplicity of time and space scales over which the watershed environment changes and to which humans must respond. The template is restricted, of course, to the data available to describe it.

Within the template, the slowly changing elements of the landscape (topography, river networks, soil texture) can be derived and left alone because they change much less frequently than the more dynamic components of the system. Land cover and land use (often determined through satellite imagery) may need to be updated on their characteristic time scale of seasonal to annual (depending on the objective). The next level of temporal resolution is that of changes in rainfall, solar radiation, humidity, and surface winds, which are the inputs (biophysical drivers) for the dynamic models themselves.

Dynamic Models of Basin Processes

With a physical template specified, models of dynamic processes of the environment, from the atmosphere to the land surface to marine circulation and productivity, can be developed, coupled, and used to evaluate resource issues. Models consist of the scientific theory of physical processes affecting a region, embodied in a computer program. While imperfect and at risk for misuse and misinterpretation, such models do summarize the cumulative understanding of a problem in ways that can be tested.

Contemporary models of land surface processes can be divided into several major components (fig. 13.4). As can be represented in a regional-scale climate model, the atmosphere's climate communicates with the land surface by distributing rainfall, temperature, and wind. A vertical component calculates the water balance of a grid cell. The water balance model is applied at each individual grid cell over the defined region and separates precipitation into evapotranspiration (a calculation that requires knowing solar radiation, temperature, and ideally surface winds), soil moisture change (a calculation that requires information about soil texture and how much water reaches the soil surface, after being intercepted by the tree canopy), and runoff from the land surface to streams. The actual rates at which these processes occur fundamentally depend on such attributes as soil texture, rooting depth, slope, and other physical characteristics, which must be described for each cell.

A horizontal component then takes the runoff generated by each grid cell

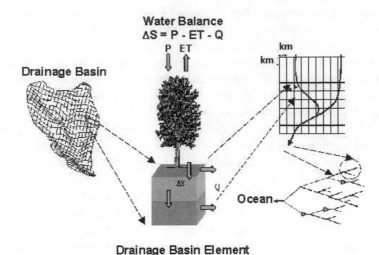

Figure 13.4. A typical hydrology model for a drainage basin.

(as the surplus from the tipping bucket) and routes it (transports it) downstream. The combined surface and subsurface flow generated at each individual grid cell is routed to the stream network according to, for example, assumptions about how long the water should take to reach the nearest stream. Once the water enters the stream reach, it is routed to the ocean through the stream network (represented by the stick diagram). Downstream discharge is then compared (but not calibrated) against observed data from stream-gauging stations. Water storage in reservoirs, and withdrawals from reservoir and channel reaches, can be included in routing models. Water for irrigation can be withdrawn from the appropriate reach or reservoir and added to the grid cell as throughfall.

Application of a Numerate Ethics to a Specific Region: The Puget Sound Basin of Washington State

For a numerate ethics to be relevant to a specific region, such issues as the following must be addressed:

- What is important to the region?
- What is required of an integrated modeling system to provide decision support at the scales required by managers and decision makers?
- What are the trade-offs between those requirements and information availability?

As a test case, the general framework sketched out in the previous section will be applied to the Puget Sound basin (Pacific Northwest, USA). The application is based on the PRISM (Puget Sound Regional Synthesis Model) project. The central metaphor for capturing the interactive and dynamic knowledge bases and the issues of the region is via the creation and execution of a "virtual Puget Sound."

The Region: Its Issues and Jurisdictions

The Pacific Northwest is a region of extreme contrasts in physical geography, land use, and rainfall. Water is the unifying theme across most sectors of the Pacific Northwest economy and culture, from the traditionally important sectors—forestry, fisheries, agriculture, energy—to the recreation and quality-of-life issues that have become central to the explosively growing non–resource-based sectors. Salmon are not only an icon of the region but a reminder of how integrally linked climate, land surface processes, and the oceans are.

The most populated sector of the Pacific Northwest is the Puget Sound basin, a region of about 30,000 km², with a classic partitioning of multiple jurisdictions crossing drainage basin boundaries (fig. 13.5). There are eleven

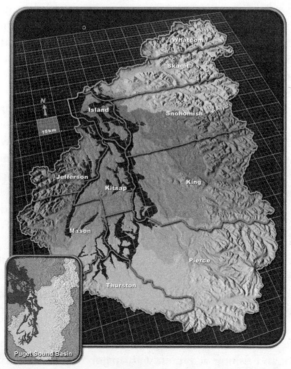

Figure 13.5. Puget Sound basins overlapped with county boundaries.

primary river basins divided among eight counties, which in turn are made up of numerous municipalities, which themselves fall under state and federal government. These governing bodies are then responsible for enforcing a set of laws and regulations with regional consequences.

Stewardship of this region poses a series of interrelated questions, typical of those raised in many other regions, which must be confronted by current and future managers:

- What are the responses of the land surface to changes induced by urban pressures and overall population growth and from climate variability on seasonal to interannual and decade time scales?
- What impacts are discernible with respect to freshwater and marine water quality, agriculture, forestry, fisheries, and coastal erosion and hazards, and what management capacities and policy response strategies are needed?
- How can water resources best be accommodated to meet flow needs for agriculture, endangered species of salmon, and domestic and industrial consumption?

Under the Washington Growth Management Act (GMA) of 1990–1991, most of the state's counties and their constituent municipalities are required to do comprehensive land-use planning for management of urban growth and protection of prime natural resource lands and environmentally critical areas. The GMA also requires monitoring of growth, including the spatial and temporal concurrency of urban growth and infrastructure improvements. These monitoring requirements have been among the most difficult for local and regional governments to accomplish.

Responsibilities for water resource planning and management are divided. User agencies include the Washington State departments of ecology, natural resources, and fish and wildlife, with their mandates for basinwide water resource planning, administration of water permits, and protection of instream flows. At a regional level, the Puget Sound Water Quality Action Team is responsible for implementing the Puget Sound Water Quality Management Plan and the federally approved Comprehensive Conservation and Management Plan under Section 320 (the National Estuary Program) of the Clean Water Act. The plan identifies activities for implementation at the local government level. Local government agencies include the Tri-County (King, Pierce, and Snohomish) coordination for salmon recovery, the Hood Canal Coordinating Council, and planning offices of the twelve basinwide counties.

The joint growth and water resource issues are accentuated with the listing of chinook salmon as threatened under the Endangered Species Act (ESA). This will require significant changes in urban development, pollution control, forestry, farming, and fishing activities, with major implications for resource management and land-use planning throughout much of the Pacific

Northwest. Listing species under the ESA will increase information requirements, including the need for monitoring forest and agricultural practices, urban growth, and land-cover or land-use change. Players in the ESA arena are many, including the U.S. Fish and Wildlife; NOAA/National Marine Fisheries Service; Washington departments of natural resources, fish and wildlife, and agriculture, local governments throughout the region; and habitat restoration groups.

A Virtual Puget Sound: A High-Resolution Integrated Model

The virtual Puget Sound (VPS) centers on coupling dynamic ecosystem simulation models with models of human behavior and socioeconomic forecast (fig. 13.6). Each model performs its own predictions based on its own input data. The time and space scales of each submodel then provide, essentially by definition, what the relevant and feasible space and time scales of each set of processes are.

The base physical template on which the VPS is built consists of layers of different temporal resolution (fig. 13.7). Digital elevation data, from which river networks are derived, change only on geological time scales. Soils and their attributes are then distributed across the elevation models. River networks are set by the elevation but may wander on decade time scales (particularly with human intervention). Vegetation may respond on an annual basis (as well as seasonal cycles), and is represented through LANDSAT time series data (e.g., fig. 13.2). With the template in place, the more dynamic properties of how water and energy are transferred from the atmosphere to the land surface and across the land surface can be represented. This template is also being

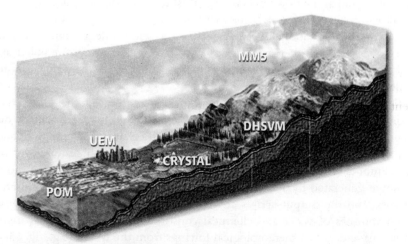

Figure 13.6. Linked models of the virtual Puget Sound.

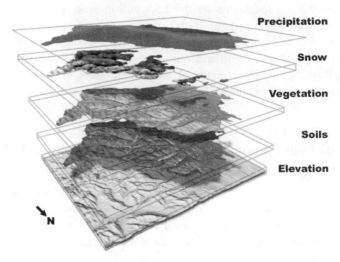

Figure 13.7. The physical template basis for the virtual Puget Sound, illustrated here for the Snoqualmie River basin.

shared with regional agencies as the most complete land-cover source in the region for purposes ranging from habitat inventories to assessing extent of impervious surfaces for calculating taxes.

Meteorological forcing for the surface hydrology model is provided by a so-called mesoscale atmospheric model (the MM5), designed to predict regional-scale atmospheric circulations and surface exchanges. The MM5 produces 48-hr weather forecasts at 12-km spatial resolution for the entire Pacific Northwest and at 4-km resolution over Washington state (e.g., fig. 13.8). This model is initialized using both observations (satellite and in situ) and large-scale output from National Weather Service models. Model outputs are being used in regional weather forecasting. Past "climates" will be assembled and used as the basis for seasonal to annual climate alternatives for water resource models and for global change assessment.

Finer-scale surface water movement is represented via the Distributed Hydrology-Soil-Vegetation Model (DHSVM), a physically based, spatially distributed hydrologic model that explicitly solves the water-and-energy balance over a topographic grid with cells typically 30–200 m in dimension. A hydrological model routes the output of this spatially explicit data through a model landscape generated by a three-dimensional land-surface, elevation, and river network, and the output arrives at the coastal interface in the form of estimated volumes of water and chemical constituents. DHSVM uses as inputs spatial image data and meteorological forcings from the MM5 (e.g., fig. 13.9).

Surface Temperatures   Surface Winds

Figure 13.8. Model fields of surface temperature and surface winds from the MM5 mesoscale circulation model. (C. Mass, pers. comm.)

Immediate output from the model is starting to be used for flood forecasting and for generating in-stream flow alternatives for salmon.

This hydrology process model is then linked to a water resource model (CRYSTAL) predicting the availability and potential uses of water in Puget Sound (fig. 13.10). This model integrates the separate water supply systems to better use existing regional resources by viewing Puget Sound as a single watershed. The goal of the model is to illustrate the value and opportunities of a regional approach to water management, particularly in meeting the needs of both fish and people. Answering this challenge is becoming increasingly important as in-stream requirements are modified to address the impending salmon listing under the ESA. The model simulates water system response to different scenarios (e.g., "How will increased flow requirements for the salmon affect the reliability of the urban water supply? When might water use curtail-

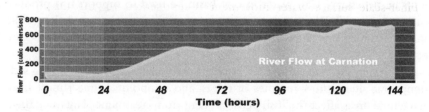

Figure 13.9. Application of the DHVSM (D. Lettenmaier, pers. comm.) to a snow-storm in the Snoqualmie River basin, followed by rapid melting and rapid river rise.

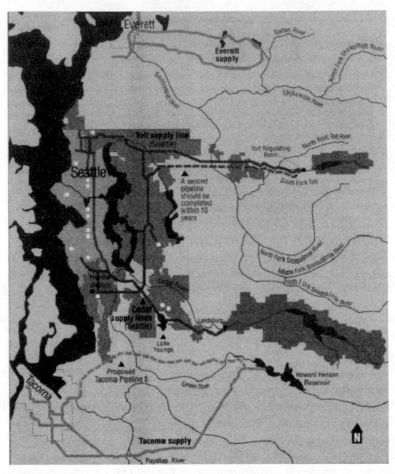

Figure 13.10. The CRYSTAL water resources model (R. Palmer, pers. comm.) for allocating water between the principal utility districts of Seattle, Tacoma, and Everett.

ments be necessary? Can water in one basin be used to support fish production in another?"). With such tools, regional decision makers and the public can better understand the consequences of important policy and infrastructure decisions.

Changes in the land surface affect nearshore marine waters. Increasing sediment flow, altered flow regimes of rivers, and nonpoint source runoff from agricultural areas affect shellfish beds. Effluent from treatment plants can affect plankton communities. A numerical ocean circulation model (the Princeton Ocean Model, or POM), used extensively by coastal and estuarine researchers, captures the circulation of Puget Sound. The model, simulating Puget Sound

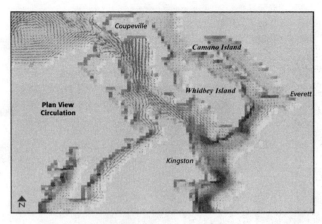

Figure 13.11. A snapshot of modeled POM (M. Kawase, pers. comm.) surface vectors of tidal currents over 24 hours.

circulation and stratification for a model year, is forced by realistic tides and river flows from the hydrology model (fig. 13.11). An immediate application for the model is assessing the best location for a proposed major sewage treatment plant.

The coupled model is driven by not only the biophysical system dynamics but by explicit links to human alteration of the land surface by projecting environmental pressures of urbanization under various management practices. These human pressures are reflected in the state of land cover, air and water quality, and application of management programs in forestry, agriculture, and fisheries. At various time steps, a variety of feedback loops in the coupled model simulates socioeconomic responses to environmental changes and predicts the dynamics of the altered landscape (fig. 13.12).

The aggregate of the specific submodels, each of which addresses its own specific issues, is the value added by an interdisciplinary synthesis that provides the basis for a regional numerate ethics.

Numerate Literacy: End-to-End Information Networking and Visualization

The virtual Puget Sound raises some difficult technical issues. Modern society is increasingly confronted, if not characterized, by requirements to generate, process, and, it is hoped, understand high volumes of digital information representing extremely complex phenomena. Determining the overall sequence of acquisition, processing, use, and communication of such information is a fundamental challenge for a new generation of managers.

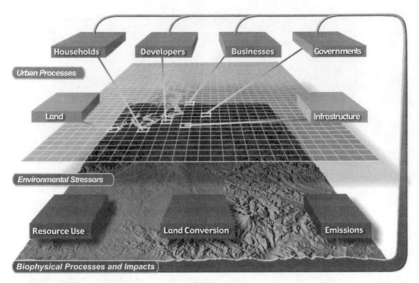

Figure 13.12. Schematic diagram of the UrbanSim model (M. Alberti, pers. comm.) for describing changes in the demography of the Puget Sound basin and the consequences for the environment.

Data Management

How to solve the information management and computational issues of linking such complicated models and observations and then making the products accessible to a wide variety of users constitutes a significant challenge in information technology (fig. 13.13). There are approximately 6 million grid cells across the Puget Sound domain, with thirty-eight levels of atmosphere, three layers of soil, and thirty-two layers of marine environment, on which dynamical calculations are performed. The data, even for one specific submodel, come in many different formats and resolutions: spatially, from cm (rarely) to 10 m (often) to ~1 km (common); temporally, from every second to once per year or less. Adding to the problems, data come from many sources. This produces more possible variations of collected data, processed forms of collected data, transformed submodel outputs, and hypothetical data constructed by users who want to see how some process works or to test a hypothesis. The challenge is to efficiently store and analyze data from multiple data sources in metadata-referenced mass storage and knowledge bases.

The Visual Interface

Such complex information must be conveyed to multiple parties, from the student and the scientist involved in developing the information systems to the

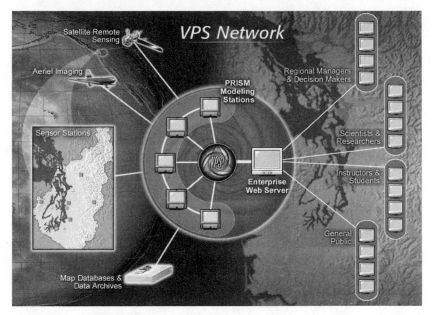

Figure 13.13. Information networks and interfaces needed to gather, process, and distribute complex information.

end user making decisions (fig. 13.14). Recent advances in visualization technology combined with the dramatic increase in computer communication, including the World Wide Web, are making this possible. For example, the virtual Puget Sound is being brought to life by the wrapping of linked models with a visual interface, creating a user-friendly, interactive virtual environment. This resource can then be made available to many different types of users via the Internet. Interface development will include Web-based tools to access database structures, create interactive visualizations, and extract customized information from the models and data.

Toward a Sustainable Future

Water is one of the foremost examples of a common-pool resource in which sustainability cannot be accomplished by individuals acting out of self-interest alone; there must be intergenerational commons institutions to ensure sustainability. The vitality of watersheds is the result of all the day-to-day decisions of their inhabitants. How to do it? We can indeed generalize from one scale to the next. The new generation of earth system science provides necessary capabilities for addressing cross-scale issues in a quantitative way, which can allow improved capabilities to provide scenarios of future

Figure 13.14. A schematic of the visualization of complex information.

outcomes. But these capabilities alone are not sufficient. Other requirements also must be met.

Tools for systematic synthesis of information leading to a coherent information base that can be applied to regional evaluation must be developed. A large amount of data is available in many regions, but there are few synthesis tools to bring it together. To sustain a numerate ethics, there must be a systematic identification of what information is needed, where it is, and how it must be brought together.

A predicative capability and scenario generation across multiple time and space scales is necessary. Though critical, synthesized information alone is not sufficient. The capability to use such information to evaluate resource and policy options is critical. This must be done with models and should include economic values and benefit/cost ratios for managers at levels of evaluating specific actions. As an end product, building a scaled modeling environment that addresses cumulative effects and allows adaptive management is being increasingly called for.

A process for communication between scientists of different disciplines (the model developers) and especially between scientists and policy makers must be established. Bringing together information from multiple sources, analyzing it with models, and ultimately conveying it not only to other scientists but also to policy-makers are not trivial or common tasks. They require an explicit commitment to the process of communication and display. Solutions involving building the capacity of interdisciplinary scientists (including recruiting young scientists trained in the tools of synthesis), developing means for communication, and targeting how to involve policymakers in the process must be proactively sought. Technical issues of information transfer and visualization must be incorporated into the process.

Hardin (1998) concludes that the tragedy of the commons is well tailored for contemporary resource issues, as expedited by interdisciplinary synthesis. But the difficulties should not be underestimated: "The more specialties we try to stitch together, the greater are our opportunities for mistakes, and the more numerous are willing critics." Large teams of specialists have had considerable difficulty communicating the causes and long-term implications to each other, let alone to the general public. The melding of contemporary earth science tools specifically focused on legally mandated resource issues has enormous potential to effect a managed commons. Numerate literacy, executed by the interdisciplinary capabilities of today's science community and mediated by social and political scientists and practitioners, empowers the viable commons of tomorrow.

Acknowledgments

This chapter is based on extensive discussions with my colleagues in the PRISM project, in particular Dr. Miles Logsdon. Figures are based on content provided by Mark Stoermer and Hunter Hadaway (Center for Environmental Visualization, UW). Funding has been provided by the University of Washington University Initiative Fund, the National Science Foundation, and the National Aeronautics and Space Administration. CAMREX contribution number 103.

References

Beard, D. P. 1996. *Creating a Vision of Rivers for the 21st Century.* Remarks at the International Dam Summit, Nagaragawa, Japan. International Rivers Network.

Hardin, G. 1998. "Essays on Science and Society." *Science* 280 (5364):682–83.

Ostrom, V., and E. Ostrom. 1977. "Public Goods and Public Choices." In *Alternatives for Delivering Public Services: Toward Improved Performance,* edited by E. S. Savas, 7–49. Boulder, CO: Westview Press.

Vitousek, P. M., H. A. Mooney, J. Lubchenco, and J. Melillo. 1997. "Human Domination of Earth's Ecosystems." *Science* 277:494–99.

Chapter 14

Integrating Scale and Social Justice in the Commons

MICHEL GELOBTER

An Americas perspective on the commons would be hopelessly incomplete without the recognition that this continent, in the last five hundred years, suffered a tragedy of the commons of speed and scale unparalleled in human history. Such radical changes in American ecological and resource regimes could not have occurred in the absence of deep social change. Indeed, the history of the American commons is linked to a number of human tragedies that include mass expropriation, genocide, and slavery.

Tragedies in the management of common-pool resources (CPRs) are less about natural resources themselves than they are about the social resources and institutions that determine CPR outcomes. The hope that CPRs can be managed sustainably depends on this fact. CPR users are not bound, as Hardin implies in his classic article, to an inexorable run to resource exhaustion (Hardin 1968). Often, but still too infrequently, they build institutions committed to the renewal of shared natural resources (Ostrom chapter 1, this volume). Such institutions, as well as the health or the "tragedy" of a resource pool, are defined within an anthropocentric frame, within the context of human action and institutions at many scales.

A number of observers have noted that the social structures that bound and define resource commons share the fundamental characteristics of commons themselves. For example, Feeny et al., in an analysis of fisheries argue,

> The creation of a new institution itself is indeed a form of collective action and thus subject to free rider problems. . . . The collapse of the California sardine industry, one of the most egregious wildlife management failures in U.S. history, thus came about

because of a "tragedy of the commons" not only in the fishery itself but also in the very legal/political processes that were supposed to counteract such problems. Too many government bodies competed with each other for political resources for any of them to account meaningfully for such diffuse, intangible, or transgenerational values as were really at stake in the sardine controversy. (Feeny, et al. 1996)

CPRs and human institutions both represent finite resources with delineated sets of users. In either context, each user reduces the overall amount of the resource available to others.

Although not usually cast as starkly as above, the idea that the social world exhibits some of the characteristics of commons is a recurring theme in the social sciences. This chapter tentatively groups diverse conceptions of the social commons (such as social structures, institutions, ideologies, norms, cultures, ethical systems, religions, and so forth) under the rubric of social pool resources (or SPRs). Unlike CPRs, SPRs are created in a wholly human context. Although they can take on physical manifestations (such as buildings, equipment, and infrastructure), their primary resource is the pool of human will of which they are constituted.

By dint of age, religion, occupation, income, gender, race, or other social characteristics, individuals contribute to many such pools simultaneously. A native fisherman can be a commercial operator and still hold a spiritual obligation to his prey. Citizens who pool resources to protect a particular commons may be both beneficiaries of that formation and, as taxpayers, victims of their own special interest. The democratic state itself, in traditional Western political thought, is no more or less than the collective pool of individual wills that supplanted the monarch in whom sovereignty previously resided (Foucault 1986).

Research on CPRs to date has focused on the conditions under which natural resources have been managed sustainably or not. The dominant approach, characterized by Baland and Platteau (1998a) as "evolutionary," posits that individuals, motivated by their interests, evolve new institutions to manage CPRs. Changes in commons management are the logical outcome of individual decisions, driven by scarcity and guided by concerns of efficiency and wealth maximization (Hayami and Ruttan 1981:22). A commons is only one of the sets of rights and obligations that may emerge. Private property regimes are the dominant alternative, or the default when individual or resource attributes are not conducive to cooperation (Baland and Platteau 1998a; Ostrom chapter 1, this volume).

While acknowledging the importance of the institutional context, this literature has focused predominantly on the challenges to self-organization posed by the intersection of resource characteristics and decision making by individual resource users (Ostrom chapter 1, this volume; Ostrom et al. 1999). The importance of preexisting SPRs (such as the state, the culture, the economy) has been subsumed to the analysis of the conditions necessary for forming new SPRs for sustainable natural resource management.

An Americas perspective, because of the very starkness of our resource history, provides an opportunity to assess the ways in which the tragedies and, at times, the stability of resources and human institutions are deeply interwoven. This chapter examines the management of the American commons from an SPR perspective. By focusing on social history and institutions, it identifies theoretical insights into how SPRs shape CPRs and how CPRs in their own right, engender change in social systems beyond those specific to the natural resource in question.

Furthermore, the SPR perspective explicitly adds a distributional dimension to the efficiency-centered, evolutionary framework. The dominant variable in evolutionary analysis of commons has been the relative effectiveness of CPR regimes for the purposes of efficient resource extraction or sustainability. When, as will be done here, the analysis is broadened to include the institutional and historical environment that shapes CPR management, we must also recognize the diversity of possible efficient outcomes that exist within a broader social context (Baland and Platteau 1997; Baland and Platteau 1998b; Howarth and Norgaard 1990). This diversity can be understood only through an analysis of the equity and justice dimensions of the commons.

The next section briefly examines the history of commons in the Americas in the context of this chapter's core arguments: that social institutions may be understood as a form of commons themselves and that the preservation of resource commons is inseparable from the development of just social institutions. The third part develops the theoretical intersection between SPRs and CPR regimes, and the fourth extends analyses of equity and justice concerns for individual CPR regimes to an understanding of the commons and justice in the broader social context. Finally, the fifth section examines atmospheric commons at the local, national, and international levels as examples of how SPRs and an environmental justice analysis can contribute to our understanding of resource problems at multiple scales.

A Brief Social History of the American Commons

In 1492, the Americas stood, by any modern standard, as idylls of common property use. The vast majority of their native communities had lived for tens of thousands of years with resource management practices that did little to exclude users and fostered sustainable extraction. Even resources that represented a significant investment of time and effort, such as the cultivated vegetable tracts managed by indigenous people in New England, were open to other forms of harvesting (hunting or gathering nonagricultural products, for example) by other kinship groups and villages (Cronon 1983: 62).

Such practices stood in sharp contrast to Europeans' imperative for commodification of resources that drove the initial exploration and settlement of these continents. Explorers and new settlers most often described the new territories in lists of "merchantable commodities" (Hakluyt 1584, as cited in Cronon 1983: 20). From the outset, colonists in the Americas "treated members of an ecosystem as isolated and extractable units" (Cronon 1983: 21).

Europe in the early sixteenth century had already faced significant resource scarcity. Combined with high population densities, this scarcity made resources the limiting factor to economic growth. In 1787, physician Joseph Warren wrote, "In England, rents are high and labour low; in America, it is just the reverse, rents are low and the rate of labour high" (Warren 1787: 168, as cited in Cronon 1983). In the economic regimes of the New World, land and resources were cheap while labor costs were high. In a description reminiscent of accounts of contemporary Amazonian agriculture, a Swedish observer in the mid-1750s described New England farmers' practice of exhausting their land (through slash-and-burn techniques) only to move to a new swath of forest: "This kind of agriculture will do for a time, but it will afterward have bad consequences, as every one may clearly see" (Kalm 1753–1761, 1770, vol. 1: 307, as cited in Cronon 1983). Colonial powers moved aggressively to make land an even cheaper input to production through aggressive expropriation of territory and delineation of property rights.

The history of the American commons richly illustrates how the rules of social collective action are deeply entwined with those of resource commons. The battles over resource regimes were more about culture, institutions, and ideas than about small groups or individual actors. Rampant privatization had a disastrous effect on native cultures and their relations to the environment. The transition from commons regimes to private property erased the very basis of native livelihood. SPRs representing millennia of tradition with the land were supplanted by externally imposed social rules and institutions. The link between the viability of native SPRs and the preservation of commons regimes was so tight that we cannot distinguish between land expropriation as a means toward native genocide and a commerce-maximizing end in itself.

Another new SPR emerged as part of new commons practices: Slavery was adopted as a solution to the high cost of labor in the New World. From its onset at the end of the fifteenth century to the last abolition in the early twentieth century, the forced migration known as the Middle Passage brought tens of millions of Africans into a system aimed primarily at facilitating a natural resource–based economy (Patterson 1982). Slavery was central to the emergence of the American plantation regimes whose stocks-in-trade included sugar, cotton, and human beings. (In one grotesque parallel to the argument made here that human and social institutions represent a form of commons, a significant economic analysis of this system conducted in the 1970s goes so far as to liken the Atlantic slave trade to a fishery [Thomas and Bean 1974].)

At times, changes in commons regimes themselves helped lower the cost of labor. Much of Mexico and what is now the southwestern United States was settled in the seventeenth and eighteenth centuries using *mercedes,* or land grants. These grants were large tracts of land that were managed communally by settlers and occupied at times cooperatively with native people. As the logic of American capitalism and Anglo-American dominance encroached on these communities, existing commons regimes were dismantled. Simultaneously, dispossessed Hispanic farmers were thrust into a sharecropper (no-wage) or low-wage economy (Pulido 1996: 131–32). The story of American commons is thus also one of the reshaping of labor pools into new SPRs, for better or for worse, into new forms that ranged from slavery to communal democracies.

Although American resources and land were first and foremost seen as commodities, the *mercedes* were an example of CPRs that served as an intermediate stage between the resources' original status as a commons and their commercialization. Such intermediate regimes served, in many cases, to pool risks and to secure European privilege. The Massachusetts Bay Company, for example, moved from apportioning land to individual settlers to giving village land grants, partially because collective claims were easier to explain to and defend from native people. Europeans also found greater security in the village form reminiscent of the common places in their home countries. New towns would then be subdivided among their owners in some mix of public and private use (Cronon 1983: 72–73). In another context, Feeny et al. describe the exclusion of Chinese from the turn-of-the-century San Francisco crab harvest as the "first and most important step . . . to produc[ing] an optimum yield for the group [Italians]" (Feeny et al. 1996). The Americas were, and still are, a testing ground for new forms of property, for institutional experimentation on where to draw the line between what is common and what is private.

Even after social structures became more democratic, racially exclusionary practices were common in and around CPRs. Access to the parks (local, state, and national) created in the United States over the last century was almost universally limited to white people until the 1960s (Caro 1975; Hurley 1995; West 2000). U.S. urban planning and infrastructure development often targeted people of color and low-income communities in such cities as Houston,

New York, and St. Louis for the management of public "bads" such as toxic waste facilities, garbage transfer stations, bus depots, and other disamenities (Bullard 1983; Bullard 1990; Bullard and Wright 1985; Hurley 1997; Miller 1993). Such facilities are a form of commons: a collective place to manage environmental "bads." Racism is a legacy of American history, and it too is a pool resource, an institutional presence in our midst.

Unfortunately, the American contribution to tragedies of the commons unfolding today remains problematic. In the colonial era, much of the destruction of local commons regimes was conducted or sanctioned by royal grant or fiat. The democratic heir to sovereign power, national government, can play a similar role. In the case of Brazil, for example, Baland and Platteau argue, "When the government heavily subsidizes the intrusion of modern business interests into traditional resource territories . . . not only deforestation but also dispossession or disenfranchisement of traditional user communities can result" (Baland and Platteau 1998a).

The same ethos that fueled our whirlwind conversion from the most communal to the most commercial geography in the world accounts for the overwhelming contemporary burden that the Americas place on the global commons. Five hundred years after Europe's discovery of America, Canada and the United States alone had contributed 33 percent of the planet's surplus CO_2, not including contributions from changes in land use. In 1993 alone, almost 28 percent of the world's fossil-fuel resources were consumed in these countries by less than 6 percent of the world's population. The statistics available are relentless in cataloging our disproportionate contemporary consumption of planetary resources (fig. 14.1).

What is it about American social structure, about the fabric of our social will, that leaves such a heavy mark on our natural resources? The next section suggests some of the ways in which social institutions come to pattern our management of commons and some of the sources of America's particular natural resource history.

Social-Pool Resources and the Commons

> "Mastery over nature inevitably turns into mastery over men."
> (Leiss 1974: 194)

The reshaping of the American (and thus the global) commons began around the same time that Europe began a cultural and material "emancipation" from nature. At a material level, Europeans had begun to experience real limits to growth in the form of resource scarcity and explosive population growth, and they responded with an unprecedented global expansion of their resource base. Equally important, European culture and thought reflected this increased

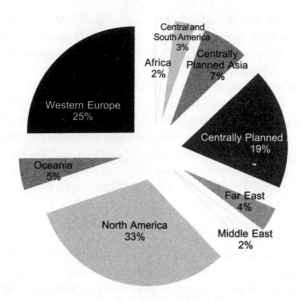

Figure 14.1. Cumulative CO$_2$ emissions as of 1996. *Sources:* Marland, et al. (1999). Global, Regional, and National CO$_2$ Emission and Gas Flaring: 1751–1996 Numeric Data Package (NDP-030; FTP site). Carbon Dioxide Information Analysis Center.

dependence on an external nature by conceptually divorcing people from their natural environments (Horkheimer 1947). Resources and the physical world would increasingly be seen as objects separate from the social world and, eventually, subservient to social order. As Heidegger put it in contemporary terms, "nature becomes 'one vast gasoline station' for human exploitation" (Harvey 1996: 134).

The price exacted on the natural and social worlds by their separation was at the heart of the political philosophy known as the Frankfurt School. Its thinkers struggled with a dialectic: How could a nature so evidently within each of us be so easily overcome and controlled outside of us? (Horkheimer 1947; Jay 1973). In their view, people had forgotten their internal linkages with nature and succumbed to a clear separation, emergent during Enlightenment, between society and nature. This separation provided a modern justification for the incorporation of colonized and enslaved people into resource management regimes as another factor to production. The domination of nature led to new forms of domination and injustice among people.

Analysis of SPRs enables us to explain the persistence, speed, and pattern of the changes seen in the Americas in the last 500 years. Many of the Frankfurt school's views were formed in the Americas during Adorno and

Horkheimer's World War II exile in Los Angeles (Davis 1992). Their experiences here as well as the preceding account of the American commons highlight the linkage between CPRs and the social-pool resources that reshape them.

The vision of nature as a resource for human use has dominated the analysis of commons regimes to date. Decision makers are presumed to be engaged in an individual calculus of costs and benefits about natural resource use with little thought of other, noncommercial or nonremunerative linkages to the commons. These assumptions clearly hold for many commons, but their usefulness can be extended by placing individual behavior in the context of the types of SPRs that enabled such views of the commons to become dominant.

SPR Types and the Role of Power

The currency of social resources is power. When herders meet to allocate a pasture, the concept of power best captures the force that determines the winners and the losers. The social resources that structure that meeting (property rights, rules of negotiation, the existence of markets) themselves embody power relations that distinguish those with greater capacity to achieve their desired outcomes from those with less. For the purposes of understanding the interaction between SPRs and CPR regimes, table 14.1 delineates two primary axes along which SPRs can be classified and defined by the types of power they embody and where that power is exercised. The table lists examples of SPRs that can influence commons regimes.

Table 14.1. Social-Pool Resources: Examples in Interactions with CPRs.

	Domain of Action	
Domain of Power	Ideological	Material
Authority	• Universities • Scientific expertise • Cultural values • Religion	• Kinship • Military • Police • Judicial system and legal resources (laws, civil rights, etc.) • Weapons
Allocation	• Economic institutions • Ideas of value • Framework for property rights • Consumer desires and values	• Banks • Initial property rights and endowments • Tax structures

The first of these axes measures the type of power on which particular social resources depend: allocation or authority (Giddens 1981; Weber 1986). Allocative power defines the social resources, such as banks and economic markets, that determine physical, material wealth. The social resources associated with authoritative power govern what Weber calls "the power to command and duty to obey." SPRs of authority are not institutions of material wealth and accumulation but instead determine politics, social standing, and spiritual or cultural significance.

The second axis focuses on the way in which SPRs act on the world. Following Gramsci (1971) and others, it differentiates between institutions that act primarily on ideas and ideology, such as universities, scientific institutions, ideas about economic value and prices, and religion, and those that act on the material world, such as biological kinship, the police or military, and financial institutions.

At a first approximation, natural resource commons themselves are SPRs that determine the allocation of resources by materially determining their usage. Depending on their broader significance, they may play an ideological role (as is the case for high-profile natural assets, such as Yosemite National Park in the United States). They may also influence social tools of authority, as by subverting (or buttressing) the power of the state over natural resources.

Such a typology of SPRs allows us to extend conventional commons analysis in a few constructive ways. First, it allows us to understand the multitude of positions held by actors within CPR regimes at any given time. From an evolutionary perspective, Ostrom et al. propose,

> Users of a CPR include (1) those who always behave in a narrow, self-interested way and never cooperate in dilemma situations (free-riders), (2) those who are unwilling to cooperate with others unless assured they will not be exploited by free-riders, (3) those who are willing to initiate reciprocal cooperation in the hopes that others will return their trust, and (4) perhaps a few genuine altruists who always try to achieve higher returns for a group. Whether norms to cope with CPR dilemmas evolve without extensive, self-conscious design depends on the relative proportion of these behavioral types in a particular setting. (Ostrom et al. 1999).

SPRs extend actors' roles beyond their relationship to an individual commons to include other factors, such as race or class, religion, and so forth, that they may bring to its management. We can thus begin to locate Native Americans, indentured white and Chinese servants, Mexican peasants, and slaves within the commons-specific typology outlined by Ostrom et al. Consideration of these social positions allows us to recognize the central role such communities played in commons regimes where heretofore their role may not have been recognized.

Second, SPRs include "prevailing norms and values" thought to play a critical role not encompassed by evolutionary analysis (Baland and Platteau 1998a). As Cronon points out, "The colonists brought with them concepts of value and scarcity which had been shaped by the social and ecological circumstances of northern Europe, and so perceived New England as a landscape of great natural wealth" (1983: 168). Efficiency and scarcity played a crucial role in the success or failure of American commons as norms core to the colonizing European culture and alien to most indigenous peoples.

Finally, the analysis of SPRs such as military and paramilitary forces of colonization enables us to explain the origins of norms themselves and the conditions that determine which ones win. Efficiency and scarcity, for example, were not the values of Native Americans, but they prevailed because of colonial power and European economic conditions. Accounting for both is central to understanding commons outcomes in the Americas.

Durrenberger and Pálsson's (1987) analysis of Icelandic fisheries illustrates how commons coevolve with social-pool resources. They argue that the need to define a resource as "common" arose only when production within the society no longer focused uniquely on subsistence. Markets emerged as a result of changes in two SPRs. First, the basis (ideology) on which the resource was valuable to stakeholders shifted from a value based on use to a value based on financial exchange. In the ensuing narrowing of the resource's cultural and social significance, the fishery thus also became more clearly aligned with the allocative domain of power. The ideological shift from use to exchange then engendered the emergence of user or social "classes." This social stratification was a material manifestation of ideological changes in that it represented real changes in people's material endowments.

Natural resource management arises in the context of social-pool resources and, in turn, influences those same institutions. The analysis of these linkages not only clarifies them but allows us to identify which social institutions and resources change and how. Such distributional implications of commons management on social resources are the topic of the next section.

Justice and the Commons

The role of social-pool resources in commons outcomes involves a distributional dimension not available within the efficiency-centered framework of evolutionary analysis. SPRs shed light on how institutions direct natural and social resources to different social groupings and how asymmetries emerge in ideological and material resources. This analytic capacity is also reciprocal: It is valuable for understanding the distributional factors in commons formation but equally useful in characterizing how commons outcomes influence social structure. SPR approaches thus bring to the fore social justice issues related to the distribution of commons resources and more profound issues of justice having to do with how CPR regimes are used to buttress various social positions.

Consider three examples of the distributional feedback between SPRs and CPRs. First, Cronon's description of social and ecological change in New England illustrates how European institutions imposed a new order on preexisting native CPR regimes and how, once native communities were inserted into a competitive market economy, changes in those regimes led further to the demise of indigenous Americans. Second, for much of American history, the driving force in CPR regimes has been competition, which helps explain how winners and losers become members of different classes as stratification takes hold. Those classes (SPRs themselves) become key variables in social struggles. Finally, the overwhelming predominance of the United States in greenhouse gas emissions has endowed its present residents with certain benefits while almost certainly changing the natural and social resource endowments its future citizens will face.

SPRs do not remain fixed in time. The struggles they embody shape commons outcomes, move into commons regimes as they are formed, and return to reengage their originating institutions in new configurations. An SPR perspective is thus complementary to the evolutionary view in that each approaches commons problems and embodies distributional concerns at different scales.

The earlier example of a San Francisco crab industry closed to all but Italian fishers at the turn of the century can be understood as the joint result of environmental justice mechanisms operating at two distinct scales. Within the specific context of the Bay Area, industry rules emerged as a result of threats to both the productivity and the exclusivity of the crab harvest. With respect to productivity, the resultant rules may have evolved from attempts to use the resource more efficiently. With respect to exclusivity, they almost certainly reflected the strong anti-Chinese sentiment that prevailed in the white community at the time. Analysis of such individual cases necessitates what we will call here a proximate approach: a focus on the efficiency and equity dimensions of results that evolve in specific cases.

Although the need for increased crab productivity may have reflected conditions in broader economic markets, the commons regime that emerged is best understood within the local dynamics of the crab market itself. On the other hand, the origins and evolution of anti-Chinese (or pro-Italian) regulation stem from broader ideologies and institutions. A structural level of analysis addresses equity and justice as they permeate broader SPRs. Elements of justice at this level extend beyond the fate of individual CPRs to explain how social structure and stratification remain persistent variables.

Proximate justice has begun recently to be examined as a factor in commons formation. The remainder of this section reviews that discussion and extends it to structural elements of justice.

Proximate Elements of Justice in CPR Regimes

Until recently, theories of common property held that inequality in individual cases might actually foster the formation of healthier resource commons. The existence of rich or powerful "patrons" was theorized to increase the likelihood that a CPR regime would be enforced and to discourage free riders (Olson 1965). Field experience as well as recent analysis by Baland and Platteau have done much to cast such ideas in question (1997, 1998b). Tables 14.2 and 14.3 summarize their findings on the relationship between distributional conditions in the social settings that determine outcomes for individual CPRs.

Not all of Baland and Platteau's findings are determinate, particularly in the regulation-free scenario (table 14.2). The indeterminacy itself is a finding toward rebutting the claim that inequity is good for commons formations: "[There is] no directly testable relation between wealth distribution and efficiency in the production of public goods." In some situations, a number of distribution or efficiency outcomes are possible. Nevertheless, their work points to a few clear ways in which injustice is potentially endemic to commons management. Although they point out that very few commons, if any, could properly be said to be unregulated, their economic analysis for this case debunks the myth of the com-

Table 14.2. Distributional Consequences and the Commons in the Absence of Regulation.

Type of Commons or Distributional Intervention	Distributional Consequence	Commons Consequence
Increased inequality of credit constraints	Indeterminate	More efficient use
Increased inequality of access rights	Possible increased welfare	
Contributions to production by the wealthy	Indeterminate	Increased production
Drastic transfers of wealth	Indeterminate	Reduced production
Transfers that increase wealth of all parties	Indeterminate	Increased production
Increased inequality	Indeterminate	No clear results

Source: Adapted from Baland and Platteau (1997).

mons patron: "It cannot be inferred that more inequality is better for efficiency."
On the contrary, their work here suggests that welfare-equalizing measures generally lead to more optimal commons management.

Baland and Platteau's analysis of the regulated case (table 14.3) yields findings that are more directly applicable. Where regulations are being created and

Table 14.3. Distributional Consequences and the Commons in the
Presence of Regulation.

Type of Commons or Distributional Intervention	Distributional Consequence	Commons Consequence
Creation of regulations	Large interests have more interest in regulations and compliance when markets change the nature of wealth; efficient solutions tend to increase the pre-existing inequality between users	More equitable distributions of wealth can lead to equally optimal outcomes
Imposition of uniform quota	If inequality is high, the better-skilled user (usually with more money) is better off	Higher inequality among users implies lower efficiency of commons use
Interagent transfers	The only intervention with unambiguously equalizing potential	Imperfect information can lead to significant distortions; monetary transfers can be viewed as exclusionary in the long run and so are problematic
Uniform tax	With high inequality, the poor suffer from regulation	More inequality means less efficient use unless discount rates are equal among users, in which case the tax is the most efficient solution
Social exclusion	Typically aimed at minority groups or weaker segments of society	

Source: Adapted from Baland and Platteau (1998b). *Note:* Many of the conclusions
here assume that the poor have higher discount rates and lower skill levels than the
rich. To a large extent, these are factors determined in the structural context discussed later.

when initial social conditions are fairly egalitarian, it is possible to create optimally efficient CPR regimes while avoiding inequitable outcomes. With other initial conditions they unfortunately find that "efficient solutions tend to increase preexisting inequality between users." Furthermore, they find that if freely accessible or market-based CPR regimes have the potential to induce changes in the distribution of wealth, the wealthy themselves may lead the charge toward regime regulation to preserve their advantage.

Baland and Platteau also examine four different regulatory regimes, finding that only one, interagent transfers, is likely to ameliorate inequity in CPR access or usage. They suggest that even that policy intervention may lead to the exclusion of less wealthy actors from the commons because (1) the poor enter into transfer arrangements with less good information, and (2) wealth transfers, particularly monetary ones, may become a form of buyout or exclusion in the long run.

Many of their results are driven by relative differences in the social opportunity structures faced by poor or less powerful participants in commons regimes. The poor come into the commons lacking the depth and breadth of skills available to more powerful participants. By dint of their lack of money, investment opportunities, health care, and the like, the poor also tend to value the present more than the rich. Their higher discount rate contributes to the economically regressive results reported by Baland and Platteau.

Finally, Baland and Platteau's findings also show that overall commons productivity is reduced by inequity. All commons participants suffer from the way social stratification reduces resource availability. The wealthy, the poor, and the commons alike pay a price for injustice.

The Structural Context of Justice across CPR Regimes

Localized social conditions, like those studied by Baland and Platteau, represent SPRs in immediate interaction with individual CPRs. Discount rates, income transfers, creation of regulations, initial social endowments, and other factors that enter into the success or failure of local commons institutions are just a few manifestations of broader SPRs within a local setting. Beyond their influence on local cases, SPRs also influence CPR outcomes on a broad scale, connecting otherwise disparate natural resource regimes to core values and cultures in their social environments.

Elements of more general social justice embedded in social structures can have a number of effects on the emergence of CPR regimes. First, widespread injustice in a society may be a strong barrier to regime formation. Dominant groups under such circumstances are likely to prefer the absence of rules or recourse with respect to commons resources over their integration into community- or state-mediated institutions. When there are large asymmetries among different SPRs and large intergroup disparities, we can expect that groups in power will cede little of it for any reason.

A second consequence for regime formation is that injustice undermines the very ground for negotiation and agreement. The historical background, material conditions, and asymmetrical political or social power reduce the likelihood of building the consensus needed for commons management. Finally, even if commons regimes emerge, unjust social conditions may contribute to violations of the commons rules or strategic and exploitive behavior with respect to the resource. The higher discount rates held by the poor reflect their lack of faith in (an unjust) social commons' ability to safeguard their future, resulting in less sustainable commons consumption. When participants become so poor that their survival is threatened, they are likely to forsake commons-sustaining practices in favor of self-sustaining ones. When, through wealth or power, powerful participants have little to fear from sanctions, they are likely to exploit the commons with little regard for its rules.

Human generations represent another major social pool, which if inadequately included in commons formation can experience injustice. Howarth and Norgaard (1990) find that "competitive exchange in natural resource markets gives rise not to a single efficient allocation but rather to an infinite number of efficient allocations that correspond to particular property rights assignments." The intergenerational survival of commons depends not only on the efficiency of allocation but on its social sustainability: Have the interests of future generations been sufficiently weighted in management plans? Have institutions been designed to reproduce the social resources needed for long-term sustainability?

Multiple generations are present as differentiated SPRs in existing commons regimes as well. When commons face challenges as a result of generationally specific migration of users in and out of urban areas, they are experiencing disjunctures in the norms of different generations that must be reconciled for the health of the commons.

Resource commons have inseparable roles as both result *and* locus of struggle among SPRs. Social structures laid the foundation for the preeminence of the European commercialization of commons in America. But, once established, CPR regimes themselves became a tool for establishing European domination of the social hierarchy in the New World (Cronon 1983). As can be seen in the second section of this chapter, some American commons were actually reformulated for the express purpose of killing off, indenturing, or enslaving specific ethnic or racial groups. In an unjust social structure, commons can become another tool for domination. They can play a critical role in the fur-

Table 14.4. Key Contributions of Injustice to Commons Failures.

Scale: PROXIMATE (distributional outcomes or equity in individual commons regimes)	STRUCTURAL (distributional and justice effects spanning multiple commons)
Regulation is more strongly influenced by the wealthy and powerful	Injustice decreases the incentives for cooperation
Injustice increases subordinate groups' discount rates and contributes to unsustainable extraction	Injustice decreases trust necessary for meaningful negotiation
Social exclusion often targets subordinate groups	Injustice increases likelihood of strategic, noncooperative behavior
Significant inequity reduces commons productivity	Commons regimes and concomitant social structures become new locales for social struggle
Overlapping generations may hold differential interests and endowments in the commons, leading to conflict	Inadequate attention to preserving intergenerational social resources can undermine long-term sustainability

ther elaboration of social stratification and injustice. They may also be used by subordinate members of society as a new terrain of struggle for justice.

This section has described how justice and commons regimes are intertwined for individual cases as well as for SPRs at larger scales. It has specified some of the influences of justice on commons evolution and, in turn, helped us to understand the role of commons in shaping social power (table 14.4). The next section provides three short case studies that illustrate these influences in action at three different scales.

Justice at Three Scales: Local, National, and International Atmospheric Commons and Environmental Justice

SPRs coevolve with commons from the local to the global scale. Which SPRs are most important in determining CPR outcomes? Which CPRs most influence justice in the allocation of social resources, human health, and well-being? At each scale of CPR, there are concomitant SPRs, themselves heterogeneous in their extents, that shape CPR outcomes. This section examines this coevolution with respect to atmospheric commons at three distinct and contemporary geographic scales: local, national, and global. Each case highlights the difficult choices we face when confronting justice across such scale disjunctures in the commons.

To explore such choices, each case consists of:

- A description of the resource and atmospheric commons and related SPRs
- A description of proximal and structural components of inequities
- A discussion of the reciprocal link between the social commons and the atmospheric commons, or how social structures and resource commons can play a mutually reinforcing role
- A summary of how incorporation of justice into the analysis of the commons provides alternative approaches to protecting them

Justice and Metropolitan Air Quality: The Local Commons

The most diverse SPR in the United States is the spatial, political, and economic entity called the metropolitan area (MA). Its formal political institutions consist of anywhere from one to several central cities defined by their historical and economic relationships to suburbs. The latter, in turn, come in a variety of forms: incorporated towns, unincorporated zones, informal townships, and improved areas.

The MA is more than the sum of its parts, and its web of suburbs and central cities inevitably leads to some form of regional planning and governance. These functions can span simple road building to the provision of mass transit or the preservation and protection of the water supply. A substantial built environment links the geography and provides key resources to residents. Within this overall commons, there are individual regimes of economic activity (business or manufacturing districts), education and its finance (local school boards and property tax), and infrastructure (freeways, subways, buses). Class and racial social power is often also a pool resource that, thanks to segregation, is strongly identified with a specific subgeography. Black city council members tend to be elected from black neighborhoods, working-class school board officials from blue-collar neighborhoods.

The atmospheric commons in an MA usually is a sink for pollution generated locally and at a distance. Depending on the pollutant and meteorology, MA residents may experience the impact of their own activities or those of upwind users. To the extent that pollution externalities are locally generated, solutions may be sought on this scale. The Clean Air Act of 1990 tries to facilitate solutions to more regional air pollution problems by establishing cross-metropolitan governance structures (ozone transport commissions, for example).

Prior work on the intersection of the social and atmospheric commons in MAs illustrates the role of the components identified earlier. For example, table 14.5 compares metropolitan inequality with air quality in up to 260 U.S. MAs. Social inequality is measured by the level of income and race segregation among submetropolitan areas (census-defined "places") measured by the

Table 14.5. Correlation between Metropolitan Area Mean Air Quality and Municipal Segregation.

	Mean Level of Pollutant in MSA (number of MSAs)						
	TSP	PM10	CO	SO_2	NO_x	Ozone	Lead
Standard deviation	0.134 *	0.195 **	0.039	−0.099	0.188 !	0.032	0.127
of median incomes	(260)	(226)	(160)	(159)	(108)	(210)	(146)
Standard deviation	−0.072	0.148 *	−0.088	−0.283 ***	0.070	0.018	−0.002
of % nonwhites	(260)	(226)	(160)	(159)	(108)	(210)	(146)

! $= 0.05 < p < 0.10$ * $= 0.01 < p < 0.05$ ** $= 0.001 < p < 0.01$ *** $= p < 000.1$

standard deviation of race and income characteristics across such areas. Air quality is measured as the mean metropolitan air pollution level for the six national ambient air quality standards. Except for sulfur dioxide's association with racial inequity, the results confirm Baland and Platteau's (1998b) finding that greater inequality can lead to less efficient commons use. In the case of MA atmospheric and social commons, greater racial and income inequity clearly leads to lower air quality for rich and poor, white and nonwhite alike (table 14.5).

An additional result from the same study is that air pollution inequality is closely associated with segregation, implying that underlying social inequities contribute to inequities in the distribution of air quality in MAs as well. Finally, although the wealthy generally contribute to more emissions than the poor by dint of their higher material consumption, car ownership patterns within MAs are evidence of potentially higher discount rates among the poor (Bingham et al. 1987). Studies in Los Angeles and other heavily polluted areas have shown that low-income people and people of color drive older, more polluting cars, despite the higher cost of fuel and the heavy impact on local air quality.

Which of the many SPRs operating at this scale contribute to these outcomes? A number of studies have suggested that the submetropolitan areas that people inhabit profoundly shape the benefits they reap from local resource and social commons, and these subareas are highly segregated by race and class (Logan 1976; Logan and Alba 1993; Logan and Molotch 1987; Logan and Zhou 1990; Schneider and Logan 1981; Schneider and Logan 1982). The fragmentation of the social structure (multiple jurisdictions, disparate financial resources, segregated social commons) itself may further hobble metropolitan areawide efforts at optimizing the atmospheric commons.

The impact of injustice in exposure to local air pollution also has negative feedbacks to the communities most polluted. Not only do they suffer disproportionate health effects and lack of access to clean air, but they also face stronger regulatory pressure in the social commons to regulate their emissions, which in turn may hinder their attempts to achieve economic growth or autonomy.

MA social institutions and atmospheric commons are closely linked. The 1990 amendments to the U.S. Clean Air Act recognized some of these linkages by requiring that pollution-control measures address transportation and land-use issues, for example. These SPRs are critical to determining pollution outcomes, but the metropolitan geography of pollution often embodies the segregated geography of class and race. Injustice reduces the viability of the MA airshed for its poor residents as well as its rich ones. Management regimes that accounted for social segregation might identify new tools for clean air.

Ambient Air Quality and Environmental Justice: The National Commons

The national commons is the least complicated of the three commons examined here. National resource and political sovereignty encompass the totality of atmospheric resources and a vast majority of the social structures within national boundaries. In the United States, the management regime atmosphere is largely described by the Federal Clean Air Act and is mainly focused on controlling air quality at the state, regional, and national levels. In democratic societies, such as the United States and Brazil, the SPRs at the national level are substantially mediated through the political process. Their rules are thus largely determined by the nation's constitution and political processes.

The distribution of air quality at the national level demonstrates how persistent, local-scale injustice is manifest in a slightly different form at the national scale as well. Within a heterogeneous U.S. distribution of air quality, studies have shown that low-income groups and people of color generally suffer higher exposure to particulate matter and ozone (the two most damaging pollutants; Gelobter 2000a) and higher exposure to air pollution spikes for most regulated pollutants (Wernette 1992). This is largely due to the disproportionate concentration of people of color in highly polluted MAs and the intractable nature of pollution in the most polluted airsheds. Similar results have been reported for Brazil (Penna and Duchiade 1991). Although distributional studies have not been conducted for many non-U.S. cities, there is good reason to believe that poor, urban populations face a disproportionate share of pollution because of their residence in large cities such as São Paolo, Mexico City, and Santiago de Chile, which routinely experience hazardous levels of air pollution.

Social institutions responsible for excessive pollution were expected to shrivel up under the onslaught of uniform air quality standards, but this has not proven to be the case (Asch and Seneca 1978; Gianessi et al. 1977; Gianessi et al. 1979). Persistent, large-scale disparities in exposure to air pollution at a national scale may be an indication of a linkage between structural social injustice and the atmospheric commons. I have described a variety of mechanisms by which widespread inequities in social regimes can cause the failure of resource commons. More specifically, unjust outcomes may be a symptom of the power of dominant national stakeholders (such as industry groups). Crenson's 1972 study of air pollution in cities around the United States showed how the mere reputation of business leaders could effectively suppress air pollution regulation. The pattern of discriminatory outcomes can thus also be seen as a reflection of how easily CPR regimes can come to embody and replicate broader patterns of social injustice.

Like natural resource commons, social-pool resources exhibit interesting congruences across scales. Is high exposure to pollution in low-income communities and among people of color persistent at a national scale because it is so in urban areas? Distributional injustices clearly have shrunken at the national level more quickly than in individual metropolises. What explains the variations, and how many more MAs must reduce disparate exposures to have a national impact? What SPRs hold the most potential as intervention points?

The feedbacks from atmospheric commons to social ones are significant. Persistent exposure to pollutants contributes to life-threatening health and social deficits in communities with people of low income and people of color. To the extent that the distribution of atmospheric resources is a reflection of underlying social power, we can see how unjustly managed atmospheric commons reinforce the asymmetries.

Unjust social conditions in the United States decrease the efficiency of commons regulation and increase the inequitable distribution of air pollution. A focus on structural injustice expands the "solution set" beyond individual stakeholders to SPRs such as the structure of cities, factors in industrial location, and the historical legacy of urban discrimination. It also places the behavior of individual actors in the commons in its strategic context: ownership of older cars in low-income communities as a manifestation of reduced expectations for the future, lack of local regulation as the influence of powerful industrial forces. An analysis of commons regimes that incorporates the influence of SPRs facilitates such insights. With proper analysis, they can lead to more effective regimes for managing common resources.

Global Warming and Environmental Colonialism: The Global Commons

The planet's atmosphere provides a number of services vital to ecosystem and human health. As human action has had greater and greater impacts on the delivery of those services, scientists and policymakers have conceptually subdivided that commons by segmenting the atmosphere based on the specific services extracted. This section focuses on justice issues with respect to climate change, the atmospheric commons that provides the planet with its heat and meteorological balance.

The threats to that commons today come from the vast increase in anthropogenic greenhouse-gas (GHG) emissions over the last 200 years. The tragedy of this commons is engendered by contributions of pollutants rather than subtractions of resources, and an emission anywhere is equally threatening to the planet's heat balance. Nevertheless, there are vast geographic differences in the share of GHG emissions released to the atmosphere, with North America's cumulative share dwarfing that of any other region (Marland et al. 1999).

Each emission of a specific GHG in any region contributes more or less equally to climate change. But there is a great deal of heterogeneity with respect to both the values of such emissions and their impacts. First, use and exchange values for emissions vary widely across the world. Emissions from commercial processes such as energy production, chemical and concrete manufacturing, or agriculture clearly occur as inputs to goods traded in markets. Therefore, they can be assigned an exchange value that permits us to compare their monetary value almost universally. On the other hand, emissions that result from individual subsistence activities, whether plowing a field with draft cattle in Thailand or driving from home to a mall in Los Angeles, may vary substantially and be very difficult to value comparatively. This is because they embody use, not exchange value, and thus are not properly valued by currency of any sort. Global comparisons of both values can be very problematic, but it is in the latter set that developing the norms for managing this commons becomes very difficult.

Global warming generates the negative externalities that abuse of the global atmospheric commons imposes. Beyond the exigencies of calculating the value of this use to globally diverse parties, a second major difficulty is how geographically, socially, and temporally diverse the externalities appear to be. General circulation models project significant geographic variation in changes in surface temperature, cloud cover, humidity, rainfall, and the impact of sea-level change. Social institutions and structure will also be affected heterogeneously. Climate-dependent activities, from transportation to tourism to agriculture, will suffer from first-order effects of climate change disproportionately to sectors that are more climate independent, such as banking, manufacturing, or entertainment. (All human activities depend more or less on climate. But it is precisely the "more or less" that generates the variety discussed here.) Of course such activities may themselves embody disparate use and exchange values, further complicating any calculus of impacts.

The difficulties in determining the value of regulating climate change are also compounded by its intergenerational dimensions. Differing assumptions about how to distribute the costs across generations, past, present, and future, have significant impacts on the choice of policies. Howarth's (1996) recent work has shown that this is one area where decisions we make about the distribution of the global atmospheric commons overlap substantially with the efficiency of such a commons. Analyzing climate change from a policy perspective necessarily entails explicitly assigning values to different social groups, both in the present and in the future.

The intersection of the commons that is the global climate system and SPRs is enormous. There is tremendous heterogeneity in both the institutions responsible for emissions and those affected by climate change. The sheer number of actors, institutions, and CPRs that may be affected poses a daunting challenge to evolutionary theories of the commons. An evolution toward norms for protection of the climate commons seems distant at best and, given the complicated interplay between the norms of use and exchange value involved with GHG emissions, not likely to be based solely on considerations of efficiency.

The field of research on the commons itself exhibits significant differences in norms in this arena. Oran Young (1995) contrasts two schools of thought on the problem of CPRs that have emerged to cope with the many scales of global resource issues. The first is the traditional CPR literature, which was the starting point for this chapter. Its focus is the development of codes of conduct and social practices of individuals for commons management. The second is the literature of international resource regimes, which focuses on collective-action problems (factors that influence the formation of regimes) instead of on individual users of a resource. For problems such as climate change, Young argues that both approaches must be used to bridge the varied scales at which humans affect the CPR (Young 1995).

With such heterogeneity in use values, exchange values, impacts, and analytic approaches, the possibilities for injustice are, unfortunately, rather large, and concerns over justice appear to be a major barrier to reaching effective international environmental agreements. The most immediate manifestation of their centrality is the dilemma faced by policymakers about what specific mechanisms should be used and how much money should be pledged to achieve justice in sharing the economic burdens of existing international environmental agreements (King 1993a, 1993b, 1993c, 1993d; King and Munasinghe 1991, 1992, 1993; Mintzer 1993; Pierce and Barett 1993; Wolf 1993; Workshop on Cross-National Environmental Problems 1994). At a deeper level, progress in controlling GHGs is significantly hampered by divergent assessments of which allocation rules should be used to determine relative rights to and responsibility for the sources of global change (Grubb et al.

1992). Most fundamentally, there remains serious debate over the importance of linking justice and international environmental protection and sustainability at all (Ahuja 1992; Beckerman 1992; Hammond et al. 1990; Jodha 1992; Sebenius 1991; Shue 1992; Susskind and Ozawa 1990). This lack of agreement about mechanisms, allocations, and the legitimacy of justice concerns themselves may be a case of preexisting inequities that impede regulation by fostering recalcitrant behavior among dominant users of the commons.

If justice in commons regimes depends, as does efficiency, on evolving shared norms for the present and the future, the norm disjunctures between stakeholders are daunting, to say the least. One problem in analyzing injustice in such global CPRs as the climate system is the lack of specific theoretical frameworks. One possible approach, suggested by Amartya Sen's work on inequality, is to explicitly recognize equality "domains," conceptual spaces in which equality is sought according to a domain-specific measure (1992). Sen cites the example of utilitarianism: "In fact, the equality that utilitarianism seeks takes the form of equal treatment of human beings in the space of gains and losses of utilities. There is an insistence on equal weights on everyone's utility gains in the utilitarian objective function" (Sen 1992: 13). The same is true for economics, where monetary units must hold equal weights across a given field of analysis.

The seminal work in Western thought this century, Rawls's *A Theory of Justice* (Rawls 1971), restricts its domain of analysis to the nation-state and to one period in time and is thus of limited value in analyzing justice in global CPRs. But more recent commentators have begun adapting Rawls's framework or proposing alternatives better suited to exploring the concept of justice in an international, intergenerational context (Dreze and Sen 1989; Sen 1992; Stone 1993).

One provocative domain for analysis was proposed by Agarwal and Narain in 1991. Crystallizing the disproportionate impact that North Americans and others had on global climate in 1991, they wrote a response to a report by the World Resources Institute (WRI) on international responsibility for emissions. Agarwal and Narain (1991) proposed GHG allocation rules based on the human need to survive. Rebutting WRI's assumption of the international equivalence of emissions, *Global Warming in an Unequal World* made an early and explicit case for the ethical and distributional nature of efforts to apportion GHG emissions:

> Can we really equate the carbon dioxide contributions of gas guzzling automobiles in Europe and North America or, for that matter, anywhere in the Third World with the methane emissions of draught cattle and rice fields of subsistence farmers in West Bengal

or Thailand? Do these people not have the right to live? But no effort has been made in WRI's report to separate out the "survival" emissions of the poor from the "luxury" emissions of the rich. (Agarwal and Narain 1991:3)

Figure 14.2 represents a test of this distinction with respect to current emissions of CO_2 drawn from prior work (Gelobter 2000b). It shows the best-fit polynomial, a segmented linear relationship with one knot at the break-point between emissions that significantly contribute to life expectancy and those that do not: 1.93 tons/capita. (This functional form was the best fit among linear and nonlinear models with zero or more breakpoints.) Thus, the equation for "survival emissions" (when per capita CO_2 emissions < 1.93) is

life expectancy (LE) = 48.9 + 11.23 * (per capita CO_2 emissions) + ∈
and for "luxury emissions" (when per capita CO_2 emissions > 1.93):
LE = 70.5 + .11 * (per capita CO_2 emissions) + ∈)

The two spline segments represent two distinct relationships between increases in survival and increases in CO_2 emissions. The first segment models countries for which CO_2 use contributes to survival: As emissions rise, so does life expectancy. This is not true for countries on the second half of the curve: Emissions there show no significant relationship with increased life expectancy.

Agarwal and Narain's (1991) suggestion of luxury versus survival as an approach to justice appears to raise a statistically valid distinction that itself leads to new possibilities for GHG regimes. For example, allocation scenarios could incorporate this domain of justice by setting caps based on an emission's survival value instead of on commercial value. The luxury-versus-survival framework also highlights the need within existing proposals to focus on how negotiated allocations will affect subsistence activities throughout the world.

Efforts to measure global inequities notwithstanding, it would be naive to claim that justice issues have not been systematically addressed because of a lack of theoretical frameworks. A more important cause of the paucity of the debate is the political and cultural differences in the conceptions of justice for international policy processes (Ahuja 1992; Jodha 1992; Kasperson and Dow 1991; Sen 1992). Although the three levels outlined earlier sketch a topography of the debate over justice, a major barrier to international cooperation on such issues is the lack of forums in which the broad range of understandings of and frameworks for justice held by globally diverse stakeholders can be discussed, understood, and perhaps negotiated (*Financial Times* 1992).

Finally, structural inequity is also a barrier to the emergence of a sustainable regime for global climate, and the Americas' historical role in such inequity is undeniable. North America, in particular, has a legacy and a continuing level of

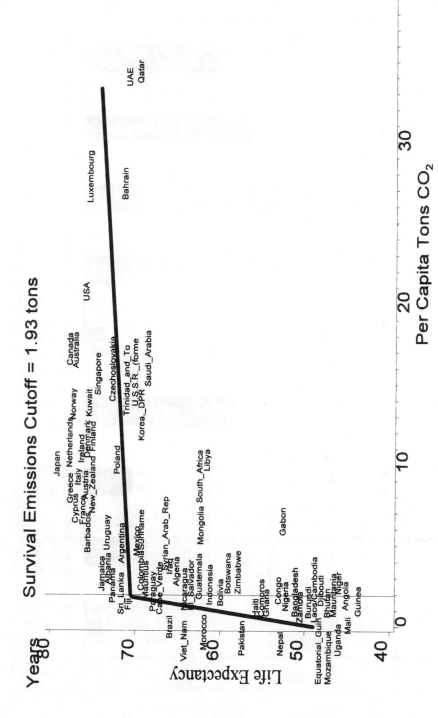

Figure 14.2. Survival versus luxury emissions of CO_2 (1992).

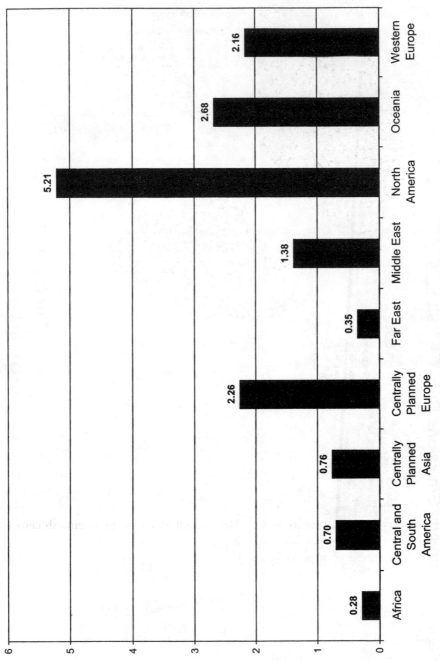

Figure 14.3. Per capita CO$_2$ commercial emissions, 1996. *Source:* Marland et al. 1999.

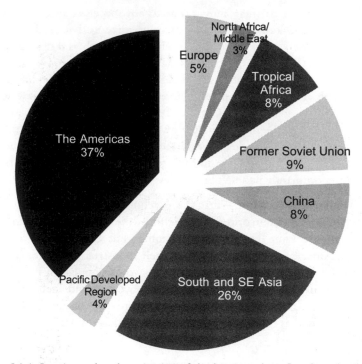

Figure 14.4. Continental-scale estimates of the biotic carbon flux from land cover change: 1850 to 1980.

industrial emissions that dwarf those of any other region (fig. 14.3). Taken together, changes in land use in the Americas further account for almost 40 percent of such carbon fluxes from 1850 to 1980 (fig. 14.4). In the global climate commons, North America is the prime free-rider.

An SPR and justice perspective not only indicates who the prime free-riders are but also places the genesis of inequity firmly back within the social systems that interact with the commons. Tremendous asymmetries in power have been at play in the Americas' history. The United States, as the twentieth century's dominant superpower, has been able to consume much more than its share of resources thanks to its might and wealth. The foundations of that might and wealth lie to a large extent in the Americas' history as a commons colonized and then almost wholly molded into a "merchantable commodity."

The importance of feedbacks from commons to SPRs is highlighted by the leverage that, at least in some ways, poorer, less powerful nations may acquire in international relations as a result of climate change. Climate change has emerged as a key planetary concern concurrent with these nations' power to influence it through their emissions. The climate system as a resource commons is as vulnerable to their activities as to anyone else's and, should they choose a path to modernization as resource intensive as that used in Europe or the Americas, they are likely to disrupt climate as much as if not more than have their industrialized counterparts.

The power to disrupt climate (and other valued commons) is no longer perceived as purely a function of physicobiological factors, like the raw rate of population growth, as it was by Garrett Hardin more than twenty years ago. Then, he argued that "the most rapidly growing populations on earth today are (in general) the most miserable" (Hardin 1968). Indeed, Hardin's argument on population itself casts the problem in SPR terms. He blamed the world's poor countries (predominantly people of color), even though, as Amartya Sen argues,

> It is important to address first the psychologically tense issue of racial balance in the world. . . . The third world is right now going through the same kind of demographic shift that Europe and North America experienced during their industrial revolution. In 1650 the share of Asia and Africa in the world population is estimated to have been 78.4 percent, and it stayed around there even in 1750. . . . Even now the combined share of Asia and Africa (71.2 percent) is considerably *below* what its share was in 1650 or 1750. (Sen 1994)

The early "tragedy of the commons" argument shifted the debate away from the influence of social institutions such as partriarchy (the restriction of women's liberty) and social patterns of modern capitalism (the need for low-wage labor for production and cross-national stratification to fuel high consumption). With Darwinian arguments such as "conscience is self-eliminating," Hardin and others argued implicitly for SPRs built around biology rather than other possible institutions to promote fair markets or gender equality (Hardin 1968).

In this sense, less powerful nations and peoples have already won an important victory. Policymakers and international negotiators have begun to understand that the consumption of CPRs is certainly mediated by SPRs such as institutions of production and individual consumption. Trade-offs for climate stability must operate in a way to influence both in the right ways. We cannot ask to start reducing consumption in places where daily survival is still in question. Nor can many social institutions as we know them survive another iteration of the GHG pulse created by Western industrialization.

For now, the prospects of less developed countries or future generations sharing equally in global commons regimes are more rhetorical than real. It is not at all clear, in the mix of costs and benefits shaped by the use values, exchange values, discount rates, and impacts of emissions, that less developed countries have the leverage to seriously reshape global institutions in exchange for their participation in a sustainable climate regime. Nor have climate negotiations to date seriously grappled with incorporating the needs of future generations.

Conclusion

To understand and better manage commons, we must, at least for analytic purposes, recognize the links between social collectivities and natural ones. Just as nature is both an intrinsic part of individuals and an external force at times alien to our beings, so too is society shot through with the natural world, and yet outside of it. Endowed with great natural resources and an even greater capacity to consume them, the Americas are one place where better balance must be struck between our externalization and our internalization of common-pool resources.

Reintegrating social structures with nature is not an easy task. The case studies examined here illustrate the grounded complexity of justice and the nature of the SPRs within and through which social groups struggle over CPR outcomes. The geographic place, the marketplace, and international political and economic regimes each have significant influence over how resource commons form, how effective they can be, and how their resources are partitioned among social groups. The study of justice in the commons diverges from and complements more traditional CPR studies in its emphasis on social institutions while also helping us to analytically bridge local, regional, national, and international distributional outcomes in CPR regimes.

The language and practice of commons research must stretch to incorporate the insights that a focus on justice enables. Equity and distributional concerns are a new dimension from which to explore the critical factors in commons regimes. Linking the history of practices and institutions to their implications for CPRs begins to address the justice of outcomes while improving our understanding of their efficiency. Further research in this arena promises to enrich the possibilities for commons formation and survival.

More than two decades ago, Garrett Hardin argued that "injustice is preferable to ruin" (Hardin 1968). Today, we know that resource commons emerge, exist, fail, or succeed in a human context shaped by history, by difference, and by commonality. The strength of our social commons lies in no small measure in how its members come to see each other and the resources they must depend on as part of an integrated whole. The question is thus no longer which injustices are necessary for the survival of commons, but instead which ones to remedy first to alleviate suffering and to promote a sustainable future for our societies *and* our resources.

Acknowledgments

Thanks to Dick Norgaard for his constructive comments and to S. Max Edelson for suggestions on the historical section of this chapter. I have depended heavily for the history in the second section on William Cronon's 1983 study of native and colonist approaches to ecology, *Changes in the Land*. Although I consulted some primary historical material, most pre–nineteenth-century writings cited in the text were originally cited in Cronon's work

References

Agarwal, A., and S. Narain. 1991. *Global Warming in an Unequal World: A Case of Environmental Colonialism*. New Delhi: Centre for Science and Environment.

Ahuja, D. R. 1992. "Estimating National Contributions of Greenhouse Gas Emissions: The CSE-WRI Controversy." *Global Environmental Change* (June 1992) 2, no. 2:83–87.

Asch, P., and J. J. Seneca. 1978. "Some Evidence on the Distribution of Air Quality." *Land Economics* 54, no. 3 (August): 278–97.

Baland, J.-M., and J.-P. Platteau. 1997. "Wealth Inequality and Efficiency in the Commons Part I: The Unregulated Case." *Oxford Economic Papers* 49:451–82.

———. 1998a. "Division of the Commons: A Partial Assessment of the New Institutional Economics of Land Rights." *American Journal of Agricultural Economics* (August) 80, no. 3:644–65.

———. 1998b. "Wealth Inequality and Efficiency in the Commons Part II: The Regulated Case." *Oxford Economic Papers* no. 50 (January): 1–22.

Beckerman, W. 1992. "Economic Growth and the Environment: Whose Growth? Whose Environment?" *World Development* 20:481–96.

Bingham, T. H., D. W. Anderson, and P. C. Cooley. 1987. "Distribution of the Generation of Air Pollution." *Journal of Environmental Economics and Management* 14, no. 1:30–40.

Bullard, R. D. 1983. "Solid-Waste Sites and the Black Houston Community." *Sociological Inquiry* 53 (2–3): 273–88.

———. 1990. *Dumping in Dixie: Race, Class, and Environmental Quality*. Boulder, CO: Westview Press.

Bullard, R. D., and B. H. Wright. 1985. "Endangered Environs: Dumping Grounds in a Sunbelt City." *Urban Resources* 2, no. 2.

Caro, R. A. 1975. *The Power Broker*. New York: Vintage Books.

Crenson, M. 1972. *The Unpolitics of Air Pollution*. Baltimore: Johns Hopkins University Press.

Cronon, W. 1983. *Changes in the Land*. New York: Hill & Wang.

Davis, M. 1992. *City of Quartz: Excavating the Future in Los Angeles*. New York: Vintage Books.

Dreze, J., and A. Sen. 1989. *Hunger and Public Action*. Oxford: Clarendon Press.

Durrenberger, E. P., and G. Pálsson. 1987. "The Grass Roots and the State: Resource Management in Icelandic Fishing." In *The Question of the Commons: The Culture and*

Ecology of Communal Resources, edited by B. J. McCay and J. M. Acheson, 370–92. Tucson: University of Arizona Press.

Feeny, D., S. Hanna, and A. F. McEvoy. 1996. "Questioning the Assumptions of the 'Tragedy of the Commons' Model of Fisheries." *Land Economics* (May) 2, no. 2:187–205.

Foucault, M. 1986. "Disciplinary Power and Subjection." In *Power,* edited by S. Lukes, 229–42. Oxford: Basil Blackwell.

Gelobter, M. 2000. *Race, Class, and Outdoor Air Pollution: The Dynamics of Environmental Discrimination in America.* In press.

———. 2000. "Trading Survival for Luxury: An Empirical Examination of Greenhouse Gas Allocation Rules." In press.

Gianessi, L. P., H. M. Peskin, and E. Wolff. 1977. "The Distributional Implications of National Air Pollution Damage Estimates." In *The Distribution of Economic Well-Being,* edited by F. T. Juster, 85–102. Cambridge: Ballinger Publishing.

———. 1979. "The Distributional Effects of Uniform Air Pollution Policy in the U.S." *Quarterly Journal of Economics* (May) vol. 93, no. 2:281–301.

Giddens, A. 1981. *A Contemporary Critique of Historical Materialism.* London/Berkeley: Macmillan/University of California Press.

Gramsci, A. 1971. *Selections from the Prison Notebooks,* translated by Q. Hoare Geoffrey Nowell-Smith. London: Lawrence & Wishart.

Grubb, M., J. Sebenius, A. Magalhaes, and S. Subak. 1992. "Sharing the Burden." In *Confronting Climate Change,* edited by I. M. Mintzer, 305–22. New York: Cambridge University Press.

Hakluyt, R. 1584. "Discourse Concerning Western Planting." In *Original Writings and Correspondences of the Two Richard Hakluyts,* edited by E. G. R. Taylor II, 211–327. London: Hakluyt Society, 1935.

Hammond, A. L., E. Rodenberg, and W. Moomaw. 1990. "Accountability in the Greenhouse." *Nature* 347:705–6.

Hardin, G. 1968. "The Tragedy of the Commons." *Science* 162, no. 1:243–48.

Harvey, D. 1996. *Justice, Nature, and the Geography of Difference.* Cambridge, MA: Blackwell Publishers.

Hayami, Y., and V. Ruttan. 1981. *Asian Village Economy at the Crossroads.* Baltimore: Johns Hopkins University Press.

Horkheimer, M. 1947. *The Eclipse of Reason.* New York: Oxford University Press.

Howarth, R. B. 1996. "Climate Change and Overlapping Generations." *Contemporary Economic Policy* (October) vol. 17, no. 4:100–111.

Howarth, R. B., and R. B. Norgaard. 1990. "Intergenerational Resource Rights, Efficiency, and Social Optimality." *Land Economics* 66, no. 1:1–11.

Hurley, A. 1995. *Environmental Inequalities: Class, Race, and Industrial Pollution in Gary, Indiana, 1945–1980.* Chapel Hill: University of North Carolina Press.

———. 1997. *Common Fields: An Environmental History of St. Louis.* St. Louis: Missouri Historical Society Press.

Jay, M. 1973. *The Dialectical Imagination: A History of the Frankfurt School and the Institute of Social Research, 1923–1950.* Boston: Little, Brown.

Jodha, N. S. 1992. "A Comment on 'Global Warming in an Unequal World.'" *Global Environmental Change* (June 1992) vol. 2, no. 2:97–98.

Kalm, P. 1753–61, 1770. *Travels in North America,* edited by A. B. Benson. New York: Dover Press, 1964.

Kasperson, R. E., and K. M. Dow. 1991. "Developmental and Geographical Equity in Global Environmental Change." *Evaluation Review* 15, no. 1:149–71.

King, K. 1993a. "Incremental Costs for the Global Environmental Benefits: A Survey of Analytical and Strategic Issues." Paper prepared for the Program for Measuring Incremental Costs for the Environment (PRINCE) Workshop, 8–9 February, New Delhi.

———. 1993b. "Issues to Be Addressed by the Program for Measuring Incremental Costs for the Environment (PRINCE)." Working Paper no. 8, Global Environmental Facility.

———. 1993c. "Incremental Cost of Actions to Prevent the Loss of Biodiversity." Paper prepared for the GEF Incremental Cost Seminar, November 19, Washington, DC.

———. 1993d. "Incremental Costs as an Input to Operational Decision-Making." Paper prepared for the GEF Incremental Cost Seminar, November 19, Washington, DC.

King, K., and M. Munasinghe. 1991. "Incremental Costs of Phasing Out Ozone Depleting Substances." Environmental Working Paper no. 47. Washington, DC: The World Bank, Environment Department.

———. 1992. "Cost-Effective Measures to Limit the Emissions of Greenhouse Gases in Developing Countries." Divisional Working Paper, 1992, 30. Washington, DC: The World Bank, Environment Department.

———. 1993. "Draft Report of Country Incremental Costs of Phasing Out Ozone-depleting Substances." Draft Report. Washington, DC: The World Bank, Environment Department.

Leiss, W. 1974. *The Domination of Nature.* Boston: Beacon Press.

Logan, J. R. 1976. "Industrialization and the Stratification of Cities in the Suburban Region." *American Journal of Sociology* 82, no. 2:333–48.

Logan, J. R., and R. D. Alba. 1993. "Locational Returns to Human Capital: Minority Access to Suburban Community Resources." *Demography* 30, no. 2:243–68.

Logan, J. R., and H. Molotch. 1987. *Urban Fortunes: The Political Economy of Place.* Berkeley: University of California Press.

Logan, J. R., and M. Zhou. 1990. "The Adoption of Growth Controls in Suburban Communities." *Social Science Quarterly* 71, no. 1:118–29.

Marland, G., R. J. Andres, T. A. Boden, C. Johnston, and A. Brenkert. 1999. *Global, Regional, and National CO_2 Emission Estimates from Fossil Fuel Burning, Cement Production, and Gas Flaring: 1751–1996 Numeric Data Package (NDP-030).* Carbon Dioxide Information Analysis Center. Accessed January 1999. FTP site. Available at http://cdiac.esd.ornl.gov/ndps/ndp030.html.

Miller, V. D. 1993. "Building on Our Past, Planning Our Future: Communities of Color and the Quest for Environmental Justice." In *Toxic Struggles: The Theory and Practice of Environmental Justice,* edited by R. Hofrichter, 128–35. Philadelphia: New Society Publishers.

Mintzer, I. M. 1993. "Implementing the Framework Convention on Climate Change:

Incremental Costs and the Role of Global Environmental Facility." Global Environmental Facility. GEF Working Paper no. 4. Washington, DC: The World Bank.

Olson, M. 1965. *The Logic of Collective Action: Public Goods and the Theory of Groups.* Cambridge, MA: Harvard University Press.

Ostrom, E. 2000. "Reformulating the Commons." In *Protecting the Commons: A Framework for Resource Management in the Americas,* edited by J. Burger, E. Ostrom, R. B. Norgaard, D. Policansky, and B. D. Goldstein. Washington, DC: Island Press.

Ostrom, E., J. Burger, C. B. Field, R. B. Norgaard, and D. Policansky. 1999. "Sustainability—Revisiting the Commons: Local Lessons, Global Challenges." *Science* 284, no. 5412:278–82.

Patterson, O. 1982. *Slavery and Social Death: A Comparative Study.* Cambridge, MA: Harvard University Press.

Penna, M. L., and M. P. Duchiade. 1991. "Air Pollution and Infant Mortality from Pneumonia in the Rio de Janeiro Metropolitan Area." *Bulletin of the Pan American Health Organization* 25, no. 1:47–54.

Pierce, D., and S. Barett. 1993. "Incremental Costs and Biodiversity Conservation." Unpublished manuscript, prepared for the GEF Incremental Cost Seminar, November 19, Washington, DC.

Pulido, L. 1996. *Enviornmentalism and Economic Justice: Two Chicano Struggles in the Southwest.* Society, Environment, and Place. Tucson: University of Arizona Press.

Rawls, J. 1971. *A Theory of Justice.* Cambridge, MA: Harvard University Press.

"Risks of Too Much Hot Air." 1992. *Financial Times,* May 28, 1992.

Schneider, M., and J. R. Logan. 1981. "Fiscal Implications of Class Segregation: Inequalities in the Distribution of Public Goods and Services in Suburban Municipalities." *Urban Affairs Quarterly* 17, no. 1 (September):23–37.

———. 1982. "Suburban Racial Segregation and Black Access to Local Public Resources." *Social Science Quarterly* 63, no. 4:762–70.

Sebenius, J. K. 1991. "Designing Negotiations towards a New Regime: The Case of Global Warming." *International Security* 15, no. 4:110–148.

Sen, A. 1992. *Inequality Reexamined.* Cambridge, MA: Harvard University Press.

———. 1994. "Population: Delusion and Reality." *New York Review of Books* (September 22) vol. 41, no. 15:62.

Shue, H. 1992. "The Unavoidability of Justice." In *The International Politics of the Environment,* edited by A. Hurrell and B. Kingsbury. New York: Clarendon Press.

Stone, C. D. 1993. *The Gnat Is Older Than Man.* Princeton, NJ: Princeton University Press.

Susskind, L., and C. Ozawa. 1990. "Environmental Diplomacy: Strategies for Negotiating More Effective International Agreements." Report of the MIT–Harvard Public Disputes Program.

Thomas, R. P., and R. N. Bean. 1974. "The Fishers of Men: The Profits of the Slave Trade." *Journal of Economic History* 34 no. 4:885–94.

Warren, J. 1787. "Observations on Agriculture." *American Museum* 2, no. 4:345–47.

Weber, M. 1986. "Domination by Economic Power and by Authority." In *Power,* edited by S. Lukes, 28–36. Oxford: Basil Blackwell.

Wernette, D. R. 1992. "Minorities, Age Groups, and Air Quality Non-Attainment Areas: An Analysis of Regional and Urban Patterns." Argonne National Laboratory,

Report of the Environmental Assessment and Information Sciences Division. USDOE contract no. W-31-109-Eng-38.

West, P. C. 1993. "The Tyranny of Metaphor: Interracial Relations, Minority Recreation, and the Urban/Wildland Interface." In *Culture, Conflict, and Communication in the Wildland/Urban Interface,* edited by A. W. Ewert, D. J. Chavez, and A. W. Magill. Boulder, CO: Westview Press.

Wolf, A. 1993. "Incremental Costs and the Global Environmental Facility." Unpublished manuscript. United Nations Development Program.

Workshop on Cross-National Environmental Problems. 1994. "The Costs of Incremental Costs: Consequences for GEF/UNDP Project Evaluation." New York: Columbia University, Report of the Program on Environmental Policy, School of International and Public Affairs.

Young, O. R. 1995. "The Problem of Scale in Human/Environment Relationships." In *Local Commons and Global Interdependence: Heterogeneity and Cooperation in Two Domains,* edited by R. O. Keohane and E. Ostrom, 24–75. London/Thousand Oaks, CA: Sage Publications.

Conclusion

JOANNA BURGER, RICHARD B. NORGAARD, AND ELINOR OSTROM

This volume illustrates how common-pool resources span a number of variables: scale (small to global), location of effects (local to far reaching), and degree of mobility (stationary to highly mobile). Grazing and forest common-pool resources tend to be relatively small-scale, local resources; water common-pool resources tend to be more regional resources; while the atmosphere as a common-pool resource can range from local to regional to global. As the scale of common-pool resources expands, the impacts of one user's activities shift from immediate to more distant users. Common-pool resources can be stationary, such as medicinal plants in a forest, to highly mobile, such as fish that travel great distances in the oceans. Similarly, this volume illustrates that common-pool institutions have arisen under different social and political conditions. While the differences documented in this volume are considerable, are they sufficient to give us hope that we will be able to develop common-pool institutions for global resources such as biodiversity and climate maintenance where the impacts of today's use affect people in the future? The history of the Americas also shows how profound equity and justice issues are intertwined with the governance and management of common-pool resources. Can we learn from past mistakes and apply them to the challenges of building global common-pool institutions whose success depends on how well they promote justice?

Ostrom provides a theoretical framework in chapter 1 to help us understand when and how common-pool institutions will arise and be reformulated over time. In this framing, resource users reformulate their institutions when they estimate that the benefits from such a change will exceed both immediate and long-term costs. This is more likely when commons users can communicate with a common language, engage in face-to-face bargaining, and have the ability to change at least some of the rules over time that affect the use of the resource. Having a supportive legal structure at the macro level that facilitates a self-organizing role for users is key to successful adaptation of common-pool institutions and management of common-pool resources. Further, being able to monitor both the resource and the users and provide low-cost and reliable information is critical. Effective conflict resolution, by either local officials or external authorities, is another essential element of long-term success. Often users themselves can create associations to increase the flow of information, create rules that encourage compliance, and find ways to decrease monitoring and sanctioning costs. Ultimately, successful self-organization is more likely when management programs lead to net benefits for users.

Major Themes of the Book

Several themes run consistently through the chapters, whether the common-pool resource in question is fisheries, wildlife, forests, land, medical care, water, or the atmosphere. Consistent themes include the following:

- Historical factors play a major role in both creating the problems surrounding particular common-pool resources and fashioning a solution for their management. This is particularly clear for the Americas, where European invasion was sufficiently recent to allow careful analysis of historical factors.
- Degradation of local or global common-pool resources will continue until steps are taken to address the problem.
- Major progress is being made toward equitable and satisfactory management of some common-pool resources, but management of others will require more innovative solutions and involvement at a larger scale.
- A variety of disciplines, tools, and approaches are required to analyze common-pool resources and to develop and formulate appropriate paradigms for their management.
- Rules and institutions to manage common-pool resources work best when there is an obvious need and a willingness on the part of the commoners to address the problems.
- A commons analysis can usefully be broadened to include human resources as common-pool resources, particularly with respect to medical care and environmental justice.
- New spatial tools such as the GIS will have a major future role in both assessing resources and monitoring their distribution, as well as the pattern of use by the users.
- Common-pool resources will not be managed in a sustainable manner until adequate attention is given to the human dimensions of resource manage-

ment, including equity and justice, for all who need or want to use the resources.

Historical Constraints to Solutions

A thread that runs through the book is the impact of the recent exploitation of common-pool resources by Europeans. Resource degradation was telescoped in the Americas by the invasion of Europeans both because the duration was short and because the European perspective of commodity exchange and land tenure so clearly differed from that of the native peoples living in the Americas. The importance of historical analysis to understanding commons resources is most clear in the chapter by Sarukhán and Larson on the evolution of common property from pre-Hispanic times to present-day rural Mexico. Successful examples of the rational use of resources exist, although many social, political, and economic factors can disrupt these uses. Successful traditional systems are disrupted with recent resettlement of landless peoples from semiarid regions to the tropical forest areas. Resettlements result in deforestation, forest fragmentation, and establishment of unproductive cattle ranching. Unsound national agrarian policies and lack of economic support by government agencies has led to ecological degradation on government-owned and privately owned land, as well as on some socially owned lands (*ejidos*). An overall problem is the absence of ecological and environmental laws governing the agricultural sector, despite their overall presence for hunting, fishing, and environmental protection. For many countries, including rural Mexico, a tension exists between orthodox policies designed to encourage national economic growth and social land tenure systems that protect local communities and can facilitate common-pool resource management.

Sarukhán and Larson argue that the central issue is whether communal property systems can lead to more sustainable use of resources. If they can, the problem shifts to whether the human resources and social values of rural populations can exist within the mainstream development of the country. Modern forestry and agricultural sectors can be integrated as part of the mosaic of the rural landscape and its economic development. Global consumers could help by recognizing and valuing the products that indigenous peoples produce from socially and ecologically sustainable systems. Indigenous peoples should be accorded the right to a fair share of the economic value of their resources. In examining equity issues concerning common-pool resources, Gelobter argues persuasively that the speed and scale of changes in the American commons was partially responsible for the critical need to consider social resources in any analysis of the institutions and structures governing the use of common-pool resources. Both history and social resources emerge as key factors in the development of different methods of managing resources, as is readily apparent in the discussion of fisheries later in this Conclusion.

Global Resources, Local and Regional Solutions

From an Americas perspective, we see that a number of common-pool resources, including grazing lands, forests, wildlife, fisheries, and other marine resources, have impacts, for example, on biodiversity, across regional or global scales, but management of the resources requires local or regional institutions and solutions. Moreover, common–pool resource management problems, such as those involving grazing lands and forests, typically can be addressed more easily at a regional or local scale. Gibson provides some examples of how the wise use of forests and their products (including associated water resources) can be managed by native peoples in Guatemala. From a manager's viewpoint, this involves trying to understand the conditions under which communities construct institutions to govern their forest resources. Gibson notes that the emergence of institutions and rules to govern forests wisely frequently hinges on the community's dependence on the forest resources and the perceived scarcity of those resources. The importance of users having homogeneous values clearly emerged in Gibson's analysis of Guatemalan forests. In other cases from Indiana, he found that values about preserving forests (and their products) are insufficient by themselves. Institutions and methods are necessary to screen new members of a community for similar values so that the already-established values among users (or commoners) can be maintained and enforced.

The significance of having similar values in managing common-pool resources is evident in Begossi's analysis of fishing communities in Brazil. In her examination of several coastal and riverine fishing communities, she illustrates how a wide variety of different rules governing access and exclusion operate when subsistence and commercial fishers are using the same fish resources. This is equally true in the United States, where regulatory bodies may enforce different quotas or size limits on different fishery sectors, leading to disputes. Important variables determining the degree of cooperation and rules for access in the Brazilian fishing communities include unpredictability of the fishery environment, technology, risk, kinship ties, territoriality, resource competition, market demands, and the presence of protected areas. The complex interrelationships between these variables determined the types of rules and the degree of cooperation that Begossi found in Brazilian fishing communities.

The two key conditions suggested by Gibson and others (Ostrom, chapter 1, this volume) for the evolution of resource management exist here as well; the fish stocks are necessary for the livelihood and survival of the local community, and the fish are limited. The traditional fishing community values are augmented by tourist demands. If income from tourism is siphoned off outside the community, this creates a nonviable conflict. In some cases laws and regulations external to the Brazilian communities are required to manage the resource, and in one case, comanagement has evolved.

In contrast, McCay provides an analysis of the management of fisheries within the Americas from a national and international perspective. She tackles the difficult analysis of a common-pool resource that is inherently national and multinational but relies largely on national institutions and rules for management. In contrasting Canadian and U.S. management systems, she notes that the persistence of open access as an ideological position (or as a de facto outcome of enforcement difficulties) hinders development of management that benefits both the resource and the resource users. Many management problems are caused by a lack of information and social barriers, resulting in a recent policy of delegating some management authority to the resource users or local communities. This becomes more difficult, however, when there are many users such as tourists, recreational fishers, commercial fishers, and conservationists (see chapters 7 and 9 by Policansky and Burger, respectively).

Complex Objectives and Complex Resource Systems

The ideal model of a commons consists of commoners with shared values managing a resource system that is fairly easy to understand. However, many of the case studies examined in this book center on complexity. Resource users sometimes have little in common. Common-pool resources are frequently complex in themselves and are interrelated with other complex common-pool resources. Fisheries and wildlife resources are inherently complex even when you consider only harvesting in a sustainable manner. These complexities become much more problematic when an array of users want to use the resource in incompatible ways. Commercial fishers, recreational fishers, and conservationists all view fish differently. Hunters, wildlife photographers, Native Americans, and wildlife managers all view game differently. And commercial and recreational fishers, clammers in the water, boaters and personal watercraft operators, and landowners all view the use of estuarine waters differently.

The management of fisheries and marine resource commons, usually dealt with as issues of subsistence or commercial use, was broadened by Policansky to include recreational fisheries and by Burger to include resource conflicts between recreational boaters, nesting birds and other natural resources, and other users. Both of these examples illustrate that there are many dimensions to the common-pool resources themselves and to the users, uses, and possible institutions and rules to govern them.

The conflict between recreational boaters, particularly people operating personal watercraft, and a wide range of other users illustrates that the development of management regimes for common-pool resources, such as open-water surfaces, can occur rapidly. In this case, data showing an undisputed negative effect on a resource (declines in reproductive success of colonies of birds) served as the focal point for very different users. Despite their conflicts, they were able to acknowledge the immediate need for a solution allowing use by all in common but reducing the negative effects on some natural resources. It was not essential to have data showing a negative effect on all resources, only on one that was of critical social and biological interest. This case clearly illustrates the characteristics of common-pool resources that are more likely to generate an interest in organizing to find solutions, as suggested by Ostrom and Gibson (chapters 1 and 3, this volume).

Conflicts over game are increasingly more complex, given the different views of consumptive and nonconsumptive users (for example, hunters versus photographers and nature lovers) as well as the interests of local farmers and other landowners who do not want to see their crops, lawns, or property destroyed by migrating mammals. This case is illustrated in the analysis by Clark for elk. As with many common-pool resources, the institutions and rules governing the management of elk are in dispute, largely because of the different objectives of the users. Adaptive management with recurrent evaluations is the current solution (chapter 4, this volume).

Regional Commons

Water common-pool resources tend to be managed on a regional basis. Their management provides an excellent example of the importance of history. For most of the Americas there are diverse and complex institutions and rules for managing water rights that have their origins in institutions predating European invasion and those established during early colonization. Any solution for managing water resources today must take into account the historical evolution of such resources.

Schlager and Blomquist undertake an analysis of the rules and institutions that govern the use of water resources, contrasting the California and Colorado systems. Both states have addressed depletion and degradation associated with subtractability and difficulty of exclusion. Unlike many other common-pool resources, water typically can be easily measured and monitored and its flow predicted. It also can be stored for future use (unlike fish in the ocean or elk on the range). Extensive economic development in the Southwest has been paralleled by social, economic, legal, and political changes that form the basis for the evolution of solutions to the management of water. Although defining and limiting rights of access and use are difficult, coordinating and managing water resources is easier with these social structures in place. As regional populations grow and demand increases, the ability to manage is greatly strained. Unfortunately, both the users and the uses of water are increasing in the Southwest, creating additional pressures on the social institutions that manage water resources. The challenges of allocating and protecting water supplies and water quality are now very complex, making it difficult to move forward.

Nontraditional Commons

Natural resources strained by growing demand were the focus of Hardin's (1968) original view of the commons, and most attention has been devoted to natural resources. However, a commons analysis can profitably be applied to other, less traditional resources, such as medical care and the human dimensions of equity. In both cases, social-pool resources are at the heart of the issue. In the case of medical care, Gochfeld and colleagues argue that providers are the resource and patients are the users or commoners. While many natural resources are ultimately regulated by the government, other entities play a role in regulating access, including employers and insurance plans. Traditional economic analysis has identified a surplus of physicians competing for patients and procedures as the driver of increased costs. However, the commons analysis of Gochfeld et al. suggests that access to providers is restricted not by scarcity of the resource (as it is in many natural resources) but by the for-profit managed care insurance plans. Thus reducing the resource by limiting the number of clinicians in training will not solve the dilemma. Gochfeld et al. further suggest that a more aggressive role of the government in ensuring access and empowerment of the users is essential for solving the problem. Both of these are paradigms long suggested for managing fishers and fisheries (see chapters 5 and 8 by Begossi and McCay, respectively). In the case of equity, Gelobter argues that understanding social-pool resources and taking into account equity and justice in the distribution, use, and management of resources lead to benefits along both racial and economic continua.

Local to Global Issues

The spatial scale of common-pool resources emerges as one of the most important aspects affecting the use of the resource and possible solutions. Although the tools to examine resources, and both uses and users, on a regional or global scale were minimal until very recently, Richey shows that sophisticated spatial techniques such as GISs will greatly enhance our ability to measure and monitor a wide range of natural and social resources, making management of common-pool resources possible—and, we argue, in a more just and equitable manner.

Within the twentieth century, local actions of people have fundamentally altered the composition and function of the global atmosphere in harmful ways, providing an example of air degradation on a global scale. This degradation will continue unless decisive steps are taken to address both regional and global atmospheric issues. Although we are making progress on a few high-profile issues, such as ozone depletion, acid rain, and climate change, many other issues still must be addressed (see chapter 10 by Harrison and Matson).

Although Middaugh does not deal directly with changes in contaminants in the atmospheric commons, the serious ecological, sociological, and public health impacts of global pollution in the Arctic are discussed. Because the degradation of air is a classic common-pool resource problem taken to a global scale, international cooperative efforts are needed to minimize further anthropogenic pollution. Middaugh documents that at the local level in Arctic communities the sociological and public health consequences are dramatic, particularly if contaminant levels keep indigenous peoples from their traditional diets. In the name of avoiding pollutants in fish and other indigenous foods, some people may switch to Western, high-fat foods, with dire public health consequences.

Finally, Gelobter uses the atmospheric commons to demonstrate the effects of local, national, and international levels of individual (or corporate) action and the coevolution of social-pool resources with commons issues at all three levels. The social commons and the atmospheric commons are linked reciprocally, and each can play a reinforcing role in its own management. Gelobter suggests that incorporating justice into the analysis of commons can provide an alternative approach to protecting them. This is particularly true with global commons such as the atmosphere. He demonstrates that greater racial and income inequality leads to lower air quality for rich and poor, and white and nonwhite, in metropolitan areas.

At the national level, particularly for democracies, atmospheric commons can be managed by national laws, but environmental justice concerns are still paramount. Yet to some extent, national injustices are a function of metropolitan injustices. At the global level, there is a large heterogeneity both in the institutions responsible for emissions and in the people affected by climate change. Clearly several analytical approaches are necessary to manage both the resource itself and the environmental justice issues surrounding the resource. However, such an analysis depends on common conceptions of justice. Nowhere is the question of the role of the Americas, particularly North America, more critical to managing a commons than in the case of the atmospheric commons, where changes in land use accounted for almost 40 percent of the carbon fluxes from 1850 to 1980: North America is the prime free rider. We suggest that in the future, water resources may acquire the same importance, significance, and imperatives as the atmospheric commons (see chapter 6 by Schlager and Blomquist).

Gelobter's argument can be summarized as follows. The speed and scale of change in the American commons highlights the fact that the social setting surrounding changes in common-pool resources is itself a common-pool resource (which he called a social-pool resource). Both are finite resources with sets of users. The social-pool resources that influence natural resource commons extend beyond the immediate social system in which the resources are harvested or managed to broader social institutions, structures, and history. Analysis of these broader social domains can extend the policy "toolbox" for resource management, helping us understand the feedback between social and natural resources. Once common-pool resources are analyzed with social resources in mind, the criteria for measuring common-pool resource performance must be extended from simple efficiency to distributional outcomes. Justice and equity concerns become central to choosing the optimal approach for long-term sustainability.

The complexities of integrating common-pool resources with social-pool resources will become increasingly important as it becomes clear that managing the former entails managing, or at least understanding clearly, the latter. All the chapters illustrate the importance of taking into account not only the physical constraints of the resource but also the human dimensions of resource use and management. When intergenerational aspects and environmental justice are added, the task becomes daunting but even more important to managing our planet's resources.

In the distant past when there were too many people for the available resource, they starved or migrated, particularly to urban areas. But every year, the options for migration are further reduced. Clearly to manage the earth's common-pool resources, natural resource management and social structure must incorporate intergenerational aspects and environmental justice. No longer can natural scientists and social scientists examine and manage their respective resources. They must help to integrate diverse local peoples with local governing rules and institutions into a multilayer web where constraints ranging from local to global can be addressed. The Americas provide a unique tapestry for such analysis and integration because of our exceptional history including both common-pool and social-pool resources.

Acknowledgments

We thank all of the authors of the chapters in this volume for their continued willingness to participate in this process and for the excellent chapters they have produced. Our work over the year of this project has been supported by the Consortium for Risk Evaluation with Stakeholder Participation (CRESP; funding through a cooperative agreement with the U.S. Department of Energy, AI no. DEFC01-95-EW55084, DE-FG-26-OONT-40938; Joanna Burger), NIEHS (ESO 5022; Joanna Burger), the New Jersey Endangered and Nongame Project (Joanna Burger), and the Ford and MacArthur foundations (Elinor Ostrom).

About the Contributors

Alpina Begossi is a researcher at the Nucleo de Estudos e Pesquisas Ambientais (Center of Environmental Studies and Research) at the Universidade Estadual de Campinas (UNICAMP), Brazil. She teaches human ecology and ethnoecology as a member of the Graduate Group in Ecology at UNICAMP, the Universidade do Amazonas, and at INPA, Manaus. Her main research topics include artisanal fishing, ethnoichthyology and ethnobotany, and diet and the use of ecological models to analyze human foraging strategies.

William Blomquist is associate professor and chair of political science at Indiana University–Purdue University at Indianapolis. He has published research on institutional arrangements for water resource management in Southern California for more than fifteen years. Currently he serves as facilitator for an interagency effort to improve coordination of water resources planning in Orange County, California. He is the author of *Dividing the Waters: Governing Groundwater in Southern California*.

Joanna Burger is a Distinguished Professor of Biology at Rutgers University, where she is a member of the Institute for Marine and Coastal Sciences and the Environmental and Occupational Health Sciences Institute. An ecologist, behavioral toxicologist, and risk assessor interested in the social and biological aspects of risk assessment and management, she was director of the Graduate Program in Ecology and Evolution at Rutgers from 1978 to 1993. She has served on the governor's Endangered and Nongame Species Council since 1980 and has served on numerous National Research Council committees. She currently serves on the National Academy of Science's Board on Biology. She has written more than 300 papers on behavior, ecology, and ecological risk. Her books include *The Black Skimmer: Social Dynamics of a Colonial Species, The Common Tern Breeder Biology and Behavior of Seabirds and Other Marine Vertebrates, A Naturalist along the New Jersey Shore, Interactions of Animals,* and *The Parrot That Owns Me.*

Tim Clark is an adjunct professor in the School of Forestry and Environmental Studies and a fellow in the Institution for Social and Policy Studies at Yale University. He is also board president of the Northern Rockies Conservation Cooperative in Jackson, Wyoming. He received his Ph.D. in zoology from the University of Wisconsin–Madison in 1973. His interests include interdisciplinary problem solving, professionalism, organizational development, and policy sciences, and he has written more than 300 papers are those topics. His books and monographs include *Greater Yellowstone's Future: Prospects for Ecosystem Science, Management, and Policy, Averting Extinction: Reconstructing Endangered Species Recovery,* and *Foundations of Natural Resources Policy and Management.*

Christopher B. Field is a staff scientist with the Department of Plant Biology at the Carnegie Institution of Washington and a professor by courtesy with Stanford University. He is an ecologist interested in the responses of ecosystems to global changes, the global carbon cycle, and feedbacks between ecosystems and climate. He has served on many committees of the International Geosphere–Biosphere Programme and the U.S. National Research Council. Currently he is a member of the National Research Council's Board on Environmental Studies and Toxicology as well as cluster coordinator for biogeochemistry projects led by the Scientific Committee on Problems of the Environment.

Michel Gelobter is an assistant professor in the Graduate Department of Public Administration at the Newark Campus of Rutgers University and academic director for the Community–University Consortium for Regional Environmental Justice (CUCREJ), where he works with community-based environmental justice organizations and academics in New Jersey, New York, and Puerto Rico. Among other appointments, he served as the first director of the Program on Environmental Policy at Columbia University's School of International and Public Affairs and as director of Environmental Quality and assistant commissioner for the New York City Department of Environmental Protection.

Clark Gibson is assistant professor of political science at Indiana University. Much of his research explores the politics of natural resources management, especially forests and wildlife in Africa and Latin America. His recent book,

Politicians and Poachers: The Political Economy of Wildlife Policy in Africa, examines the politics of wildlife management at multiple levels in Zambia, Kenya, and Zimbabwe. A recent co-edited volume, *People and Forests: Communities, Institutions, and Governance* (co-editors Elinor Ostrom and Margaret McKean), explores how people construct rules about forest use at the local level.

Michael Gochfeld is a professor in the Department of Environmental and Community Medicine at the University of Medicine and Dentistry of New Jersey (UMDNJ)–Robert Wood Johnson Medical School and a member of the Environmental and Occupational Health Sciences Institute. He chairs the academic section of the American College of Occupational and Environmental Medicine. A board-certified physician in occupational medicine, he specializes in environmental toxicology, occupational health and safety, and ecology. His books include *Butterflies of New Jersey* (with J. Burger), *Environmental Medicine,* and *Protecting Workers at Hazardous Waste Sites.*

Bernard D. Goldstein is the director of the Environmental and Occupational Health Sciences Institute, a joint program of Rutgers, the State University of New Jersey, and the UMDNJ–Robert Wood Johnson Medical School. He is a board-certified physician in internal medicine and hematology and in toxicology. He has been chair of the Department of Environmental and Community Medicine at the UMDNJ–Robert Wood Johnson Medical School since 1980. He is also principal investigator of the Consortium for Risk Evaluation with Stakeholder Participation (CRESP). Dr. Goldstein served as acting dean of the UMDNJ–School of Public Health from 1998 to 1999, the first year of its formation. He is a member of the Institute of Medicine, where he has chaired the Section on Public Health, Biostatistics, and Epidemiology. His numerous publications include the book *Methods for Assessing Exposure of Humans and Non-Human Biota.*

John Harrison is a Ph.D. candidate in the Department of Geological and Environmental Sciences at Stanford University. He has worked on atmospheric quality issues with the Environmental Defense Fund and is currently researching the impacts of agricultural intensification on greenhouse gas production in the Yaqui Valley, Mexico.

Jorge Larson, a biologist from the National University of Mexico, trained in population and community ecology of plants. Since 1992 he has been analyst and advisor to the National Commission for the Knowledge and Use of Biodiversity. He served as technical coordinator of the Mexican delegation to the negotiations of the Cartagena Protocol on Biosafety. With the support of a grant from the Fund for Leadership Development of the MacArthur Foundation, he is conducting research on the relationship between intellectual property rights and biological resource use and conservation in Mexico.

Pamela Matson is the Richard and Rhoda Goldman Professor in the Department of Geological and Environmental Sciences and the Institute of International Studies and the Sant Director of the Earth Systems Program at Stanford University. She is an ecologist and biogeochemist, and her research focuses on the effects of natural and anthropogenic disturbances on biogeochemical cycling and trace gas exchange in tropical ecosystems. Together with economists and agronomists, she has analyzed economic drivers and environmental consequences of land-use decisions in the developing world's agricultural systems and identified alternative practices that are economically and environmentally viable. She is currently a science advisory committee member for the International Geosphere–Biosphere Programme and serves on the National Research Council's Board on Sustainable Development and the U.S. SCOPE Committee. She was elected to the American Academy of Arts and Sciences in 1992 and to the National Academy of Sciences in 1994. In 1995, Dr. Matson was selected as a MacArthur Fellow and in 1997 was elected a Fellow of the American Association for the Advancement of Science.

Bonnie McCay is the Board of Governor's Distinguished Service professor at Rutgers University and a member of the Institute for Marine and Coastal Sciences. She is an anthropologist and human ecologist interested in the institutional and human dimensions of the use and management of common-pool resources. She has served on the science committee of the Mid-Atlantic Fisheries Management Council since 1979 and been a member of numerous National Research Council committees; currently she serves on the council's Ocean Studies Board. Her books include *The Question of the Commons, Oyster Wars and the Public Trust,* and *Community, State and Market on the North Atlantic Rim.*

John P. Middaugh is the state epidemiologist for the Alaska Division of Public Health, a position he has held since 1980. Board certified in internal medicine and preventive medicine, he received training in epidemiology as a commissioned officer in the U.S. Public Health Service in the Epidemic Intelligence Service, Centers for Disease Control and Prevention. Former president of the American Society for Circumpolar Health and a founding member of the International Union for Circumpolar Health, he has been active in public health practice and environmental research in Alaska and the Arctic.

Richard B. Norgaard is professor of energy and resources and of agricultural and resource economics at the University of California–Berkeley. He has worked across the disciplines of biology and economics over the past quarter century, conducting research on the biological control of agricultural pests, the potential for environmentally sustainable development in the Amazon, and the economics of biological diversity. A member of the Office of Technology Assessments Advisory Panel on Technologies to Maintain Biological Diversity, the National Academy of Sciences Panel on Biodiversity Research Priorities, and the Scientific Advisory Committee of the Biodiversity Support Program, he also served for six years on the U.S. Scientific Committee on Problems of the Environment (SCOPE) hosted by the National Research Council. A respected international transdisciplinary scholar, he currently serves (1998–2001) as president of the International Society for Ecological Economics.

Elinor Ostrom is the Arthur F. Bentley Professor in the Department of Political Science at Indiana University. She is the codirector with Vincent Ostrom of the Workshop in Political Theory and Policy Analysis, and with Emilio Moran of the Center for the Study of Institutions, Population, and Environmental Change (CIPEC). Her primary interest is the evolution of institutions and strategic behavior within institutions. She is a member of the American Academy of Arts and Sciences and a recipient of the Frank E. Seidman Prize in Political Economy and the Johan Skytte Prize in Political Science. Her books include *Governing the Commons; Rules, Games, and Common-Pool Resources;* and *Local Commons and Global Interdependence: Heterogeneity and Cooperation in Two Domains.*

David Policansky is associate director of the Board on Environmental Studies and Toxicology at the National Research Council, where he has directed studies on applied ecology and natural resource management. He is a member of the Ecological Society of America and the American Fisheries Society and chairs the advisory council to the University of Alaska's School of Fisheries and Ocean Sciences. His interests include population biology, fisheries, natural resource management, and the use of science in informing policy. In addition to his work on National Research Council reports, his recent publications have been on fisheries, the role of science in decision making, and common-property resources.

Jeffrey Richey is a professor of oceanography at the University of Washington and an adjunct professor in the College of Forest Resources and the Quaternary Research Center. He is a systems ecologist and biogeochemist interested in the dynamics of large-scale river basins and their interaction with the coastal zone, under natural and anthropogenic conditions. He has led research programs on the Amazon basin, Southeast Asia, and the Pacific Northwest. He has served on numerous national and international panels, including the National Research Council's U.S. National Committee for

SCOPE and committees of the International Geosphere–Biosphere Programme and the World Bank. His books include *Biogeochemistry of Major World Rivers* and *The Biogeochemistry of the Amazon Basin*.

José Sarukhán is a professor at the Instituto de Ecología, U.N.A.M., and coordinator of the National Commission for the Knowledge and Use of Biodiversity of Mexico. His professional areas of interest include plant population ecology, systems ecology, and biodiversity. He was president of the Mexican Academy of Sciences from 1981 to 1982 and vice-president for science from 1986 to 1987, then served as president of the National University of Mexico (UNAM) from 1989 to 1997. Since 1998 he has served as chairman of DIVERSITAS and is a member of the World Commission on the Ethics of Scientific Knowledge and Technology of UNESCO. He is a member of the board of the World Resources Institute. He is a foreign member of the U.S. National Academy of Sciences. His books include *Arboles Tropicales de Mexico, Manual de Malezas del Valle de Mexico,* and *Mexico Confronts the Challenges of Biodiversity* (editor).

Edella Schlager is an associate professor in the School of Public Administration and Policy at the University of Arizona. She is a political scientist specializing in institutional analysis and natural resource policy. She has sat on a National Academy of Sciences panel and is a member of the scientific advisory committee for the Minerals Management Service of the Department of the Interior.

Index